`D1015751`

10 BIBLIOGRAPHIES

OF

20TH CENTURY RUSSIAN LITERATURE

edited by Fred Moody

ardis / ann arbor

10 BIBLIOGRAPHIES OF 20TH CENTURY RUSSIAN LITERATURE

CONTENTS

EDITOR'S NOTE

Eight of the bibliographies in this collection (those on Annenskii, Blok, Mayakovsky, Grin, Aksenov, Versification, Akhmadulina, and Brodsky) were originally published in *Russian Literature Triquarterly*. The bibliographies of Evreinov and Kuprin make their first appearance in this volume.

Unless otherwise stated in their titles, all bibliographies can be considered complete through 1972. The addenda following the bibliographies of Annenskii, Grin, Aksenov and Brodsky are casual and incomplete: their completeleness obtains only through 1972. The copious addenda following Christine Rydel's bibliography of Akhmadulina make it complete through 1976. Corrections have been made by the compilers of any errors discovered in their bibliographies between the date of original publication and their appearance in this volume; Vasilii Aksenov has kindly supplied corrections for the bibliography of his works.

Fred Moody

10 BIBLIOGRAPHIES OF 20TH CENTURY RUSSIAN LITERATURE

A SELECTED BIBLIOGRAPHY OF WORKS BY AND ABOUT

ALEXANDER KUPRIN (1870-1938)

Compiled by

Nicholas J.L. Luker

INTRODUCTION

Three bibliographies of Kuprin's work and of critical material on it are readily available to the researcher. However, while the first two are now over twenty years out of date, the third, though very recent, deals only with Kuprin in English. All three, therefore, are far from full in the light of the wealth of new work on Kuprin, most of it Soviet, produced during the 1960s.

The first bibliography, to be found in Vladimir Boutchik, *La Littérature russe en France* (Paris, 1947), is only skeletal and of little help to those investigating Kuprin today.

The second compilation, K.E. Pavlovskaia's "A.I. Kuprin. Publikatsiia ego proizvedenii i literatura o nem," (*Uchenye zapiski saratovskogo Universiteta imeni Chernyshevskogo*, LIII, 1955, pp. 196-248), is admirably detailed and infinitely more valuable, but records critical material on Kuprin published only up to 1953 and includes no Western sources. The two decades since have seen the publication of three large collected editions of Kuprin's work, each more complete than its predecessor, and of six major critical studies in Russian.

The third bibliography, Christina Thompson's *Kuprin in English: A Bibliography of Works By and About Him* (*Russian Language Journal,* East Lansing, Michigan, Vol. XXX, No. 105 (Winter, 1976), pp. 99-108), provides most welcome detail on articles and stories by Kuprin in English translation (see Section 3, pp. 103-06), detail which is not reproduced here. But as a whole the compilation is needlessly repetitive, contains several inaccuracies, includes items of little value for serious research and yet omits a number of recent publications altogether, notably the article on *The Duel* by Gareth Williams (1967) (see below, section 5a), one of the extremely few critical pieces on Kuprin in English.

Easily the best edition of Kuprin available at present is the recent *Sobranie sochinenii v deviati tomakh*, Moscow ("Khudozhestvennaia literatura"), 1970-73. This includes detailed notes on each work, frequently with reference to contemporary critical comment, a useful introductory essay by F.I. Kuleshov in Volume 1 (see below), and an index in Volume 9.

The bibliography below offers a selection of sources, both Western and Russian, which the compiler found most useful in his recent research work on Kuprin.

In the lists which follow, exact page references are given wherever possible and the abbeviation sb. is used to denote *sbornik*.

1. COLLECTIONS OF KUPRIN'S WORK
(a) In Russian

MINIATURY. Kiev, 1897.
RASSKAZY. St. Petersburg: "Znanie", Vol. 1, 1903; Vol. 2, 1906.

POLNOE SOBRANIE SOCHINENII V DEVIATI TOMAKH. St. Petersburg-Petrograd: "A.F. Marks", 1912-15.
ZHIDKOE SOLNTSE (Sb.) "Moskovskoe Knig.", 1916.
RASSKAZY DLIA DETEI. Paris: "Sever", 1921.
NOVYE POVESTI I RASSKAZY. Paris: "Tov-a N.P. Karbasnikov", 1927.
KUPOL' SV. ISAAKIIA DALMATSKOGO. Riga: "Literatura", 1928.
ELAN', rasskazy. Belgrade, 1930.
ZHANETA, roman (sb.), Paris: "Vozrozhdenie", 1934.
SOCHINENIIA V TREKH TOMAKH. Moscow: Gos. izd. khud. lit., 1953.
SOBRANIE SOCHINENII V SHESTI TOMAKH. Moscow: "Goslitizdat", 1957-58.
SOBRANIE SOCHINENII V DEVIATI TOMAKH. Moscow, "Pravda", 1964.
SOBRANIE SOCHINENII V DEVIATI TOMAKH. Moscow: "Khud. lit.", 1970-73.

(b) In translation

THE RIVER OF LIFE AND OTHER STORIES. Dublin and London: Maunsel, 1916. Tr. S. Koteliansky and J.M. Murry.
A SLAV SOUL AND OTHER STORIES. London: Constable, 1916. Tr. S. Graham.
THE BRACELET OF GARNETS AND OTHER STORIES. London: Duckworth, 1919. Tr. Leo Pasvolsky.
SASHA. London: Stanley Paul, 1920. Tr. Douglas Ashby.
THE GARNET BRACELET AND OTHER STORIES. Moscow: "Foreign Languages", 1950.
THE DUEL AND SELECTED STORIES. New York: New American Library, 1961. Tr. Andrew MacAndrew.
GAMBRINUS AND OTHER STORIES. Freeport, NY: Books for Libraries, 1970. Tr. B. G. Guerney.
A SLAV SOUL AND OTHER STORIES. Freeport, NY: Books for Libraries Press, 1971. (Reprint of London, 1916 edition.)

2. INDIVIDUAL WORKS

(a) Some works not included in SOB. SOCH. editions listed above.

ANRI ROSHFOR. EGO ZHIZN', DEIATEL'NOST' I SMERT'. St. Petersburg-Moscow: "Osvobozhdenie", 1914. Pamphlet.
ARMEE UND REVOLUTION IN RUSSLAND. Vienna: NEUE FREIE PRESSE, No. 15103 (September 8, 1906), pp. 2-3. Article.
BOR'BA I BOKS. GERKULES, Nos. 2-3 (February 19, 1916), p. 9. Article.
ELEGII V PROZE. ZHURNAL DLIA VSEKH, No. 1 (1902), cols. 552-60. Prose pieces.
KIEVSKII BEDLAM (OCHERK). Kiev: KIEVSKOE SLOVO, Nos. 2799 (October 27), and 2802 (October 30), 1895, both p. 1.
RODINA. MOSKVA, No. 3 (1958), pp. 118-19. Sketch.

(b) Individual works in translation

THE SWAMP. In SHORT STORIES BY RUSSIAN AUTHORS. London and Toronto: Dent, 1924. Tr. R.S. Townsend.
TEMPTATION. In SELECTED RUSSIAN SHORT STORIES. London: Oxford Univ. Press, 1925. Tr. A.E. Chamot.

YAMA (THE PIT). New York: Modern Library, 1932. Tr. B.G. Guerney.
SULAMITE (SULAMITH). Paris, 1922. Tr. Marc Semenoff and S. Mandel.

3. MAIN BIOGRAPHICAL SOURCES

B.M. Kiselev, RASSKAZY O KUPRINE. Moscow: "Sov. pisatel'", 1964.
K.A. Kuprina, KUPRIN—MOI OTETS. Moscow: "Sov. Rossiia", 1971.
M.K. Kuprina-Iordanskaia, GODY MOLODOSTI. Moscow: "Khud. lit.", 1966.
N.K. Verzhbitsky, VSTRECHI S A.I. KUPRINYM. Penza: "Penzenskoe knizh.", 1961.

4. CRITICAL STUDIES OF KUPRIN

Afanas'ev, V.N., ALEKSANDR IVANOVICH KUPRIN, Kritiko-biograficheskii ocherk.
    Moscow: "GIKhL", 1960.
Berkov, P.N., ALEKSANDR IVANOVICH KUPRIN, Kritiko-biograficheskii ocherk.
    Moscow-Leningrad: "ANSSSR", 1956.
Dynnik, A., A.I. KUPRIN: OCHERK ZHIZNI I TVORCHESTVA. E. Lansing, MI: RUS-
    SIAN LANGUAGE JOURNAL, 1969.
Krutikova, L.V., A.I. KUPRIN. Leningrad: "Prosveshchenie", 1971.
Kuleshov, F.I., TVORCHESKII PUT' KUPRINA. Minsk: "MVSSO BSSSR", 1963.
Rotshtein, E.M., A.I. KUPRIN. ZABYTYE I NESOBRANNYE PROIZVEDENIIA.
    "Penzenskoe", 1950.
Volkov, A., TVORCHESTVO A.I. KUPRINA. Moscow: "Sov. pisatel'", 1962.

5. CRITICAL AND BIOGRAPHICAL ARTICLES AND ESSAYS

(a)

A. "Zhurnal'noe obozrenie," RUSSKAIA MYSL', No. 1 (1905), p. 134.
Adamovich, Georgy, "Kuprin," ODINOCHESTVO I SVOBODA (New York, 1955),
    pp. 243-49.
Afanas'ev, V., "Kuprin i stsena," TEATRAL'NAIA ZHIZN', No. 2 (1958), pp. 59-60.
Afanas'ev, V., "Sovremennitsa POEDINKA," OGONEK, No. 36 (1960), p. 19.
Afanas'ev, V., "Zabytye ocherki A.I. Kuprina," RADUGA, No. 1 (1969), pp. 113-23.
Aldanov, M., "Pamiati A.I. Kuprina," SOVREMENNYE ZAPISKI (Paris), No. 43 (1938),
    pp. 317-24).
Anichkov, E., "Literaturnye obrazy i mneniia," NAUCHNOE OBOZRENIE, No. 5
    (1903), pp. 147-58.
Anichkov, E., "Rasskazy ZNANIIA, 1903," LITERATURNYE OBRAZY I MNENIIA
    (1904), pp. 74-96.
A. R—ov., "Zametki o tekushchei literature," ZHIZN' I ISKUSSTVO, No. 26 (1897), p.
    2.
Arsen'eva, L., "O Kuprine," GRANI (Frankfurt), No. 43, pp. 125-32.
Asheshov, N., "Rasskazy A. Kuprina," VESTNIK I BIBLIOTEKA SAMOOBRAZOVA-
    NIIA, No. 17 (1903), pp. 745-48.
Aspiz, E.M., "S A.I. Kuprinym v Danilovskom," LITERATURNAIA VOLOGDA, No. 5
    (1959), pp. 180-81).
Aspiz, E.M., "A.I. Kuprin v Balaklave," KRYM, No. 23 (1959), pp. 131-36.
Ayaks (A. Izmailov), "Novaia p'esa A.I. Kuprina," BIRZHEVYE VEDOMOSTI, No.
    13133 (September 8, 1912), pp. 5-6.

Bartenev, A., "A. Kuprin. GRANATOVYI BRASLET, Sob. Soch. Tom VII, Moscow, 1911," ZHATVA, No. 1 (1912), pp. 228-30.

Batiushkov, F.D., "Psikhologiia i politika v poslednikh rasskazakh A. Kuprina," RECH', No. 253 (December 28, 1906), p. 2.

Batiushkov, F.D., "Chekhov i Kuprin," SEVERNYE ZORI, No. 1 (December 11, 1909), cols. 19-25.

Batiushkov, F.D., "Stikhiinyi talant" (A.I. Kuprin), K.N. BATIUSHKOV, F.D. BA-TIUSHKOV, A.I. KUPRIN (sb. statei), Vologda: "Vologodskii gosud. ped. Instit., 1968.

B---n, V., ZHURNAL DLIA VSEKH, No. 8 (1905), p. 519.

Bogdanovich, A., "Kriticheskie zametki," MIR BOZHII, No. 2 (1897), p. 8.

Bogdanovich, A., "Kriticheskie zametki," MIR BOZHII, No. 4 (1903), pp. 7-11.

Borisov, L., "Nemnozhko o Kuprine," NEVA, No. 8 (1956), pp. 162-64.

Botsianovsky, VI., "YAMA Kuprina," NOVAIA RUS', No. 107 (April 21, 1909).

Botsianovsky, VI., "A. Kuprin. SOBYTIIA V SEVASTOPOLE," REZETS, Nos. 15-16 (1939), pp. 24-26.

Brusianin, V.V., "Deti v proizvedeniiakh A.I. Kuprina," DETI I PISATELI (Moscow, 1915), pp. 204-72.

Bunin, Ivan, "Kuprin," VOSPOMINANIIA (Paris, 1950), pp. 141-58.

Chukovsky, K., "Zhevanaia rezinka," RECH', No. 160 (June 14, 1909), p. 2.

Chukovsky, K., "Kuprin v YAME," RECH', No. 161 (June 15, 1909), p. 3.

Chukovsky, K., "Novaia kniga A.I. Kuprina," NIVA, No. 45 (1914), pp. 867-70.

Chukovsky, K., "Kuprin," NOVYI MIR, No. 3 (1962), pp. 190-210.

Chukovsky, K., "Kuprin," SOB. SOCH. KUPRINA V DEVIATI TOMAKH (Moscow, 1964), Vol. I, pp. 3-40.

Diu-Kir, I., "Zhurnal'noe obozrenie," VSEMIRNYI VESTNIK, No. 2 (1905), pp. 219-20.

Drozd-Boniachevsky, "POEDINOK Kuprina s tochki zreniia stroevogo ofitsera." St. Petersburg, 1910.

Ezerskaia, B., "Po sledam geroev rasskaza Kuprina NATASHA," RADUGA, No. 9 (1970), pp. 107-110.

Friche, V., "Ocherki sovremennoi literatury," PRAVDA, (Sept.-Oct. 1905), pp. 420-25.

Frid, S., "U A.I. Kuprina," BIRZHEVYE VEDOMOSTI, No. 13764 (Sept. 21, 1913), pp. 7-8.

Gippius, Z.N., RUSSKAIA MYSL', No. 11 (1911), pp. 28-29.

Golikov, V.G., "YAMA Kuprina," VESTNIK ZNANIIA, No. 6 (1915), pp. 360-69.

Gornfel'd, A., "Kuprin-romantik," RUSSKIE VEDOMOSTI, No. 38 (Feb. 17, 1911), p. p. 3.

Gura, I., "Pis'ma A.I. Kuprina k F.D. Batiushkovu iz Danilovskogo," Almanac SEVER (Vologda, 1963), pp. 152-58.

Gura, I., "Povest' A.I. Kuprina POEDINOK," VOPROSY ZHANRA I STILIA, red. V. V. Gura (Vologda, 1967), pp. 84-116.

I., "Literaturnye otgoloski," RUSSKIE VEDOMOSTI, No. 340 (December 11, 1903), p. 4.

I., "Literaturnye otgoloski," RUSSKIE VEDOMOSTI, No. 91 (April 22, 1909), p. 2.

Izmailov, A., "Literatura i zhizn'," RODNAIA NIVA, No. 32 (1905), pp. 279-80.

Izmailov, A., "Literaturnye Besedy," RUSSKOE SLOVO, No. 72 (March 1906), p. 2.

Izmailov, A., "Pod krasnym fonarem," RUSSKOE SLOVO, No. 91 (April 22, 1909), p. 2.

Izmailov, A., "Pesni zemnoi radosti," LITERATURNYI OLIMP (Moscow, 1911), pp. 339-69.

Izmailov, A., "Khrestomatiia novoi literatury," NOVOE SLOVO, No. 3 (1914), pp. 116-18.

Izmailov, A., "A.I. Kuprin," RUSSKOE SLOVO, No. 278 (December 3, 1914), p. 6.

Jackson, R.L., "A.I. Kuprin's RIVER OF LIFE," in DOSTOEVSKY'S UNDERGROUND MAN IN RUSSIAN LITERATURE. The Hague: Mouton, 1958. pp. 108-12.

Kataev, V., "Tvorchestvo Aleksandra Kuprina," OGONEK, No. 22 (1954), p. 16.

Kogan, P., OCHERKI PO ISTORII NOVEISHEI RUSSKOI LITERATURY, Vol. 3, Vyp. I, izd. 2 (Moscow, 1911), pp. 3-65.

Koltonovskaia, E., "Novyi rasskaz iz voennoi zhizni," A. Kuprin, POEDINOK, VEST-NIK I BIBLIOTEKA SAMOOBRAZOVANIIA, No. 28 (1905), cols. 886-90.

Koltonovskaia, E., "Poet zhizni," VESTNIK EVROPY, No. 1 (1915), pp. 302-18.

Koretskaia, I.V., "A.I. Kuprin," SOCHINENIIA V TREKH TOMAKH (Moscow, 1953), pp. III-XXXIX.

Koretskaia, I.V., "Chekhov i Kuprin," LITERATURNOE NASLEDSTVO, Vol. 68 (Moscow, 1960), pp. 363-94.

Koretskaia, I.V., "Gor'kii i Kuprin," GOR'KOVSKIE CHTENIIA 1964-5 (Moscow, 1966) pp. 119-61.

Korolenko, V., RUSSKOE BOGATSTVO, No. 8 (1904), p. 148.

Kranikhfel'd, V., "Zhurnal'nye otgoloski," MIR BOZHII, No. 4 (1906), otdel II, pp. 72-3.

Kranikhfel'd, V., "Literaturnye otkliki," SOVREMENNYI MIR, No. 6 (1909), pp. 98-102.

Krinitsky, Mark, "Kak pisat' rasskazy," ZHENSKII ZHURNAL, No. 1 (1927), p. 5.

Krutikova, L., "Lektsiia A.I. Kuprina o literature," RUSSKAIA LITERATURA, No. 3, (1962), pp. 187-93.

Kuleshov, F.I., "Kuprin-ocherkist," UCHENYE ZAPISKI. Minsk: Belorusskogo gosud. univ. im. Lenina, 1954. Vyp. 18 (seriia filologicheskaia), pp. 117-33.

Kuleshov, F.I., "Ranniaia proza Kuprina," UCHENYE ZAPISKI, Tom II, STAT'I O LIT-ERATURE. Sakhalin: Iuzhno-sakhalinskii gosud. ped. instit., 1959. pp. 107-70.

Kuleshov, F.I., "Iz neizdannykh stikhotvorenii A.I. Kuprina," in above, pp. 179-86.

Kuleshov, F.I., "Aleksandr Ivanovich Kuprin," in A.I. Kuprin, SOB. SOCH. V DEVIATI TOMAKH (Moscow, 1970-73), Vol. I, pp. 5-38.

Kuprina, K.A., "Perepiska I.E. Repina i A.I. Kuprina," NOVYI MIR, No. 9 (1969), pp. 193-210.

Kuprina-Iordanskaia, M.K., "Iz vospominanii ob A.I. Kuprine," OGONEK, No. 36 (1945), pp. 8-9.

Kuprina-Iordanskaia, M.K., "Iz vospominanii o D.N. Mamin-Sibiriak," D.N. MAMIN-SIBIRIAK (mat. nauchnoi konferentsii). Sverdlovsk, 1953. pp. 162-79.

Ledré, Charles, TROIS ROMANCIERS RUSSES. Paris, 1935. pp. 81-123.

Less, A., "Riadom s Kuprinym," DON, No. 5 (1958), pp. 179-81.

Liubimov, L., "Na chuzhbine," NOVYI MIR, No. 2 (1957), pp. 177-206.

Liubimov, L., "Iz tvorcheskoi laboratorii Kuprina," RUSSKAIA LITERATURA, No. 4 (1961), pp. 164-67.

Lunacharsky, A., "O chesti," PRAVDA (Sept.-Oct. 1905), pp. 164-81.

L'vov, V., "Zhretsy i zhertvy," OBRAZOVANIE, No. 7 (1905), pp. 85-106.

L'vov, V., "Nochnoi koshmar," OBRAZOVANIE, No. 2 (1908), pp. 49-50.

L'vov-Rogachevsky, V., SOVREMENNYI MIR, No. 3 (1911), pp. 352-54.

Manych, P.D., VESTNIK LITERATURY, No. 8 (1905), pp. 161-68.

Mikhailova, L., "Sochineniia A.I. Kuprina," NOVYI MIR, No. 9 (1954), pp. 252-59.

Mikhailovsky, B.V., "Tvorchestvo A.I. Kuprina," RUSSKAIA LITERATURA XX VEKA (Moscow, 1939), pp. 47-58.

Nevedomsky, M., "O sovremennom khudozhestve," MIR BOZHII, No. 8 (1904), pp. 29-31.

Nikolaev, N.N., "YAMA, povest' A.I. Kuprina," EFEMERIDY (sb. statei), Kiev, 1912, pp. 308-17.

7

Nikulin, L., "Ob odnom ocherke A.I. Kuprina," OGONEK, No. 34 (1957), p. 14.

Nikulin, L., ed., A.I. Kuprin, RODINA, MOSKVA, No. 3 (1958), pp. 118-24.

Nikulin, L., "Kuprin i Bunin," OKTIABR', No. 7 (1958), pp. 204-18.

Nikulin, L., CHEKHOV. BUNIN. KUPRIN. Moscow, 1960. pp. 267-325.

Nord, Lidia, "Vozvrashchenie A.I. Kuprina," INZHENERY DUSH. Buenos Aires, 1954. pp. 60-64.

Norvezhsky, Oskar, "Kuprin v KAPERNAUME," VESTNIK LITERATURY, Nos. 6 & 7 (1908), pp. 125-29.

Ol'minsky M., PO LITERATURNYM VOPROSAM (sb. statei), Moscow-Leningrad, 1932. pp. 36-38.

Osharova, T., "Kuprin v rabote nad finalom POEDINKA," RUSSKAIA LITERATURA, No. 3 (1966), pp. 179-85.

Pachmuss, Temira, ZINAIDA HIPPIUS. AN INTELLECTUAL PROFILE. Southern Illinois Univ. Press, 1971. PP. 339-45.

Paustovsky, K., "Potok zhizni" (Zametki o proze Kuprina), Paustovsky, K., SOB. V SHESTI TOMAKH, Vol. 5. Moscow, 1958. pp. 629-55.

Persky, Serge, "Alexandre Kouprine," LES MAÎTRES DU ROMAN RUSSE CONTEMPORAIN. Paris, 1912. pp. 313-25.

Pilsky, P.M., "Vo mrake kasty," RUSSKAIA MYSL', No. 11 (1905), pp. 64-79.

Pilsky, P.M., "A. Kuprin," KRITICHESKIE STAT'I. St. Petersburg, 1910. pp. 91-105.

Pilsky, P.M., "Radosti zemli. O Kuprine," A.I. Kuprin, KUPOL' SV. ISAAKIIA DALMATSKOGO. Riga, 1928. pp. 2-8.

Plotkin, L.A., "A.I. Kuprin," LITERATURNYE OCHERKI I STAT'I. Leningrad, 1958. pp. 413-45.

Prutskov, N.I., "Khudozhestvennaia struktura povesti A. Kuprina MOLOKH," VOPROSY IZUCHENIIA RUSSKOI LITERATURY XI-XX VEKOV. Moscow-Leningrad, 1958. pp. 235-40.

Ptukh (Sadovsky, B.), "Ne ostupites'!", VESY, No. 6 (1909), pp. 82-86.

Sedykh, Andrei, "A.I. Kuprin," DALEKIE, BLIZKIE. New York, 1962. pp. 7-17.

Sementkovsky, R.I., LITERATURNYE PRILOZHENIIA K 'NIVE', No. 2 (1897), cols. 408-09.

Shaginian, M., "Literaturnyi dnevnik. Russkii Mopassan," PRIAZOVSKII KRAI (Rostov-on-Don), No. 174 (July 5, 1911), p. 2.

Shapir, N., "A.I. Kuprin," SEVERNYE ZAPISKI, No. 12 (1914), pp. 18-37.

Shirmakov, P.P., ed., "Neizvestnaia p'esa A.I. Kuprina, GRAN' STOLETIIA," LENINGRADSKII AL'MANAKH, No. 11 (1956), pp. 373-82.

Shirmakov, P.P., "Novoe ob A.I. Kuprine," RUSSKAIA LITERATURA, No. 2 (1962), pp. 205-12.

Skabichevsky, A., "Literatura v zhizni i zhizn' v literature," NOVOE SLOVO, No. 4 (1897), pp. 163-67.

Skif, N., "Zhurnal'noe i literaturnoe obozrenie. Gor'kii i Kuprin," RUSSKII VESTNIK, No. 12 (1906), pp. 570-87.

Smolensky, "Otkrytie vesenniago sezona," BIRZHEVYE VEDOMOSTI, No. 9793 (March 13, 1907).

Sobolev, Yu., "A.I. Kuprin," OBSHCHESTUDENCHESKII LITERATURNYI SBORNIK (Moscow, 1910), pp. 137-78.

Sobolev, Yu., "Zametki o novykh knigakh," PUT', no. 7 (1913), pp. 46-47.

Starodum, N. Ya., "POEDINOK, roman A. Kuprina," RUSSKII VESTNIK, No. 6 (1905) pp. 689-726.

Strel'tsov, R., SOVREMENNIK, No. 4 (1914), p. 122.

Struve, Gleb, "Alexander Ivanovich Kuprin (1870-1938)," SLAVONIC AND EAST EUROPEAN REVIEW, Vol 17 (1938-39), pp. 689-90.

Struve, Gleb, RUSSKAIA LITERATURA V IZGNANII. New York, 1956. pp. 99-101,

267-68.

Teleshov, N., ZAPISKI PISATELIA. Moscow, 1943. pp. 59, 68, 87.

Unkovsky, V., "O Kuprine, Poslednie gody," GRANI (Frankfurt), No. 21, pp. 79-82.

Vernon, L., "La vie littéraire en Russie," LA REVUE (Paris),No. 14 (July 15, 1911), p. 243.

Verzhbitsky, Nik., "Khudozhnik za rabotoi," DAL'NII VOSTOK, No. 1 (1956), pp. 149-69.

Verzhbitsky, Nik., "Vstrechi s Kuprinym," ZVEZDA, No. 5 (1957), pp. 116-41.

Verzhbitsky, Nik., "K biografii Kuprina," ZVEZDA, No. 12 (1960), pp. 179-81.

Veselovsky, Yu. A., "Literaturnye otgoloski III," VESTNIK ZNANIIA, No. 8 (1903), pp. 137-40.

V.G., "O knigakh," ZLATOSVET, No. 6 (1914), p. 18.

Viacheslavov, P., "Zabytye stranitsy Kuprina," DON, No. 6 (1965), pp. 172-80.

Vishnevsky, Ivan, "A.I. Kuprin," POVESTI I RASSKAZY. L'vov, 1958. pp. 3-17.

Vladin, A., "Kak zhivet i rabotaet A.I. Kuprin," ILLIUSTRIROVANNAIA ROSSIIA (Paris), No. 4 (January 28, 1926), pp. 8-9.

Volkov, A.A., "A.I. Kuprin," ISTORIIA RUSSKOI LITERATURY, Vol X, Literatura 1890-1917 godov. Moscow-Leningrad: ANSSSR, 1954. pp. 529-42.

Volkov, A.A., "A.I. Kuprin na Ukraine," SOVETSKAIA UKRAINA, No. 9 (1960), pp. 149-63.

Volkov, A.A., "A.I. Kuprin," RUSSKAIA LITERATURA XX VEKA. Moscow, 1966. pp. 277-303.

Vorovksy, V.V., "A.I. Kuprin," LITERATURNO-KRITICHESKIE STAT'I. Moscow, 1956. pp. 273-87.

Williams, Gareth, "Romashov and Nazansky: Enemies of the People," CANADIAN SLAVONIC PAPERS, Vol. IX, No. 2 (1967), pp. 194-200.

Zaikin, Ivan M., V VOZDUKHE I NA ARENE (Vospominaniia). Kuibyshev, 1963. pp. 28-38.

Zhegalov, N., "Vydaiushchiisia russkii realist," CHTO CHITAT', No. 12 (1958), pp. 26-7.

(b) Anonymous articles

"MINIATURY, ocherki i rasskazy A. Kuprina, Kieve,1897," RUSSKAIA MYSL', No. 3 (1898), pp. 91-92.

"A. Kuprin. MINIATURY, Kiev, 1897," RUSSKOE BOGATSTVO, No. 4 (1898). pp. 25-28.

NOVOE DELO, No. 2 (1902), p. 275.

NOVOE DELO, No. 12 (1902), p. 322.

"Nasha tekushchaia zhizn'," RUSSKOE BOGATSTVO, No. 2 (1903), pp. 148-50.

RUSSKAIA MYSL', No. 8 (1904), pp. 240-41.

PETERBURGSKIE VEDOMOSTI, No. 149 (June 21, 1905), p. 2.

"A.I. Kuprin. Tom III, Kn. Izd-vo MIR BOZHII, St. Petersburg, 1907," RUSSKOE BO-GATSTVO, No. 2 (1907), otdel II, pp. 160-62.

"Tom VI, A. Kuprin, Sochineniia, Izd-vo 'Progress', St. Petersburg, 1909," RUSSKOE BOGATSTVO, No. 9 (1909), pp. 112-14.

"A.I. Kuprin. Rasskazy, tom 7, Moskovskoe Kn.-izd-vo," SOVREMENNIK, No. 1 (1912). pp. 361-65.

"Avtobiografiia A.I. Kuprina," OGONEK, No. 20 (1913).

6. GENERAL SOURCES

Corbet, Charles, LA LITTÉRATURE RUSSE. Paris, 1951. pp. 163-64.

Field, Andrew, ed., THE COMPLECTION OF RUSSIAN LITERATURE. London, 1971. p. 283.

Gorelov, A., PODVIG RUSSKOI LITERATURY. The Hague, 1969. pp. 336-47.

Hare, R., RUSSIAN LITERATURE FROM PUSHKIN TO THE PRESENT DAY. London, 1947. pp. 180-81.

Holthusen, Johannes, TWENTIETH CENTURY RUSSIAN LITERATURE. New York, 1972. pp. 51-52.

Lavrin, Janko, A PANORAMA OF RUSSIAN LITERATURE. London, 1973. pp. 211-13.

Mirsky, D.S., A HISTORY OF RUSSIAN LITERATURE. London, 1964. pp. 388-89.

Moore, Harry T. and Parry, Albert, TWENTIETH-CENTURY RUSSIAN LITERATURE. S. Illinois Univ. Press, 1974. pp. 8-9, 18, 44-45.

Olgin, Moissaye J., A GUIDE TO RUSSIAN LITERATURE (1820-1917). New York, 1971. pp. 245-50.

Slonim, M., FROM CHEKHOV TO THE REVOLUTION, RUSSIAN LITERATURE 1900-1917. Oxford Univ. Press, 1962. pp. 173-77.

Tkhorzhevsky, Ivan, RUSSKAIA LITERATURA. Paris, 1950. pp. 518-20.

A BIBLIOGRAPHY OF WORKS BY AND ABOUT

INNOKENTII FEDOROVICH ANNENSKII

Compiled by

Felix Philipp Ingold

A. INTRODUCTORY NOTE

The present bibliography—chronologically arranged and divided into four sections (O. - III.)—contains the writings by I. F. Annenskii and criticism of them (from 1881 up until 1972). We have included not only individual publications, newspaper and review articles, book chapters devoted entirely or partly to I.F.A., but also Annenskiiana in Russian and foreign almanacs, anthologies, and reviews, as well as references to I.F.A. in encyclopedias, handbooks, histories of literature, etc. —*Not* registered were the first printings of Annenskii's poems, since all references to them are given in Fedorov's notes to Innokentii Annenskii, *Stikhotvoreniia i tragedii* (Leningrad, 1959), pp. 581-625. For transliteration from Russian we have used J. Thomas Shaw's System II.

B. ABBREVIATIONS AND SIGLA

A.

FO - *Filolgicheskoe obozrenie*
LM - *Literaturnaia mysl'*
LN - *Literaturnoe nasledstvo*
LS - *Literaturnyi sovremennik*
MB - *Mir bozhii*
MV - *Moskovskie vedomosti*
NZ - *Novyi zhurnal*
RM - *Russkaia mysl'*
RS - *Russkaia shkola*
VE - *Vestnik Evropy*
VL - *Voprosy literatury*
WdS - *Welt der Slaven (Die)*
ZMNP - *Zhurnal ministerstva*
        narodnago prosveshcheniia
ZsP - *Zeitschrift für slavische*
        Philologie

B.

Bln - Berlin
L - Leningrad
Ln - London
M - Moskva
Mchn - München
NY - New York

P - Paris
Pb - Peterburg
Pg - Petrograd
SPb - Sankt-Peterburg
Zch - Zürich

C.

ch. - *chast'*
enc. - encyclopedia (or handbook, etc.)
inc. - *incipit*
kn. - *kniga*
khr. - *khronika*
otd. - *otdel; otdel'nyi*
ott. - *ottisk*
rev. - *review (article)*
sgd - *signed (by)*
t. - *tom*
tir. - *tirazh*
vyp. - *vypusk*
= - *in*

C. TABLE OF CONTENTS

O. BIBLIOGRAPHIES

1. [Arkhippov, Evgenii] "Bibliografiia Innokentiia Annenskago (Sostavlennaia Evgeniem Arkhippovym)" = ZHATVA 1914 V pp. 308-20 [single edition M 1914]

2. Vladislavlev, I. V. RUSSKIE PISATELI (Opyt bibliograficheskogo posobiia po russkoi literature 19-20 stoletiia) M-L [4th edition] 1924 pp. 151-2.

3. Nikitina, E. F. RUSSKAIA LITERATURA OT SIMVOLIZMA DO NASHIKH DNEI. M 1926 pp. 257-8.

4. [Beletskii, A. I. et al., eds] "Innokentii Annenskii—poet, kritik i perevodchik" = NOVEISHAIA RUSSKAIA LITERATURA: KRITIKA, TEATR, METODOLOGIIA (Temy, Bibliografiia) Ivanovo-Voznesensk 1927 p. 132.

5. Vladislavlev, I. V. LITERATURA VELIKOGO DESIATILETIIA (1917-1927), Vol. I M-L 1928 pp. 35-36.

6. [Budanova, N. F.] "Annenskii Innokentii Fedorovich" = ISTORIIA RUSSKOI LITERATURY KONTSA XIX-NACHALA XX VEKA (Bibliograficheskii ukazatel', pod redaktsiei K. D. Muratovoi) M-L 1963 pp. 96-98.

7. TSENTRAL'NYI GOSUDARSTVENNYI ARKHIV LITERATURY I ISKUSSTVA SSSR (Putevoditel': literatura) M 1963 pp. 17, 33-34, 35, 41, 49, 53, 76, 108, 160, 161, 181, 673 [F. 6; ed. khr. 462; archival materials and MSS, 1872-1910].

8. Setchkarev, Vsevolod. "Bibliography" = his STUDIES IN THE LIFE AND WORK OF INNOKENTIJ ANNENSKIJ. The Hague, 1963. pp. 260-63.

9. Tarasenkov, An[atolii] RUSSKIE POETY XX VEKA (1900-1955) M 1966 pp. 17-18.

I. THE WRITINGS OF I. F. ANNENSKII

1881

10. [rev.] "Małecki, Antoni d-r, GRAMMATYKA HISTORICZNO-PORÓWNAWCZA JĘZYKA POLSKIEGO, Lwów, 1879" = ZMNP 1881 ch. 214 mart otd. ii pp. 170-9 [sgd I.A.]

1883

11. "Iz nabliudenii nad iazykom i poezii russkago severa [Innokentiia Annenskago] " = SBORNIK V CHEST' V. I. LAMANSKAGO SPb [fevral'] 1883 pp. 196-211 [single edition SPb 1883].

12. [rev.] "A. Budilovich. NACHERTANIE TSERKOVNO-SLAVIANSKOI

GRAMMATIKI, PRIMENITEL'NO K OBSHCHEI TEORII RUSSKAGO I DRUGIKH
RODSTVENNYKH IAZYKOV. Varshava, 1883." = ZMNP 1883 ch. 227 mai otd. ii
pp. 127-37.

1888

13. PERVYE SHAGI V IZUCHENII SLOVESNOSTI (Dva soobshcheniia v sobranii
prepodovatelei russkago iazyka pri Pedagogicheskom Muzee voenno-uchebnykh
zavedenii) SPb 1888 [23pp.]
14. [rev.] "SLOVO O POLKU IGOREVE, kak khudozhestvennyi pamiatnik Kievskoi
druzhinnoi Rusi. E. Barsova. Dva toma. M. 1887" = ZMNP 1888 ch. 256 aprel' otd. ii
pp. 501-512.

1890

15. "Obrazovatel'noe znachenie rodnago iazyka" = RS 1890 ianvar' pp. 21-44.
16. "O formakh fantasticheskago u Gogolia [Rech', chitannaia na godichnom akte
gimnazii Gurevicha 15-go sentiabria 1890 goda] " = RS 1890 dekabr' pp. 93-104.

1891

17. "Ob esteticheskom otnoshenii Lermontova k prirode [Chitano na godichnom akte
v kollegii Pavla Galagana, v Kieve, 1-go oktiabria, 1891 goda] " = RS 1891 dek. pp. 73-83.

1892

18. "Goncharov i ego Oblomov" = RS 1892 apr. pp. 71-95.
19. "Pedagogicheskiia pis'ma (Ia. P. Gurevichu)" = RS 1892 iiul'/avgust pp. 146-67
[pis'mo pervoe].
19a. = RS 1892 noiabr' pp. 65-86 [pis'mo vtoroe].

1893

20. [rev.] "Tri shkol'nykh izdaniia Sofokla EDIPA TSARIA [otzyv o knigakh] "
= ZMNP 1893 ch. 287 mai otd. ii. pp. 282-87.
21. [rev.] "Illiustrirovannoe sobranie grecheskikh i rimskikh klassikov. Gerodot. [...]
Ob-iasnil G. fon Gaaze. Tsarskoe Selo, 1892." = FO 1893 tom IV pp. 235-38.
22. [rev.] "Gerodot. GREKO-PERSIDSKIIA VOINY. Ob-iasnil G. fon Gaaze. S.-Peter-
burg. 1883." = FO 1893 tom V pp. 136-8.

1894

23. [transl.] VAKKHANKI, TRAGEDIIA EVRIPIDA (Stikhotvornyi perevod s sobliu-
deniem metrov podlinnika, v soprovozhdenii grecheskago teksta i tri ekskursa dlia
osveshcheniia tragedii, so storony literaturnoi, mifologicheskoi i psikhologicheskoi)
SPb 1894 [172pp.].

1895

24. "Pedagogicheskiia pis'ma (Ia. P. Gurevichu)" = RS 1895 fevral' pp. 87-103 [pis'-
mo tret'e].

1896

25. KRATKII SVOD MNENII PEDAGOGICHESKIKH SOVETOV GIMNAZII I PRO-
GIMNAZII S.-PETERBURGSKAGO UCHEBNAGO OKRUGA [...] ZA No. 12930 I
ZAKLIUCHENIE PO VYSHEOZNACHENNYM MNENIIAM DIREKTORA 8-I S. PETER-
BURGSKOI GIMNAZII I.F. ANNENSKAGO. SPb 1896.

26. [transl.] "RES. Tragediia, pripisyvaemaia Evripidu." = ZMNP 1896 ch. 307 sentiabr' otd. V pp. 100-45 [I].

    26a. = ZMNP 1896 oktiabr' pp. 1-32 [II].

27. [rev.] "ILIADA Gomera v perevode N. M. Minskago. Moskva. 1896." - "DAFNIS I KHLOIA. Drevne-grecheskii roman Longusa. Perevod D. S. Merezhkovskago. S.-Peterburg. 1896." = FO 1896 tom XI otd. ii pp. 58-66.

1897

28. "Iz nabliudenii nad iazykom Likofrona (O nachal'nom zvukopodobii)" = COMMEN-TATIONES PHILOLOGICAE (Sbornik statei v chest' Ivana Vasil'evicha Pomialovskago [...] ot uchenikov i slushatelei) SPb 1897 pp. 55-80.

29. [transl.] "GERAKL. Tragediia Evripida." - ZMNP 1897 ch. 312 iiul' otd. V pp. 36-48 [I]

    29a. = ZMNP 1897 avgust pp. 49-96 [II]

    29b. = ZMNP 1897 ch. 313 sentiabr' pp. 97-132 [III]

1898

30. "A. N. Maikov i pedagogicheskoe znachenie ego poezii" = RS 1898 fev. pp. 40-61 [I]

    30a. = RS 1898 mart pp. 53-66 [II]

31. [rev.] "A. Tambovskii, ANAKREONT. Sobranie ego sochinenii v perevodakh russkikh pisatelei. S.-Peterburg. 1898." = FO 1898 tom XIV pp. 47-49.

32. [transl.] "FINIKIIANKI, tragediia Evripida [stikhotvornyi perevod I. F. Annenskago]" = MB 1898 aprel' pp. 1-72 ["Vmesto predisloviia" pp. 1-2; text pp. 3-72.]

33. "Iunyia zhertvy, ili Fesei Vakkhilida" = ZMNP 1898 ch. 317 mai otd. V pp. 54-7.

34. [transl.] "IFIGENIIA — ZHERTVA. Antichnaia tragediia." - ZMNP 1898 ch. 316 mart otd. V. pp. 97-147 [I]

    34a. = ZMNP 1898 aprel' pp. 1-27 [II]

35. "Posmertnaia IFIGENIIA Evripida (Posleslovie k perevodu IFIGENII — ZHERTVY" = ZMNP 1898 ch. 317 mai pp. 67-83.

1899

36. PUSHKIN I TSARSKOE SELO. (Rech', proiznesennaia direktorom Imperatorskoi Nikolaevskoi gimnazii Innokentiem Annenskim 27 maia 1899 goda na Pushkinskom prazdnike v Imperatorskom Kitaiskom Teatre v Tsarskom Sele) SPb 'Tipografiia Shumakher' 1899 [39pp.]

37. "Ion i Apollonid (Chitano v godichnom sobranii Obshchestva klassicheskoi filologii i pedagogiki v Peterburge 20 ianvaria 1899 goda)" = FO 1899 tom XVI [razdel statei] pp. 2-44.

38. [transl.] "ELEKTRA. Tragediia Evripida." = ZMNP 1899 ch. 322 aprel' otd. V. pp. 11-48 [I]

    38a. = ZMNP 1899 ch. 323 mai pp. 49-72 [II]

1900

39. [transl.] RES, TRAGEDIIA (perevod s grecheskago I. F. Annenskago) [Posleslovie Sokolova] SPb 'Tipografiia P. O. Iablonskago' 1900 [30pp.]

40. [transl.] "OREST. Tragediia Evripida." = ZMNP 1900 ch. 327 ianvar' otd. V. pp. 19-48 [I]

    40a. = ZMNP 1900 fevral' pp. 46-96 [II]

    40b. = ZMNP 1900 ch. 328 mart pp. 97-103 [III]

41. MIF OB ORESTE U ESKHILA, SOFOKLA I EVRIPIDA (Etiud Innokentiia Annenskago) SPb 1900 [72pp.; otd. ott. iz ZMNP 1900 VII-VIII ("Khudozhestvennaia obrabotka mifa ob Oreste, ubiitse materi v tragediiakh Eskhila, Sofokla i Evripida")]

1901

42. MELANIPPA-FILOSOF (Tragediia Innokentiia Annenskago [posviashchaetsia Borisu Vasil'evichu Varneke] [Vvodnyia zamechania I. Annenskago]) SPb 'Tipo-litografiia M.P. Frolovoi' 1901 [x + 11-82 pp.]

43. [transl.] Evripid, AL'KESTA (Drama, perevel s grecheskago stikhami i snabdil predisloviem "Poeticheskaia kontseptsiia AL'KESTY Evripida" I. Annenskii) [II] SPb 'Tipografiia V.S. Balashov i K⁰' 1901 [93 pp.]

1902

44. "Khudozhestvennyi idealizm Gogolia (Rech', proiznesennaia 21-go fevralia 1902 goda)" = RS fevral' pp. 114-25

45. TSAR' IKSION (Tragediia v 5 deistviiakh, s muzykal'nymi antraktami) SPb 'Tipografiia M.P. Frolovoi' 1902 [viii + 9-90 pp.]

46. "Antichnaia tragediia (publichnaia lektsiia)" = MB 1902 XI pp. 1-42

47. [transl.] Evripid, IPPOLIT (Tragediia, perevel s grecheskago stikhami i snabdil predisloviem "Tragediia Ippolita i Fedry" I.F. Annenskii) SPb 'Senatskaia tipografiia' 1902 [87 pp.]

1903

48. [transl.] Evripid, MEDEIA (Tragediia, perevel s grecheskago stikhami i snabdil predisloviem "Tragicheskaia Medeia" I. F. Annenskii) SPb 'Senatskaia tipografiia' 1903 [110pp.]

1904

49. TIKHIIA PESNI (S prilozheniem sbornika stikhotvornykh perevodov "Parnastsy i prokliatye") [SPb 1904] [iv + 130 pp.] [sgd Nik. T-o]

50 RAZBOR STIKHOTVORNAGO PEREVODA LIRICHESKIKH STIKHOTVOR-ENII GORATSIIA, P.F. PORFIROVA, SDELANNYI I.F. ANNENSKIM [otd. ott. iz "Otcheta o XV prisuzhdenii Pushkinskikh premii"] SPb 1904

1905

51. F.M. DOSTOEVSKII Kazan' 'Tipo-lit. Nerova' 1905 [16 pp.] [otd. ott. iz OBNOVLENIIA XXXV (dated: January 1906 in Tsarskoe Selo)]

1906

52. "Laodamiia (Liricheskaia tragediia v 4 deistviiakh i s muzykal'nymi antraktami)" [Predislovie avtora] = SEVERNAIA RECH' [SPb] 1906 pp. 137-208 [tir.: 500]

53. KNIGA OTRAZHENII (Problema Gogolevskago iumora. —Dostoevskii do / katastrofy. —Umiraiushchii Turgenev. —Tri / sotsial'nykh dramy. —Drama nastro- / enii. —Bal'mont-lirik.) SPb ['Izdanie Br. Bashmakovykh'] 1906 [213 pp.]

54. [transl.] TEATR EVRIPIDA (Polnyi stikhotvornyi perevod s grecheskago / vsekh p'es i otryvok, / doshedshikh do nas pod etim imenem. / V trekh tomakh, / s dvumia vvedeniiami, stat'iami ob otdel'nykh p'esakh, ob-iasnitel'nym ukazatelem i snimkom s antichnago biusta Evripida / I.F. Annenskago) SPb 'Tipografiia Knigoizdatel'skago T-va Prosveshchenie' vol. I [all published] 190[6] [introductory note dated 20. IX. 1906] [x + 628 pp.]

1907

55. LAODAMIIA (Liricheskaia tragediia) [SPb 1907] [single edition of (52)]

56. "Geine i ego "Romantsero' " = PEREVAL 1907 IV pp. 27-34

57. [rev.] "Aleskandr Kondrat'ev: SATIRESSA. Mifologicheskii roman. Kn-vo 'Grif.' Moskva. 1907." = PEREVAL 1907 IV pp. 62-3

58. [rev.] "Prof. F. Zelinskii: SOPERNIKI KHRISTIANSTVA. Iz zhizni idei (vol. III). S.-Peterburg. VII + 406[pp.] . 1907." = PEREVAL 1907 VIII p. 63

59. "Brand" = PEREVAL 1907 X pp. 42-8

60. "Antichnyi mif v sovremennoi frantsuzskoi poezii [Anne Vladimirovne Borodinoi] " = GERMES 1908 VII pp. 177-85 [I]

   60a. = GERMES 1908 VIII pp. 209-13 [II]

   60b. = GERMES 1908 IX pp. 236-40 [III]

   60c. = GERMES 1908 X pp. 270-88 [IV]

   60d. [SINGLE EDITION] SPb 1908

61. [rev.] "O romanticheskikh tsvetakh: N. Gumilev, ROMANTICHESKIE TSVETY (Stikhi), Parizh 1908" = RECH' 1908 no. 308 [15.XII.1908] [sgd. I.A.]

62. [rev.] "D. N. Ovsianiko-Kulikovskii: TEORIIA PROZY I POEZII. Moskva. 1908." = ZMNP 1908 XI otd. iii pp. 123-5

63. "Perevody D. S. Merezhkovskogo" [with I. Kholodniak] = ZMNP 1908 XII otd. iii pp. 236-9

64. [rev.] "SINTAKSIS RUSSKAGO IAZYKA, sostavil F. V. Rzhiga [...] " = ZMNP 1908 XII otd. iii pp. 240-3

65. [rev.] "Arkadii Sosnitskii: TEORIIA SLOVESNOSTI [...] " = ZMNP 1908 XII otd. iii pp. 239-40

1909

66. VTORAIA KNIGA OTRAZHENII (Iznaka poezii. Belyi ekstaz. / Iuda. Geine prikovannyi. Problema Gamleta. / Brand-Ibsen. Iskusstvo mysli/ [s chertezhom]) SPb ['Tipografiia M. M. Stasiulevicha'] 1909 [135 pp.]

67. "O sovremennom lirizme" = APOLLON 1909 I pp. 12-42 [I]

   67a. = APOLLON 1909 II pp. 3-29 [II]

   67b. = APOLLON 1909 III pp. 5-29 [III]

68. "Teatr L. Andreeva [ANFISA] " = GOLOS SEVERA 1909 [6.Xii.1909] p. 3

69. "Lekont de Lil' i ego ERINNII" = EZHEGODNIK IMPERATORSKIKH TEATROV 1909 vyp. V pp. 57-93

70. Ksenofont VOSPOMINANIIA O SOKRATE (v izbrannykh otryvkakh, s vvedeniem, primechaniiami i 8 risunkami) [ob-iasnil I. F. Annenskii] ch. I (tekst) ch. II ("Ocherk drevne-grecheskoi filosofii," pp. 3-51; "Ob-iasnitel'nyia primechaniia," pp. 52-100) SPb 1909

71. "Pis'mo v redaktsiiu [S. K. Makovskomu] " = APOLLON 1909 II [Khronika] p. 34

72. [transl.] FRANTSUZSKIE LIRIKI XIX VEKA (Perevody v stikhakh i biobibliograficheskiia primechaniiia Valeriia Briusova) SPb 1909 [3 poems transl. by I. F. A.]

1910

73. KIPARISOVYI LARETS (Vtoraia kniga stikhov [posmertnaia]) Moskva 'Knigoizdatel'stvo Grif' 1910 [110 pp.; oblozhka A. Arnshtama]

74. [rev.] "I. Bunin, [Sobranie sochinenii] , tt. I-V, Pb., 1902-1909." = ZMNP 1910 II otd. iii pp. 233-7

1911

75. "Chto takoe poeziia?" (Posmertnaia stat'ia Innokentiia Annenskago [napisanna v 1903 godu—nabrosok vstupleniia k pervoi knige stikhov]) = APOLLON 1911 VI 51-7

76. "Estetika MERTVYKH DUSH i eia nasled'e" (Posmertnaia stat'ia) = APOLLON 1911 VIII pp. 50-8

77. "O Sologube" = O F. SOLOGUBE (Kritika. Stat'i i zametki) [A. Chebotarev-skaia, ed.] Pb 1911, pp. 99-112 [reprinted from APOLLON 1909 I pp. 32-42]

78. ["Avtobiografiia"] = PERVYE LITERATURNYE SHAGI (Avtobiografii so-vremennykh russkikh pisatelei, sobral F. F. Fidler) M 1911 pp. 171-2

1912

79. ANTOLOGIIA SOVREMENNOI POEZII ["Chtets deklamator" IV] Kiev [2nd edition] 1912 pp. 593-600 [10 poems by I. F. A.; 5 poems trans. by I. F. A.]

80. ["Lichnost' Oblomova"] = I. A. GONCHAROV, EGO ZHIZN' I SOCHINENIIA (Sbornik istoriko-literaturniykh statei) [V. I. Pokrovskii, ed.] M [izd. 3-e, dopolnennoe] 1912 pp. 142-6

1913

81. FAMIRA-KIFARED (Vakkhicheskaia drama) [Izd. posmertnoe] M 'Izdanie V. P. Portugalova' 1913 [128 pp.; tir: 100]

82. SOVREMENNYE RUSSKIE LIRIKI 1907-1912 (Stikhotvoreniia) [Evg. Shtern, ed.] SPb 1913 [6 poems by I. F. A.]

83. [transl.] CHTETS DEKLAMATOR kn. III Kiev [3rd edition] 1913 [1 poem transl. by I. F. A.]

84. [transl.] Siulli-priudom [:Sully Prudhomme] IZBRANNYE STIKHOTVORENI-IA V PEREVODAKH RUSSKIKH POETOV (Sbornik, sostavlennyi P. N. Petrovskim) M 1913 [6 poems transl. by I. F. A.]

85. [transl.] MIROVAIA MUZA (Antologiia sovremennoi poezii zapadnoevropei-skoi i russkoi) [S. Gorodetskii, ed.] [I] SPb 1913 [1 (?) poem transl. by I. F. A.]

1914

86. AL'MANAKH 'GRIF' 1903-1913 [S. Krechetov, red.] M 1914 [2 poems by I. F. A.; 1 portrait; 1 facsimile]

87. IZBRANNYE STIKHI RUSSKIKH POETOV [Seriia sbornikov po periodam; period III; vyp. ii: A. Blok—M. Shaginian] SPb 1914 [9 poems by I. F. A.]

88. ANTHOLOGIE DES POETES RUSSES [Jean Chuzeville, ed.] P 1914 [4 poems by I. F. A., in French]

1915

89. [transl.] Verlen, P. [:Paul Verlaine] IZBRANNYE STIKHOTVORENIIA V PE–REVODAKH RUSSKIKH POETOV [sostavil P. N. Petrovskii; s biograficheskim ocherkom Valeriia Briusova] ["Universal'naia Biblioteka" 780] M [2nd edition] 1915 [1 poem transl. by I. F. A.]

1916

90. [transl.] TEATR EVRIPIDA (Perevod / so vvedeniiami i poslesloviiami / I. F. Annenskago / pod redaktsiei i s kommentariem / F. F. Zelinskago) ["Pamiatniki mirovoi literatury"/Antichnye pisateli/Evripid] vol. I M 'Izdanie M. i S. Sabashnikovykh' 1916 [xiv + 406 pp.]

91. "Iz posmertnykh stikhotvorenii" = AL'MANAKH MUZ Pg 1916

1917

92. [transl.] TEATR EVRIPIDA (Perevod [...] I. F. Annenskago [...]) vol. II M 1917 [xxiv + 516 pp.]

1918

93. FAMIRA-KIFARED (Vakkhicheskaia drama) SPb 'Izdanie Z. I. Grzhebina' 1919 [91 pp.; oblozhka N. Radlova, kontsovki A. B., V. Belkina, D. Mitrokhina, S. Sudeikina] 93a. OP.CIT. Pg 'Giperborei' 1919 [95 pp.; 8 ill.]

1920

94. STRANITSY LIRIKI (Izbrannye stikhotvoreniia sovremennykh russkikh poetov, sobral A. Derman) Simferopol' 1920 [1 poem by I. F. A.]

1921

95. PUSHKIN I TSARSKOE SELO [reprinted from (36)] Pb 'Parfenon' 1921 [30 pp.]
96. [trans.] TEATR EVRIPIDA (Perevod [...] I. F. Annenskago pod redaktsiei [...] F. F. Zelinskago) vol. III M 1921 [iv + 548 pp.]

1922

97. CHTETS DEKLAMATOR (Sbornik russkoi poezii) Bln 1922 [6 poems by I. F. A.]
98. TSARSKOE SELO V POEZII (so stat'ei E. F. Gollerbakha) [N. O. Lerner, red.] SPb 1922 [3 poems by I. F. A.]

1923

99. TIKHIE PESNI (s prilozheniem sbornika stikhotvornykh perevodov "Parnastsy i prokliatye") [izd. 2-oe, posmertnoe] Pg 'Academia' 1923 [sgd INNOKENTII ANNEN-SKII (NIK. T-O); 140 pp.; tir.: 1000]
100. KIPARISOVYI LARETS (Vtoraia kniga stikhov, posmertnaia) [Izdanie vto-roe, pod redaktsiei Valentina Krivicha] Pb 'Kartonnyi domik' 1923 [159pp.; tir.: 2000]
101. POSMERTNYE STIKHI INNOKENTIIA ANNENSKOGO (s portretom i 2 faksimile, pod redaktsiei Valentina Krivicha) Pb "Kartonnyi domik' 1923 [168 pp.; tir.: 2000]

1924

102. RUSSKAIA LIRIKA [kn. D. Sviatopolk-Mirskii, ed.] P 1924 [3 poems by I. F. A.]

1925

103. RUSSKAIA POEZIIA XX VEKA (Antologiia russkoi liriki ot simvolizma do nashikh dnei) [I. S. Ezhov, E. I. Shamurin, eds] M 1925 [36 poems by I. F. A.]
104. Krivich, Valentin [:V. I. Annenskii] "Innokentii Annenskii po semeinym vos-pominaniiam i rukopisnym materialam" = LM III [L] 1925 pp. 208-55 [hitherto unpub-lished poems, letters, journals by I. F. A., PASSIM]

1927

105. Grossman, L[eonid] OT NEKRASOVA DO ESENINA: RUSSKAIA POEZIIA 1850-1925gg. (Sbornik stikhotvorenii s bio-bibliograficheskimi primechaniiami) M 1927 [1 poem by I. F. A.]

1929

106. RUSSIAN POEMS [Ch. F. Coxwell, ed.] Ln 1929 [6 poems by I. F. A., in English]

1930

107. [transl.] REVOLIUTSIONNAIA POEZIIA ZAPADA XIX VEKA [A. Gatov, red.] M 1930 [1 poem transl. by I. F. A.]

1933

108. "Petersburg" = CZAS [Kraków] 1933 no. 88 [15.IV.1933] [1 poem by I. F. A., in Polish (transl. by Julian Tuwim)]

1935

109. [transl.] LIRIKA DREVNEI ELLADY V PEREVODAKH RUSSKIKH POET-OV (sobral i kommentiroval Ia[kov] Golosovker) [M-L] 'Academia' 1935 [37 texts transl. by I. F. A.]

1937

110. "To shelestiashchemu listvoi..." [inc.] = LN vol. XXVII-XXVIII M 1937 p. 670 [sgd NIKTO]

1939

111. STIKHOTVORENIIA (Vstupitel'naia stat'ia, redaktsiia i primechaniia A. Fedorova) [L] 'Sovietskii pisatel' ' ["Biblioteka poeta" Malaia seriia 54] 1939 [307 pp.; tir.: 10,000]

1940

112. Malkina, E. P. "Innokentii Annenskii" = LS 1940 VI-VII pp. 6-7 [pis'mo I. F. Annenskogo k N. P. Begichevoi ot 20 ianvaria 1907 g.]

1946

113. ANTHOLOGIE DE LA POESIE RUSSE (précedée d'une introduction à la poésie russe; choix, traduction et commentaires de Jacques David) vol. I [1740-1900] P 1946 [3 poems by I. F. A., in French]

1947

114. DWA WIEKA POEZJI ROSYJSKIEI [M. Jastrun, S. Pollak, eds] Warszawa 1947 [4 poems by I. F. A., in Polish]
115. ANTHOLOGIE DE LA POESIE RUSSE [E. Rais, J. Robert eds] [P] 1947 [19 poems by I. F. A., in French]

116. A BOOK OF RUSSIAN VERSE [translated into English by various hands and edited by C. M Bowra] Ln 1947 [2 poems by I. F. A., in English]

1948

117. A SECOND BOOK OF RUSSIAN VERSE [translated into English by various hands and edited by C. M. Bowra] Ln 1948 [2 poems by I. F. A., in English]

1952

118. RUSSKAIA LIRIKA OT ZHUKOVSKOGO DO BUNINA (Izbrannye stikhotvoreniia) [A. A. Bogolepov, ed.] NY 1952 [8 poems by I. F. A.]

1954

119. DWA WIEKA POEZJI ROSYJSKIEJ [M. Jastrun, S. Pollak eds] Warszawa [3rd edition] 1954 [3 poems by I. F. A., in Polish]
120. Tuwim, Julian Z ROSYIJSKIEGO [S. Pollak, red.] vol. I Warszawa 1954 [1 poem by I. F. A., in Polish]

1955

121. Czechowicz, Józef WIERSZE WYBRANE [S. Pollak, J. Śpiewak eds.] Warszawa 1955 [1 poem by I. F. A., in Polish]

1958

122. [transl.] Longfello, G. [:Henry Longfellow] IZBRANNOE (vstupitel'naia stat'ia i primechaniia B. Tomashevskogo) M 1958 [1 poem transl. by I. F. A.]

1959

123. STIKHOTVORENIIA I TRAGEDII (vstupitel'naia stat'ia, podgotovka teksta i primechaniia A. V. Fedorova) ["Biblioteka poeta" Bol'shaia seriia Vtoroe izdanie] [L 1959] [668 pp.; tir.: 15,000] [the most complete I. F. A.-Edition; contains many of A.s hitherto unpublished poems and letters]
124. Tuwim, Julian DZIEŁA vol. IV ["Przekłady poetyckie" 1] [S. Pollak, red.] Warszawa 1959 [1 poem by I. F. A., in Polish]
125. VERSDICHTUNG DER RUSSISCHEN SYMBOLISTEN (Ein Lesebuch) [J. Holthusen, D. Tschizewskij eds] ["HsT" 5/6] Wiesbaden 1959 [9 poems by I. F.A., in Russian]

1960

126. [transl.] TEATR EVRIPIDA (Medeia. Kiklop. Ippolit. Geralk. Elektra. Orest. Ifigeniia v Avlide) [Perevod I. F. Annenskogo, redaktsiia, vstupitel'naia stat'ia i primechaniia V. V. Golovni] M 1960
127. Guenther, Johannes von NEUE RUSSICHE LYRIK (Mit einer Einleitung von Juri Semjonov) ["Fischer Bücherei" 328] [Frankfurt am Main/Hamburg 1960] [8 poems by I. F. A., in German]
128. POESIA RUSSA DEL NOVECENTO (Versioni, saggio introduttivo, profili bio-bibliografici e note a cura di A. M. Ripellino) ["Universale Economica" 313-314] Milano 1960 [8 poems by I. F. A., in Italian]
129. Podhorski-Okolów, Leonard WYBÓR POEZJI [S. Pollak, ed.] Warszawa 1960 [1 poem by I. F. A., in Polish]

1961

130. Ocup, Nikolai SOVREMENNIKI P 1961 [1 unpublished poem by I. F. A., p. 18]

131. Granoff, Katia ANTHOLOGIE DE LA POESIE RUSSE DU XVIIIe SIECLE A NOS JOURS [Préface de Brice Parain] [P 1961] [5 poems by I. F. A., in French]

132. [Pis'mo I. F. Annenskogo k A. A. Bloku] = UCHENYE ZAPISKI TARTU-SKOGO UNIVERSITETA vyp. 104 Tartu 1961 p. 306

1962

133. Trifonov, N. A. [ed.] RUSSKAIA LITERATURA XX VEKA (dorevoliutsion-nyi period) [Khrestomatiia] M 1962 [4 poems by I. F. A.]

134. THE PENGUIN BOOK OF RUSSIAN VERSE (Introduced and edited by Dimitri Obolensky) ["The Penguin Poets" D 57] [Marmondsworth Middlesex 1962] [8 poems by I. F. A., in Russian/English]

1963

135. Czechowicz, Józef WIERSZE [S. Pollak, A. Jaworski ET AL., eds] Lublin 1963 [1 poem by I. F. A., in Polish]

136. RUSSISCHE LYRIK 1185-1963 (ausgewählt und übersetzt von Hans Baumann) Gütersloh 1963 [1 poem by I. F. A., in German]

1965

137. "O romanticheskikh tsvetakh" = NZ kn. 78 1965 pp. 285-7 [REPRINTED from (61)]

138. LA POESIE RUSSE (Anthologie réunie et publiée sous la direction de Elsa Triolet) [P 1965] [3 poems by I. F. A., in Russian/French]

139. [transl.] Bodler, Sharl' [: Charles Baudelaire] LIRIKA (sostavil E. Etkind, predislovie P. Antokol'skogo) M 1965 [3 poems transl. by I. F. A.]

140. POESIA RUSSA DEL NOVECENTO Milano [2nd edition] 1965 [the same as (128), 8 poems by I. F. A., in Italian]

1966

141. RUSSKIE POETY (Antologiia v chetyrekh tomakh) [D. D. Blagoi ET AL., eds] vol. III M 1966 [5 poems by I. F. A.]

142. MODERN RUSSIAN POETRY (An Anthology with Verse Translations, edited and with an Introduction by Vladimir Markov and Merrill Sparks) [Ln] 1966 [12 poems by I. F. A., in Russian/English]

1967

143. MODERN RUSSIAN POETRY Indianapolis-NY [1967] [the same as (142)]

144. PESN' LIUBVI (Lirika russkikh poetov) M 1967 [1 poem by I. F. A.]

145. SEŠITY PRO MLADOU LITERATURU [Praha] 1967 XI [3 poems by I. F. A., in Czech; transl. by Ivan Wernisch]

146. "Was ist Dichtung?" = 66 RUSSISCHE ESSAYS (Von Puschkin bis Pasternak) [E. Müller-Kamp, ed.] Mn [1967] pp. 380-90 [(75) in German]

1968

147. TRI VEKA RUSSKOI POEZII [N. Bannikov, red.] M 1968 [7 poems by I. F. A.]
148. "Budzik" [and] "Leże na dnie" = TWÓRCZOSC [Warszawa] 1968 VII pp.8-9 [2 poems by I. F. A., in Polish; transl. by Adam Ważyk]
149. [transl.] ZARUBEZHNAIA POEZIIA V RUSSKIKH PEREVODAKH (Ot Lomonosova do nashikh dnei) [E. Vinokurov, L. Ginzburg, eds] M 1968 [2 poems transl. by I. F. A.]
150. KLEINER DREHORGELGRUSS [Peter Schifferli, ed.] Zch 1968 [1 poem by I. F. A., in German]
151. [transl.] MASTERA RUSSKOGO STIKHOTVORNOGO PEREVODA [E. Etkind, ed.] vol. II L 1968 [poems no. 485-502 transl. by I. F. A., pp. 93-104

1969

152. [transl.] Evripid TRAGEDII (Perevod s drevnegrecheskogo Innokentiia Annenskogo, vstupitel'naia stat'ia i kommentarii V. Iarkho) ["Biblioteka antichnoi literatury (Gretsiia)"] vol. I M 1969 [contains A's translations of "Alkesta," "Medeia," "Geraklidy," "Ippolit," Andromakh," "Gekuba," Gerakl," "Ifigeniia v Tavride," "Kiklop," pp. 7-672]
152a. Evripid TRAGEDII (Perevod s drevnegrecheskogo Innokentiia Annenskogo i S. Shervinskogo, kommentarii V. Iarkho) vol. II M 1969 [A's translations of "Elektra," "Elena," "Finikianki," "Ion," "Orest," "Vakkhanki," "Ifideniia v Avlide," pp. 5-570]
153. KNIGI OTRAZHENII [I/II] ["Slavische Propyläen" 50] Mchn 1969 [reprinted from (53) and (66)]
154. [transl.] FRANTSUZSKIE STIKHI V PEREVODE RUSSKIKH POETOV XIX-XXvv. [E. Etkind, ed.] M 1969 [22 poems transl. by I. F. A.]
155. FERNER LEIERKASTENKLANG (Drehorgelgeschichten) [Peter Schifferli, ed.] Zch 1969 [1 poem in prose ("Sentimental'noe vospominanie") by I. F. A., in German, pp. 7-13]

1970

156. ANTHOLOGIE DE LA POESIE RUSSE (La Renaissance du XXe siècle) [N. Struve, ed.] [Coll. "af" 35] [P 1970] [8 poems by I. F. A., in Russian/French]
157. [transl.] Bodler, Sharl' [:Charles Baudelaire] TSVETY ZLA [N. I. Balashov, I. S. Postupal'skii, eds] M 1970 [5 poems transl. by I. F. A.]

1971

158. "Innokenty Annensky on Mikhail Lermontov" [and] "Innokenty Annensky on Fyodor Dostoevsky" = THE COMPLECTION OF RUSSIAN LITERATURE (A Cento, compiled by Andrew Field) Ln 1971 pp. 57-62 [I], 108-13 [II] [in English]

1972

159. "Iz neopublikovannykh pisem Innokentiia Annenskogo" [I] [I. I. Podol'skaia, ed.] = IZVESTIIA AN SSSR [Seriia literatury i iazyka] 1972 V pp. 462-9
159a. ["Pis'ma I. F. Annenskogo k E. M. Mukhinoi" (II) = IZVESTIIA AN SSSR (Seriia literatury i iazyka) 1973 I pp. 49-57]
160. RUSSIAN LITERATURE TRIQUARTERLY IV Fall 1972 pp. 46-50 [5 poems by I. F. A., in English]

n. d.

161. RUSSKII PARNAS [A. Eliasberg, D. Eliasberg, eds] Leipzig n. d. [6 poems by
I. F. A.]
162. CHTETS DEKLAMATOR NY n. d. [4 poems by I. F. A.]
163 OSENNIAIA ANTOLOGIIA [E. Nikolaeva, ed.] [2nd edition] [without pub-
lisher's colophon, n. d.] [5 poems by I. F. A.]

II. WRITINGS ON I. F. ANNENSKII

1901

164. Sokolov, P. [rev.] "Melanippa-filosof" = MV 1901 no. 342 [12.XII.1901]
pp. 3-4
165. [rev.] "Melanippa-filosof. Tragediia Innokentiia Annenskago. S.-Pb., 1901
(X + 81 str.)" = OBZOR KNIG [1901] pp. 86-109 [sgd -r-]

1902

166. Sokolov, P. [rev.] "Tsar' Iksion" = MV 1902 no. 118 [1.V.1902] pp. 2, 3, 4
167. [anon.] [rev.] "Melanippa-filosof (1901)" [and] "Tsar' Iksion (1902)" =
S.-PETERBURGSKIIA VEDEMOSTI 1902 no. 150 [5.VI.1902]
168. Varneke, B. "Original'naia tragediia [Melanippa-filosof] " = TEATR I ISKUS-
STVO 1902 II pp. 26-8

1904

169. Avrelii [: Valerii Briusov] [rev.] "NIK-TO. Tikhiia pesni [...] , SPb., 1904" =
VESY 1904 IV pp. 62-3

1905

170. [enc.] "Annenskii, Innokentii Fedorovich" = ENTSIKLOPEDICHESKII SLO-
VAR' [Izd. F. A. Brokgauz i I. A. Efron] dopolnitel'nyi tom [I] SPb 1905 p. 122

1906

171. Blok, Aleksandr [rev.] "Nik. T-o. Tikhiia pesni [...] " = SLOVO [Literaturnoe
prilozhenie, no. 5] 1906 no. 403 [6.III.1906]
172. Chukovskii, K. "Ob esteticheskom nigilizme" [rev.: KNIGA OTRAZHENII
SPb 1906] = VESY 1906 III-IV pp. 79-81

1907

173. Varneke, B. [rev.] "TEATR EVRIPIDA. Polnyi stikhotvornyi perevod [...]
I. F. Annenskogo. Tom pervyi. SPb. 1907 [...] " = GERMES 1907 I pp. 8-11
174. Varneke, B. V. [rev.] "Teatr Evripida, t. 1, SPb., 1907" = ZMNP 1907 V otd.
ii pp. 226-37
175. Zelinskii, F. [: Tadeusz Zieliński] "Evripid v perevode I. F. Annenskago" =
PEREVAL 1907 XII pp. 40-6 [II]
176. Liatskii, Evgenii "Voprosy iskusstva v sovremennykh ego otrazheniiakh" =
VE 1907 IV [vi-x] pp. 659-87 [on A's KNIGA OTRAZHENII, pp. 665-6]
177. Tsybul'skii, St. [rev.] "Teatr Evripida" = S.-PETERBURGSKIIA VEDEMOSTI
1907 no. 18 [24.I.1907] p. 2

178. Zelinskii, F. IZ ZHIZNI IDEI (nauchno-populiarnyia stat'i) SPb [2nd edition] pp. 231-38 PASSIM
179. Nilender, Vladimir [rev.] "Teatr Evripida. Polnyi stikhotvornyi perevod I. F. Annenskago" = VESY 1908 IV pp. 51-3
180. [anon.] "Referat [I. F. Annenskago], soobshchennyi v zasedanii Obshchest-va Klassicheskoi Filologii i Pedagogiki [26. II.1908] " = GERMES 1908 V p. 139
181. Aleksandrovich, Iu. POSLE CHEKHOVA (Ocherk molodoi literatury posled-niago desiatiletiia, 1898-908) M 1908 p. 213

1909

182. Burnakin, A. "Muchenik krasoty" = ISKRA 1909 III p. 7-9
183. Chukovskii, K. "I. Annenskii" = RECH' 1909 no. 336 [7.XII.1909] p. 4
184 Chukovskii, K. "I. F. Annenskii—nekrolog" = UTRO ROSSII no. 47
185. Kholodniak, I. [rev.] "I. F. Annenskago TEATR EVRIPIDA, t. I." = ZMNP 1909 VII otd. iii pp. 86-9
186. Erberg, Konst[antin] "O vozdushnykh mostakh kritiki" = APOLLON 1909 II pp. 59-62 PASSIM
187. Gumilev, N. [rev.] "Zhurnal VESY, 1909g., IX" [and] "Zhurnal OSTROV, 1909g., II" = APOLLON 1909 III [Khronika] p. 46
188. Gumilev, N. [rev.] "I. F. Annenskii. Vtoraia kniga otrazhenii. Pb. 1909" = RECH' 1909 [11./24.V.1909] p. 3
189. [anon.] "Pokhorony I. F. Annenskago" = RECH' 1909 [5.XII.1909]
190. [anon.] ["I. F. Annenskii (nekrolog)"] = APOLLON 1909 III otd. i p. 49
191. "Segodnia pokhoroniat..." [nekrolog] = SOVREMENNOE SLOVO 1909 [4.XII.1909] p. 1 [sgd. A.O.]
192. Mukhin, A. A. "I. F. Annenskii (nekrolog)" = GERMES 1909 XX pp. 608-12.
193. [anon. (:Sergei Makovskii)] "Otvet redaktsii [Annenskomu] " = APOLLON 1909 II [Khronika] p.34 [cf. (71)]
194. [anon.?] [rev. VTORAIA KNIGA OTRAZHENII] = RUSSKOE BOGAT-STVO 1909 XII

1910

195. Zelinskii, F. "Innokentii Fedorovich Annenskii kak filolog-klassik" = APOLLON 1910 IV [Khronika] pp. 1-9
196. Chulkov, Georgii "Traurnyi estetizm (I. F. Annenskii—kritik)" = APOLLON 1910 IV [Khr.] pp. 9-10
197. Voloshin, Maksimilian "Liki tvorchestva (I. F. Annenskii lirik)" = APOLLON 1910 IV [Khr.] pp. 11-6
198. Ivanov, Viacheslav "O poezii Innokentiia Annenskago" = APOLLON 1910 IV [Khr.] pp. 16-24
199. Burnakin, A. "Esteticheskoe donkikhotstvo" = NOVOE VREMIA 1910 no. 12398 [17.IX.1910] p. 4
200. [Gurevich, Liubov'] "Pamiati I. F. Annenskago" = RM 1910 I otd. ii pp. 163-6 [sgd. L. G.]
201. Gurevich, L. "Zametki o sovremennoi literature" = RM 1910 I otd. ii pp. 73-4
202. Gurevich, L. "Zametki o sovremennoi literature" = RM 1910 V otd. ii p. 167
203. [anon.] [rev: KIPARISOVYI LARETS] = BIRZHEVYIA VEDEMOSTI 1910 no. 11809 [11. VII.1910]
204. [anon.][rev.: KIPARISOVYI LARETS] = KIEVSKAIA MYSL' 1910 no. 205 [27.VII.1910]

205. Briusov, V. [rev.] "I. Annenskii. KIPARISOVYI LARETS, M., 1910" = RM 1910 VI otd. ii pp. 162-3

206. Briusov, V. "Zhan Moreas [: Jean Moréas] " = RM 1910 V otd. ii p. 206

207. Gumilev, N. "Pis'ma o russkoi poezii" = APOLLON 1910 VIII otd. ii pp. 59-60 [rev: KIPARISOVYI LARETS et al.]

208. Gofman, Viktor [rev.] "I. Annenskii. KIPARISOVYI LARETS. M. 1910" = NOVYI ZHURNAL DLIA VSEKH 1910 no. 21 p. 122

209. [anon.] "I. F. Annenskii—nekrolog" = ISTORICHESKII VESTNIK 1910 ianvar' p. 387

210. Varneke, B. V. "I. F. Annenskii [nekrolog] " = ZMNP 1910 mart otd. iv pp. 37-48

211. [Vol'kenshtein, V. M.] [rev: KIPARISOVYI LARETS] = SOVREMENNYI MIR 1910 V [sgd. V. V-n]

1911

212. [enc.] "Annenskii, Innokentii Fedorovich" = NOVYI ENTSIKLOPEDICHE-SKII SLOVAR' [...] K. K. ARSEN'EVA vol. II SPb [1911] col. 921-2 [sgd F. Z.]

1912

213. [Krivich, Valentin (: Valentin I. Annenskii) TSVETOTRAVY (Stikhi; posviashchaetsia "Svetloi pamiati ushedshago ottsa moego") M 1912]

214. Buldeev, Aleksandr "I. F. Annenskii, kak poet" = ZHATVA 1912 kn. III pp. 195-219

215. Gurevich, Liubov' LITERATURA I ESTETIKA (Kriticheskie opyty i etiudy) M 1912 pp. 100-1 ET PASSIM

216. Briusov, Valerii DALEKIE I BLIZKIE (Stat'i i zametki o russkikh poetakh ot Tiutcheva do nashikh dnei) M 1912 pp. 159-60

1913

217. Erberg, Konstantin [: K. A. Siunnerberg] TSEL' TVORCHESTVA M. 1913 pp. 224-9, PASSIM

218 Bobrov, Sergei "Zhizn' i tvorchestvo Artiura Rimbo [: Arthur Rimbaud] " = RM 1913 X otd. ii p. 154

219. Bobrov, Sergei "Chuzhoi golos" = RAZVOROCHENNYE CHEREPA (Ego Futuristy) [SPb] 1913 IX pp. 5-8

220. Mandel'shtam, Osip [rev.] "In. Annenskii: FAMIRA-KIFARED, Vakkhicheskaia drama, Izd. Portugalova. M. 1913" = DEN' [prilozhenie "Literatura, iskusstvo, nauka.."] 1913 [8.X.1913]

1914

221. Gumilev, N. "Pis'mo o russkoi poezii" = APOLLON 1914 I-II pp. 128-30 [rev: FAMIRA-KIFARED]

222. Punin, N. "Problema zhizni v poezii I. F. Annenskago" = APOLLON 1914 X pp. 47-50

223. Chulkov, Georgii "Zakatnyi zvon (I. Annenskii i Anna Akhmatova)" = OT-KLIKI 1914 IX pp. 2-3

224. Arkhippov, Evgenii "Graal' pechali (Lirika E. A. Boratynskago)" = ZHATVA 1914 V pp. 257-74, PASSIM

225. Kriuchkov, Dmitrii "Kritik—intuit (Innokentii Annenskii)" = OCHAROVAN-NYI STRANNIK (Al'manakh intuitivnoi kritiki i poezii) [SPb] 1914 vyp. III pp. 12-4

226. Khovin, Viktor "Poeziia talykh sumerek (I. Annenskii)" = OCHAROVANNYI STRANNIK 1914 vyp. IV pp. 8-10
227. Al'ving, Arsenii [rev.] "Innokentii Annenskii—FAMIRA-KIFARED. Vakkhicheskaia drama. Izd. posmertnoe. M. 1913." = ZHATVA 1914 kn. V pp. 296-8
228. Chuzeville, Jean "Innocent Annensky" = ANTHOLOGIE DES POETES RUSSES P 1914 pp. 139-40

1915

229. Arkhippov, Engenii "Nikto i nichei" = his MIRTOVYI VENETS M 1915 pp. 77-86
230. Mitrofanov, P. P. "Innokentii Annenskii" = RUSSKAIA LITERATURA XX VEKA (1890-1910) [S. A. Vengerov, red.] ch. II t. 2 M 1915 pp. 281-96
231. Vengerov, S. A. KRITIKO-BIOGRAFICHESKII SLOVAR' RUSSKIKH PISATELEI I UCHENYKH (Ot nachala russkoi obrazovannosti do nashikh dnei) vol. I vyp. 1 Pg [2nd edition] 1915 p. 24

1916

232. Ivanov, Viacheslav "O poezii Innokentiia Annenskago" = his BOROZDY I MEZHI (Opyty esteticheskie i kriticheskie) M 1916 pp. 289-311 [cf. (198)]
233. Bal'mont, Konstantin "Poet vnutrennei muzyki" [Bylo proizneseno 30-go noiabria (1916g.) v Kamernom teatre (v Moskve), pered ispolneniem FAMIRY KIFAREDA] = UTRO ROSSII 1916 no. 337 [3.XII.1916] p. 7

1917

234. Zelinskii, F. "Predislovie redaktora" = TEATR EVRIPIDA, vol. II M 1917 pp. vii-xxiii [I. F. A. as a translator]
235. Rozanov, V. V. "Perevodchik i redaktor (k izdaniiu perevodov I. F. Annenskago)" = NOVOE VREMIA 1917 [14.I.1917 (I)]
235a. = NOVOE VREMIA 1917 [24. I. 1917 (II)]
235b. = NOVOE VREMIA 1917 [16.I.1917] [reply to V. V. Rozanov (235) by A's son, Valentin I. Annenskii]

1920

236. Adariukov, V. "Zhizn' i tvorchestvo I. F. Annenskogo" = ZHIZN' ISKUSSTVA 1920 no. 241 [13.I.1920] p. 2 [I]
236a. [reply by Gollerbakh, E.] = ZHIZN' ISKUSSTVA 1920 no. 342 [14.I.1920] p. 1 [II]

1921

237. Tairov, Aleksandr ZAPISKI REZHISSERA [M] 1921 pp. 44-5 et PASSIM

1922

238. Mandel'shtam, Osip O PRIRODE SLOVA Khar'kov 1922 [PASSIM]
239. Khodasevich, Vladislav "Ob Annenskom [chitano v Peterburgskom DOME ISKUSSTV na vechere, posviashchennom pamiati I. F. Annenskogo, 14 dek. 1921g.] = EPOPEIA [Bln] 1922 II pp. 34-56
239a. = FENIKS [M] 1922 kn. I pp. 122-36
240. Gollerbakh, Erikh V. V. ROZANOV (Zhizn' i tvorchestvo) Pb 1922 p. 83 [Rozanov on I. F. A.]

241. Adamovich, Georgii "Pamiati Annenskogo" = TSEKH POETOV kn. II-III [Bln] [1922?] pp. 92-7

242. Makovskii, Sergei "Innokentii Annenskii (po lichnym vospominaniiam)" = VERETENO kn. I Bln 1922 pp. 231-47

243. Eliasberg, Alexander RUSSISCHE LITERATURGESCHICHTE IN EINZEL-PORTRÄTS (Von Puschkin bis Majakowskij) Mn 1922 p. 150

1923

244. Larin, B. "O Kiparisovym lartse" = LM 1923 II pp. 149-58

245. Gizetti, A. "Poet mirovoi disgarmonii (Inn. Fed. Annenskii)" [v osnovu etoi stat'i leg doklad, chitannyi vo Vserossiiskom Literaturnom Obshchestve 18 aprelia 1914g.] = PETROGRAD kn. I Pg-M 1923 pp. 47-71

246. Gumilev, Nikolai PIS'MA O RUSSKOI POEZII Pg 1923 pp. 27-8, 75-6, 85-8, 180-4 ET PASSIM

247. Medvedev, P. [rev.] "I. Annenskii (k vykhodu 2-m izdaniem KIPARISOVOGO LARTSA)" = ZAPISKI PEREDVIZHNOGO TEATRA 1923 no. 49 pp. 2-3

248. Bobrov, Sergei [rev.] "Innokentii Annenskii. Posmertnye stikhi [...] SPb., 1923 [...]" = PECHAT' I REVOLIUTSIIA 1923 III pp. 262-3

1924

249. Sviatopolk-Mirskii, Kn. D. RUSSKAIA LIRIKA (Malen'kaia antologiia ot Lomonosova do Pasternaka) P 1924 pp. 194-5 [on I. F. A.]

250. Luther, Arthur GESCHICHTE DER RUSSISCHEN LITERATUR Leipzig 1924 p. 428

1925

251. Shamurin, E. I. "Osnovnye techeniia v dorevoliutsionnoi russkoi poezii XX veka" = RUSSKAIA POEZIIA XX VEKA M 1925 pp. xxv-xxvi [on I. F. A., cf. (103)]

252. [Mirskii, D. S.] MODERN RUSSIAN LITERATURE (by Prince D. S. Mirsky) Ln 1925 p. 106

253 Krivich, Valentin [: V. I. Annenskii] "Innokentii Annenskii po semeinym vospominaniiam i rukopisnym materialam" = LM 1925 III pp. 208-55 [cf. (104)]

254. [enc.] MASARYKŮV SLOVNÍK NAUČNÝ díl I Praha 1925 p. 192

1926

255. [enc.] BOL'SHAIA SOVETSKAIA ENTSIKLOPEDIIA vol. II M 1926 col. 783

1927

256. Gollerbakh, E. "Iz zagadok proshlogo (I. Annenskii i Tsarskoe Selo)" = KRAS-NAIA GAZETA [vechernyi vypusk] 1927 [3.VII.1927] p. 2

257. Grossman, Leonid BOR'BA ZA STIL' (Opyty po kritike i poetike) M 1927 p. 144

258. Sakulin, P. DIE RUSSISCHE LITERATUR ["Handbuch der Literaturwissenschaft" 116] Bln-Potsdam 1927 pp. 208-9

259 [Lavrin, Janko] RUSSIAN LITERATURE (by Janko Lavrin) Ln [1927] p. 67

1928

260. Voitolovskii, L. OCHERKI ISTORII RUSSKOI LITERATURY XIX I XX VEKOV [ch. 2] M 1928 pp. 233-6

1929

261. [enc.] Blagoi, D. "Annenskii I. F." = LITERATURNAIA ENTSIKLOPEDIIA vol. I [M] 1929 col. 164-7
262. Tynianov, Iurii ARKHAISTY I NOVATORY L 1929 pp. 16-7
263. Rozanov, Iv. N. PUTEVODITEL' PO SOVREMENNOI RUSSKOI LITERA-TURE M [2nd edition] 1929 pp. 53-4, 61-2
264. Pozner, Vladimir PANORAMA DE LA LITTERATURE RUSSE CONTEMP-ORAINE P [1929] pp. 40-6 ET PASSIM
265. [enc.] Lo Gatto, E. "Annenskii I. F." = ENCICLOPEDIA ITALIANA DI SCIENZE, LETTERE ED ARTI vol. III [Milano] 1929 p. 394 [sgd E. L. G.]
266. Piast, Vladimir A. VSTRECHI M 1929 pp. 137-8, 146

1930

267. [enc.] OTTŮV SLOVNÍK NAUČNÝ [Nové doby] vol. I Praha 1930 p. 182
268. [enc.] MALAIA SOVETSKAIA ENTSIKLOPEDIIA vol. I M 1930 col. 335

1931

269. Adamovich, G. V. "Vecher u Annenskogo" = CHISLA 1931 pp. 214-6

1934

270. Derzhavin, Konstantin KNIGA O KAMERNOM TEATRE (1914-1934) L 1934 pp. 65-70

1937

271. Dukor, I. "Problemy dramaturgii simvolizma" = LN vol. XXVII-XXVIII M 1937 pp. 120, 123 seqq., 147 seqq., 165
272. Gofman, V. "Iazyk simvolistov" = LN M 1937 pp. 86, 88-9

1939

273. Fedorov, A. "Innokentii Annenskii" = In. Annenskii STIKHOTVORENIIA [L] 1939 pp. 3-30 [cf. (111)]
274. Evgen'ev, A. "Stikhotvoreniia Innokentiia Annenskogo" = LITERATURNOE OBOZRENIE 1939 no. 14 pp. 31-5 [rev: (111)]
275. Aleksandrov, V. "Innokentii Annenskii" = LITERATUNRYI KRITIK 1939 V-VI pp. 115-34
276. Mikhailovskii, B. V. RUSSKAIA LITERATURA XX VEKA (s devianostykh godov XIX veka do 1917g.) M 1939 [on I. F. A. cf. pp. 72-3, 95-8, 100-1]

1940

277. Iablonko, B. P. I. F. ANNENSKII (k tridtsatiletniiu [sic] so dnia smerti) Baku [Azerbaidzhanskii Gos. Universitat (sic) im. S. M. Kirova] 1940
278. Malkina, E. "Innokentii Annenskii" = LITERATURNYI SOVREMENNIK 1940 V-VI pp. 210-3 [rev: (111)]
279. Golovin, A. Ia. VSTRECHI I ZNAKOMSTVA M-L 1940 pp. 98-9

1941

280. [enc.] HRVATSKA ENCIKLOPEDIIA sv. I Zagreb 1941 p. 462 [sgd N. F.]

1945

281. [enc.] SCHWEIZER LEXIKON vol. I Zch [1945] col. 386

1947

282. [enc.] A DICTIONARY OF MODERN EUROPEAN LITERATURE [H. Smith, ed.] Ln 1947 p. 24

1948

283. [enc.] WINKLER PRINS ENCYCLOPAEDIE vol. II Amsterdam-Brussel 1948 p. 100

1949

284. Strakhovsky, Leonid. I. [ed.] A HANDBOOK OF SLAVIC STUDIES Cambridge, Mass. 1949 p. 446

285. Makovskii, Sergei "Iz vospominanii ob Innokentii Annenskom" = NOVOSEL'E [P-NY] 1949 no. 39-41 pp. 117-29

1950

286. Ivask, Iurii "O poslevoennoi emigrantskoi poezii" = NZ kn. 23 1950 pp. 195-214 [on I. F. A. pp. 196-9 ET PASSIM]

287. Lo Gatto, Ettore STORIA DELLA LETTERATURA RUSSA Firenze 1950 p. 459

288. Tkhorzhevskii, Ivan RUSSKAIA LITERATURA P [2nd edition] 1950 pp. 425-30, PASSIM

289. [enc.] BOL'SHAIA SOVETSKAIA ENTSIKLOPEDIIA vol. II [M] [2nd edition] [1950?] p. 462

1951

290. [enc.] DIE WELTLITERATUR [E. Frauwallner ET AL., eds] vol. I Wien [1951] p. 60

1952

291. Lo Gatto, Ettore STORIA DEL TEATRO RUSSO vol. II Firenze 1952 pp. 148-9

292. Ivanov, Georgii PETERBURGSKIE ZIMY NY 1952 pp. 49, 139, 154

1953

293. Slonim, Marc MODERN RUSSIAN LITERATURE FROM CHEKHOV TO THE PRESENT NY 1953 pp. 101-2 ET PASSIM

1954

294. Khodasevich, Vladislav LITERATURNYE STAT'I I VOSPOMINANIIA NY 1954 pp. 159-73 [the same as (239; 239a)]

295. LITERATURNYI SOVREMENNIK (Al'manakh) Mchn 1954 p. 204 [a note on I. F. A. by Vl. F. Markov]

1955

296. Adamovich, Georgii "Poeziia v emigratsii" = OPYTY kn. IV 1955 pp. 52-3 [on I. F. A.]

297. Makovskii, Sergei PORTRETY SOVREMENNIKOV NY 1955 pp. 221-68 ["Innokentii Annenskii"]

298. Lettenbauer, Wilhelm RUSSISCHE LITERATURGESCHICHTE Frankfurt-Wien 1955 pp. 298-9

1956

299. Iur'eva, Zoia "Innokentii Annenskii o Gogole" = NZ kn. 55 1956 pp. 136-48

300. [enc.] DICTIONARY OF RUSSIAN LITERATURE [W. E. Harkins, ed.] NY [1956] p. 8

301. Shcherbina, V. R. A. N. TOLSTOI M 1956 pp. 25, 37-8 [cit. from Tolstoi's letters to I. F. A.]

302. Veidle, V. "O spornom i besspornom" = OPYTY kn. VII 1956 pp. 42-3 [on I. F. A.]

1957

303. [enc.] DICTIONARY OF RUSSIAN LITERATURE Ln [1957] p. 8 [cf. (300)]

304. [enc.] DICTIONNAIRE BIOGRAPHIQUE DES AUTEURS DE TOUS LES TEMPS ET DE TOUS LES PAYS vol. I P 'Laffont-Bompiani' [1957] pp. 50-1

305. Pertsov, V. "Realizm i modernisticheskie techeniia v russkoi literature nachala XX veka" = VL 1957 II pp. 50-69, PASSIM

306. Stender-Petersen, Adolf GESCHICHTE DER RUSSISCHEN LITERATUR vol. II Mchn 1957 pp. 515-6

1958

307. Setschkareff, Vsevolod "Laodamia in Polen und Russland (Studien zum Verhältnis des Symbolismus zur Antike)" = ZsP 1958 I pp. 1-32 [on Wyspiański, ANNENSKII, Sologub, Briusov]

308. Khardzhiev, N. I. "Tema i metod Annenskogo" = LN vol. LXV M 1958 pp. 408-10

309. Lettenbauer, Wilhelm RUSSISCHE LITERATURGESCHICHTE Wiesbaden [2nd edition] 1958 pp. 222-3 [cf. (298)]

310. Fridlender, G. M. "Osnovnye linii razvitiia russkoi literaturnoi kritiki ot 90-kh godov XIX veka do 1917g." = ISTORIIA RUSSKOI KRITIKI vol. II M-L 1958 pp. 410, 413

311. Lo Gatto, Ettore STORIA DELLA LETTERATURA RUSSA CONTEMPORANEA Milano [2nd edition] 1958 pp. 294-6

312. [enc.] MALAIA SOVETSKAIA ENTSIKLOPEDIIA vol. I M [3rd edition] 1958 col. 423

313. [enc.] DICTIONNAIRE DES OEUVRES DE TOUS LES TEMPS ET DETOUS LES PAYS vol. I P 'Laffont-Bompiani' [1958] p. 462 [on KIPARISOVYI LARETS]

1959

314. Ivask, George "Annenskij und Čechov" = ZsP 1959 II pp. 363-74

315. VERSDICHTUNG DES RUSSISCHEN SYMBOLISMUS [J. Holthusen ET AL., eds] Wiesbaden 1959 p. 108 ET PASSIM [cf. (125)]

316. Fedorov, Andrei "Poeticheskoe tvorchestvo Innokentiia Annenskogo" = I. A. STIKHOTVORENIIA I TRAGEDII [L 1959] pp. 5-60 [cf. (123)]
317. [enc.] DIZIONARIO UNIVERSALE DELLA LETTERATURA CONTEMPO-RANEA vol. I [Verona 1959] p. 138

1960

318. Poggioli, Renato THE POETS OF RUSSIA 1890-1930 Cambridge, Mass. 1960 pp. 170-3
319. Mirsky, D. S. A HISTORY OF RUSSIAN LITERATURE [Francis J. Whitfield, ed.] NY-Ln 1960 pp. 446-8 ET PASSIM
320. [enc.] LEXIKON DER WELTLITERATUR IM 20. JAHRHUNDERT vol. I Freiburg-Basel-Wien 1960 col. 65-6

1961

321. Otsup, Nikolai LITERATURNYE OCHERKI P 1961 pp. 23-5
322. Otsup, Nikolai SOVREMENNIKI P 1961 pp. 7-22, 23-5 ET PASSIM
323. Adamovich, Georgii "O nas i o frantsuzakh" = MOSTY kn. VIII 1961 p. 108
324. Akhmatova, A. A. "Korotko o sebe" = her STIKHOTVORENIIA (1909-1960) M 1961 p. 7
325. [enc.] TEATRAL'NAIA ENTSIKLOPEDIIA vol. I [M 1961] col. 221

1962

326. Makovskii, Sergei "Innokentii Annenskii—kritik" = his NA PARNASE SE-REBRIANOGO VEKA Mn 1962 pp. 123-42
327. Slonim, Marc FROM CHEKHOV TO THE REVOLUTION (Russian Literature 1900-1917) NY 1962 pp. 84, 101-2, 110
328. [enc.] Nikonov, V. A. "Annenskii Innokentii Fedorovich" = KRATKAIA LI-TERATURNAIA ENTSIKLOPEDIIA vol. I [M 1962] col. 237
329. [enc.] WIELKA ENCYKLOPEDIA POWSZECHNA PWN vol. I Warszawa [1962] p. 276
330. Rozhdestvenskii, Vs. A. STRANITSY ZHIZNI (Iz literaturnykh vospominanii) M-L 1962 p. 19

1963

331. Setchkarev, Vsevolod STUDIES IN THE LIFE AND WORK OF INNOKENTIJ ANNENSKIJ ["Slavistic Printings and Reprintings" 36] The Hague 1963
    331a. [rev.] = WdS 1964 IV pp. 440-5 [J. Holthusen]
    331b. [rev.] = THE RUSSIAN REVIEW 1965 I pp. 77-80 [G. Struve]
332. Holthusen, Johannes RUSSISCHE GEGENWARTSLITERATUR vol. I [1890-1940] ["Dalp Taschenbücher" 328] Bern-Mchn [1963] pp. 49-51
333. [enc.] LEXIKON DER WELTLITERATUR [G. von Wilpert, ed.] vol. I Stuttgart [1973] p. 62
334. [enc.] ENTSIKLOPEDICHESKII SLOVAR' V DVUKH TOMAKH [B. A. Vvedenskii ET AL., eds] vol. I [M 1963] p. 54
335. [enc.] DER GROSSE BROCKHAUS [zweiter Ergänzungsband] Wiesbaden [16th edition] 1963 p. 31
336. ANFÄNGE DES RUSSISCHEN FUTURISMUS [D. Tschiževskij, ed.] ["HsT" 7] Wiesbaden 1963, passim ["Einführung"]
337. Blok, Aleksandr SOBRANIE SOCHINENII vol. VIII M-L 1963 pp. 151-2, 163 [B's letters to I. F. A.], 132, 299-300

338. [enc.] Lo Gatto, Ettore "Annenskij I. F." = DIZIONARIO LETTERARIO BOMPIANI DEGLI AUTORI DI TUTTI I TEMPI E DI TUTTE LE LETTERATURE vol. I. Milano 1963 p. 84 [sgd E. L. G.]

1964

339. Ginzburg, L [idiia] O LIRIKE M-L 1964 pp. 330-71

340. Poggioli, Renato I LIRICI RUSSI 1890-1930 (Panorama storico-critico) Milano 1964 pp. 200-3

341. Busch, Wolfgang "Zwei vergessene Uebersetzungen von I. F. Annenskij" = ZsP 1964 II pp. 265-70

342. Busch, Wolfgang HORAZ IN RUSSLAND (Studien und Materialien) ["Forum Slavicum" 2] Mchn 1964 pp. 209-11 ET PASSIM

343. ISTORIIA RUSSKOI LITERATURY [D. D. Blagoi, ed.] vol. III M 1964 pp. 762-3

344. Mirskij, Dmitrij S. GESCHICHTE DER RUSSISCHEN LITERATUR Mchn 1964 pp. 412-4 ET PASSIM

345. [enc.] DIE LITERATUREN DER WELT IN IHRER MÜNDLICHEN UND SCHRIFTLICHEN UEBERLIEFERUNG [W. von Einsiedel, ed.] [1964] p. 752

346. [enc.] DAS GROSSE DUDEN-LEXIKON vol. I Mannheim [1964] p. 270

347. Makovskii, Sergei "Nikolai Gumilev po lichnym vospominaniiam" = NZ kn. 77 1964 pp. 159, 161

347a. [rev.] Terapiano, Iu. K. = RM [P] 14.XI.1964 [on I. F. A. and Gumilev]

1965

348. Bazzarelli, Eridano "Appunti sugli epiteti composti nella lingua poetica di I. Annenskij" = STUDI DI LETTERATURA, STORIA E FILOSOFIA IN ONORE DI BRUNO REVEL Firenze 1965 pp. 95-9

349. Bazzarelli, Eridano LA POESIA DE INNOKENTIJ ANNENSKIJ ["Civiltà letteraria del Novecento" sez. russa I] [Milano 1965]

350. Struve, Gleb "Innokentii Annenskii i Gumilev" = NZ kn. 78 1965 pp. 279-85 [cf. (137)]

351. Ripellino, Angelo Maria IL TRUCCO E L'ANIMA ["Saggi" 365] Torino 1965 pp. 249-50, 356-7 ET PASSIM

352. LA POESIE RUSSE [Elsa Triolet, ed.] [P 1965] p. 190 [cf. (138)]

353. "Griadushchee, sozrevshee v proshedshem (Beseda s Annoi Akhmatovoi)" = VL 1965 IV pp. 183-9, PASSIM

354. [enc.] ENCYCLOPEDIA OF POETRY AND POETICS [A. Preminger, ed.] Princeton, N.J. 1965 p. 526 ["Modern Poetics (Slavic)", sgd V. S.]

1966

355. Gromov, P. A. BLOK, EGO PREDSHESTVENNIKI I SOVREMENNIKI M-L 1966 pp. 218-35 ET PASSIM

356. Gifford, Henry "Imitation as a Poetic Mode" = ACTES DU IVᵉ CONGRES DE L'ASSOCIATION INTERNATIONALE DE LITTERATURE COMPAREE [F. Jost, ed.] The Hague-P 1966 pp. 912-6 [I. F. A. and Baudelaire]

357. Sechkarev, Vsevolod "Gumilev—dramaturg" = Nikolai Gumilev SOBRANIE SOCHINENII vol. III Washington 1966 pp. iii-xxxvii [on I. F. A. pp. ix seqq.]

358. [rev.] Ivask, Iurii "Poety-liriki Drevnei Ellady i Rima (v perevodakh Ia. Golosovkera)" = NZ kn. 84 1966 pp. 294-5 [on I. F. A. as a translator]

359. SOVETSKIE PISATELI (Avtobiografii) vol. III M 1966 p. 31 [Anna Akhmatova on I. F. A., cf. (324)]

360. [Pasternak, B. L.] "Krai, stavshii mne vtoroi rodinoi" = VL 1966 I p. 175 [on I. F. A. as a translator]
361. Orlov, Vl. "Na rubezhe dvukh epokh" = VL 1966 X p. 113
362. Nilsson, N. A. "THE DEAD BEES—Notes on a Poem by Nikolaj Gumilev" = ORBIS SCRIPTUS Mchn 1966 p. 579 [on I. F. A. and Acmeism]
363. Plank, D. L. PASTERNAK'S LYRIC (A study of sound and imagery) The Hague 1966 pp. 65, 83, 85, 93, 99
364. [enc.] BROCKHAUS ENZYKLOPÄDIE [17th edition of Der Grosse Brockhaus] vol. I Wiesbaden 1966 p. 544
365. [enc.] DTV-LEXIKON vol. I [Mchn 1966] p. 154
366. Kviatkovskii, A. POETICHESKII SLOVAR' M 1966, PASSIM [numerous cit. from poems by I. F. A.]

1967

367. Adamovich, Georgii KOMMENTARII Washington D. C. 1967 p. 176
368. Karlinskii, Semen "Veshchestvennost' Annenskogo" = NZ kn. 85 1967 pp. 69-79
369. Etkind, Efim "Baudelaire en langue russe" = EUROPE 1967 avril-mai pp. 252-61, PASSIM [I. F. A. as a translator]

1968

370. Goupy, Armelle "Annenskii i iskusstvo perevoda" = VI. MEZINÁRODNÍ SJEZD SLAVISTŮ V PRAZE (Resumé přednášek [...]) Praha 1968 p. 336
370a. Goupy, Armelle "L'Art de traduire selon Annenskij" = COMMUNICA-TIONS DE LA DELEGATION FRANCAISE ET DE LA DELEGATION SUISSE (VIe Congrès International des Slavistes) P 1968 pp. 39-53
371. Ivask, Iurii "Poety dvadtsatogo veka" = NZ kn. 91 1968 pp. 91-102, PASSIM
372. Ivask, Iurii "Epokha Bloka i Mandel'shtama (O novoi russkoi poezii)" = MOSTY kn. XIII-XIV [NY] 1968 pp. 220-3
373. Etkind, Efim "Poeticheskii perevod v istorii russkoi poezii" = MASTERA RUSSKOGO STIKHOTVORNOGO PEREVODA vol. I L 1968 pp. 60 seqq. [cf.(151)]
374. ZARUBEZHNAIA POEZIIA V RUSSKIKH PEREVODAKH M 1968 pp. 38-40 [N. Vil'mont on I. F. A; cf. (149)]
375. Struve, Nikita "Vosem' chasov s Annoi Akhmatovoi" = Anna Akhmatova SOCHINENII vol. II [Washington D. C.?] 1968 p. 341 [interview 1965]
376. Ripellino, A. M. POESIE DI CHLÉBNIKOV [Torino 1968] pp. lxx, lxxv ["Tentativo di esplorazione del continente Chlébnikov"]
377. Dobin, E. POEZIIA ANNY AKHMATOVOI L 1968 p. 29
378. Shapovaloff, Lubov A. "Aesthetics and Poetics of Innokentij Annenskij" = DA 29:879 A [University of Washington] 1968
379. [enc.] DIE WELTLITERATUR [Frauwallner, Giebisch, Heinzel, eds] [Ergänzungsband A-F] Wien [1968] p. 21
380. [enc.] KINDLERS LITERATUR LEXIKON [Werke] vol. IV Zch [1968] col. 506-8 [on KIPARISOVYI LARETS]

1969

381. Dolgopolov, L. K. "Poeziia russkogo simvolizma" = ISTORIIA RUSSKOI PO-EZII vol. II L. 1969 pp. 274, 290-1
382. Iarkho, V. [ed.] Evripid TRAGEDII vol. I M 1969 pp. 596-8 [on I. F. A. as a translator] [cf. (152)]
383. Markov, Vladimir RUSSIAN FUTURISM (A History) Ln [1969], PASSIM [cf. index]

33

1970

385. Struve, N. [ed.] ANTHOLOGIE DE LA POESIE RUSSE [P 1970] p. 22

384. Khardzhiev, N. [and] V. Trenin POETICHESKAIA KUL'TURA MAIAKOV-SKOGO M 1970 pp. 197-200 [cf. (308)]

385. Struve, N. [ed.] ANTHOLOGIE DE LA POESIE RUSSE [P 1970] p. 22 [cf. (156)]

386. Ingold, Felix Philipp "Das 'Bild' der Poesie bei Innokentij Annenskij" = WdS 1970 II pp. 125-46

387. Ingold, Felix [Philipp] INNOKENTIJ ANNENSKIJ (Sein Beitrag zur Poetik des russischen Symbolismus) [Diss Basel 1968] Bern 1970 [mimeographed edition; not for sale]

388. Agushi, Irina "The Poetry of Georgij Ivanov" = HARVARD SLAVIC STUDIES vol. V 1970 pp. 116, 125-7

389. Mandel'shtam, Nadezhda VOSPOMINANIIA NY 1970 pp. 198, 257-8

390. Mandel'shtam, Osip [rev: FAMIRA-KIFARED] = VESTNIK RStKhrD kn. 97 P-NY 1970 III p. 120 [reprinted from (220)]

391. Adamovich, Georgii "Spory o Nekrasove" = MOSTY kn. XV 1970 p. 164

392. VI. MEZINARODNI SJEZD SLAVISTŮ V PRAZE 1968 (Akta sjezdu) vol. II Praha 1970 pp. 400, 449-50

393. Golovashenko, Iu. REZHISSERSKOE ISKUSSTVO TAIROVA M 1970 pp. 25, 74, 120-1 ET PASSIM

394. Tairov, A. ZAPISKI REZHISSERA (Stat'i, besedy, rechi, pis'ma) M 1970 pp. 17-25 (PASSIM), 153-76 (PASSIM), 510, 565 ET PASSIM

395. Volkov, A. A. RUSSKAIA LITERATURA XX VEKA (dooktiabr'skii period) M [5th edition] 1970 pp. 387-90, PASSIM

396. Nebol'sin, Arkadii "Poeziia poshlosti" = NZ kn. 101 1970 pp. 97-106

1971

397. Pascal, Pierre LES GRANDS COURANTS DE LA PENSEE RUSSE CON-TEMPORAINE [Lausanne 1971] p. 39

398. Terapiano, Iu. "Innokentii Annenskii i Osip Mandel'shtam" = RM [P] no. 2850 [8.VII.1971]

399. Mandel'shtam, Osip SOBRANIE SOCHINENII vol. II [NY] [2nd edition] 1971 pp. 252-3, 344-5, 415-6

400. RUSSKAIA LITERATURA KONTSA XIX–NACHALA XX V. (1901-1907) [B. A. Bialik ET AL., eds] M 1971 pp. 290-6 ET PASSIM

401. [enc.] MEYERS ENZYKLOPAEDISCHES LEXIKON, vol. II Mannheim-Wien-Zch 1971 p. 254

1972

402. Mandel'shatm, Nadezhda VTORAIA KNIGA P 1972 pp. 37, 57, 93, 127, 134, 266, 391, 435, 512

403. RUSSKAIA LITERATURA KONTSA XIX–NACHALA XX V. (1908-1917) [B. A. Bialik ET AL., eds] M 1972, PASSIM [cf. index]

404. Tatishchev, Nikolai PIS'MO V ROSSIIU P 1972 pp. 130-2 [on I. F. A. as a translator (Evripid)]

405. Pollak, Seweryn NIEPOKOJE POETÓW (O poezji rosyjskiej XX wieku) Kraków [1972] pp. 25-7 ET PASSIM

406. Berberova, N. KURSIV MOI (Avtobiografiia) ["Tsentrifuga" 3] Mchn 1972 pp. 133-4, 635 ET PASSIM

407. Podol'skaia, I. I. [ed.] "Iz neopublikovannykh pisem Innokentiia Annenskogo" = IZVESTIIA AN SSSR 1972 V pp. 462-6 ["Vstupitel'naia stat'ia;" cf. (159)]

34

408. [enc.] ILUSTROWANA ENCYKLOPEDJA TRASZKI, EVERTA I MICHAL-
SKIEGO [St. Lam, red.] vol. VI [supplement] col. 78

ADDENDUM

409. [enc.] Nikonov, V. A. "Annenskii Innokentii Fedorovich" = BOL'SHAIA
SOVETSKAIA ENTSIKLOPEDIIA vol. II M [3rd edition] 1970 p. 41

III. TAIROV'S STAGING OF *FAMIRA-KIFARED*

410. "FAMIRA-KIFARED" I. ANNENSKOGO V MOSKOVSKOM KAMERNOM
TEATRE [postanovka A. Tairova; khudozhnik: A. Ekster; muzyka A. Fortera; svet po
sisteme A. Zal'tsmana; PREMIERE 2-ogo noiabria 1916g.] [cf. (81) (233)]
  410a. Derzhavin, Konstantin [ed.] KNIGA O KAMERNOM TEATRE
    (1914-1934) L 1934 pp. 55/57, 58/59 [photographs of Ekster's stage-
    decorations]
  410b. KTO, CHTO, KOGDA V KAMERNOM TEATRE (1914-1924) M n.d.
    (with ill.]
411. [critical accounts of Tairov's staging of FAMIRA-KIFARED:]
    411a. = RUSSKOE SLOVO 9.XI.1916
    411b. = TEATR 9.XI.1916
    411c. = NOVOSTI SEZONA 10.XI. 1916
    411d. = VECHERNIIA IZVESTIIA [M] 10.XI.1916
    411e. = RUSSKIIA VEDEMOSTI 10.XI.1916
    411f. = TEATRAL'NAIA GAZETA 12.XI.1916
    411g. = RAMPA 1.XII.1916
    411h. = APOLLON 1917 I

FURTHER ADDENDA

ad I (The Writings of I. F. Annenskii)

    DIE NEUESTE RUSSISCHE DICHTUNG [von N. A. Otzoup] Breslau 1930 [1
poem by I. F. A., in German]
    LE RUSSE VIVANT [par C. Frioux, A. P. Aleksitch, N. N. Lopatnikova] P [21970]
[1 poem by I. F. A., in Russian]

ad II (Writings on I. F. Annenskii)

    Gumilev, N. "Zhizn' stikha" = APOLLON 1910 VII otd. ii pp. 11-12

ADDENDA, 1973-1975
(Critical Writings on I.F. Annenskii)

1. Ivask, George, "Chelovek (sonet Innokentiia Annenskogo)," = ZAPISKI (Russkaia
    akademicheskaia gruppa v SShA), VII (1973), pp. 251-260.
2. Petrova, I.V., "Annenskii i Tiutchev (K voprosu o traditsiiakh)," = [Sbornik statei:]
    ISKUSSTVO SLOVA. Moskva, 1973. pp. 277-288.
3. Chernyi, Konstantin M., POEZIIA INNOKENTIIA ANNENSKOGO (Avtoreferat dis-
    sertatsii). Moskva [MGU] , 1973. 24 pp.
4. Tucker, Janet G., INNOKENTII ANNENSKII AND THE ACMEIST DOCTRINE. In-

diana [PhD] , 1973.

5. Struve, Nikita, "Valeur expressive des mêtres ternaires," = COMMUNICATIONS DE LA DELEGATION FRANÇAISE (VIIe Congrès international des slavistes). Paris, 1973. pp. 335-340, PASSIM.

6. Prutskov, N.I., "A.P. Chekhov i I.F. Annenskii ('Dama s sobachkoi'/'Razluka')," = id., ISTORIKO-SRAVNITEL' NYJ ANALIZ PROIZVEDENII KHUDOZHEST-VENNOI LITERATURY. Leningrad, 1974. pp. 192-202.

7. Karlinsky, Simon, "Frustrated Artists and Devouring Mothers in Chekhov and Annenski," = MNEMOZINA (Studia [. . .] in honorem V.Setchkarev), München, 1974. pp. 229-231.

8. Tucker, Janet, "Innokenty Annensky as Critic," = RLT, XI (1975), pp. 379-392.

9. Fedorov, A.V., "Proza A. Bloka i 'Knigi otrazhenii' In. Annenskogo (Opyt tipologicheskogo sravneniia)," = TEZISY I VSESOIUZHOI (III) KONFERENTSII [. . .] Tartu, 1975. pp. 90-95.

BLOK'S "THE TWELVE": A BIBLIOGRAPHY OF CRITICISM (1918-70)

Compiled by Munir Sendich

I. NOTE

The following bibliography embraces the 1918-1970 criticism of "The Twelve": articles, reviews, book chapters devoted entirely or partly to the poem, and thesis synopses. It excludes, however, introductory notes in many translations of the poem and parenthetical remarks on the poem, particularly those in memoir literature. All items in the bibliography were verified either *de visu*, or against bibliographical listings in books on Blok, Symbolism or on Soviet Russian literature, as well as against the more noteable bibliographies of Blok, such as:

1. Blium, E., Gol'tsev, V. "Literatura o Bloke za gody revoliutsii. Bibliografiia (1918-1928)," in O BLOKE. Ed. E. F. Nikitina. M. "Nikitinskie subbotniki," 1929. 335-81.

2. Nikitina, E. F., Shuvalov, S. V. "Literatura o Bloke," POETICHESKOE ISKUS-STVO BLOKA. M. "Nikitinskie subbotniki," 1926. 174-91.

3. Kolpakova, E., and others. "Materialy k bibliografii Aleksandra Bloka za 1928-1957 gody," UCHENYE ZAPISKI VIL'NIUSSKOGO GOSUDARSTVENNOGO PEDAGO-GICHESKOGO INSTITUTA, VI (1959), 289-355.

4. Pomirchii, R. E. "Materialy k bibliografii A. Bloka za 1958-1970 gody," BLOKOV-SKII SBORNIK II' Eds. Z. G. Mints and others. Tartu: "Tartuskii gosud. univer." 1972. pp. 528-82.

5. Pyman, Avril, "Materialy k bibliografii A. Bloka," BLOKOVSKII SBORNIK [I]. Eds. Iu. Lotman and others. Tartu: "Tartuskii gosud. univer." 1964. pp. 557-73.

II. TABLE OF ABBREVIATIONS

KO — Knizhnoe obozrenie
KR — Kniga i revoliutsiia
KU — Knizhnyi Ugol
LZ — Literatura i zhizn'
MG — Molodaia gvardiia
NM — Novyi Mir
NZ — Novyi Zhurnal [New York]
PR — Pechat' i revoliutsiia
RU — Rannee Utro
RESL — Revue des etudes slaves

RLit — Russkaia literatura
RSLit — Russkaia sovetskaia literatura
RS — Russkii Sovremennik
SZ — Sovremennye Zapiski [Paris]
TP — Tsekh Poetov
VF — Voprosy filologii
VLit — Voprosy literatury
VRLit — Voprosy russkoi literatury [L'vov]
ZM — Zapiski mechtatelei
ZS — Zeitschrift für Slawistik [Berlin]

III. BIBLIOGRAPHY

1918

1. Brik, O. "Neumestnoe politikanstvo." KU, No. 2.
2. Eikhenval'd, Iu. "Lirik nashego vremeni." TEATRAL'NYI KUR'ER, No. 11.
3. Eikhenval'd, Iu. "Otrazheniia." RU, No. 117.
4. Aldanov, Mark. ARMAGGODON. Petersburg, 1918.
5. Georgiev, A. [Evdokimov, I. V.]. "Poema 'Dvenadtsat' ' Aleksandra Blok." IZVESTIIA VOLOGODSKOGO GUBISPOLKOMA. No. 84-85.
6. Gizetti, A. "Stikhiia i tvorchestvo." MYSL', I (1918), 2-3.
7. Ivanov-Razumnik, R. " 'Dvenadtsat'.' " ZNAMIA TRUDA, No. 180.

8. Ivanov-Razumnik, R. "Ispytanie v groze i bure." NASH PUT', No. 1. Reprinted in his ALEKSANDR BLOK. ANDREI BELYI. Petrograd: "Alkonost," 1919. pp. 119-63.

9. I. [Ivanov-Razumnik, R.]. "Vniz po lesenke." PONEDEL'NIK. No. 2.

10. Ivnev, R. "Poety i poetika." ANARKHIIA. No. 32.

11. Leonidov, O. "Retsenzii na poemy 'Dvenadtsat' ' i 'Solov'inyi sad'. " SVOBODNYI CHAS, No. 6.

12. Osinskii, N. "Intelligentskii gimn Oktiabr'skoi revoliutsii (A. Blok–'Dvenadtsat')." VECHERNYE IZVESTIIA [Moskovskogo Soveta Rabochikh i Krasnoarmeiskikh deputatov]. August 21, 1918.

13. Rostin, E. " 'Dvenadtsat' ' Bloka." PONEDEL'NIK, No. 17.

14. Shershenevich, V. "Vdrug revoliutsionnoe." RU, No. 28.

15. Shleiman, P. " 'Dvenadtsat'.' " KOLOS'IA [Khar'kov] , No. 7.

1919

16. Chernyi, Boris. "Demokratizatsiia poezii." OTKLIKI, No. 4.

17. Mochul'skii, K. "Poema razrusheniia." ODESSKII LISTOK, No. 117.

18. Spaskii, S. "Poeziia sovremennosti." ZAREVO ZAVODOV, No. 1.

19. Voloshin, Maks. "Poety revoliutsii." KAMENA, Kn. 2 (1919), 13-15.

1920

20. Ivanov-Razumnik, R. RUSSKAIA LITERATURA XX VEKA. Petrograd, 1920.

21. L'vov-Rogachevskii, V. OCHERKI PO ISTORII NOVEISHEI RUSSKOI LITERATURY. M. 1920.

22. Shershenevich, V. "Putevoditel' po poezii." OGNI [Voronezh] , No. 2.

1921

23. Antsiferov, N., Ed. NEPOSTIZHIMYI GOROD. SBORNIK STATEI OB ALEKSANDRE BLOKE. Petrograd: "Kartonnyi domik," 1921.

24. Eikhenbaum, B. "Mig soznaniia." KU, No. 7.

25. Eikhenval'd, Iu. "Pamiati Bloka." KUL'TURA TEATRA, No. 7-8.

26. Gollerbakh, E. "Iz vospominanii o Bloke." NM, No. 253.

27. Guber, P. "Poet i revoliutsiia." LETOPIS' DOMA LITERATOROV, No. 1.

28. Gurian, W. "Alexander Blok." HOCHLAND, XIX (Oct. 1921-March 1922), 118-25.

29. Kuzmin, M. "A. Blok." ZHIZN' ISKUSSTVA, No. 804.

30. Lavretskii, V. "Poet revoliutsionnyikh iskanii." PUT', No. 153.

31. Leo. L. [Pseud.]. "Dvenadstat' ", RUL' [Berlin] , No. 237. August 28, 1921.

32. Nikolsky, Yuriy. "Two Poets of Bolshevism." LIVING AGE, Vol. 311 (Nov. 19, 1921), 384-86.

33. OB ALEKSANDRE BLOKE. [Stat'i N. Antsiferova, Iu. Verkhovskogo, V. Zhirmunskogo, V. Piasta, A. Slonimskogo, Iu. Tynianova, B. Eikhenbauma, B. Engel'gardta.] Peterburg: "26-aia gosud. tipografiia," 1921.

34. Pil'skii, Petr. "Dvenadtsat'." SEGODNIA [Riga] , No. 260.

35. Pozdniak, A. "Ot prekrasnoi damy k 'Dvenadtsati'." VOSKHOD, No. 1.

36. Rubinshtein, D. "Pamiati A. A. Bloka." TRUD, No. 132 (August 10, 1921).

37. Struve, Petr. " 'Dvenadtsat' ' Aleksandra Bloka." RUSSKAIA MYSL' [Sofia] , No. 1-2, pp. 6-7.

38. Tolstoi, A. N. "Padshii angel." POSLEDNIE NOVOSTI [Paris] , No. 413.

39. Treplev, M. "Dva literaturnykh vechera." RUL', No. 293 (Dec. 3, 1921).

40. Tsshokher, A. "Iz vospominanii ob A. Bloke." ISKUSSTVO [Vitebsk], No. 4-6, pp. 4-5.

41. Tyrkova, A. "Iz vospominanii o Bloke." RUL', No. 256 (August, 1921).

42. Wescott, Glenway. "Alexander Blok." POETRY [Chicago] , XIX (Dec. 1921), 149-51.

1922

43. Adamovich, Georgii. "Smert' Bloka." TP, No. 3.
44. Ashukin, N. "A. A. Blok." SPOLOKHI [Berlin] , No. 6-7.
45. Beketova, M. A. "Glava piatnadtsataia," in her ALEKSANDR BLOK. BIOGRAFI-
    CHESKII OCHERK. P. "Alkonost," 1922. pp. 255-70.
46. Belyi, A., Ivanov-Razumnik, R., Shteinberg, A. PAMIATI ALEKSANDRA BLOKA.
    Petersburg: "Vol'fila," 1922.
47. Briusov, V. "Vchera, segodnia i zavtra russkoi poezii." PR, No. 7.
48. Chukovskii, K. KNIGA OB ALEKSANDRE BLOKE. Berlin: "Epokha," 1922.
49. Chukovskii, K. "Poslednie gody Bloka." ZM, No. 6, 155-83. Reprinted in his ALEK-
    SANDR BLOK KAK CHELOVEK I POET. P. "A. F. Marks," 1924.
50. Fedin, K. "Nemetskii perevod 'Dvenadtsati'." KR, No. 5, 49-51.
51. Gorodetskii, S. "Vospominaniia o Bloke." PR, No. 1.
52. Kniazhnin, V. N. ALEKSANDR ALEKSANDROVICH BLOK. P. "Kolos," 1922.
53. Lundberg, E. "Die jüngste russische Literatur." DIE NEUE RUNDSCHAU (1922),
    pp. 921-32.
54. Lundberg, E. ZAPISKI PISATELIA. Berlin, 1922.
55. Mandel'shtam, O. "A. Blok (7 avg. 1921 - 7 avg. 1922 g.)." ROSSIIA, No. 1.
56. Medvedev, P. N. "Tvorcheskii put' Bloka," in SBORNIK PAMIATI BLOKA.
    Petersburg: "Poliarnaia zvezda," 1922.
57. Nadezhdin, L. "Blok i revoliutsiia." NOVYI PUT' [Riga] , March 3, 1922.
58. Otsup, Nikolai. "O poezii Aleksandra Bloka." TP, No. 3.
59. Pil'skii, P. "Aleksandr Blok." SEGODNIA, No. 3 (August 6, 1922).
60. Sumarokov, A. "Moia vstrecha s Blokom." NOVYI BYT [Ivanov-Voznesensk] , No. 1.
61. Tolstoi, A. N. "Pamiati Bloka." NAKANUNE [Berlin] , No. 13 (1922).
62. Trotskii, L. D. "Vneoktiabr'skaia literatura," PRAVDA [Moscow] , No. 221, 238
    (October 1922).
63. Zorgenfrei, V. A. "Blok." ZM, No. 3, 23-27.
64. Zorgenfrei, V. A. "Aleksandr Aleksandrovich Blok." ZM, No. 6, 123-54.

1923

65. Anichkov, E. NOVAIA RUSSKAIA POEZIIA. Berlin: Izd. Ladyzhnikova," 1923.
66. Babenchikov, M. ALEKSANDR BLOK I ROSSIIA. M. 1923.
67. Hippius, Zinaida. "Moi lunnyi drug. Rasskaz pro A. Bloka." OKNO [Paris] , No. 1.
    Reprinted in her ZHIVYE LITSA. Prague: "PImaia," 1925. I, 3-79.
68. Kogan, R. "Drama Bloka." PR, No. 5.
69. Oksenov, I. "O kompozitsii 'Dvenadtsati.' " KR, No. 125, 26-28.
70. Piast, V. VOSPOMINANIIA O BLOKE. Petersburg: "Atenei," 1923.
71. Trotskii, L. D. "Aleksandr Blok," in his LITERATURA I REVOLIUTSIIA. M. 1923,
    pp. 115-26.
72. Zhukov, P. "Miatezhnyi Blok." LITERATURNYI EZHENEDEL'NIK, No. 31.

1924

73. Blok, G. P. "Geroi 'Vozmezdeiia'." RS, No. 3.
74. Zamiatin, Evg[egnii] . "Vospominaniia o Bloke." RS, No. 3, 187-94.

1925

75. Gorbachev, G. E. "Sub"ektivno-antiburzhuaznyi i ob"ektivno-reaktsionnyi mistitism
    i tvorchestvo A. Bloka," in his KAPITALIZM I RUSSKAIA LITERATURA. L. 1925.
76. L'vov-Rogachevskii, V. NOVEISHAIA RUSSKAIA LITERATURA. M. 1925.
77. Mirsky. D. S. MODERN RUSSIAN LITERATURE. London: Oxford U., 1925. p. 108.

78. Iushchenko, Andrei. LICHINA I LIK. [O poemakh A. Bloka 'Dvenadstat' ' i Alekseia
    Masainova 'Lik Zveria.' (Seriia: "Otkliki zhizni." Obzor vydaiushchikhsia proizvedenii
    sovremennosti)]. Paris, 1925.
79. PIS'MA ALEKSANDRA BLOKA. Intro. and notes by S. M. Solov'ev, G. I. Chulkov, A.
    D. Skaldin, and V. N. Kniazhnin. Leningrad: "Kolos," 1925.

1926

80. Tsingovatov, A. Ia. A. A.BLOK. ZHIZN' I TVORCHESTVO. M. 1926.

1927

81. Gor'kii, M. ZAMETKI IZ DNEVNIKA. M. 1927.

1928

82. Medvedev, P. N. DRAMY I POEMY ALEKSANDRA BLOKA. Leningrad, 1928.

1929

83. Legras, Jules. "Poesie d'hier," in his LA LITTERATURE EN RUSSIE. Paris: Armand
    Colin, 1929. pp. 203-207.

1930

84. Lavrin, Janko. "Alexander Blok." LIFE AND LETTERS. V, 28 (1930), 174-76. Re-
    printed, slightly revised, in his ASPECTS OF MODERNISM. FROM WILDE TO
    PIRANDELLO. London, 1935. pp. 115-38; and in his FROM PUSHKIN TO MA-
    YAKOVSKY. London, 1948. pp. 254-60.
84a. Nemerovskaia, O., and Vol'pe, Ts. SUD'BA BLOKA. L. 1930.

1931

85. Adamovich, Georgii. "Aleksandr Blok." SZ, Kn 47 (1931).

1932

86. Bowra, C. M. "The Position of Alexander Blok." THE CRITERION [London], XIX,
    44 (1932), 422-38.

1933

87. Blagoi, D. "Aleksandr Blok," in his TRI VEKA. IZ ISTORII RUSSKOI POEZII XVIII,
    XIX i XX vv. M. 1933. pp. 323-40.

1936

88. Goodmann, Th. "Blok und die Revolution," in his ALEXANDER BLOK. Konigsberg:
    "Klutke," 1936. pp. 79-87.
89. Orlov, V. "Aleksandr Blok," in ALEKSANDR BLOK. STIKHOTVORENIIA. POEMY.
    TEATR. L. 1936.
90. Stepanov, N. "V. V. Khlebnikov," in VELEMIR KHLEBNIKOV. IZBRANNYE
    STIKHOTVORENIIA. M. 1936. p. 65.

1937

91. Orlov, V. "Blok v pechati." LITERATURNOE NASLEDSTVO. Kn. 27-28 (1937),
    512-35.
92. Shklovskii, V. "O proshlom i nastoiashchem v proizvedeniiakh A. Bloka." ZNAMIA,
    No. 11. pp. 278-88.

1939

93. Lednitzky, Wacław. "Christ et revolution dans la poesie russe et polonaise," MELANGES
    EN L'HONNEUR DE JULES LEGRAS. Paris: Librairie Droz [Travaux publies par
    l'Institut d'etudes Slaves, XVII, 1939], 91-121.

1943

94. Bowra, C. M. "Alexander Blok," in his THE HERITAGE OF SYMBOLISM. London, 1943. pp. 144-79.

1945

95. Rozhdestvenskii, V. A. "Vospominaniia ob Aleksandre Bloke." ZVEZDA, NO. 3.

1946

96. Bonneau, Sophie. "Blok et le Christ," and "Le Quatrième Monde: l'Amour, la Russie éternelle," in her L'UNIVERS POETIQUE D'ALEXANDRE BLOK. Paris: Institut d'études slaves, 1946, pp. 187-94 and 253-93. Reprinted as "La Russie et la Revolution de Blok," in her [Sophie Laffitte], A. BLOK. Paris: Seghers, 1958. pp. 72-87, with revisions.

97. Orlov, V. "Lirika i poemy A. Bloka," in A. Blok, POLNOE SOBRANIE STIKHOTVORENII V DVUKH TOMAKH. Ed. V. Orlov. M. 1946.

98. Timofeev, L. E. ALEKSANDR BLOK: OCHERK ZHIZNI I TVORCHESTVA. M. 1946.

1947

99. Guenther, Johann von. "Alexander Blok. Der Versuch einer Darstellung," in Alexander Blok, GESAMMELTE DICHTUNGEN. Munich: Weissmann Verlag, 1947. 409-97.

1948

100. Colin, R. Guershoon. "The Russian Genius: Alexander Blok." THE PENGUIN RUSSIAN REVIEW., No. 4 (1948), 110-33.

101. Mochul'skii, K. " 'Dvenadtsat'." in his ALEKSANDR BLOK. Paris: YMCA, 1948. pp. 397-411.

1951

102. Labry, Raoul. "Alexander Blok et Nietzsche." RESL, XXVII (1951), 201-208.

1953

103. Slonim, Marc. "Blok and the Symbolists," MODERN RUSSIAN LITERATURE. New York: Oxford Univ. Press, 1953. pp. 204-10.

1955

104. Timofeev, L. I. A. BLOK. M. 1955.

1956

105. Adamovich, Georgii. "Nasledstvo Bloka." NZ, Kn. 44. 73-87.

106. Annenkov, Iu. "Ob Aleksandre Bloke." NZ, Kn. 47 (1956), 108-32.

107. Anon. "Romantic Poet of Russia." LONDON TIMES LITERARY SUPPLEMENT (August 10, 1956), 474.

108. Orlov, V. ALEKSANDR BLOK. M. 1956.

109. Tarasenkov, A. "Zametki o poezii Bloka," POETY. M. 1956.

1957

110. Aksenova, E. "A. Blok. 'Dvenadtsat'.' " VLit. No. 7, 33-53.

111. Baade, M. "Die deutsche Literaturkritik zu dem Poem 'Die Zwölf' won Alexander Blok." WISSENSCHAFTLICHE ZEITSCHRIFT DER HUMBOLDT-UNIVERSITAT ZU BERLIN, VII, No. 1 (1957-58), 107-117.

112. Laffitte, Sophie. "Le symbolisme occidental et Alexandre Blok." RESL, XXXIV (1957), 88-94.

113. Lunacharskii, A. "Blok i revoliutsiia," STAT'I O LITERATURE. M. 1957, 402-18.

114. Timofeev, L. I. ALEKSANDR BLOK. M. 1957.
115. Zelinskii, K. "Na velikom rubezhe." ZNAMIA, No. 11. pp. 160-99.

1958

116. Budrin, V. "Pervaia poema ob Oktiabre (protiv traditsionnogo tolkovanii poemy A. Bloka 'Dvenadtsat'.')," PRIKAM'E, No. 24. pp. 118-23.
117. Pomerantseva, E. V. "Aleksandr Blok i fol'klor." RUSSKII FOL'KLOR. MATERI- ALY I ISSLEDOVANIIA, III (1958), 203-24.
118. Vengrov, N. "A. Blok," ISTORIIA RUSSKOI SOVETSKOI LITERATURY. M. 1958. pp. 255-80.
119. Zavalishin, Vyacheslav. "Aleksandr Blok (1880-1921)," EARLY SOVIET WRITERS. New York, 1958. pp. 5-22.

1959

120. Aksenova, E. "Pozitsiia pisatelia v simvolike proizvedeniia," KHUDOZHESTVEN- NOE VYRAZHENIE POSITSII PISATELIA. Vladimir, 1959. pp. 75-98.
121. Dolgopolov, L. K. "Dvenadtsat' Al. Bloka (Ideinaia osnova poemy)." VOPROSY SOVETSKOI LITERATURY, VII (1959), 134-80.
122. Drabkina, E. Ia. "Dvenadtsat'." NM, No. 4 (1959), 17. Reprinted in her CHERNYE SUKHARI. M. 1959.
123. Remenik, G. POEMY ALEKSANDRA BLOKA. M. 1959.
124. Smirnov, R. I. "Nekotorye voprosy ideino-khudozhestvennoi spetsifiki poemy A. A. Bloka 'Dvenadtsat'.' " UCHENYE ZAPISKI IRKUTSKOGO PED' UNIVERSITETA [Kafedra literatury, vyp. 15, 1959.] , pp. 87-129.
125. Shtut, S. M. "Dvenadtsat' A. Bloka," NM, No. 1 (1959), 231-46. Reprinted in his KAKOV TY, CHELOVEK. M. 1964. pp. 55-92.
126. Shubin, E. "Poema A. Bloka 'Dvenadtsat'.' " in FILOLOGICHESKII SBORNIK STU- DENTCHESKOGO NAUCHNOGO OBSHCHESTVA LGU, II (1959), 37-52.

1960

127. Kish, Sir Cecil. "The Coming of the 1917 Revolution." ALEXANDER BLOK: PROPHET OF REVOLUTION. London, 1960. 123-41. Reprint New York, 1961.
128. Medvedev, Pavel. "P'esa iz zhizni Isusa," V LABORATORII PISATELIA. M. 1960. pp. 310-12.
129. Mints, Z. G. "Poema 'Dvenadtsat' ' i mirovozrenie Aleksandra Bloka epokhi revoliutsii." TRUDY PO RUSSKOI I SLAVIANSKOI FILOLOGII [Uchenye zapiski Tartuskogo gosudarstvennogo universiteta, III, vyp. 98, 1960] . pp. 247-78.
130. Ognev, V. F. "Ideia i obraz." LZ, No. 115 (1960), 1-2.
131. Orlov, V. N. "Aleksandr Blok. Vstupitel'nyi ocherk," in A. Blok, SOBRANIE SOCHI- NENII V VOS'MI TOMAKH. M. 1960. I, vii-lxiv.
132. Poggioli, Renato. THE POETS OF RUSSIA: 1890-1930. Cambridge, 1960. 205-208.
133. Pyman, Avril. "Sil'noe vpechatlenie." SMENA [Leningrad] , No. 206 (Aug. 31), p. 3.
134. Reeve, F. D. "Structure and Symbol in Blok's 'The Twelve'." AMERICAN SLAVIC AND EAST EUROPEAN REVIEW, XIX (1960), 259-75. Reprinted in his ALEK- SANDR BLOK: BETWEEN IMAGE AND IDEA. New York, 1962. pp. 202-218.
135. Timofeev, L. I. "Poema Bloka 'Dvenadtsat' ' i ee tolkovateli." VLit, No. 7 (1960), 116-27. Reprinted, slightly revised in his SOVETSKAIA LITERATURA. M. 1960. pp. 507-22.

1961

136. Chekarlieva, N. "A. A. Blok i revoliutsiia." EZIK I LITERATURA [Sofia] , No. 3 (1961), 43-58.

137. Futrell, Michael. "Alexander Blok." SURVEY, No. 36. pp. 119-20.
138. Kopelev, L. "Muzhestvo i dobrota poeta." MOSKVA, No. 9. pp. 211-13.
139. Muchnic, Helen. "Alexander Blok," FROM GORKY TO PASTERNAK. New York, 1961. pp. 154-75.
140. Pyman, Avril. "Aleksandr Blok v Anglii." RLit, No. 1. pp. 214-220.
141. Sergievskii, I. V. " 'Dvenadtsat'.' Gor'kii i Blok," in his IZBRANNYE RABOTY. M. 1961. pp. 92-127.
142. Timofeev, L. I. "Poetika kontrasta v poezii Aleksandra Bloka." RLit, No. 2. pp. 98-107.

1962

143. Dolgopolov, L. K. "Poemy Bloka 'Vozmezdie,' 'Dvenadtsat'.' " [Avtoreferat dissertatsii na soiskanie uchen. step. kand. filol. nauk, LGU, 1962.]
144. Kembal, Robin. Review of Reeve, ALEKSANDR BLOK in the RUSSIAN REVIEW, No. 2 (1962), pp. 203-205.
145. Orlov, V. N. POEMA ALEKSANDRA BLOKA "DVENADTSAT'." STRANITSA IZ ISTORII SOVETSKOI LITERATURY. M. 1962. 2nd enlarged ed. M. 1967.
146. Sharypkin, D. M. "Blok i Ibsen." SKANDINAVSKII SBORNIK, vyp. 6. pp. 159-75.
147. ["The Twelve" in Poland] , SLAVIC ORIENTALIS, No. 2. pp. 183-200.
148. Timofeeva, V. V. IAZYK POETA I VREMIA. POETICHESKII IAZYK MAIAKOV-KOVSKOGO. M. 1962. pp. 121-28.

1963

149. Alexandrova, Vera. A HISTORY OF SOVIET LITERATURE. New York, 1963. pp. 8-12.
150. Bednyi, Demian. "Pisat' pravdu zhizni." NM, No. 4. pp. 216-20.
151. Felichkin, Iu. M. "Lingvisticheskaia kharakteristika odnogo iz frantsuzskikh perevodov 'Dvenadtsati' A. Bloka." TRUDY SAMARKANDSKOGO UNIVERSITETA [Voprosy grammatiki i iazyka, XXII, vyp. 132, 1963] , 15-22.
152. Levin, V. I. "Poema Aleksandra Bloka 'Dvenadtsat' ' glazami sovetskogo i amerikan-skogo issledovatelia." IZVESTIIA AKADEMII NAUK SSSR [Seriia literatury i iazyka, XXII, vyp. 5, 1963] , 386-96.
153. Mints, Z. G., and Chernov, I. A. Review of Reeve, ALEKSANDR BLOK, in RLit, No. 3 (1963), 213-17.
154. Orlov, V. N. PUTI I SUD'BY. M. 1963.
155. Papernyi, Z. S. "Blok i revoliutsiia," SAMOE TRUDNOE. M. 1963. pp. 66-99.
156. Selivanovskii, A. P. "Ocherki po istorii russkoi sovetskoi poezii," V LITERATUR-NYKH BOIAKH. M. 1963. pp. 319-20, 330-43, 350-51.
157. Struve, Gleb. "The Transition from Russian to Soviet Literature." LITERATURE AND REVOLUTION IN SOVIET RUSSIA. 1917-62. Eds. Max Hayward, et al. London: Oxford Univ. Press, 1963. pp. 1-27.
158. Timofeev, L. I. "Blok v nachale Oktiabr'skoi revoliutsii," TVORCHESTVO ALEK-SANDRA BLOKA. M. 1963. pp. 134-68.
159. Vengrov, Natan. "Aleksandr Blok v gody Velikogo Oktiabria," in his PUT' ALEK-SANDRA BLOKA. M. 1963. pp. 358-412.

1964

160. Baade, M. "Zur Aufnahme von Aleksandr Bloks Poem 'Die Zwölf' in Deutschland." ZS, IX (1964), 175-95 and 551-73.
161. Dolgopolov, L. K. " ' Dvenadtsat' ' i vozrozhdenie epicheskoi poezii," POEMY BLOKA I RUSSKAIA POEMA KONTSA XIX NACHALA XX VEKOV. M. 1964. pp. 145-81.
162. " 'Dvenadtsat' ' Blok v podpol'e." VLit, No. 1. p. 247.
163. Erlich, Victor. THE DOUBLE IMAGE. Baltimore, 1964. pp. 68-119.
164. Gorelov, A. "'Skvoz' viugi," OCHERKI O RUSSKIKH PISATELIAKH. L. 1964. pp. 659-740.

165. Nag, Martin. "Ibsen og Blok og 'Deus Caritatis'." EDDA [Oslo], No. 4. pp. 324-38.
166. Pavlovich, N. A. "Vospominaniia ob Aleksandre Bloke," BLOKOVSKII SBORNIK. Tartu, 1964. pp. 446-506.
167. Serdiuk, V. "Poema, rozhdennaia Oktiabrem." VF [Frunze], No. 2. pp. 38-56.
168. Smirnov, R. I. "Posleoktiabr'skaia poeziia A. A. Bloka." " 'Dvenadtsat',' 'Skify.' " [Avtoreferat diss. na soiskanie oechen. step. kand. filol. nauk, Irkutskii univ., 1964].
169. Timofeev, L. I. "O poetike Bloka," SOVETSKAIA LITERATURA. METOD. STIL'. POETIKA. M. 1964. pp. 476-522.

1965

170. Baade, M. Review of Orlov, POEMA ALEKSANDRA BLOKA 'DVENADTSAT' '. ZS, X (1965), 318-23.
171. Boiko, V. F. "Rozhdenie 'Dvenadtsati'," ZHIMOLOST. STIKHI. Saratov, 1965. pp. 51-54.
172. Makhulin, V. S. "K voprosu o narodno-poeticheskoi osnove poemy A. Bloka 'Dvenadtsat'." FILOLOGICHESKII SBORNIK [Alma-Ata], IV (1965), 40-58.
173. Mendeleeva-Blok, L. D. "Tri epizoda iz vospominanii ob Aleksandre Bloke," in DEN' POEZII 1965. M. 1965. pp. 306-20.

1966

174. Blair, Katherine H. "Ideas and Rules," in her REVIEW OF SOVIET LITERATURE (London, 1966), 58-71.
175. Farber, L. M. SOVETSKAIA LITERATURA PERVYKH LET REVOLIUTSII, 1917-1920 GG. M. 1968. pp. 105-34.
176. Flaman, Francois. "A propos d'un vers encore obscur des 'Douze' de A. Blok." RESL, XLV (1966), 91-92.
177. Gromov, Pavel. "Problemy liriki i eposa v tvorchestve Bloka epokhi revoliutsii," A. BLOK: EGO PREDSHESTVENNIKI I SOVREMENNIKI. M. 1966. pp. 484-568.
178. Makarenkova, A. "Otkliki na poemu Bloka 'Dvenadtsat' ' v provintsial'noi presse." TRUDY PO RUSSKOI I SLAVIANSKOI FILOLOGII [Uchenye zapiski Tartuskogo universiteta, IX, vyp. 184, 1966], 253-56.
179. Nilsson, Nils Ake. "Blok och De tolv." ORD OCH BILS [Stockholm], LXXV, No. 2 (1966), 141-46.
180. Pertsov, V. O. "O Velimire Khlebnikove." VLit, No. 7. pp. 61-62.
181. Solov'ev, Boris. "Dvenadtsat'." POET I EGO PODVIG. TVORCHESKII PUT' ALEKSANDRA BLOKA. M. 1966. pp. 634-700. Reprinted in 1967 and 1971.
182. Surpin, M. L. "O finale poemy A.BLOKA 'DVENADTSAT' ' FILOLOGICHESKIE NAUKI. [Nauchnye doklady vysshei shkoly, No. 4, 1966], pp. 16-27.
183. Vasil'kovskii, A. T. "Vazhneishie zhanrovye osobennosti russkoi poemy pervykh posleoktiabr'skikh let." VRLit, No. 3. pp. 80-83.

1967

184. Alianskii, S. M. "Vstrechi s Blokom." NM, No. 6. pp. 159-206. Reprinted in his VSTRECHI S ALEKSANDROM BLOKOM. M. 1969.
185. Babovic, Miloslav. "Prva poema o Oktobru: 'Dvenaestorica' A. A. Bloka." SAVREMENIK [Beograd], No. 13 (1967), pp. 353-67.
186. Blot, Jean. "Alexandre Blok et 'Les Douze'." PREUVES, No. 196. pp. 76-77.
187. Chukovskii, N. K. "Chto ia pomniu o Bloke." NM, No. 2. pp. 229-37.
188. Dolgopolov, L. "Ritmy i kontrasty. Zametki o poeme Bloka 'Dvenadtsat'." VOLGA, No. 5 (1967), 163-72.
189. Flaker, A. "Sovetskaia literatura v Iugoslavii s 1918 po 1934 god." SOVETSKOE SLAVIANOVEDENIE, No. 6. pp. 21-28.
190. Ivanov, G. "Dorogi 'Dvenadtsati'." KO, No. 38 (Sept. 16, 1967), p. 12.

191. Janicevic, Jovan. "Prva poema o Oktobru i njen pesnik." KNIZHEVNE NOVINE [Beograd] , No. 313 (Oct. 28, 1967), 8.
192. Maksimov, D. E. "Akhmatova o Bloke." ZVEZDA, No. 12. pp. 187-91.
193. Obrazovskaia, L. A. "Velikii Oktiabr' v russkoi sovetskoi poeme," MATERIALY I TEZISY DOKLADOV XV ITOGOVOI NAUCHNOI KONFERENTSII. Orenburg, 1967. pp. 7-8.
194. OKTIABR'SKAIA LITERATURA I SLAVIANSKIE LITERATURY. SBORNIK STATEI. M. MGU, 1967. pp. 18-19, 56, 79, 220, 235.
195. Orlov, V. N. "Tainyi zhar," in A. Blok, STIKHOTVORENIIA I POEMY. M. 1967. pp. 5-18.
196. Ozmitel', V. M. "Russkaia sovetskaia poema 1917-21 gg." [Avtoreferat dissertatsiii na soiskanie uchen. step. kand. filol. nauk, Alma-Atskii universitet, 1967.]
197. Snow, Ch. P. "Velichaishee iz dostizhenii." PRAVDA, No. 242 (Aug. 30, 1967), p. 4.

1968

198. Antokol'skii, P. G. "Aleksandr Blok," in A. Blok, STIKHOTVORENIIA. POEMY. TEATR. M. 1968. pp. 5-22.
199. Isaev, D. " 'Dvenadtsat' ' v izdatel'stve 'Liesma.' " KO, No. 18 (April 27, 1968), 8-9.
200. Krasnova, L. "Nabliudeniia nad simvolikoi krasnogo tsveta v poetike A. Bloka." VRLit, No. 3. pp. 49-56.
201. Livshits, V. "Simvolicheskie obrazy v poeme A. Bloka 'Dvenadtsat','" in AKTUAL'- NYE VOPROSY ISTORII LITERATURY. Tula, 1968. pp. 93-111.
202. Nazarenko, V. A. "Vtoroe solntse. Zametki o realizme." MG, No. 6. pp. 299-304.
203. Nebol'sin, S. "Aleksandr Blok v sovremennom zapadnom literaturovedenii." VLit, No. 9, pp. 189-96.
204. Rudnev, P. A. "O stikhe poemy A. Bloka 'Dvenadtsat'.' " in RUSSKAIA LITERATURA XX VEKA. DOOKTIABR'SKII PERIOD. SBORNIK STATEI. Kaluga, 1968. pp. 227-38.
205. Slonimskii, Iu. I. ["The Twelve" and Dance Language] , in his V CHEST' TANTSA. M. 1968. pp. 340-41.
206. Solov'ev, V. "Slushaite revoliutsiiu." TVORCHESTVO, No. 11 (1968), pp. 17-19.

1969

207. Gorelov, A. E. "Pochemu A Bloku primpomnilsia A. Diurer," in DEN' POEZII L. 1969. pp. 28- 30.
208. Mikhailov. A. ["The Twelve" as an Epic] , in his REVOLIUTSIIA, GEROI, LITERA- TURA. M. 1969. pp. 156-62.
209. Pertsov, V. O. ["The Twelve" and Mayakovsky's "Khorosho"] , in his POETY I PROZAIKI VELIKHIKH LET. M. 1969. pp. 59-60.
210. Ruhle, Jurgen. "Stars in the October Sky," LITERATURE AND REVOLUTION. Trans. and ed. Jean Steinberg. New York, 1969. pp. 4-19.
211. Skatov, N. N. "Nekrasov i Aleksandr Blok," in PROBLEMY REALIZMA V RUSSKOI I ZARUBEZHNOI LITERATURE. METOD I MASTERSTVO. [Tezisy dokladov na II mezhvuzovskoi nauchn. konf. literaturovedov. Mai, 1969.] Vologda, 1969. pp. 107-108.
212. Turkov, A. ALEKSANDR BLOK. M. 1969. pp. 267-304.

1970

213. Dement'ev, A., et al. " 'Dvenadtsat','" in RUSSKAIA SOVETSKAIA LITERATURA. Ed. A. Dement'ev. M. 1970. pp. 89-92.
214. Gorelov, A. GROZA NAD SOLOV'INYM SADOM. ALEKSANDR BLOK. L. 1970. pp. 366-509.
215. Orlov, V. N. "Ob Aleksandre Bloke," in A. Blok, IZBRANNYE PROIZVEDENIIA.

L. 1970. pp. iii-xxxii.

216. Orlov, V. N. "Poeziia Aleksandra Bloka," in A. Blok, STIKHOTVORENIIA I POEMY. M. 1970. pp. 3-22.

217. Volkov, A. A. " 'Dvenadtsat',' " in his RUSSKAIA LITERATURA XX VEKA. M. 1970. pp. 484-90.

218. Vykhodtsev, P. S. "Dvenadtsat'," in ISTORIIA RUSSKOI SOVETSKOI LITERATU-RY. Ed. P. S. Vykhodtsev. M. 1970. pp. 52-53.

ADDENDA

219. Adams, V.T., "Vospriiatie A. Bloka v Estonii," in BLOKOVSKII SBORNIK. TRU-DY NAUCHNOI KONFERENTSII, POSVIASHCHENNOI IZUCHENIIU ZHIZNI I TVORCHESTVA A.A. BLOKA MAI 1962 GODA. Tartu: Tartuskii gosudar-stvennyi universitet, 1964, pp. 5-27.

220. Aksenova, E.M."Poema 'Dvenadtsat' ' v strukture tvorchestva Bloka," in her STRUKTURA TVORCHESKOI INDIVIDUAL'NOSTI PISATELIA. Vladimir, 1970, pp. 105-48.

221. Al'fonsov, V. "Aleksandr Blok," in his SLOVA I KRASKI. OCHERK IZ ISTORII TVORCHESKIKH SVIAZEI POETOV I KHUDOZHNIKOV. M., 1966, pp. 11-88.

222. Alianskii, S.M. "Ob illiustratsiiakh k poeme Bloka 'Dvenadtsat','" in BLOKOVSKII SBORNIK. TRUDY NAUCHNOI KONFERENTSII, POSVIASHCHENNOI IZU-CHENIIU ZHIZNI I TVORCHESTVA A.A. BLOKA MAI 1962 GODA. Tartu: Tartuskii gosudarstvennyi universitet, 1964, pp. 437-445.

223. Anon. "Blok and the 'Reality of Other Worlds'." TIMES LITERARY SUPPLE-MENT (January 23, 1969), p. 76.

224. Anon. [Ekranizatsiia poemy 'Dvenadtsat' ' v Bratislave.] ISKUSSTVO KINO, No. 4 (1968), p. 125.

225. Anon. "New Tendencies in Russian Thought." TIMES LITERARY SUPPLEMENT, No. 992 (January 20, 1921), pp. 33-34.

226. Anon. "Jauni materiāli par Aleksandru Bloku." KAROGS [Riga] , No. 11 (1960), p. 156.

227. Anon. "Ob Aleksandre Bloke. K 50-letiiu opublikovaniia poemy 'Dvenadtsat' ' (1918—3 marta—1968)." ZVEZDA, No. 3 (1968), pp. 171-200.

228. Anon.[Review of THE TWELVE'] VISTI [Kiev] , No. 18 (April 13, 1919).
229. Anon. "Slushaite muzyku revolutsii." SOVETSKII EKRAN, No. 21 (1967), p. 14.
230. Antokol'skii, P. "Aleksandr Blok." NM, XXXI, No. 11 (1955), 240-46.
231. Antokol'skii, P. "Aleksandr Blok," in his POÈTY I VREMIA. M., 1957, pp. 49-73.
232. Antonov, Nikolai. "Aleksandŭr Blok i 'Dvenadesette'." EZIK I LITERATURA
     [Sofia] , XXV, No. 1 (1970), 45-48.
233. Assev, N.N. "Sovetskaia poeziia za shest' let." VLit, No. 10 (1967), p. 179.
234. Assev, N.N. "Zametki o russkom stikhe." MG, No. 3 (1957), pp. 210-11.
235. Ashukin, N. "Dvenatsat'.'" KNIZHNYE NOVOSTI, No. 7 (1938), p. 42.
236. Auzin'sh, A. "Aleksandr Blok," in his LIRIKA. Riga: Liesma, 1968, pp. 5-12.
237. Baade, M. " Aleksandr Blok: 60 Jahre deutsche Rezeptionsgeschichte." ZS, XII
     (1967), pp. 328-63.
238. Baade, M. "Grundfragen der Übersetzung von Dichtung Aleksandr Bloks ins
     Deutsche." ZS, XIV (1969), 1-11.
239. Babev, Dim. "Aleksandŭr Blok." LISTOPAD [Sofia] , Kn. 11 (1921), pp. 55-56.
240. Badalich, Josip. "'Dvanaestorica' A.A. Bloka u prijevodima Jugoslavenskih književ-
     nosti." KNJIŽEVNA SMOTRA, No. 11 (1970), pp. 5-6, 130-34.
241. B[akalov] , G. "Poèma za ruskata revoliutsiia. Aleksandŭr Blok. 'Dvenadesette.'"
     RAB. VESTNIK [Sofia] , No. 27 (July 15, 1922), Lit. Pril. No. 3.
242. Bakina, M.A. "Oplech u A. Bloka." RUSSKAIA RECH, No. 4 (1969), pp. 101-02.
243. "[Beseda s khudozhnikom A. Goncharovym.] " LITERATURNAIA GAZETA, No.
     8 (January 18, 1966), p. 3.
244. Bucharin; N.I. "Pět básníků v revoluci." TVORBA, IX (1934), 308-09.
245. Daskalova, E. " 'Dvenadtsat' u nas." SEPTEMVRI [Sofia] , No. 11 (1959), pp. 98-
     104.
246. Daskalova, E. "Oktomvriiskata poèma na Aleksandŭr Blok 'Dvenadtsat' v Bŭlgariia."
     EZIK I LITERATURA [Sofia] , XXII, No. 5 (1967), pp. 59-70.
247. Druzhin, Valerii. "Poet uslyshavshii revoliutsiiu." OKTIABR' No. 11 (1970), pp.
     202-06.
248. Dudevski, Khr. "Vliianieto na sŭvetskata literatura vŭrkhu dve bulgarski poem." IZ-
     VESTIIA NA INSTITUTA ZA LITERATURA, Nos. 14-15 (1964), pp. 152-59.
249. Fedin, K. "A. Blok." KR, No. 1 (13) (1921).
250. Fedin, K. "Vechnye sputniki: Aleksandr Blok," in his PISATEL', ISKUSSTVO,
     Vremia. M., 1957, pp. 34-44.
251. Gaidarov, VI. "A.A. Blok." RLit, No. 4 (1961), pp. 209-14.
252. Genin, L.E. "Ekho Oktiabria. Nachalo rasprostraneniia sovetskoi literatury v Ger-
     manii." NEVA, No. 10 (1967), pp. 186-91.
253. Gifford, Henry. "Pasternak and the 'Realism' of Blok." OXFORD SLAVONIC
     PAPERS, XIII (1967), pp. 96-106.
254. Gol'tsev, V.V. "'Dvenadtsat' ' Bloka," in IZBRANNYI BLOK. M., 1930, pp. 49-56.
255. Gorelov, A. "Petrukha i ego kritiki." SIBIRSKIE OGNI, No. 8 (1970), pp. 168-77.
256. Gor'kii, M. "A.A. Blok," in his O PISATELIAKH. M., 1928, pp. 87-97.
257. Hippius, Z. "Mon ami lunaire." MERCURE DE FRANCE [Paris] , CLXI (January
     15, 1923), pp. 289-326.
258. Holthusen, Johannes. "Nachwirkungen der Tradition in A. Bloks Bildsymbolik,"
     in SLAWISTISCHE STUDIEN ZUM V. INTERNATIONALEN SLAWISTEN-
     KONGRESS IN SOFIA 1963. Ed. Maximillian Braun and Erwin Koschmeider.
     Göttingen: Vandenhoeck & Ruprecht, 1963, pp. 437-44. (Opera Slavica 4.)
259. Ivanov-Razumnik, R. "Blok i revoliutsiia." ZNAMIA, No. 10 (1921).
260. Ivanov-Razumnik, R. OTKROVENIE V GROZE I BURE. Berlin: Skify, 1922.
261. Jackson, S. "In 'Correspondence.'" STAND [London] , No. 9 (1954/55), pp. 16-18.
262. Jasinowski, B. WSCHODNIE CHRZEŚCIJAŃSTWO A ROSJA. NA TLE ROSBIO-
     RU PIERWIASTKÓW CYWILIZACJI WSCHODU I ZACHODU. Wilno, 1933,

pp. 92-95.

263. Karwin, J. "A. Błok, 'Dwunastu.'" PRZEGLAD WIECZORNY, No. 183 (1919).

264. Kisch, Cecil. "Aleksander Blok on Russia." MANCHESTER GUARDIAN WEEKLY (March 22, 1951), p. 13.

265. Kluge, Rudolf-Dieter. "Die Revolutions-dichtung 'Dvenadcat'"; "Die Gestalt Christi in Bloks Versepos 'Dvenadcat,'" in his WESTEUROPA UND RUSSLAND IM WESTBILD ALEKSANDR BLOKS. Munich: Verlag Otto Sagner, 1967, pp. 244-55; 255-60.

266. Kokhan, P.S. "Aleksandŭr Blok i revoliutsiiata." NOVO VREME [Sofia], Kn. 9 (1922), pp. 284-88. Reprinted in NARSTUD [Sofia], Kn. 3-4 (1924), pp. 25-28.

267. Kokhan, P.S. "A. Blok i revoliutsiia." PR, No. 2 (1921).

268. Kopylenko, O. [Review of V. Bobyns'kyi's translation of THE TWELVE into the Ukrainian.] CHERVONYI SHLIAKH, X, No. 9 (1924).

269. Koriakov, M. "Soviet Literature; Dictatorship of Mediocrity." THOUGHT, XXVI (Spring 1951), 77-80.

270. Krasnova, L.V. "Poema Aleksandra Bloka 'Dvanadtsat' ' v perekladi Volodymyra Sosiury." UKRAINS'KOE LITERATURNOZNAVSTVO vyp. 4 (1968), pp. 20-6.

271. Krasnova, L.V. "Slushaite revoliutsiiu!" L'VOVSKAIA PRAVDA, No. 156 (August 6, 1967), p. 3.

272. Krasovtsova, N.I., ed. OKTIABRISKAIA REVOLIUTSIIA I SLAVIANSKIE LITERATURY. SBORNIK STATEI. Moscow: MGU, 1967, pp. 18-19; 56; 79; 220; 235.

273. Kruk, Ivan T. "Aleksandr Aleksandrovich Blok," in RUSSKAIA LITERATURA XX VEKA. Ed. Ivan Kruk. Kiev: Vyshcha shkola, 1970, pp. 312-58.

274. Kruk, Ivan T. "Izuchenie Poemy A. Bloka 'Dvenadtsat' ' v vuze. Opyt ideino-esteticheskogo analiza." METODIKA PREPODAVANIIA RUSSKOGO IAZYKA I LITERATURY. [Kiev], vyp. 5 (1970), pp. 128-47.

275. Kruk, Ivan T. "Slushaia muzyku revoliutsii," in his POEZIIA ALEKSANDRA BLOKA. Moscow: Prosveshchenie, 1970, pp. 212-58.

276. Kucharzewski, J. OD BIAŁEGO CARATU DO CZERWONEGO. Tom II. Warsaw, 1925, p. 54.

277. Kudasova, V. "Stikhiia v poeme A. Bloka 'Dvenadtsat' '." SB. NAUCH. STUD. RABOT VLADIM. PED. INST., vyp. 2, No. 1 (1970), pp. 105-27.

278. Kudin, O. "Tvorchist' Volodymyra Sosiury," in his VOLODYMYR SOSIURA. Tom 1. Kiev: Derzhlitvydav Ukrainy, 1957, p. 12.

279. Kuptsov, I. "Padenie chernogo vechera." MOSKOVSKII KOMSOMOLETS, No. 204 (September 1, 1967), p. 4.

280. Lavrin, J. "Alexander Blok," in his ASPECTS OF MODERNISM FROM WILDE TO PIRANDELLO. [New York] : Nott, 1935, pp. 115-38.

281. Lezhnev, A. "Russkaia khudozhestvennaia literatura revoliutsionnogo desiatiletiia." SIBIRSKIE OGNI, No. 1 (1928), pp. 203-06.

282. Libedinskaia, L. "Pal'nem-ka pulei v sviatuiu Rus'," in her ZHIZN' I STIKHI. M., 1970, pp. 133-44.

283. Libedinskaia, L. "Podvig poeta. 50 let poeme A. Bloka 'Dvenadtsat' '!" LITERATURNAIA GAZETA, No. 5 (January 31, 1968), p. 4.

284. Lukich, Sveta. "Ruski pesnichki princip i Aleksandr Blok." BORBA [Belgrade], XXXI (February 6, 1966), p. 35.

285. Lunacharskii, Anatolii V. KLASSIKI RUSSKOI LITERATURY. M., 1937, pp. 418-23.

286. Makovskii, Sergei. "Aleksandr Blok," in his NA PARNASE "SEREBRIANOGO VEKA." Munich: Izdatel'stvo Tsentr. ob"edineniia polit. emigrantov iz SSSR, 1962, pp. 143-75.

287. Mashbits-Verov, I. "Tema Rossii i revoliutsiia," in his RUSSKII SIMVOLIZM I PUT' ALEKSANDRA BLOKA. Kuibyshev: Knizhnoe izdatel'stvo, 1969, pp. 313-48.

288. Matveev, A. "Literatura i revoliutsiia." SVOBODNYI TRUD [Voronezh], No. 1 (1919).

289. Mikhailov, A. "Epos revoliutsii." LITERATURNAIA ROSSIIA, No. 37 (September 8, 1967), pp. 2-3.

290. Mikhailovskii, B.V. "Tvorchestvo A.A. Bloka," in his RUSSKAIA LITERATURA XX VEKA. M., 1939, pp. 259-83.

291. Milev, Geo. "Aleksandŭr Blok." VEZNI [Sofia], Kn. 1 (1921), pp. 1-3.

292. Miller, A. "In 'Correspondence.'" STAND [London], No. 9 (1954/55), pp. 18-22.

293. Mirsky, D. "Ob Aleksandre Bloke." ZVEZDA, No. 8 (1936), pp. 243-56.

294. Nag, Martin. "Blok, Maiakovski, Milev." LITERATURNA MISEL [Sofia], XIII, No. 5 (1969), 41-45.

295. Naumov, E.I. "Pervaia sovetskaia p'esa." UCHENYE ZAPISKI LENINGRAD-SKOGO UNIVERSITETA. SERIIA FILOLOGICHESKIKH NAUK, No. 13 (1948), pp. 253-59; 264.

296. Nest'eva, M. "'Dvenadtsat'.'" SOVETSKAIA MUZYKA, No. 11 (1964), pp. 24-27.

297. Nikiforov, S.D. "O iazyke poemy 'Dvenadtsat' ' A.A. Bloka." RUSSKII IAZYK V SHKOLE, Nos. 3-4 (1946), pp. 1-5.

298. Nikolesku, T. "Novyi pisatel' i novaia literatura." INOSTRANNAIA LITERATU-RA, No. 12 (1967), pp. 178-79.

299. Oksenov, Iv. "A. Blok. 'Dvenadtsat'.'" KR, No. 5 (1920).

300. Orlov, V. "Nekotorye itogi i zadachi sovetskogo blokovedeniia," in BLOKOVSKII SBORNIK. TRUDY NAUCHNOI KONFERENTSII POSVIASHCHENNOI IZU-CHENIIU ZHIZNI I TVORCHESTVA A.A. BLOKA MAI 1962 GODA. Tartu: Tartuskii gosudarstvennyi universitet, 1964, pp. 507-521.

301. Orlov, V. "Novoe ob Aleksandre Bloke." NM, XXXI, No. 11 (1955), 150-62.

302. Osetrov, E. "Naidi epitet i glagol edinstvennyi." OCHERK TVORCHESTVA. M., 1956, pp. 203-52.

303. Panov, Lazar. "Aleksandŭr Blok." NOVO ZVENO [Sofia], Kn. 2-3 (1923), pp. 34-36.

304. Pavlovich, N.A. "Istoriia odnogo perevoda." GOLOS RIGI, No. 185 (August 7, 1961), p. 6.

305. Pazurkiewicz, St. "A. Blok." KURIER LITERACKO-NAUKOWY, No. 45 (1926).

306. Pertsov, V. "'Dvenadtsat' A. Bloka," in his O KHUDOZHESTVENNOM MNOGO-OBRAZII. M., 1967, pp. 199-210.

307. Plotniek, A. "'Divpadsmit' solo atkal." LITERATURA UN MĀKSLA [Riga], No. 28 (1968), pp. 2-3.

308. Police, Branimir. "Dva sechanja na A. Bloka." 15 DANA, X, Nos. 9-10 (1967), 7-9.

309. Popov, V.P. "Poema Oleksandra Bloka 'Dvanadtsat' ' vperekladi Vasylia Bobyns'-kono." UKRAINS'KOE LITERATUROZNAVSTVO [Lvov], No. 4 (1968), pp. 27-32.

310. Poźniak, T. "Błok i Dostojewski." SLAVIA ORIENTALIS [Warsaw], XIV, No. 4 (1965), 419-34.

311. Prokushev, Iu. L. "Poeziia Oktiabria." ZNANIE (1963), pp. 4; 13-18; 36; 43; 46.

312. Pryhodii, Mykh, I. VZAIEMODIIA RADIANS'KYKH LITERATUR; VZAIE-MOZV' IAZKY ROSSIS'KOI TA UKRAINS'KOI LITERATUR V PROTSESI IKH STANOVLENIIA 1917-1925. Kiev: Dnipro, 1966, pp. 166-68; 308-09; 356.

313. Przybylski, Ryszard. "Muzyka rewolucjii 'Dwunastu' Aleksandra Błoka." POEZJA [Warsaw], III, No. 10 (1967), 18-33.

314. Putilev, B.N. "O nekotorykh problemakh fol'kloristiki." VOPROSY SOVETSKOI LITERATURY, IV (1956), p. 23.

315. Rod'ko, N. "Blok pod karandashom tsenzora." VLit, No. 3 (1963), p. 254.
316. Rod'ko, N. "Perevody A. Bloka na Zapadnoi Ukraine," in TEZISY DOKLADOV VI UKRAINSKOI KONFERENTSII SLAVISTOV, 13-18 Oct. 1964 g. Chernovitsy, pp. 137-38.
317. Rogoż, St. "O 'bolszewickim' poemacie A. Błoka." PRZEGLAD WSPOLCZESNY, No. 14 (1923), pp. 450-54.
318. Roshchin, P.F. POEMA A. TVARDOVSKOGO "VASILII TERKIN." POSOBIE DLIA UCHITELIA. M., 1956, pp. 27-28.
319. Rosimov, G. [Geo. Milev]. "Vŭrkhu 'Dvenadesette.'" VEZNI [Sofia], Kn. 2 (1920) pp. 77-80.
320. Rühle, Jürgen. "Gestirn am oktoberhimmel Alexander Block—Sergei Jessenin—Wladimir Majakowski." MONAT [Berlin], XII, No. 140 (1959/60), 68-79.
321. Selivanovskii, A.P. "Oktiabr' i dorevoliutsionnye poeticheskie shkoly," in his V LITERATURNYKH BOIAKH. M., 1959, pp. 247-56. Republished in 1963, pp. 330-41.
322. Sergievskii, I. "'Dvenadtsat'.'" LITERATURNYI KRITIK, Nos. 10-11 (1937), pp. 211-16.
323. Shcheglov, M. "Spor o Bloke," in his LITERATURNO-KRITICHESKIE STAT'I. M., 1934, pp. 178-80.
324. Shklovskii, V. "Siuzhet v stikhakh," in POETICHESKII SBORNIK, M., 1934, pp. 178-80.
325. Sillat, N. "Die Quellen der Tschastuschkaelemente in dem Poem 'Die Zwölf' von Alexander Blok." WISSENSCHAFTLICHE ZEITSCHRIFT DER KARL MARX-UNIVERSITAT [Leipzig], XIII, No. 5, pp. 1001-04.
326. Smolenskii, Vladimir. "Mistika Aleksandra Bloka." VOZROZHDENIE No. 37 (1955), pp. 110-27; No. 38 (1955), pp. 91-102.
327. Stepun, Fedor. "Istoriosofskoe i politicheskoe mirosozertsanie Aleksandra Bloka." VOZDUSHNYE PUTI, IV (1965), pp. 241-55.
328. Stoianov, Liudmil. "Aleksandŭr Blok." KHIPERION [Sofia], Kn. 8 (1922), pp. 484-94.
329. Sumskoi, S. "Al. Blok i revoliutsiia." SOTSIALISTICHESKII VESTNIK [Berlin], No. 18 (October 15, 1921).
330. Tager, E. "Mensch der Furchtlosen Aufrichtigkeit (A. Block, ein Dichter der Russischen Revolution)." AUFBAU, No. 10 (1946), pp. 1023-27.
331. Taranovskii, Kiril. "Certain aspects of Blok's Symbolism," in STUDIES IN SLAVIC LINGUISTICS AND POETICS IN HONOR OF BORIS O. UNBEGAUN. New York: New York University, Press, 1968, pp. 249-60.
332. Tarasenkov, A.K. "Zametki o poezii Bloka," in his STAT'I O LITERATURE. M., 1958, pp. 236-72.
333. Testena, Falco. "'Los doce' de Alejandro Blok." NOSOTROS [Buenos Aires], No. 40 (1922), pp. 206-16.
334. Tikhonov, N. "Kak ia rabotaiu." LITERAURNAIA UCHEBA, No. 5 (1931), p. 96.
335. Timofeeva, V.V. IAZYK POETA I VREMIA. POETICHESKII IAZYK MAIAKOVSKOGO. M., 1962, pp. 212, 218.
336. Tkhorzhevskii, I. "La révolution et le poète Blok," in his DE GORKI À NOS JOURS. LA NOUVELLE LITTERATURE RUSSE. Paris: La Renaissance, 1945, pp. 33-47.
337. Trofimuk, S. "Storinky ioho bytvy." ZHOVTEN' [Kiev], No. 3 (1968), pp. 128-31.
338. Ureta, Alberto. "La poesìa rusa contemporanea." MERCURIO PERUANO [Lima], XVI (1927), 429-41.
339. Volkov, A.A. "A.A. Blok," in his RUSSKAIA LITERATURA XX V. DOOKTIABR'SKOI PERIOD. M., 1964, pp. 445-71.
340. Wojnarowska, A. "A. Błok, 'Dwunastu.'" ROBOTNIK, No. 239, No. 244, No. 258

(1921).

341. Wrocki, Czesław. "A. Błok, 'Dwunastu.'" NAPRZOD, Nos. 221/222 (1922).
342. Zawodzinski, A. "A. Błok wieszcem swojego narodu." TWÓRCZOŚĆ, No. 11 (1946), pp. 79-96.
343. Zelinskii, K.L. NA RUBEZHE DVUKH EPOKH. LITERATURNYE VSTRECHI 1917-1921 GODOV. M., 1962, pp. 169-77.
344. Zharovtseva, I. "Festival' pol'skikh kukol." TEATR, No. 9 (1970), p. 129.
345. Zhirmunskii, V.M. "Anna Akhmatova i Aleksandr Blok." RLit, XIII, No. 3 (1970), 57-82.
346. Zhirmunskii, V.M. POEZIIA ALEKSANDRA BLOKA. Petersburg, 1922, pp. 34-40.
347. Zidarov, K. "Aleksandŭr Blok." SEPTEMVRI [Sofia] , X, No. 11 (1957), 277-80.
348. Zlydnev, V.I. "Sviazi L. Stoianova s russkoi i sovetskoi literaturoi," in RUSSKO-BOLGARSKIE LITERATURNYE SVIAZI XX VEKA. M., 1964, pp. 155-61.

INDEX

A BIBLIOGRAPHY OF WORKS BY AND ABOUT

N.N. EVREINOV

Compiled by C. Moody

This is the first attempt to compile a comprehensive bibliography of the work of
N.N. Evreinov in the Russian theatre. Although after his departure from the Soviet Union
in 1925 Evreinov continued to work in the theatre until his death in Paris in 1953, the im-
portant part of his contribution to the twentieth century theatre was accomplished in Russia. Of items published after 1925, therefore, only those which refer to Evreinov's Russian
period are included. A sizable collection of material relating to Evreinov's life outside his
native country was made by his widow, A.A..Evreinova. Part of this she retains in Paris,
part was sent to the Soviet Union where it is housed in the Central State Archive of Literature and Art (ЦГАЛИ) and part is in the Russian archive of Columbia University.
    The problems involved in compiling an Evreinov bibliography are considerable. Since
Evreinov has not yet been 'rehabilitated' in the Soviet Union, no Soviet scholar has attempt-
ed to review the bibliographical material. Nor has any of his work been republished in the
Soviet Union. The published work devoted to Evreinov in the West is also extremely limi-
ted. The only short bibliography to have appeared in the Soviet Union, B.V. Kazanskii's
Metod teatra (Analiz sistemy N.N. Evreinova), 1925, is so inaccurate as to be virtually use-
less. The present bibliography was compiled from the catalogues of book and serial holdings
of the Public Library and the State Institute of Theatre, Music and Cinematography in
Leningrad and the Lenin Library and the All—Russian Theatre Society in Moscow. Additional material was provided by A.A. Evreinova in Paris.
    The bibliography is divided into three sections:
    A. Books, articles and other writings by N.N. Evreinov.
    B. Dramatic works by N.N. Evreinov.
    C. Books, articles and reviews concerning the work of N.N. Evreinov in
        Russia.
    The bibliography is as complete as the sources have allowed. It is possible, however,
that omissions remain and the compiler would be grateful for information about these should
they be discovered.

A

Книги, статьи и другие работы Н.Н.Евреинова

1 История театра

(a) Общая

1 Histoire du Théâtre Russe. Paris, 1948.
История русского театра с древнейших времен до 1917 года.
   1-ое изд., New York, 1955.
   2-ое изд., Letchworth, 1972. Introduction by C. Moody.
2 История телесных наказаний в России. Изд., В.К.Ильиничика, СПБ., (Дата?)
3 О русском театре не русского происхождения и не русского уклада.
   ТЕАТР И ИСКУССТВО, СПБ., 45:834-7; 46:858-60; 47:879-80; 48:898-900, 1915.
4 Крепостные актеры. Исторический очерк.
   1-ое изд., дирекции императорских театров, СПБ., 1911.
   2-ое изд., заново переработ. и значительно дополн., изд., Л., 1925.

(б) Народные истоки театра

5 Театральное мастерство православного духовенства. ЖИЗНЬ ИСКУССТВА, ПТГ.,
   712-14 (6-8 апр.) : 1-2, 1921. (Перепечатано в: ТЕАТРАЛЬНЫЕ НОВАЦИИ,ПТГ.,1923)
6 Происхождение драмы. Первобытная трагедия: роль козла в истории ее возник-
   новения. (Фольклор-очерк.) Монография по истории и теории театра. Вып. 1,
   изд., Петрополис, ПТГ., 1921.
7 О музыке древне-русских козлоголосований. Реферат на курсах муз. педаго-
   гов. ПТГ., 13 дек. 1921.
8 Первобытная драма германцев. (Из пра-истории театра германо-скандинавских
   народов.) Изд., Полярная звезда, ПТГ., 1922.
9 Тайна Распутина. (О мифологической маске.) Изд., Былое, ПТГ., 1924.
10 Зачатки трагедии в древней Руси — (компендии подготовляемой к печати работы „Ряженая коза и начало древне-русской трагедии") . ЖИЗНЬ ИСКУССТВА,
   ПТГ., 697-9 (19, 20, 22 марта) : 1, 1921.
11 Тайна черной полумаски. (Разоблачение.) В сборн. „Арена", изд., Время, ПТГ.,
   1924, 15-22.
12 Азазел и Дионис. О происхождении сцены в связи с зачатками драмы у семи-
   тов. Предисловие — Б.Н.Кауфман. Изд., Академия, Л., 1924.

2 Теория театра

(a) Книги

13 Введение в монодраму. Реферат, прочитанный в Москве в лит.-худ. кружке
   16 окт. 1908, ТЕАТР И ИСКУССТВО, СПБ., 9:166-8; 10:183-4; 11:200-1; 13:
   241-3, 1909.
   1-ое книж. изд., Н.И.Бутковская, обложка — маска Н.В.Зарецкого, СПБ., 1909.
   2-ое книж. изд., автор, СПБ., 1913.
14 Театр как таковой. 1-ое изд., Современное искусство, Н.И.Бутковская. С теа-
   тральным портретом Кульбина, СПБ., 1912.

Содержание

2-ое изд., Academia, Berlin, 1923. Повторение издания 1912 года с добавлением трех разделов:

15 Pro Scena Sua. Изд., Прометей, Н. Н. Михайлова, обложка С. Судейкина, 1915.
Содержание

16 В. Ф. Комиссаржевская и толпа.
   (Ранее напечатано в АПОЛЛОН, СПБ., 6:28-31, 1910.)
17 Актер в кинематографе.
18 Tangelfoot.
19 Грядущий лицедей.
   (Ранее напечатано в ТЕАТР И ИСКУССТВО, СПБ., 8:152-54, 1909.)
   ПОСЛЕДНИЕ ПРОБЛЕМЫ ТЕАТРА
20 Художники в театре Комиссаржевской.
   (Ранее напечатано в сборн. ,,Алконост'', СПБ., 1911, 122-38.)
21 О наготе на сцене.
   (Ранее напечатано в ТЕАТР И ИСКУССТВО, СПБ., 45:851-5, 1910.)
22 Сценическая ценность наготы.
   (Ранее напечатано в ТЕАТР И ИСКУССТВО, СПБ., 27:469-71, 1908.)
23 Язык тела.
   (Ранее напечатано в ТЕАТР И ИСКУССТВО, СПБ., 48:853-4, 1909.)
24 Далькроз и его школа.
   (Ранее напечатано в ТЕАТР И ИСКУССТВО, СПБ., 5:107-8, 1912.)

16 Тезис лекции ,,Театр для себя'', которая будет прочитана 19 ноября в зале СПБ. Городской Думы. БИРЖЕВЫЕ ВЕДОМОСТИ, СПБ., 15 нояб. 1915.

17 Театр для себя. В 3-х частях. Изд., Современное искусство, Н. И. Бутковская.

Часть первая (теоретическая). Обложка и рисунки Н. И. Кульбина. СПБ., 1915.
Содерж. Взвитие занавеса. Театрократия. К философии театра.
      1 ,,Театр'' и театр.
      2 Воля к театру.
      3 Малолетние преступники.
      4 Преступление, как аттрибут театра.
      5 Каждая минута — театр.
      6 Дон Кихот и Робинсон.
         (Ранее напечатано в ТЕАТР И ИСКУССТВО, СПБ., 30:547-50; 31: 565-67, 1915.)
      7 Режиссура жизни.
      8 Актеры для себя.
      9 Эксцессивный ,,театр для себя'':
            1 Театральная гипербулия.
            2 Король-безумец.
            3 Русские оригиналы.
            4 Эротический ,,театр для себя''.
            5 Пантомимы.

Часть вторая (прагматическая). Обложка и рисунки Ю. П. Аненкова. СПБ., 1916.
Содерж. 1 Мы, аристократы театра.
      2 Урок профессионалам.
         (Ранее напечатано в ТЕАТР И ИСКУССТВО, СПБ., 51:1054-8, 1913.)
      3 Об отрицании театра.
         (Ранее напечатано в сборн. ,,Стрелец'', СПБ., 1915, 35-51.)
      4 Театр пяти пальчиков.
         (Ранее напечатано в ТЕАТР И ИСКУССТВО, СПБ., 52:994-5, 1914.)
      5 Театр в будущем.
         (Ранее напечатано в СТОЛИЦА И УСАДЬБА, СПБ., 7 (1 апр.): 20-2, 1914.)
      6 Мой любимый театр.

Часть третья (практическая). Обложка и рисунки Н.И.Кульбина, СПБ., 1917.
Содерж. „Театр для себя" как искусство.
    1 Общественный театр на взгляд познавшего искусство „театра для себя".
    2 Об устройстве „Спектаклей для себя".
        1 Theatrum extra habitum mea sponte.
        2 За.
        3 Страхование успеха „спектаклей для себя".
    3 Суд понимающих.
    Пьесы из репертуара „театра для себя".
    Занавес падает.

18 Что такое театр. Книжка для детей. Изд., Светозор, ПТГ., 1921.
19 Театральные инвенции. Изд., Время, М., 1922.
Содерж. 1 Что весит на весах космоса — ленточка в косичке вертлявой девочки.
    2 В чем мой monument aere ferennis.
    3 Жизненность и театральность.
    4 Театр — зеркало жизни.
    5 Какими мы любим себя.
    6 Тайна настоящих актеров.
        (Ранее напечатано в ТЕАТР КАК ТАКОВОЙ, 2-ое изд., СПБ., 1922.)
20 Театральные новации. Изд., Третья стража, ПТГ, 1923.
Содерж. 1 Pro Scena Sua.
    2 О декоративном искусстве древне-русского театра:
        1 Древняя Русь перед декоративным соблазном.
        2 Театральные новшества петровской Руси.
        3 В комедийной хоромине.
    3 О русском театре не русского происхождения и не русского уклада.
        (Ранее напечатано в ТЕАТР И ИСКУССТВО, СПБ., 45:834-7; 46:858-600; 47:879-80; 48:898-900, 1915.)
    4 Театральное мастерство православного духовенства.
        (Ранее напечатано в ЖИЗНЬ ИСКУССТВА, ПТГ., 712-14 (6-8 апр.): 1-2, 1921.)
    5 Метод художественной реконструкции театральных постановок.
        (Ранее напечатано в ЖИЗНЬ ИСКУССТВА, ПТГ., 634-6 (17-19 дек.): 1, 1920.)
    6 Естественность на сцене:
        1 Вторая натура.
        2 Мельпомена и Мин Хуан. (Ранее напечатано в ТЕАТР И ИСКУССТВО, СПБ., 38:741-4, 1913.)
        3 Дань марионеткам.
    Поминальная анафора.

21 Театр у животных. О смысле театральности с библиографической точки зрения. Л.-М., 1924.
22 The Theatre in Life. Edited and translated by A.I. Nazaroff with introduction by O.M. Sayler. New York, Brentanos 1927; London, Harrop 1927..

(б) Статьи

23 Апология театральности. УТРО, СПБ., 8 сент. 1908.
    (Перепечатано в ТЕАТР КАК ТАКОВОЙ, СПБ., 1912.)
24 Театрализация жизни. ПРОТИВ ТЕЧЕНИЯ, 2, 1911.
    (Перепечатано в ТЕАТР КАК ТАКОВОЙ, СПБ., 1912.)

25 К вопросу о пределах театральной иллюзии. ТЕАТР И ИСКУССТВО, СПБ., 36: 680-83, 1912.
(Перепечатано в ТЕАТР КАК ТАКОВОЙ, СПБ., 1912.)
26 Театр и искусство. ТЕАТР И ИСКУССТВО, СПБ., 5:107-8, 1912.
27 Театр пяти пальчиков. ТЕАТР И ИСКУССТВО, 52:994-5, 1914.
(Перепечатано в ТЕАТР ДЛЯ СЕБЯ, часть 2, СПБ., 1916.)
28 Театр в будущем. Кинотофон — театр будущего. СТОЛИЦА И УСАДЬБА, СПБ., 7:20-22, 1914.
(Перепечатано в ТЕАТР ДЛЯ СЕБЯ, часть 2, СПБ, 1916.)
29 Дон Кихот и Робинсон. ТЕАТР И ИСКУССТВО, СПБ., 30:547-50; 31:565-67, 1915.
(Перепечатано в ТЕАТР ДЛЯ СЕБЯ, часть 1, СПБ., 1915.)
30 Театр без изюминки. Выдержки из статьи Евреинова в сборн. ,,Стрелок''. О театре и театральности. СПБ., 1915.
(Ранее напечатано в БИРЖЕВЫЕ ВЕДОМОСТИ, 25 марта, 1915.)
31 Об отрицании театра в сборн. ,,Первый стрелец'' под ред. А. Беленсона, СПБ., 1915.
(Перепечатано в ТЕАТР ДЛЯ СЕБЯ, часть2, СПБ., 1916.)
32 Реферат статьи ,,О традиции театра'' в сборн. ,,Первый стрелец'', под ред. А.Бе-
ленсона СПБ., 1915.
(Ранее напечатано в ТЕАТРАЛЬНАЯ ГАЗЕТА, СПБ., 17:3-4, 1915.)
33 Естественность на сцене. ИСКУССТВО, СПБ., 1:2-3, 1916.
34 Имя богу моему в театрах. ИСКУССТВО, Тифлис, 6:1919.
35 Театротерапия. ЖИЗНЬ ИСКУССТВА, ПТГ., 578-9:1, 1920.
36 Сцена театра и сцена жизни. ЖИЗНЬ ИСКУССТВА, ПТГ., 640-1:1, 1920.
37 Демон театральности. Л. Андреев и проблема театральности в жизни. ЖИЗНЬ
ИСКУССТВА, 830:2; 831:2, 1922.
38 Театр и Эшафот. Лекция в Киеве, Харькове, Одессе и других городах в 1918-
-24 г. г. (Опубликовано?)
39 Сценическая ценность наготы. ТЕАТР И ИСКУССТВО, СПБ., 27:469-71, 1908.
40 О наготе на сцене. ТЕАТР И ИСКУССТВО, СПБ., 45:851-5, 1910.
(Перепечатано в PRO SCENA SUA, СПБ., 1915.)
41 Нагота на сцене. Иллюстрирован. сборн. статей под ред. Н.Н.Евреинова, СПБ., 1911.
42 Из речи Н.Н.Евреинова о наготе в зале Фил. Общества. ЖИЗНЬ ИСКУССТВА,
ПТГ., 8:6-7, 1923.
43 Театральные инвенции. МАСКИ, М., 1:77, 1912.
(Перепечатано в ТЕАТР КАК ТАКОВОЙ, СПБ., 1912.)

3 Современный театр

44 В. Ф. Комиссаржевская и толпа. АПОЛЛОН, СПБ., 6:28-31, 1910.
(Перепечатано в PRO SCENA SUA, СПБ., 1915.)
45 Н. Н. Евреинов и др. Письмо редакции о книге Туркина о В.Ф.Комиссаржевской,
где ее биография и факты из ее жизни извращены. РЕЧЬ, СПБ., 21 нояб. 1910.
46 Художники в театре В. Ф. Комиссаржевской — в сборн.,,Алконост'', СПБ., 1911, 122-38.
(Перепечатано в PRO SCENA SUA, СПБ., 1915.)
47 Начало конца (памяти В.Ф.Комиссаржевской). МУЗЫ, СПБ., 4, 1914.
48 К семнадцатому сентября. Памяти В.Ф.Комиссаржевской. ФИГАРО, Одесса, 7, 1918.
49 В. В. Стрельская. ТЕАТР И ИСКУССТВО, СПБ., 3:48-9, 1907.
(Перепечатано в PRO SCENA SUA, СПБ., 1915.)

50 Бабушка скончалась. Памяти В.В.Стрельской. ТЕАТР И ИСКУССТВО, СПБ., 3:47-9, 1915.

51 Сатирическая доминанта в творчестве Ильи Саца. К десятой годовщине со дня его смерти, 11 октября 1912. ЖИЗНЬ ИСКУССТВА, ПТГ., 858:2; 859:7; 860:3, 1922. (Перепечатано в ИЛЬЯ САЦ, 1923, 27-37.)

52 ,,Гадибук" в постановке Вахтангова. ЕВРЕЙСКИЙ ВЕСТНИК, М., 5-6, 1922.

53 Тайна театрального имени. О ,,Гадибук" в постановке Вахтангова в Хабима-театре. КРАСНАЯ ПАНОРАМА, М., 7 (12 июля) : 14-15, 1923.

54 Апология театральности. Статья по поводу смерти Е.Вахтангова. ТЕАТР, Берлин, 1:6-7, 1923.

55 О театральности Оскара Уайльда. ТЕАТР И ИСКУССТВО, СПБ., 6:119-20, 1916.

56 Слава Т.П.Карсавиной. Статья в сборн. ,,Карсавина". Изд. общества ,,Интимный театр", СПБ., 1914.

57 Еще при жизни Собина о нем говорили. НАШ РУПОР, М., 2:3, 1924.

58 Мартынов. К 50-летию со дня смерти. АПОЛЛОН, СПБ., 10:23-30, 1910.

59 Гордон Крэг. Сборн. статей под ред. и с предисловием Н.Н.Евреинова, (статьи Ю.А.Аненкова, Б.Казанского, В.Н.Соловьева и др.) изд., Третья стража, СПБ., 1912.

60 Непостижимый волшебник. (Макс Рейнгардт.) ТЕАТР И ИСКУССТВО, СПБ., 14:291-2, 1911.

61 Макс Рейнгардт. Монография о знаменитом режиссере-реформаторе. Сборн. статей под ред. Н.Н.Евреинова. Изд. Третья стража, СПБ., (Дата?)

62 Памяти Н.Н.Вентцеля, автора нескольких ,,кривозеркальных" пародий. ЖИЗНЬ ИСКУССТВА, ПТГ., 619-21:2, 1920.

63 О премии Островского. ,,По ступеням заповедника Коржовского. ТЕАТР, М., 1450:8-9, 1914.

64 Предисловие к описи памятников русского театра. Собрание Л.И.Жевержеева, СПБ., Вып. XX, 1907.

66 Язык тела. Новые течения в танце — Танцы Мод Аллан. ТЕАТР И ИСКУССТВО, СПБ., 48:853-4, 1909. (Перепечатано в PRO SCENA SUA, СПБ., 1915.)

67 Рецензия Н.Н.Евреинова на гастрольные спектакли японской актрисы Занако. ТЕАТР И ИСКУССТВО, СПБ., 49:876, 1909.

68 Далькроз и его школа. ТЕАТР И ИСКУССТВО, СПБ., 5:107-8, 1912. /перепечатано в PRO SCENA SUA, СПБ., 1915.)

69 На экзаменах андалузских танцовщиц. ТЕАТР И ИСКУССТВО, СПБ., 24:502-5, 1913. (Перепечатано в PRO SCENA SUA, СПБ., 1915.)

70 Грядущий лицедей. ТЕАТР И ИСКУССТВО, СПБ., 8:152-4, 1909. (Перепечатано в PRO SCENA SUA, СПБ., 1915.)

71 Урок профессионалам. ТЕАТР И ИСКУССТВО, СПБ., 51:1054-8, 1913. (Перепечатано в ТЕАТР ДЛЯ СЕБЯ, часть 2, СПБ., 1916.)

72 О некоторых ходячих терминах. К переизданию ,,Театра как такового". ЖИЗНЬ ИСКУССТВА, ПТГ., 867:6, 1922.

73 Искусство и революция. ИСКУССТВО, Тифлис, 9, 1920.

74 Оригинальность за чужой счет. ЖУРНАЛ ЖУРНАЛОВ, СПБ., 1:15-16, 1915.

75 Испытание временем. В сборн. ,,Сто лет Малому театру", изд. РТО, М., 1924, 23-35.

76 Новые веяния в театре. ПЕТРОГРАДСКИЕ ТЕАТРАЛЬНЫЕ ВЕДОМОСТИ, СПБ., 36, 1910.

77 Куда мы идем. В сборн. ,,71-2", изд. Заря, СПБ., 1910.

78 О новой маске. Авто-био-реконструктивной. Изд. Третья стража, ПТГ., 1923.

79 Беседа с Н.Н.Евреиновым о новом театре, организованном в Петербурге. БИРЖЕВЫЕ ВЕДОМОСТИ, СПБ., 6 окт. 1914.

80 Рецензия о постановке ,,Анфисы" Л.Андреева. АПОЛЛОН, СПБ., 3:35-6, 1909.

81 Рецензия о постановке „Анатэмы" Л. Андреева. АПОЛЛОН, СПБ., 3:35-6, 1909.
82 Происхождение оперетты. ТЕАТР И ИСКУССТВО, СПБ., 33:643-6; 34:660-4,1913.
(Перепечатано в К ПОСТАНОВКЕ ХИЛЬПЕРИКА, СПБ, 1913.)
83 К постановке Хильперика. Реферат, прочитанный труппе Палас театр 1 авг. 1913.
Обложка Н. Калмыкова. Изд. дирекции Палас театр, СПБ., 1913.
Содерж. 1 Введение
2 Происхождение оперетты.
(Ранее напечатано в ТЕАТР И ИСКУССТВО, СПБ., 33:643-6; 34:660-4,
1913.)
3 К реформе оперетты.
4 Хильперик.
(Ранее напечатано как КОМИЧНОСТЬ ХИЛЬПЕРИКА в ОБОЗРЕНИЕ
ТЕАТРОВ, СПБ., 28 авг. 1913.)

4 Искусство режиссера

84 О праве собственности режиссера. РАМПА, М., 9:139-40, 1908.
85 Режиссер и декоратор. ЕЖЕГОДНИК ИМПЕРАТОРСКИХ ТЕАТРОВ, СПБ.,
Вып. 1: 80-9, 1909.
(Перепечатано в PRO SCENA SUA, СПБ., 1915.)
86 О секрете сердца режиссера. ТЕАТР И ИСКУССТВО, СПБ., 21:369-71, 1909.
(Перепечатано в PRO SCENA SUA, СПБ., 1915.)
87 „Режиссер" К. Гагемана. Рецензия. ЕЖЕГОДНИК ИМПЕРАТОРСКИХ ТЕАТРОВ,
СПБ., Вып. 3, 131-5, 1910.
(Перепечатанов PRO SCENA SUA, СПБ., 1915.)
88 Искусство режиссера. Альманах-справочник, изд. Н. Давингофа, СПБ., 1914-15,
55-9.

5 Статьи и другие материалы, относящиеся к собственной деятельности Н. Н. Евреи-инова

89 Беседа с Н. Н. Евреиновым о его поездке в Марокко. БИРЖЕВЫЕ ВЕДОМОСТИ,
СПБ., 8 июня 1913.
90 В Марокко (из дневника моих скитаний). СОЛНЦЕ РОССИИ, СПБ., 27:7-8,1913.
91 Беседа с Н. Н. Евреиновым о его поездке за границу. ОБОЗРЕНИЕ ТЕАТРОВ И
СПОРТА, М., 26:3, 1922.
92 Н. Н. Евреинов о своей режиссерской и литературной текущей работе. МУЗЫКА
И ТЕАТР, ПТГ., 1:4, 1922.
93 Мой юбилей. ВЕСТНИК ТЕАТРА И ИСКУССТВА, ПТГ., 3:2, 1922.

6 Статьи и другие материалы, относящиеся к собственным постановкам Н. Н. Евреинова

(a) Разное

94 „Орлеанская дева" на сцене. По поводу выступления Б. С. Глаголина в роли
Иоанны д'Арк. ЖУРНАЛ ЛИТЕРАТУРНО-ХУДОЖЕСТВЕННОГО ОБЩЕСТВА,
8-10:180-2, 1907.
95 К постановке „Орлеанской девы" Шиллера. ЖУРНАЛ ЛИТ.-ХУД. ОБЩЕСТВА
5:116-7, 1908. (Перепечатано в PRO SCENA SUA, СПБ., 1915.)

96 Беседа с Н.Н. Евреиновым о его работе в театре В.Ф. Комиссаржевской. ТЕАТР, М., 27 марта: 13-14, 1908.

97 Беседа с Н.Н. Евреиновым о постановке „Франческа да Римини" и „Саломей" в театре В.Ф. Комиссаржевской. РАННЕЕ УТРО, М., 30 авг. 1908.

98 К постановке „Саломей" О. Уайльда. ТЕАТР И ИСКУССТВО, СПБ., 43:749-53,1908.

99 Протест против запрещения постановки „Саломей". СЛОВО, СПБ., 29 окт. 1908.

100 Беседа с Н.Н. Евреиновым о постановке „Ваньки-ключника". БИРЖЕВЫЕ ВЕДО-МОСТИ, СПБ., 7 июля 1908.

101 Беседа с Н.Н. Евреиновым о постановке оперы "Hyresa Quo Vadis". ВОСКРЕС-НАЯ ВЕЧЕРНЯЯ ГАЗЕТА, СПБ., 20 мая 1912.

(б) Кривое зеркало

102 Истолкование пьесы Ф.Сологуба „Всегдашние шашни". Речь к труппе театра, готовящейся к постановке в театре „Кривое зеркало". ТЕАТР И ИСКУССТВО, СПБ., 47:916-8, 1912.

103 Беседа с Н.Н. Евреиновым о новой постановке „Сумурин" в театре „Кривое зеркало". БИРЖЕВЫЕ ВЕДОМОСТИ, СПБ., 10 янв. 1912.

104 Беседа с Н.Н. Евреиновым о постановке в театре „Кривое зеркало" „Ревизора", „В кулисах души" и оперы „Сладкий пирог". РАННЕЕ УТРО, М., 3 апр. 1913.

105 Беседа с Н.Н. Евреиновым о постановках в театре „Кривое зеркало". РУССКАЯ МОЛВА, СПБ., 7 авг. 1913.

106 Мельпомена и Мин Хуан. ТЕАТР И ИСКУССТВО, СПБ., 38:741-4, 1913.
(Перепечатано в ТЕАТРАЛЬНЫЕ НОВАЦИИ, ПТГ., 1923.)

107 Вампука, невеста африканская. Неопубликованная статья (31 стр.) В библио-теке ин-та театра, Ленинград.

108 Кривое зеркало в Царском Селе. ВОЗРОЖДЕНИЕ, Paris, 13:113-30, 1951.

109 О смехе с препятствиями. ВОЗРОЖДЕНИЕ, Paris, 40:110-115, 1955.

110 Кривое зеркало. ВОЗРОЖДЕНИЕ, Paris, 57:95-102, 1956.

111 О Кривом зеркале. НОВЫЙ ЖУРНАЛ, XXXV, 190-207, 1953.

112 Козьма Прутков — почитаемый отцом Кривого зеркала. ВОЗРОЖДЕНИЕ, 50: 101-20, 1956.

113 Об остроумии и его проявлениях. РУССКАЯ МЫСЛЬ, Paris, оет. 24, окт. 31, ноябрь 6, ноябрь 13, 1963.

114 В школе остроумия. О театре Кривое зеркало. Неопубликованная рукопись. Собств. А. А. Евреиновой.

(в) Старинный театр

115 Испанский театр 16-18 в.в. ЕЖЕГОДНИК ИМПЕРАТОРСКИХ ТЕАТРОВ, Вып. 6-7:58-64, 1909.
(Перепечатано в ИСПАНСКИЙ ТЕАТР. СТАТЬИ. ВВЕДЕНИЕ К СПЕКТАКЛЯМ 1911-12, СПБ., 1911, и в PRO SCENA SUA, СПБ., 1915.)

116 Метод художественной реконструкции театральных постановок. ЖИЗНЬ ИС-КУССТВА, ПТГ., 634-6, 1920.
(Перепечатано в ТЕАТРАЛЬНЫЕ НОВАЦИИ, ПТГ., 1922.)

117 Реферат, прочитанный в лит.-худ. кружке им. Я.П.Полонского 30 ноября на вечере, посвященном задачам Старинного театра. ТЕАТР И ИСКУССТВО, СПБ., 50:837-41, 1907.

118 Беседа с Н.Н. Евреиновым о новой серии испанских пьес в Старинном театре. ТЕАТР, М., 257:6, 1908.

7 Статьи и другие материалы, относящиеся к пьесам Н.Н.Евреинова

119 Беседа с Н.Н.Евреиновым о „Беглой". БИРЖЕВЫЕ ВЕДОМОСТИ, СПБ., 3 окт. 1913.

120 История написания арлекинады „Веселая смерть". ИСКУССТВО, ПТГ., 5-7:7, 1917.

121 Беседа с Н.Н.Евреиновым о постановке „Самого главного" в МОскве. ТЕАТРА-ЛЬНАЯ МОСКВА, М., 33:22, 1922.

8 Книги и статьи о художниках

122 Ропс. Критический очерк. Изд. Современное искусство, Н.И.Бутковская. Серия иллюстрированных монографий СПБ., Вып.4, 1910.

123 Бердслей. Очерк. Изд. Современное искусство, Н.И.Бутковская, Серия иллюстрированных монографий. СПБ., Вып. 5, 1912.

124 Кульбин. В сборн. „Кульбин", изд. Интимный театр, СПБ., 1912.

125 Его смерть. Предисловие к книге В.Каратыгина „Скрябин"; СПБ., 1915.

126 Русское театрально-декорационное искусство. Проспект. Изд. Свободное искусство, ПТГ., 1917.

127 Нестеров. Очерк. Петербург книгоиздат, Третья стража, ПТГ., 1922.

128 Оригинал о портретистах. К проблеме субъективизма в искусстве. Изд. Светозор, ПТГ., 1922.

129 Живопись и театр. О Судейкине. ГРАНИ, Frankfurt, 39:159-72, 1958; 41:174--194, 1959.

9 Разное

130 Театрализация жизни. Поэт, театрализующий жизнь. О В.Каменском, М., 1922.

131 Товарищи артисты. Призыв к деятелям искусства о помощи голодающим Поволжья. ЖИЗНЬ ИСКУССТВА, ПТГ., 798-803:4, 1921.

132 Театральное искусство на службе общественной безопасности. Популярный очерк из книги „Прикладное театральное искусство". ЖИЗНЬ ИСКУССТВА, ПТГ., 792-7:4, 1921.

133 Недоказуемое. Предисловие к книге А.Э.Беленсона „Искусственная жизнь", ПТГ., 1921.

134 Апология наркоза. Предисловие к книге В.Орта „Республика любви", ПТГ, 1918.

135 Письмо Н.Н.Евреинова редакции, /?/ СПБ., 5:77-8, 1915.

136 Беседа с Евреиновым о театре и об искусстве в Париже. ВЕЧЕРНЯЯ КРАСНАЯ ГАЗЕТА, ПТГ., 26 (3 февр.) 1926.

137 Нас было четверо. ВОЗРОЖДЕНИЕ, Paris, 21:82-94; 22:116-32; 23:89-101,1952.

138 Любовь актера. ГРАНИ, Frankfurt, 33:187-91, 1957.

Б

Драматические произведения Н. Н. Евреинова

1 Оригинальные пьесы

1 Болваны кулирские боги. Историческая пьеса в 4-х действиях и 7 картинах. Драм. соч., Том 1, СПБ., 1908, 5-163.

2 Фундамент счастья. Комедия в 3-х действиях. Драм. соч., Том 1, СПБ., 1908. 167-287.

3 Степик и Монюрочка. Комедия в 1-ом действии. Драм. соч., Том 1, СПБ., 1908, 291-314.

4 Красивый деспот. Последний акт драмы. А.С.Суворина, СПБ., 1907. Драм. соч., Том 1, 1908, 318-366.

5 Война. Драма в 3-х действиях. Драм. соч., Том 1, СПБ., 1908, 369-476.

6 Ярмарка на индикт Св. Дениса. Пьеса в 1ом действии. Драм. соч., Том 2, СПБ., 1914, 5-31.

7 Три волхва. Пьеса в 1ом действии. Драм. соч., Том 2, СПБ., 1914, 33-55.

8 Веселая смерть. Арлекинада в 1-ом действии. Драм. соч., Том 2, 1914, 56-90.

9 Такая женщина. Драматический парадокс в 1-ом действии. Драм. соч., Том 2, 1914, 91-147.

10 Бабушка. Пьеса в 1-ом действии. Драм. соч., Том 2, 1914, 151-169.

11 Неизменная измена. Пьеса в 3-х действиях. Драм. соч., Том 2, 1914, 173-269.

12 Ревизор. Режиссерская буффонада в 5 ,,построениях одного отрывка''. Драм. соч., Том 3, ПТГ., 1923, 9-29.

13 В кулисах души. Монодрама в 1-ом действии с прологом и с музыкой Н.Н.Евреинова. Драм. соч., Том 3, ПТГ., 1923, 33-41.

14 Четвертая стена. Буффонада в 2-х картинах. Драм. соч., Том 3, ПТГ., 1923,43-70.

15 Школа этуалей. Эпизод из жизни Аннушки, горничной Н.Н.Евреинова. Драм. соч., Том 3, ПТГ., 1923, 71-84.

16 Кухня смеха. Мировой конкурс остроумия. Пародия в 4-х шаржах. Драм. соч., Том 3, ПТГ., 1923, 85-130.

17 Представление любви. Монодрама в 3-х действиях. СТУДИЯ ИМПРЕССИОНИСТОВ, СПБ., 1909 и ,,Современное искусство'', ПТГ., 1917.

18 Счастливый гробовщик. Пьеса в 1-ом действии. СПБ., 1912.

19 Беглая. Оперетта. Представлена в Палас театр, 1913.

20 Самое главное. Для кого комедия, а для кого и драма. В 4-х действиях. ПТГ., 1921 и Ревель, 1921.

21 Коммуна праведных. Пьеса в 4-х действиях. СПБ., 1924.

22 Современный лодом или пьеса во вкусе публики. Драматическая пародия в 1-ом действии.

23 Таверна смерти. Пантомима. 1924.

2 Пьесы, написанные в сотрудничестве с другими авторами

24 Эоловы арфы. Монодрама в 4-х действиях. Написана в сотрудничестве с Б.Ф.Гейером.

25 Коломбина сего дня. Пантомима в 1-ом действии. Написана в сотрудничестве с художницей Мисс, музыка Евреинова.

3 Инсценировки для театра „Кривое зеркало"

26 О шести красавицах, непохожих друг на друга. Сказка Магоммада Эль Басри
   в 1-ом действии. СПБ., 1911.
27 Пан. Перевод с английского Зинаиды Венгеровой в 1-ом действии.
28 Песни Билитис. Пьеса в 1-ой картине.
29 Карагоз (Хайали-Зиль). Представление турецкого „петрушки" в 2-х картинах.
30 Врачи. Трагедия в 4-х действиях Бернарда Шоу (The Doctor's Dilemma).

4 Другие инсценировки

31 Комедия Аристофана. В 2-х действиях и 3-х картинах, приспособленная к совре-
   менному театру Н.Н.Евреиновым, СПБ., 1912.

5 Музыка Н.Н.Евреинова к постановкам в театре „Кривое зеркало"

32 Сладкий пирог.
33 Песни Билитис.
34 В кулисах души.
35 Коломбина сего дня.
36 Вечная танцовщица.

B

Книги, статьи и рецензии, относящиеся к работе Н. Н. Евреинова в России

1 Общее

1 Айхенвальд, Ю., Отрицание театра. Из лекции „Литература и театр", М., 16 марта 1913. Также в: „В спорах о театре". М., 1914, 9-38.

2 Анастасьев, А., Об отношении формалистов к МХАТ. В: „МХАТ в борьбе с формализмом". М., 1953. 6-7, 10, 29, 30-1, 40, 61-2, 71-2, 77-9, 83, 97, 104, 105, 106.

3 Арватов, Б., Евреинов и мы. ЭРМИТАЖ, ПТГ., 19:22-6. 1922.

4 Арнс, Л., Н. Н. Евреинов. ЖИЗНЬ ИСКУССТВА, ПТГ., 3:2, 1922.

5 Bakshy, Alexander. The Path of the Modern Russian Stage and Other Essays. London, 1916, 77-82, 177-8.

6 Beeson, N.B., Vsevolod Meyerhold and the Experimental Prerevolutionary Theatre in Russia 1900—1917. Michigan (Univ. Microfilms Inc.), 1960, 209—237.

7 Беленсон, А., Искусственная жизнь. ПТГ., 1921, 73-8

8 Бескин, Э. М., Об идеях Таирова, Мейерхольда и Евреинова. ТЕАТРАЛЬНАЯ ГА-ЗЕТА. ПТГ., 15:10-12, 1917.

9 Бескин, Э. М., в „Литературная энциклопедия", М., 1930, Том 4, 13-14.

10 Богуславский, А. Б. и Диев, В. А., Русская советская драматургия. Основные проблемы развития. 1917-35. М., 1963, 9-10, 20-21.

11 Брокгауз и Эфрон., Новый энциклопедический словарь. СПБ, Том 17, 235.

12 Бруксон, Я., Проблема театральности (естественность перед судом марксизма). ПТГ., 1923.

13 Бялик, Б. А., Горький в борьбе с театральной реакцией. Л.-М., 1938, 16-34, 79, 95-6, 142-9.

14 Волконский, С., Отклики театра. СПБ., 1914, 20.

15 Всеволодский-Гернгросс, В., История русского театра. Л.-М., 1929, Том 2, 244, 250, 264, 298, 302.

16 Gorchakov, N.A., The Theatre in Soviet Russia. New York, 1957, 77—85, 149—50.

17 Зноско-Боровский, Е. Е., Русский театр начала XX века. Прага, 1925, 319-43.

18 Казанский, Б. В., Метод театра (анализ системы Н. Н. Евреинова). Л., 1925.

19 Каменский, В. В., Книга об Евреинове. ПТГ., 1917.
Рецензии:
        (а) Мейерхольд, В. Э., БИРЖЕВЫЕ ВЕДОМОСТИ, ПТГ., 10 февр. 1917.
        (б) Он же. ЗРИТЕЛЬ, ПТГ., 91:20-1, 1917.
        (в) Он же. ДЕНЬ, ПТГ., 21 янв. 1917.
        (г) Он же. НОВОЕ ВРЕМЯ, ПТГ., 6 февр. 1917.
        (д) Он же. ВЕЧЕРНЕЕ ВРЕМЯ, ПТГ., 5 февр. 1917.

20 Каменский, В. В., Детство и юность Н. Н. Евреинова. (Страницы, перепечатанные из „Книги об Евреинове"). ЗРИТЕЛЬ, ПТГ., 91:20-1, 92:30-2, 94:31, 1917.

21 Кашина-Евреинова, А. А., Н. Н. Евреинов в мировом театре XX века, Paris, 1964.

22 Clark, Barret and Freedley, George, A History of Modern Drama, New York, 1947, 430, 442—5.

23 Керженцев, А., Творческий театр. М., 1919, 43-67.

24 Марков, П. А., Новейшие театральные течения. М., 1924, 32-3.

25 Миклашевский, К., Гипертрофия искусства. ПТГ., 1924, 15, 31, 52.

26 Мокульский, С. С., (Ред.), История советского театра. Л., 1933, Том 1 (1917-21), 21, 26, 50, 134-5, 137, 211, 214-17, 279-82.

27 Moody, C., История русского театра с древнейших времен до 1917 года. Letchworth, 1972, v—xxvi.

28 Назаревский, Б. В., Кризис натурализма на сцене. Критический очерк о В.Э.Мейерхольде и Н.Н.Евреинове. МОСКОВСКИЕ ВЕДОМОСТИ, 8 сент., 1913.

29 Nicoll, Allardice, World Drama. London,　1949, 1960, 719, 722-6, 772.

30 Нилли, Н., О театре будущего. Об идеях Н.Н.Евреинова и Ю.Айхенвальда. ЗАПИСКИ ПЕРЕДВИЖНОГО ТЕАТРА, ПТГ., 20:4-8, 1919.

31 Прокофьев, В., В спорах о Станиславском. М., 1962, 159, 170-4.

32 Петров, М., 50-500, М., 1960, 142-6, 149-50, 194-5, 203, 212, 215.

33 "Prospero", Темы дня. О режиссере Н.Н.Евреинове. ТЕАТР, М., 1477:9-11, 1914.

34 Редько, А.М., Лит-художественные искания в конце Х1Х и в начале ХХ века. Л., 1924, 15-3.

35 Ростиславов, А., О докладе о театральном кризисе. Возражения оппонентов — Мейерхольд, Глаголин, Евреинов и Балибин. ТЕАТР И ИСКУССТВО, СПБ., 8:154-5, 1909.

36 Sayler, Oliver M., The Russian Theatre. London, 1922, 221-44, 257-61.

37 Swierczewski, E., Jewreinow. ZYCIE TEATRU, Warsaw, 1-6: 4-5, 12-14, 20-1, 28-9, 36—7, 44——6, 1924.

38 Swierczewski, E., Jewreinow. Warsaw, 1924.

39 Czokov, F.T., N.N.Evreinov und sein werk. Vienna, (Дата?)

40 Sielicki, Franciszek, Mikolaj Jewreinow w Polsce. ACTA UNIVERSITATIS WRATISLAVIENSIS. Wroclaw, 194:63—76, 1974.

41 Slonim, Makc, The Russian Theatre from the Empire to the Soviets. London, 1963,211-7.

42 Таиров, А.Я., Записки режиссера. Статьи, беседы, речи, письма. М., 1970, 80, 188, 240, 249, 537, 542.

43 Эфрос, А., Отражение Евреинова. ТЕАТРАЛЬНОЕ ОБОЗРЕНИЕ. М., 2:5-6, 1921.

44　— Русский советский театр 1917-21. Документы и материалы. Л., 1968.

45　— Творческая характеристика Н.Н.Евреинова. ОБОЗРЕНИЕ ТЕАТРОВ И СПОРТА. ПТГ., 36:6, 1922.

46　— О кризисе современного театра и теоретических высказываниях. О театре Н.Н.Евреинова. РАМПА, СПБ., 4:49-52, 1909.

47　— Отчет о докладе Монахиевой-Мирович в женском медицинском институте. О выступление В.Э.Мейерхольда и Н.Н.Евреинова. ДЕНЬ, ПТГ., 24 нояб. 1916.

48　— Об Евреинове. ТЕАТРАЛЬНЫЙ КУРЬЕР, М., 8 окт. 1918.

2 Воспоминания о Н.Н.Евреинове

49 Алперс, Б., Театр социальной маски. М.-Л., 1931, 115-16.

50 Анненков, Ю., Дневник моих встреч. New York, 1966, Том 2, 11-141.

51 Бруксон, Я., Театр Мейерхольда. М., 1925, 118.

52 Горчаков, Н.А., О Евреинове, ГРАНИ, 20:103-11, 1953.

53 Грот, Е., Человек и театр. НОВОЕ РУССКОЕ СЛОВО, New York, 11 февр. 1968.

54 Дейч, А., Вспоминая минувшее. ЗВЕЗДА, 5:173-83, 1966.

55 Евстигнеева, Л., Журнал ,,Сатирикон'' и поэты-сатириконцы. М., 372-6, 1968.

56 Ершов, П., Рыцарь театральности. РУССКАЯ МЫСЛЬ, Paris, 12 февр. 1959.

57 Камышников, Л., Николай Евреинов и русский театр. НОВОЕ РУССКОЕ СЛОВО, New York, 21 янв. 1955.

58 Крыжицкий, Г., Режиссерские портреты. М.-Л., 1928, 36-47.

59 Крыжицкий, Г., Стрельская, Л., 1970, 127-9.

60 Лидарцева, И., Прошел год... Памяти Н.Н.Евреинова. Возрождение, Paris, 35: 169-74, 1954,

61 Lo Gatto, Ettore, Nicola Evreinov e il teatro russo. IL TEMPO, 7 мая 1964.

62 Маковский, С., На парнасе серебряного века. Munich; 1962, 333-40.

63 Мгебров, А.А., Жизнь в театре. М., 1929-32. Т.т.1 и 2.

64 Носова, В., Комиссаржевская. М., 1964.

65 Плаксин, Б., Школьные годы Н.Н.Евреинова. РУССКАЯ МЫСЛЬ, Paris, 6 февр.1969.

66 Ремизов, А., Потихоньку, скоморохи, играйте. ГРАНИ, Frankfurt, 20:101-2, 1953.

67 Румнев, А., О пантомиме, театре и кино. О драматической пантомиме в России, в частности о Мейерхольде, Таирове и Евреинове. М., 1964, 128-56.

68 Сабанеев, Л., В память Н. Н. Евреинова. РУССКАЯ МЫСЛЬ, Paris, 12 февр. 1959.

69 Чуковский, К., Современники. Портреты и этюды. М., 1962.

70 — О Комиссаржевской. Заботы и новое. М., 1965.

71 — Художественное наследство. Репин. Ак. наук, 1948.

3 Взгляды Евреинова на роль режиссера

72 Бурлюк, Д., О режиссере Н. Н. Евреинове. РУССКИЙ ГОЛОС, New York, 2 ноября 1923.

73 Бунашев, М. Н., Н. Н. Евреинов и авторское право режиссера. ТЕАТР И ИСКУССТВО, СПБ., 22:385-7, 1909.

74 — Об идеях Н. Н. Евреинова об отношении между режиссером и драматургом. ТЕАТР И ИСКУССТВО, СПБ., 20:349, 1909.

75 — О собственности режиссера. ТЕАТР И ИСКУССТВО, СПБ., 19:333, 20:349, 1909.

4 Старинный театр

(a) Первый период 1907-8, Петербургский сезон.

76 Бурнашев, В. Н., Дризен, Н. В., Евреинов, Н. Н., Проспект спектаклей. Письмо в редакцию. ТЕАТР И ИСКУССТВО, СПБ., 22:359, 1907.

77 Бурнашев, В. Н., О задачах, репертуаре и составе труппы. БИРЖЕВЫЕ ВЕДОМОСТИ, СПБ., 24 нояб. 1907.

78 Гуревич, Л., /Рецензия/. РУССКИЕ ВЕДОМОСТИ, М., 22 дек. 1907.

79 Долгов, Н., О задачах и недостатках театра. ТЕАТР И ИСКУССТВО, СПБ., 35:567-8, 1907.

80 Дризен, Н. В., Аничков, Е., Евреинов, Н. Н., Лекции о старинном театре. ТЕАТР, М., 121:20, 1907.

81 Еремеев, Н., Петербургские письма. Русский артист. М., 11:170-1, 1907.

82 Кремлев, А., Попытка реставрации средневекового театра. ТЕАТР И ИСКУССТВО, СПБ., 7:134, 8:151, 1908.

83 Кугель, А. Р., /Рецензия/. РУСЬ, СПБ., 9 дек. 1907.

84 Кугель, А. Р., /Рецензия/. ТЕАТР И ИСКУССТВО, СПБ., 16 дек. 1907.

85 Московский, С., Первые представления старинного театра. СТАРЫЕ ГОДЫ, СПБ., 1908, 41-4.

86 „Омега''. Старинный театр. Второй исторический спектакль. ПЕТЕРБУРГСКАЯ ГАЗЕТА, 16 дек. 1907.

87 Репнин, Н., Театральные впечатления. СЛОВО, СПБ., 11 дек. 1907.

88 — Еще о старинном театре. ТЕАТР, М., 55:11-12, 1907.

89 — О генеральной репетиции. РЕЧЬ, П., 7 дек. 1907.

90 — Анализ второй постановки театра. ТЕАТР, М., 139:13-14, 1907.

91 — Хроника. ОБОЗРЕНИЕ ТЕАТРОВ, М., 253:14, 1907.

92 — Об открытии сезона, о целях, репертуаре и пр. РЕЧЬ, П., 16 нояб. 1907.

93 — О пьесе Евреинова „Три волхва'' и ее постановке. ТЕАТР И ИСКУССТВО, СПБ., 39:628, 1907.

94 — Обсуждение старинного театра между Н. Н. Евреиновым и артистами. ТЕАТР И ИСКУССТВО, СПБ., 41:673, 1907.

95 — ТЕАТР И ИСКУССТВО, СПБ., 45:735, 1907.

96 — К постановке „Действа о Теофиле'' с 9 фотографиями декораций. СТОЛИЦА

И УСАДЬБА, СПБ., 71:9, 1916.
98 — ЗОЛОТОЕ РУНО, М., 11-12:117, 1907.

(б) Первый период 1907-8, Московский сезон

99 Ауслендер, С., Разбор 2-ой программы. ЗОЛОТОЕ РУНО, М., 3-4:117-20, 1908.
100 Бороздин, И., Средневековый театр. ВЕСЫ, М., 4:96-8, 1908.
101 Бенца, А., О постановках из 14 века. МОСКОВСКИЙ ЕЖЕНЕДЕЛЬНИК, М., 4:33-8, 1908.
102 Веселовский, Ю., /Рецензия/. РУССКИЕ ВЕДОМОСТИ, М., 25 марта 1908.
103 Грабарь, И., О старинном театре и пр. ВЕСЫ, М., 4:92-5, 1908.
104 Муратов, П., /Рецензия/. РУССКОЕ СЛОВО, М., 27 марта 1908.
105 О.М., У возродителя старинного театра. О программе театра и воспитании актера для него. ТЕАТР., М., 211:22, 1908.
106 Старый друг. У колыбели театра. ТЕАТР, М., 213:15-8, 1908.
107 Сурский, А., Старинный театр. РУССКИЙ АРТИСТ, М., 13:199, 1908.
108 — /Рецензия/. ТЕАТР, М., 212:12, 1908.
109 — /Рецензия/ ТЕАТР, М., 213:12, 1908.
110 — Об основании старинного театра. ТЕАТР, М., 46:11-2, 1908.
111 — ТЕАТР, М., 212:12-3, 1908.

(в) Планы второго периода 1908-9

112 — О возобновлении и репертуаре театра в сезоне 1908-9. ОБОЗРЕНИЕ ТЕАТРОВ, СПБ., 511:8, 1908.
113 — О возобновлении деятельности старинного театра. СПБ, 761:6, 1908.

(г) Второй период 1911-12, Петербургский сезон

114 Андреевский, С., /Рецензия/. ПЕТЕРБУРГСКАЯ ГАЗЕТА, СПБ., 22 ноября 1911.
115 Арабажин, К., Старинный театр. БИРЖЕВЫЕ ВЕДОМОСТИ, СПБ., 19 ноября 1911.
116 Батюшков, Ф., По поводу спектаклей старинного театра. СТУДИЯ, М., 11:3-4, 1911.
117 Бенуа, А., Художественные письма. Старинный театр. РЕЧЬ, СПБ., 6 дек. 1911.
118 Бенуа, А., /Рецензия/. РЕЧЬ, СПБ., 16, 23 ноября 1911.
119 Гуревич, Л., /Рецензия/. РУССКИЕ ВЕДОМОСТИ, М., 27 ноября 1911.
120 Гуревич, Л., Петербургские театры. Статья перед сезоном. РУССКИЕ ВЕДОМОСТИ, М., 27 ноября 1911.
121 Дризен, Н.В., Беседа перед сезоном. РАМПА И ЖИЗНЬ, М., 46:11-2, 1911.
122 Василевский, В., Петербургские этюды. РАМПА И ЖИЗНЬ., М., 51:12-3, 1911.
123 Василевский, В., — РЕЧЬ, СПБ., 20 ноября 1911.
124 Конради, П., /Рецензия/. НОВОЕ ВРЕМЯ, СПБ., 20 ноября 1911.
125 Кугель, А.Р., /Рецензия/. ТЕАТР И ИСКУССТВО, СПБ., 48:937, 1911.
126 Ростиславов, А., О постановках старинного театра. ТЕАТР И ИСКУССТВО, СПБ., 51:1002, 1911.
127 Светлов, В., /Рецензии/. ПЕТЕРБУРГСКАЯ ГАЗЕТА, СПБ., 21, 29 ноября 1911.
128 Чудновский, В., О старинном театре. РУССКАЯ ХУДОЖЕСТВЕННАЯ ЛЕТОПИСЬ, СПБ., 4:56-63, 1912.
129 Чудновский, В., /Рецензия/. АПОЛЛОН, СПБ., 1-4:42, 1912.
130 Щепкина-Куперник, Т.Л., Театр в моей жизни. М.-Л., 1948, 160-1.
131 — /Рецензия/. РЕЧЬ, СПБ., 30 ноября 1911.
132 — /Рецензия/. НОВОЕ ВРЕМЯ, СПБ., 8 янв. 1912.

133 — /Рецензия/. РЕЧЬ, СПБ., 20 ноября 1911.
134 — /Рецензия/. ПЕТЕРБУРГСКАЯ ГАЗЕТА, СПБ., 10 дек. 1911.
135 — /Рецензия/. НОВОЕ ВРЕМЯ, СПБ., 1 дек. 1911.
136 — /Рецензия/. БИРЖЕВЫЕ ВЕДОМОСТИ, СПБ., 28 ноября 1911.

(д) Второй период 1911-12, Московский сезон

137 Бескин, Э., /Рецензия/. РАННЕЕ УТРО, М., 16 февр. 1912.
138 Карабанов, Н., /Рецензия/. ТЕАТР, М., 1019:5-6, 1912.
139 Львов, Я., /Рецензия/. РАМПА И ЖИЗНЬ, М., 8:13, 1912.
140 Назаревский, Б. В. /Рецензия/. МОСКОВСКИЕ ВЕДОМОСТИ, М., 30 марта 1912.
141 Раз-ий, С., Цели и направления старинного театра. СТУДИЯ, М., 20:5-7, 1912.
142 Эфрос, Н., /Рецензия/, РУССКИЕ ВЕДОМОСТИ, М., 15 февр. 1912.
143 Эфрос, Н., /Рецензия/. РУССКИЕ ВЕДОМОСТИ, М., 7 марта 1912.
144 — /Рецензия/. РАННЕЕ УТРО, М., 21 февраля 1912.
145 — /Рецензия/. МОСКОВСКИЕ ВЕДОМОСТИ, М., 7 марта 1912.
146 — /Рецензия/. РУССКИЕ ВЕДОМОСТИ, М., 21 февр. 1912.
147 — О разногласиях в худсовете и раздвоении старинного театра. РУССКОЕ СЛОВО, М., 31 янв. 1912.
148 — /Рецензия/. РУССКОЕ СЛОВО, М., 15 февр. 1912.
149 — /Рецензия/. РУССКОЕ СЛОВО, М., 6 марта 1912.
150 — /Рецензия/. ТЕАТР, 1023:33, 1028:32, 1029:5, 1912.

(е) Спор о собственности, 1912

151 Дризен, Н. В., Беседа о том, почему появилось два старинных театра сразу. РАННЕЕ УТРО, СПБ., 12 февр. 1912.
152 — Диспут между Н. В. Дризеном и Н. Н. Евреиновым. РУССКОЕ СЛОВО, М., 31 янв. 1912.
153 — Приговор третейского суда по делу старинного театра. БИРЖЕВЫЕ ВЕДОМОСТИ, СПБ., 25 февр. 1912.
154 — Решение третейского суда. ТЕАТР И ИСКУССТВО, СПБ., 9:190, 1912.
155 — Текст решения третейского суда. ТЕАТР И ИСКУССТВО, СПБ., 10:212,1912.

(ж) Планы третьего периода 1913-15

156 — Отмена спектаклей в сезоне 1913-14 г. из-за отсутствия помещения. ТЕАТР И ИСКУССТВО, СПБ., 42:830, 1913.
157 — Об отмене. ТЕАТР И ИСКУССТВО, СПБ., 34:693, 1914.
158 — О снятии малого зала СПБ консерватории под спектакли старинного театра зимой 1914-15 г. г. ТЕАТР И ИСКУССТВО, СПБ., 22:479, 26:559, 1914.

(з) Общее

159 Волков, Н., Мейерхольд, М., 1929, Том 2, 221-2.
160 Beeson, N.B., Vsevolod Meyerhold and Experimental Prerevolutionary Theatre in Russia 1900—17, Michigan (Univer. Microfilms Inc.), 1960, 225—31.
161 Дризен, Н. В., Старинный театр. СТОЛИЦА И УСАДЬБА, СПБ., 71:8-12, 1916.
162 Дризен, Н. В., Сорок лет театра. Воспоминания 1875-1915. СПБ., 1916,
163 Мгебров, А. А., Жизнь в театре. М.-Л., 1932, Том 2, 34-66, 76-8, 82-142.
164 Мейерхольд, В. Э., О театре, М., 1913. В: ,,В. Э. Мейерхольд. Статьи, письма, речи, беседы. Часть первая. 1891-1917. М., 1968, 189-91.
165 Poggi, Tamara Baikova, Il 'Teatro Antico' e misterija—buff. Genoa, 1974.

166 Старк, Э., Старинный театр. СПБ., 1912, ПТГ., 1922.

167 Чекан, В., О старинном театре и роль в нем Н. Н. Евреинова. ЖИЗНЬ ИСКУССТВА, ПТГ., 21:4, 1922.

168 Чулков, Г., Годы странствий. Театральные воспоминания. М., 1929, 3-4, 50-60.

5 Кривое зеркало

169 Дейч, А., Творческий портрет Н. Н. Евреинова. О его работе в театре Кривое зеркало. Театральные впечатления и встречи. М., 1966.

170 Дымов, О., Всегдашние шашни. ДЕНЬ, СПБ., 20 окт. 1912

171 Зноско-Боровский, Е. Е., Влияние Н. Н. Евреинова на уровень спектаклей в театре Кривое зеркало. (1) Василь Василич помирал — Л. Урванцев. (2) Вода жизни — — Б. Гейер. (3) Гастроль рычалов. РУССКАЯ ХУДОЖЕСТВЕННАЯ ЛЕТОПИСЬ, СПБ., 15:234, 1911.

172 Зноско-Боровский, Е. Е. /Рецензия на ,,Ревизор''/. РУССКАЯ МОЛВА, СПБ., 12 дек. 1912.

173 Крыжицкий, Р., Лаборатория смеха. Воспоминания о Кривом зеркале. ТЕАТР, 8:110-20, 1967.

174 Миклашевский, К., /Рецензия на ,,Всегдашние шашни''/. ТЕАТР, ПТГ., 2 окт. 1922.

175 Moody, C., The Crooked Mirror. MELBOURNE SLAVONIC STUDIES, Melbourne 7:25-37, 1972.

176 Философов, Д., /Рецензия на ,,Ревизор'' и ,,Чествование Козьмы Пруткова''/. РЕЧЬ, СПБ., 18 янв. 1913.

177 Ховин, В., /Рецензия на ,,В кулисах души''./ ВОСКРЕСНАЯ ВЕЧЕРНЯЯ ГАЗЕТА. СПБ., 14 окт. 1912.

178 Ходотов, Н. Н., Близкое-далекое. Воспоминания о Кривом зеркале в первые годы. М.-Л., 1962.

179 — Приглашение Н. Н. Евреинова в театр Кривое зеркало главным режиссером. ТЕАТР И ИСКУССТВО, СПБ., 36:658, 1910.

180 — /Рецензии на постановки Н. Н. Евреинова в Кривом зеркале/. (1) Чужая жена и муж под кроватью. (По Достоевскому). (2) О шести красавицах, непохожих друг на друга, — драматизированная Н. Н. Евреиновым. (3) Не хвались идучи на рать. Опера-водевиль. И. Сац. ТЕАТР И ИСКУССТВО, СПБ., 40:732, 1910.

181 — /Рецензии на постановки Н. Н. Евреинова в Кривом зеркале/. (1) Песни Билитис. (2) Деревянная трагикомедия. Бенедикт. (3) Мудрый чарутта. (4) Страничка романа. Эстеррейх. (5) Замечательное представление. Пародия. ТЕАТР И ИСКУССТВО. СПБ., 43:797, 1910.

182 — /Рецензии на постановки Н. Н. Евреинова в Кривом зеркале/. (1) Слабый пол. Густав Вид. (2) Немая жена. Анатоль Франс. (3) Женщина и смерть. С. И. Антимонов. (4) Силуэты танцев. (5) Дон Лимонадо. Комическая опера Л. И. Гебек. ТЕАТР И ИСКУССТВО, СПБ., 47:892, 1910.

183 — /Рецензии на постановки Н. Н. Евреинова в Кривом зеркале/. (1) Элементы жизни. Б. Гейер. (2) Четверо. Аверченко. (3) Около балета в старину. ТЕАТР И ИСКУССТВО, СПБ., 51:988, 1910.

184 — Н. Н. Евреинов уходит из театра ,,Кривое зеркало''. ТЕАТРАЛЬНАЯ ГАЗЕТА, СПБ., 30 марта 1914.

185 — /Рецензии на постановку Н. Н. Евреиновым ,,Монумента'' Л. Андреева в Никитинском театре (Кривое зеркало) /. ТЕАТР, М., 1822:9, 1916.

186 — О гастроли театра Кривое зеркало в Польше и работе Н. Н. Евреинова в нем. ЛЕНИНГРАДСКАЯ ПРАВДА, Л., 3 апр. 1925.

6 Театр Комиссаржевской

(а) Общее

187 Альтшуллер, А. Я., В. Ф. Комиссаржевская. Л.-М., 1964, 275-8, 280-5.
188 Бейконе, М., Театр Комиссаржевской. ТЕАТР И ИСКУССТВО, СПБ., 44:764, 1908.
189 Вас, Р., Черепослов и Фантазия. БИРЖЕВЫЕ ВЕДОМОСТИ, СПБ., 24 апр. 1909.
190 ,,Забытый'', В лапах. Против работы В. Э. Мейерхольда и Н. Н. Евреинова в театре Комиссаржевской. ТЕАТР, М., 253:7-8, 1908.
191 Мгебров, А. А., Жизнь в театре, М.-Л., 1932, Том 2, 310-2, 316-8, 375-8.
192 — Приглашение Н. Н. Евреинова работать режиссером в театре В. Комиссаржевской. ТЕАТР И ИСКУССТВО, СПБ., 2:27, 1908.
193 — Приглашение Н. Н. Евреинова в театр Комиссаржевской. ОБОЗРЕНИЕ ТЕАТ-
РОВ, СПБ., 306:18, 1908.
194 — О режиссерах в театре Комиссаржевской. ТЕАТР И ИСКУССТВО, СПБ.,
32:543, 1908.
195 — О В. Ф. Комиссаржевской. АПОЛЛОН, СПБ., 6:28, 1910.

(б) Франческа да Римини

196 Гуревич, Л., /Рецензия/. СЛОВО, СПБ., 6 окт. 1908.
197 Кугель, А. Р., /Рецензия/. НОВАЯ РУСЬ, СПБ., 6 окт. 1908.
198 Львов, Я., /Рецензия/. РАМПА, СПБ., 4:61-2, 1908.
199 Тамарин, Н., /Рецензия/. ТЕАТР И ИСКУССТВО, СПБ., 41:704, 1908.
200 — /Рецензия/. РАННЕЕ УТРО, М., 5 сент. 1908.
201 — /Рецензия/. ТЕАТР, М., 31 сент. 1908.
202 — /Рецензия/. БИРЖЕВЫЕ ВЕДОМОСТИ, СПБ., 6 окт. 1908.
203 — /Рецензия/ РЕЧЬ, СПБ., 7 окт. 1908.
204 — /Рецензия/. ПЕТРОГРАДСКАЯ ГАЗЕТА, СПБ., 5 окт. 1908.
205 — /Рецензия/. РУССКОЕ СЛОВО, М., 5 сент. 1908.
206 — /Рецензия/. ГОЛОС МОСКВЫ, М., 5 сент. 1908.
207 — О беседе с Евреиновым (Раннее утро, 30 авг. 1908). ТЕАТР, М., 5 сент. 1908.
208 — /Рецензия/. ТЕАТР, 6 сент. 1908.
209 — /Рецензии на постановке в петербургском Малом театре/. РУССКАЯ МОЛВА,
СПБ., 24 марта 1913.

(в) Саломей

210 Вейконе, М., /Рецензия/. (Последняя репетиция). ТЕАТР И ИСКУССТВО, СПБ.,
44:769, 1908.
211 — О запрещении Царевны (Саломей). СЛОВО, СПБ., 29 окт. 1908.
212 — О запрещении Царевны. БИРЖЕВЫЕ ВЕДОМОСТИ, СПБ., 29 окт. 1908.
213 — О запрещении Царевны (Саломей). БИРЖЕВЫЕ ВЕДОМОСТИ, СПБ., 30 окт. 1908.

(г) Ванька-Ключник

214 Кугель, А. Р., /Рецензия/. НОВАЯ РУСЬ, СПБ., 10 янв. 1909.
215 Тамарин, Н., /Рецензия/. ТЕАТР И ИСКУССТВО, СПБ., 18 янв. 1909.
216 — /Рецензия/. САТИРИКОН, СПБ., 17 янв. 1909.
217 — /Рецензия/. ТЕАТР, 343:7, 1908.
218 /Рецензия/ ОБОЗРЕНИЕ ТЕАТРОВ, СПБ., 629:5-6, 1909.

7 „Орлеанская дева" в Малом театре, 1908

219 Бентовин, Б.И., /Рецензия/. ТЕАТР И ИСКУССТВО, СПБ., 19:335, 1908.
220 — /Рецензия/. РЕЧЬ, СПБ., 6 мая 1908.
221 — /Рецензия/. РУСЬ, СПБ., 6 мая 1908.
222 — /Рецензия/. БИРЖЕВЫЕ ВЕДОМОСТИ, СПБ., 5 мая 1908.

8 Ночные пляски

223 Гуревич, И., /Рецензия/. СЛОВО, СПБ., 12 марта 1909.
224 — /Рецензия/. НАША ГАЗЕТА, СПБ., 2 марта 1909.
225 — /Рецензия/. ВЕЧЕР, СПБ., 10 марта 1909.

9 „Козьма Прутков" в Литейном Театре, 1909.

226 Крушинин, Вс., Веселый театр. ТЕАТР И ИСКУССТВО, СПБ., 14:255, 1909.
227 „Старый воробей", Веселый театр. ОБОЗРЕНИЕ ТЕАТРОВ, СПБ., 686:6-7, 687:6, 1909.
228 — /Рецензия/. ОБОЗРЕНИЕ ТЕАТРОВ, СПБ., 696:7, 1909.
229 — /Рецензия/. РАННЕЕ УТРО, СПБ., 29 апр. 1909.
230 — /Рецензия/. РЕЧЬ, СПБ., 1 апр. 1909.
231 — /Рецензия/. СЛОВО, СПБ., 1 апр. 1909.
232 — /Рецензия/. ЛИСТОК, СПБ., 31 марта 1909.

10 „Взятие Зимнего дворца", Петроград, 1920

233 Анненков, Ю., Дневник моих встреч. New York, 1966. 118-24.
234 Пиотровский, А.И., За советский театр, М., 1925, 16-7.
235 Ripellino, A.M., Maiakovskii et le théâtre russe d'avant garde.Paris,1965, 65—9.
236 Самойлов, В.Г., Революционные празднества. Воспоминания о спектакле „Взятие Зимнего дворца". В сборн. „Театрально-декорационное искусство в СССР"., Л., 1927, 185-94.
237 Füllop—Müller, R., Das russische Theater, 1928.
238 Пиотровский, А.И., Хроника ленинградских празднеств 1919-20. В сборн. „Массовые празднества". Л., 1926.
239 — /Рецензия/. ЖИЗНЬ ИСКУССТВА, ПТГ., 31 окт. 1920.
240 — /Рецензия/. ЖИЗНЬ ИСКУССТВА, ПТГ., 12 ноября 1920.
241 — /Рецензия/. ИЗВЕСТИЯ ПЕТРОГРАДСКОГО СОБРАНИЯ РАБОЧИХ И КРАСНОАРМЕЙСКИХ ДЕПУТАТОВ, ПТГ., 6 ноября 1920.
242 — /Рецензия/. ПЕТРОГРАДСКАЯ ПРАВДА, ПТГ., 4 ноября 1920.
243 — О работе 12 режиссеров. ВЕСТНИК ТЕАТРА, 74:11-2, 1920.
244 — Русский советский театр 1917-21. Документы и материалы. Л., 1968, 274-5.

11 Прочая деятельность Н.Н.Евреинова в качестве театрального режиссера

245 Гозенпуд, А., О постановке Евреиновым оперы Моцарта „Похищение из сераля" в: „Русский советский оперный театр 1917-41", Л., 1963, 96-8.
246 Николаев-Шевырев, А., Вторая Евреиновская неделя в Свободном театре. Рецензия о программе миниатюр. ОБОЗРЕНИЕ ТЕАТРА И СПОРТА, ПТГ., 19:8, 1922.
247 Сторицын, П., Свободный театр. О деятельности Н.Н.Евреинова в Свободном театре в Петрограде. ПЕТРОГРАДСКАЯ ПРАВДА, ПТГ., 30 июня 1922.
248 Тамарин, Н., О студии Н.Н.Евреинова. ТЕАТР И ИСКУССТВО, СПБ., 18:378,1910.

249 Тамарин, Н., О постановке Н. Н. Евреиновым пьесы-феерии Ю. Беляева в театре „Луна-Парк", 1912. ТЕАТР И ИСКУССТВО, СПБ., 32:611-12, 1912.

250 Черный, В., Евреиновская неделя (Свободный театр). ЖИЗНЬ ИСКУССТВА, ПТГ, 27:2, 1922.

251 Щербаков, С., Театральное сегодня. Кривой Джимми. Оценка репертуара, краткая характеристика сезона. О приглашении Евреинова в качестве худ. рук. ЗРЕЛИЩЕ, М., 1:22, 1922.

252 — Театр лит.-худ. общества. Иллюстрированные программы сезона 1906-7 гг. Вып. 8, 65-72.

253 — О постановках „Сон осеннего заката" д'Аннунцио и „Пастораль" Кузмина в драм. студии Н. Н. Евреинова и Риглера Воронковой. ТЕАТР И ИСКУССТВО, СПБ., 18:378, 1910.

254 — Об организации художественного общества интимного театра. ТЕАТР И ИСКУССТВО, СПБ., 20:402, 1910.

255 — Сценические начинания кружка баронессы И. А. Будберг. СПБ., Альбом, 1913.

256 — О приглашении Н. Н. Евреинова в Палас-театр худ. директором. НОВОЕ ВРЕМЯ, СПБ., 19 янв. 1913.

257 — Н. Н. Евреинов отказался от приглашения Луначарского поставить первомайский спектакль в Москве. ЖИЗНЬ ИСКУССТВА, ПТГ., 721-3:1, 1921.

258 — Об открытии Н. Н. Евреиновым новой студии режисеерского мастерства в Петрограде. ЖИЗНЬ ИСКУССТВА, ПТГ., 767-9:2, 1921.

259 — О постановке Н. Н. Евреиновым серии пьес-опер 18 века в бывшем Михайловском театре. ИЗВЕСТИЯ ВЦИК И МОССОВЕТА. М., 13 июля 1922.

260 — Эксцентрический театр. Предложение организовать новый театр из группы молодых актеров и режиссеров, в числе которых Ю. Анненков и Н. Н. Евреинов. ЭРМИТАЖ, ПТГ., 8:14, 1922.

261 — Свободный театр. О постановке Евреиновских пьес. ЖИЗНЬ ИСКУССТВА. ПТГ., 51:24, 1923.

262 — Слон за роялем. Первый гротеск Н. Н. Евреинова в Доме искусств. ЖИЗНЬ ИСКУССТВА, ПТГ., 669-7:1, 1921.

263 — Кривой Джимми. Оценка программы и игры исполнителей Н. Н. Евреинова, Агнивцева и Алексеева. ЗРЕЛИЩЕ, М., 7:23, 1922.

264 — О приглашении Евреинову от Жака Копо в Париж в театр Vieux Colombier. ЖИЗНЬ ИСКУССТВА, ПТГ., 30:5, 1922.

265 — О приглашении Еыреинова в Михайловский театр поставить оперу Массене „Манон". ИЗВЕСТИЯ ВЦИК И МОССОВЕТА, М., 8 ноября 1922.

266 — О приглашении Евреинова поставить оперу Моцарта „Похищение из сераля" в Михайловском театре. ВЕЧЕРНЯЯ КРАСНАЯ ГАЗЕТА, ПТГ., 14 июля 1923.

268 — О постановке Евреиновым оперы Моцарта „Похищение из сераля". ИЗВЕСТИЯ ВЦИК И МОССОВЕТА, М., 10 мая 1923.

269 — О постановке Н. Н. Евреинова в американском театре. КРАСНАЯ ГАЗЕТА, М., 29 апреля 1925.

12 Путешествия Н. Н. Евреинова

270 Старк, Э., О беседе с Н. Н. Евреиновым, опубликованной в „Вечерней красной газете" 3 февраля 1923. ВЕЧЕРНЯЯ КРАСНАЯ ГАЗЕТА, ПТГ., 7 февр. 1923.

271 — Н. Н. Евреинов (к его возвращению в Петроград). ЖИЗНЬ ИСКУССТВА, ПТГ., 9 сентября 1920.

272 — Приезд в Москву Н. Н. Евреинова. ЭКРАН, М., 27:13, 1922.

273 — Работа Н. Н. Евреинова в Грузии. ЖИЗНЬ ИСКУССТВА, ПТГ., 552:1, 1920.

274 — Поездка Н. Н. Евреинова за границу. ВЕЧЕРНЯЯ КРАСНАЯ ГАЗЕТА, 25 янв. 1923.
275 — Возвращение Н. Н. Евреинова из-за границы. ЗРЕЛИЩЕ, ПТГ., 26:14, 1923.

13 Пятнадцатилетие творческой деятельности Н. Н. Евреинова, 1922.

276 Арнс, Л., Юбилей Н. Н. Евреинова. ЖИЗНЬ ИСКУССТВА, ПТГ., 826:2, 1922.
277 Лев, А., Спектакль из произведений Н. Н. Евреинова в театре ,,Вольная комедия''.
,,Такакя женщина'', ,,Веселая смерть'' и ,,Коломбина сего дня''. — Юбилей Евреинова. ЖИЗНЬ ИСКУССТВА, ПТГ., 826:3-4, 1922.
278 Обломов, И., Юбилей Н. Н. Евреинова. ВЕСТНИК ТЕАТРА И ИСКУССТВА, ПТГ.,
13 янв. 1922.
279 — Юбилей Н. Н. Евреинова. ВЕСТНИК ТЕАТРА И ИСКУССТВА, ПТГ., 23 дек. 1921.

14 Различные заметки, касающиеся Н. Н. Евреинова

280 Кугель, А. Р., Заметки. ТЕАТР И ИСКУССТВО, СПБ., 42:784-7, 1910.
281 Кугель, А. Р., Театральные заметки. ТЕАТР И ИСКУССТВО, СПБ., 39:726-8,1911
282 Кугель, А. Р., Театральные заметки. ТЕАТР И ИСКУССТВО, СПБ., 10:233-4, 1913.
283 Трелль, Н., Н. Н. Евреинов. ЖИЗНЬ ИСКУССТВА, ПТГ., 865:3, 1922.
284 — ВЕСТНИК ТЕАТРА И ИСКУССТВА, ПТГ., 9 дек. 1921.
285 — Строительство самодеятельного театра. В сборн. ,,Пути развития театра''.
Стенограммы доклада и заключительного слова на совещании по вопросам театра
при агитпропе ЦК ВКП/б/ в мае 1927. : а также и резолюции по докладу. Л.-М.,
1927, 261-305.

15 Рецензии на книги и статьи Н. Н. Евреинова

(a) Введение в монодраму

286 Бейконе, М., НОВАЯ РУСЬ, 24 февр. 1909.
287 Беспятов, Е., ЕЖЕГОДНИК ИМПЕРАТОРСКИХ ТЕАТРОВ, СПБ., 3:75-81, 1909.
288 Высотский, Н., РАМПА И ЖИЗНЬ, М., 17 мая 1909.
289 Глаголин, Б., Русский аргонавт. ЖУРНАЛ ТЕАТРА ЛИТ.-ХУД. ОБЩЕСТВА, СПБ.,
1:19-20, 1909-10.
290 Кугель, А. Р., ТЕАТР И ИСКУССТВО, СПБ., 39:726-8, 1911.
291 Кугель, А. Р., Утверждение театра. М., 1923, 196-201.
292 ,,Не-актер'', О театре. Против статьи Н. Н. Евреинова. ТЕАТР, М., 412:5-6, 1909.
293 Тэффи, РЕЧЬ, СПБ., 11 мая 1909.
294 Тэффи, РАМПА И ЖИЗНЬ, М., 24 февр. 1909.
295 Философов, Д., НАША ГАЗЕТА, СПБ., 24 февр. 1909.
296 — РУССКОЕ СЛОВО, М., 17 дек. 1908.
297 — О реферате, прочитанном Н. Н. Евреиновым в лит.-худ. кружке в Москве
16 декабря. ОБОЗРЕНИЕ ТЕАТРОВ, СПБ., 662:5-6, 1909.
298 — ТЕАТР И ИСКУССТВО, СПБ., 7:124, 1909.
299 — Кратко о докладе Евреинова. РЕЧЬ, СПБ., 25 февр. 1909.
300 — Заметки о лекции Н. Н. Евреинова ,,Теория монодрамы''. ЗОЛОТОЕ РУНО, М.,
4:86-8, 1909.
301 — РЕЧЬ, СПБ., 2 февр. 1909.

(б) Pro Scena Sua

302 Беспятов, Е., ТЕАТР И ИСКУССТВО, СПБ., 2:35-6, 1914.
303 Шебуев, Н., ОБОЗРЕНИЕ ТЕАТРОВ, СПБ., 2 янв. 1914.
304 Неведомов, И., Против статьи „Грядущий лицедей". РАМПА, СПБ., 8 марта 1909.

(в) Театр как таковой

305 Беспятов, Е., ТЕАТР И ИСКУССТВО, СПБ., 8:183-4, 1913.
306 Бенуа, А. А., РЕЧЬ, СПБ., 15 февр. 1913.
307 Бонч-Томашевский, МАСКИ, СПБ., 6:83, 1913.
308 Гиляровская, Н., ГОЛОС МОСКВЫ, М., 2 марта 1913.
309 Дерман, А., РУССКОЕ БОГАТСТВО, СПБ., 11:393-403, 1913.
310 Кугель, А. Р., Проблема театральности. ТЕАТР И ИСКУССТВО, СПБ., 10:233-4, 1913.
311 Соловьев, В. Н., Театральный традиционализм. АПОЛЛОН, СПБ., 3:65, 1914.
312 Юрьев, М., Против книги Н. Н. Евреинова. РАМПА И ЖИЗНЬ, М., 17 марта, 24 марта 1913.
313 — УТРО РОССИИ, СПБ., 29 дек. 1912.
314 — ВОСКРЕСНАЯ ВЕЧЕРНЯЯ ГАЗЕТА, СПБ., 17 февр. 1913.
315 — РЕЧЬ, СПБ., 24 дек. 1912.

(г) Театр для себя. Часть 1.

316 Айхенвальд, Ю., УТРО РОССИИ, СПБ., 5 дек. 1915.
317 Редько, А. Е., РУССКИЕ ЗАПИСКИ, СПБ., 3:285-97, 1916.
318 — ТЕАТР И ИСКУССТВО, СПБ., 47:884-5, 1915.
319 — ОБОЗРЕНИЕ ТЕАТРОВ, СПБ., 9 ноября 1915.
320 — О лекции автора „Театр для себя", которая состоится в зале городской Думы. БИРЖЕВЫЕ ВЕДОМОСТИ, СПБ., 19 ноября 1915.
321 — О статье урок профессионалам в журнале ТЕАТР И ИСКУССТВО, СПБ., 51:93-4, 1913, 5:106-8, 1914.

(д) Театр для себя. Часть 2.

322 Айхенвальд, Ю., УТРО РОССИИ, СПБ., 30 апр. 1916.
323 Горталов, В., НОВОСТИ ДНЯ, СПБ., 24 апр. 1916.
324 „Жакасс", ТЕАТРАЛЬНАЯ ГАЗЕТА, СПБ., 24 апр. 1916.
325 Пильский, П., СОЛНЦЕ РОССИИ, СПБ., 17:27, 1916.
326 Шебуев, Н., ОБОЗРЕНИЕ ТЕАТРОВ, СПБ., 19 янв. 1916.
327 — РАМПА И ЖИЗНЬ, М., 17:11, 1916.
328 — ТЕАТР И ИСКУССТВО, СПБ., 8:154, 1916.

(е) Театр для себя. Часть 3.

329 Кугель, А. Р., ТЕАТР И ИСКУССТВО, ПТГ., 41:716-18, 1917.

(ж) Что такое театр

330 Эфрос, А., ТЕАТРАЛЬНОЕ ОБОЗРЕНИЕ, ПТГ., 2:5, 1921.
331 Филиппов, В., КУЛЬТУРА ТЕАТРА, ПТГ., 1-2:61-2, 1922.
332 — ВЕСТНИК ТЕАТРА И ИСКУССТВА, ПТГ., 2 дек. 1921.
333 — ВЕСТНИК ТЕАТРА, М., 1:23, 1922.
334 — ЕЖЕГОДНИК АКАДЕМИЧЕСКИХ ТЕАТРОВ, ПТГ., 3:25, 1921.

(з) Нагота на сцене

335 Зноско-Боровский, Е., РУССКАЯ ХУДОЖЕСТВЕННАЯ ЛЕТОПИСЬ, СПБ., 2: 172-3, 1911.
336 Шебуев, Н., ОБОЗРЕНИЕ ТЕАТРОВ, СПБ., 7 мая 1911.

(и) Кульбин

337 Бенуа, А. А., РЕЧЬ, СПБ., 12 окт. 1912.
338 — НОВАЯ СТУДИЯ, СПБ., 12 окт. 1912.
339 — ВЕЧЕРНЕЕ ВРЕМЯ, СПБ., 3 окт. 1912.

(к) Бердслей

340 — НОВОЕ ВРЕМЯ, СПБ., 14 июля 1912.
341 — ОДЕССКИЕ НОВОСТИ, Одесса, 28 июля 1912.

(л) Оперетта

342 — НОВОСТИ СЕЗОНА, СПБ., 4 авг. 1913.

(м) Театр и эшафот

343 Варнеке, Б., О лекции Евреинова в Киеве, Харькове и Одессе в 1918 г. ОДЕС-СКИЕ НОВОСТИ, Одесса, 14 авг. 1918.
344 „Висмонд", ЮЖНАЯ МЫСЛЬ, Одесса, 19 сент. 1918.
345 — ЖИЗНЬ ИСКУССТВА, ПТГ., 566-7:3, 1920.

(н) Происхождение драмы

346 Кекиг, М., ЭКРАН, М., 13:9, 1921.
347 — ЭКРАН, М., 23:12, 1921.
348 — ВЕСТНИК ТЕАТРА И ИСКУССТВА, ПТГ., 9 дек. 1921.

(о) Театральные новации

349 Бескин, Э.М., ВЕСТНИК РАБОТНИКОВ ИСКУССТВ, ПТГ., 3-4:58-9, 1922.

(п) Первобытная драма германцев

350 Крыжицкий, Г., ЕЖЕГОДНИК АКАДЕМИЧЕСКИХ ТЕАТРОВ, ПТГ., 1о:20, 1922.
351 — ЖИЗНЬ ИСКУССТВА, ПТГ., 858:4, 1922.

(р) Оригинал о портретистах

352 Соболев, Ю., ЭХО., ПТГ., 3:32, 1923.

(с) История обрядового театра

353 Соболев, Ю., ВЕЧЕРНЯЯ КРАСНАЯ ГАЗЕТА, ПТГ., 20 февр. 1923.

(т) О новой маске

354 Кугель, А.Р., Театральные заметки. ЖИЗНЬ ИСКУССТВА, ПТГ., 36:5-7, 1923.
355 — ВЕЧЕРНЯЯ КРАСНАЯ ГАЗЕТА, ПТГ., 3 июля 1923.
356 — ЛИТЕРАТУРНЫЙ ЕЖЕГОДНИК, 18 июля 1923.

(у) Театр у животных

357 — Немного о животных и много о себе. ВЕЧЕРНЯЯ КРАСНАЯ ГАЗЕТА, ПТГ.,
29 июня 1924.

(ф) Тайна Распутина

358 — ВЕЧЕРНЯЯ КРАСНАЯ ГАЗЕТА, ПТГ., 2 окт. 1924.

16 Рецензии на постановки пьес Н.Н.Евреинова

(а) Война

359 Беляев, Ю., НОВОЕ ВРЕМЯ, СПБ., 31 дек. 1908.
360 — ТИФЛИССКИЕ ЛИСТЫ, Тифлис, 4 окт. 1907.
361 — Война, поставленная труппой Л.Б.Яровской в Тифлисе. ОБОЗРЕНИЕ ТЕАТ-
РОВ, СПБ., 228:14, 1907.
362 Янов, В.М., ТЕАТР И ИСКУССТВО, СПБ., 37:605-6, 1907.

(б) Красивый деспот

363 Беляев, Ю., НОВОЕ ВРЕМЯ, СПБ., 31 дек. 1906.
364 Беляев, Ю., ИЛЛЮСТРИРОВАННАЯ ПРОГРАММА МАЛОГО ТЕАТРА, СПБ.,
10:85-92, 1907.
365 Герасимов, В., Обозрение сезона в театре Соловцова в Киеве. „Красивый деспот''.
В МИРЕ ИСКУССТВ, Киев, 4:18-20, 1907.
366 Старк, Э., ТЕАТР И ИСКУССТВО, СПБ., 2:30-2, 1907.
367 Старк, Э., ПЕТЕРБУРГСКИЕ ВЕДОМОСТИ, СПБ., 19 дек. 1906.
368 — ПЕТЕРБУРГСКИЕ ЛИСТЫ, СПБ., 17 дек. 1906.
369 — БИРЖЕВЫЕ ВЕДОМОСТИ, СПБ., 6 сент. 1906.

(в) Коммуна праведных

370 — Заметки о пьесе. ЖИЗНЬ ИСКУССТВА, СПБ., 49:20, 1924.
371 — ВЕЧЕРНЯЯ КРАСНАЯ ГАЗЕТА, СПБ., 24 ноября 1924.
372 — Евреинов кончил свою пьесу. ВЕЧЕРНЯЯ КРАСНАЯ ГАЗЕТА, ПТГ., 1 июля
1924.

(г) Самое главное

373 Агатов, В., ЗАРЯ ВОСТОКА, Тифлис, 18 ноября 1922.
374 Беленсон, А.Э., ЖИЗНЬ ИСКУССТВА, ПТГ., 682-4:1, 1921.
375 Беленсон, А.Э., Самое главное о самом главном. ИСКУССТВЕННАЯ ЖИЗНЬ,
СПБ., 1921, 73-8.
376 Чаговец, В., ИСКУССТВО, Киев, 1:6-7, 1922.
377 Гринвальд, Я., ТРУДОВОЙ ДОН, Ростов-на-Дону, 25 ноября 1922.

378 Dybovski, R., Wrazenia z teatrów moskiewskich. Przeglad Warszawski, t. 1, 1922, 209-12.

379 Евгеньев, Е., ЖИЗНЬ ИСКУССТВА, ПТГ., 2:13-4, 1921.

380 Марков, П. А., Постановка В. Г. Сахновским в драматическом театре в Москве. ТЕАТРАЛЬНОЕ ОБОЗРЕНИЕ, М., 2:6-7, 1921.

381 Старк, Э., Постановка в Театре Вольной Комедии. ВЕЧЕРНЯЯ КРАСНАЯ ГАЗЕТА, ПТГ., 17 марта 1924.

382 Шебуев, Н., ТЕАТРАЛЬНОЕ ОБОЗРЕНИЕ, М., 1:14-5, 1921.

383 Шкловский, В., ЖИЗНЬ ИСКУССТВА, ПТГ., 780-5:20, 1921.

384 Янтарев, Е., Постановка в драматическом театре (Москва). ЭКРАН, М., 8:5-6, 1921.

386 — Сравнение постановок в театре Вольной Комедии и Драматическом (Москва). ЭКРАН, М., 10:7-8, 1921.

387 — ЗРЕЛИЩЕ, Свердловск, 1:6, 1925.

388 —"Самое главное" в Драматическом театре (Одесса). ЗРИТЕЛЬ, Одесса, 9:8,1922.

389 — ВОРОНЕЖСКАЯ КОММУНА, Воронеж, 31 окт. 1922.

390 — ИЗВЕСТИЯ, Казань, 10 мая 1923.

391 — Альманах „Возрождение", Том 2, М., 1923, 301-33.

392 — О второсортгости. ЛИТЕРАТУРНАЯ ГАЗЕТА, М., 106:3-4, 1958.

393 — ИСКУССТВО И ТРУД, М., 2:17-8, 1921.

394 — Постановка в Краснозаводском театре. ПРОЛЕТАРИЙ, Харьков, 14 ноября 1923.

395 — ПРОЛЕТАРИЙ, Харьков, 22 ноября 1923.

396 — ВЕЧЕРНЯЯ КРАСНАЯ ГАЗЕТА, ПТГ., 16 авг. 1923.

397 — „Самое главное" в Германии. ЖИЗНЬ ИСКУССТВА, ПТГ., 742-5:2, 1921.

398 — „Самое главное" в Париже. КУЛЬТУРА, Саратов, 1:14, 1922.

(д) Веселая смерть

399 Воронов, В., РЕЧЬ, СПБ., 21 апр. 1916.

400 Крушинин, В., ТЕАТР И ИСКУССТВО, СПБ., 14:255, 1909.

401 Мамонтов, С., Постановка в театре Незлобина. РУССКОЕ СЛОВО, СПБ., 14 ноября 1912.

402 П. Ю., ТЕАТР И ИСКУССТВО, СПБ., 17:343, 1916.

403 Рабинович, М., Постановка в театре Соловцова. ТЕАТР И ИСКУССТВО, СПБ., 16:337-9, 1910.

404 Регинин, В., БИРЖЕВЫЕ ВЕДОМОСТИ, СПБ., 1 апр. 1909.

405 — Постановка в Литейном театре. ТЕАТР И ИСКУССТВО, СПБ., 46:877, 1911.

406 — БИРЖЕВЫЕ ВЕДОМОСТИ, СПБ., 9 ноября 1911.

407 — Постановка в театре Незлобина. РУССКИЕ ВЕДОМОСТИ, СПБ., 14 ноября 1912.

408 — Постановка в театре Незлобина. РАМПА И ЖИЗНЬ, М., 47:5-7, 1912.

409 — О пьесе в Незлобинском театре. ТЕАТР И ИСКУССТВО, СПБ., 48:945,1912.

410 — БИБЛИОТЕКА ТЕАТРА И ИСКУССТВА, СПБ., 2:57, 1909.

411 — ВЕЧЕР, СПБ., 1 апр. 1909.

412 — ЖИЗНЬ ИСКУССТВА, ПТГ., 840:6, 1922.

413 — ЖИЗНЬ ИСКУССТВА, ПТГ., 792-7:5, 1921.

(е) Коломбина сего дня

414 — ЗРИТЕЛЬ, СПБ., 7:16, 1916.

415 — ТЕАТРАЛЬНАЯ ГАЗЕТА, СПБ., 6 марта 1916.

416 — ТЕАТР, М., 1822; 19, 1916.

(ж) Карагез

417 Бентович, В. А., ДЕНЬ, СПБ., 2 февр. 1916.
418 — ТЕАТР И ИСКУССТВО, СПБ., 2:16, 1916.

(з) Кухня смеха

419 „М-В", А., РЕЧЬ, СПБ., 25 окт. 1913.
420 — ТЕАТР, М., 1460:30, 1914.
421 — НОВОЕ ВРЕМЯ, СПБ., 26 окт. 1913.
422 — РУССКОЕ СЛОВО, СПБ., 27 окт. 1913.
423 — БИРЖЕВЫЕ ВЕДОМОСТИ, СПБ., 25 окт. 1913.

(и) Кулисы души

424 Арнс, Л., ЖИЗНЬ ИСКУССТВА, ПТГ., 814:1, 1921.
425 Василевский, Л., РЕЧЬ, СПБ., 1 апр. 1909.
426 Iwaszkiewicz, J., Ksiazka o sycykù. Krakow, 1956 , 56—7.
427 П. Ю., ТЕАТР И ИСКУССТВО, СПБ., 43: 817, 1912.
428 — БИРЖЕВЫЕ ВЕДОМОСТИ, СПБ., 29 марта 1913.
429 — РАННЕЕ УТРО, СПБ., 29 марта 1913.
430 — ТЕАТР И ИСКУССТВО, СПБ., 14:236, 1915.

(к) Беглая

431 Анчар, БИРЖЕВЫЕ ВЕДОМОСТИ, СПБ., 8 ноября 1913.
432 М. В., ДЕНЬ, СПБ., 9 ноября 1913.
433 Каратыгин, В. Г., РЕЧЬ, СПБ., 10 ноября 1913.
434 Кречетов, С., РАМПА И ЖИЗНЬ, СПБ., 45:17, 1913.
435 Скиталец, РАННЕЕ УТРО, СПБ., 1 дек. 1913.
436 Шебуев, Н., ОБОЗРЕНИЕ ТЕАТРОВ, СПБ., 9 ноября 1913.
437 — ТЕАТР И ИСКУССТВО, СПБ., 43:855, 1913.
438 — РУССКОЕ СЛОВО, СПБ., 29 авг. 1913.
439 — ТЕАТР, М., 1355:11-12, 1913.

(л) Ревизор

440 Данилов, С. С., Гоголь и театр, М., 1936, 294-5.
441 Данилов, С. С., Ревизор на сцене, М., 1934, 71-2.
442 Кугель, А. Р., РАННЕЕ УТРО, СПБ., 12 ноября 1913.
443 П. Ю., ТЕАТР И ИСКУССТВО, СПБ., 51:1009, 1912.
444 Тверской, К., РАБОЧИЙ И ТЕАТР, Л., 15:12, 1925.
445 Яшин, В., ТЕАТР, М., 1222:4-5, 1913.
446 — РУССКОЕ СЛОВО, СПБ., 17 февр. 1915.
447 — БИРЖЕВЫЕ ВЕДОМОСТИ, СПБ., 12 дек. 1912.
448 — БИРЖЕВЫЕ ВЕДОМОСТИ+ СПБ., 19 дек. 1913.
449 — БИРЖЕВЫЕ ВЕДОМОСТИ, СПБ., 9 сент. 1916.
450 — ТЕАТР, М., 1471:37, 1914.

(м) Ярмарка на Индикт Св. Дениса

451 — ОБОЗРЕНИЕ ТЕАТРОВ, СПБ., 249:13, 1907.

452 — ТЕАТР И ИСКУССТВО, СПБ., 45:735, 1907.

(н) Эоловы арфы

453 — ТЕАТР, М., 1822:19, 1916.

(о) Четвертая стена

454 Лебедев, Н., РЕЧЬ, СПБ., 24 дек. 1915.
455 — ТЕАТР И ИСКУССТВО, СПБ., 1:7, 1916.

(п) Школа этуалей

456 Василевский, Л., РЕЧЬ, СПБ., 16 сент. 1911.
457 Лебедев, Н., ПЕТРОГРАДСКАЯ ГАЗЕТА, СПБ., 13 ноября 1911.
458 — /Рецензия/. БИРЖЕВЫЕ ВЕДОМОСТИ, СПБ., 14 ноября 1911.
459 — /Рецензия/ ТЕАТР И ИСКУССТВО, СПБ., 47:900, 1911.
460 — /Рецензия/ ТЕАТР, М., 1032:19, 1912.

(р) Три волхва

461 Кугель, А.Р., Театральные заметки. ТЕАТР И ИСКУССТВО, СПБ., 5о:845-7, 1907.

(с) Фундамент счастья

462 — ПЕТЕРБУРГСКИЙ ДНЕВНИК ТЕАТРАЛА , СПБ., 6:5, 1905.
463 — ТЕАТР И ИСКУССТВО, СПБ., 6:84, 1905.
464 — /Рецензия/ БИРЖЕВЫЕ ВЕДОМОСТИ, СПБ., 2 февраля 1905.

(т) Степик и Монюрочка

465 Беляев, Ю., НОВОЕ ВРЕМЯ, СПБ., 24 дек. 1905.
466 Кугель, А.Р., МОЛВА, СПБ., 24 дек. 1905.
467 — СЛОВО, СПБ., 24 дек. 1905.

(у) Таверна смерти (пантомима).

468 — /Рецензия/. НОВАЯ РАМПА, ПТГ., 25:12, 1924.

(ф) Сказка о шести красавицах, не похожих друг на друга

469 — /Рецензия/. КРАСНАЯ ГАЗЕТА, ПТГ., 23 окт. 1922.

(х) Представления любви

470 — /Рецензия/. НОВОЕ ВРЕМЯ, СПБ., 3 авг. 1910.

(ц) Такая женщина

471 — /Рецензия/. НОВОЕ ВРЕМЯ, СПБ., 4 ноября 1908.

472 Василевский, Л., /Рецензия/. РЕЧЬ, СПБ., 4 ноября 1908.

473 Глаголин, Б., /Рецензия/. ПЕТЕРБУРГСКИЕ ВЕДОМОСТИ, СПБ., 4 сент. 1908.

474 Гурьевин, Л., /Рецензия/. СЛВО, СПБ., 13 сент. 1908.

475 Лев, А., /Рецензия/. ЖИЗНЬ ИСКУССТВА, ПТГ., 826:3-4, 1922.

476 Осипов, М., /Рецензия/. ОБОЗРЕНИЕ ТЕАТРОВ, СПБ., 4 сент. 1908.

477 — /Рецензия/. ТЕАТР, М., 250:12, 1912.

478 — /Рецензия/. НОВОЕ ВРЕМЯ, СПБ., 10 сент., 1908.

479 — /Рецензия/. ТЕАТР И ИСКУССТВО, СПБ., 36:616, 1908.

480 — /Рецензия/. ТЕАТР И ИСКУССТВО, СПБ., 29:468, 1907.

481 — /Рецензия/. ВЕЧЕР, СПБ., 3 сент. 1908.

18 Рецензии на сборники драматических произведений Н. Н. Евреинова, 1908, 1914, 1923 г. г.

(а) Том 1

482 Поза, Маркиз, /Рецензия/. РУССКИЙ АРТИСТ, СПБ., 12-13:204-5, 1907.

483 — /Рецензия/. БИРЖЕВЫЕ ВЕДОМОСТИ, СПБ., 3 окт. 1904.

484 — /Рецензия/. БИРЖЕВЫЕ ВЕДОМОСТИ, СПБ, 2 февр. 1905.

(б) Том 2

485 — /Рецензия/. ВОСКРЕСНОЕ ВЕЧЕРНЕЕ ВРЕМЯ, СПБ., 2 марта 1914.

(в) Том 3

486 — /Рецензия/. ЖИЗНЬ ИСКУССТВА, ПТГ., 2:23, 1924.

19 Критический разбор драматических произведений Н. Н. Евреинова

487 Collins, Christopher, Nikolai Evreinov as a playwright. RUSSIAN LITERATURE TRIQUARTERLY, Michigan, 2:373—398, 1972, and
Theatre as Life. Evreinov. Five Modern Plays. Michigan, 1973, xi—xxviii.

MAYAKOVSKY: A BIBLIOGRAPHY OF CRITICISM (1912-1930)

Compiled by Gerald Darring

1. Introduction

This bibliography is essentially a summary of Soviet critical commentary on Mayakovsky during the poet's lifetime. A section of pre-Revolutionary items has been included for the sake of completeness, but I have not concentrated on the earlier period as much as on the years after the Revolution. The list includes short monographs and brochures, chapters from books, articles devoted wholly or in part to Mayakovsky, reviews of works about Mayakovsky, and reviews of Mayakovsky's works and performances of his plays. I have tried to omit items of purely biographical interest, but I have included every item containing some critical evaluation of Mayakovsky as poet, playwright, critic, actor, film writer, editor, and literary theoretician.

The items are place in chronological order primarily for convenience in locating commentaries on specific works and in making cross references to Soviet bibliographies, which are almost always chronologically arranged. Moreover, chronological organization is helpful to anyone desiring to read through all of the material; and it is precisely this kind of reading which will help one see what Mayakovsky meant to his contemporaries and what his exact pos tion was in Soviet intellectual and artistic currents on the time.

Mayakovsky took the critics seriously, commenting on their reviews privately, in his poetry, in his theoretical writings, even in his suicide note. For their part, the critics had a significant influence on him, esepcially after the Revolution: in some of the changes from the first to the second variant of *Mystery-Bouffe,* in the toning down of certain Futurist elements of his poetry, in the reduced prominence of the love theme except for two brief periods, in his various public changes of position, and perhaps even in his decision to commit suicide. The study of the critics is particularly fruitful, therefore, in the case of Mayakovsky, because he was a self-styled "public poet, the common property of the liberated proletariat; and we cannot separate his poetry from the events of his time, or his poems from what his contemporaries thought and wrote about them.

Since this is what I sought to clarify in my research, I have not included emigre sources except those (such as Roman Jakobson's) which formed a part of the "literary atmosphere" of the Soviet Union.

2. Major Bibliographies Consulted.

_____. V. Maiakovskii, *Sobranie sochinenii.* M. 1928. I, 337-56. [203 items, 1913-28.]

_____. V. Maiakovskii, *Polnoe sobranie sochinenii* M. 1936. XI, 575-96. [197 items, 1929-30.]

Poliak, L., Reformatskaia, N., *Literaturnyi kritik,* 4 (1936), 244-62. [159 items, 1918-30.]

Matsuev, N., *Khudozhestvennaia literature,* Vol. I (M.-Odessa, 1926) [30 items, 1917-25] ; Vol. II (M. 1929) [9 items, 1926-27] ; Vol. III (M. 1936) [44 items, 1928-30] .

Vladislavlev, I., *Literatura velikogo desiatiletiia* Vol. I (M.-L. 1928). [65 items, 1917-27.]

Vitman, A., Pokrovskaia, N., Ettinger, M., *Vosen' let russkoi khudozhestvennoi literatury* (M.-L. 1926). [56 items, 1917-25.]

Vladislavlev, I., *Russkie pisateli* (M.-L. 1924). [21 items, 1918-23.]

Istoriia russkoi literatury kontsa XIX-nachala XX veka (M.-L. 1963). [16 items, 1914-30.]

NOTE. The bibliography which follows is the most complete list covering the period 1912-1930.

3. ABBREVIATIONS

Iz - *Izvestiia*   NM - *Novyi mir*
KG - *Krasnaia gazeta*   O - *Oktiabr'*
KN - *Krasnaia nov'*   PR - *Pechat' i revoliutsiia*
Kn - *Knigonosha*   Pr - *Pravda*
KR - *Kniga i revoliutsiia*   VM - *Vecherniaia Moskva*
LG - *Literaturnaia gazeta*   ZI - *Zhizn' iskusstva*
NLP - *Na Literaturnom postu*

4.BIBLIOGRAPHY

1912

1. Anon., note on Mayakovsky's public reading. *Obozrenie teatrov,* No. 1915 (Nov. 19, 1912).

1913

2. Izmailov, A. "Rytsari oslinogo khvosta," *Birzhevye vedomosti* (SPb.), evening, Jan. 25, 1913.

3. Izmailov, A. "Rytsari zelenogo osla," *Birzhevye vedomosti* , evening, Dec. 3, 1913.

4. Anon., comment on Mayakovsky's lecture in Kharkov, Dec. 14. *Utro* (Khar'kov), No. 2171 (Dec. 16, 1913).

1914

5. Abramovich, N."O futurizma v literature,"*Novaia zhizn',* 5 (1914), 105-114.

6. Boduen-de-Kurtene, "Galopom vpered," *Vestnik znaniia,* 5 (1914), 10.

7. Briusov, V. "Zdorovogo smysla tar-tara-ry. Dialog o futurizme," *Russkaia mysl',* 3 (1914), section 2, 83-95.

8. Briusov, V. "God russkoi poezii," *Russkaia mysl',* 5 (1914), section 3, 25-31.

9. Chukovskii, K. "Futuristy," *Litsa i maski.* SPb, 1914.

10. Ivanov, G. "Ispytanie ognem (voennye stikhi)," *Apollon,* 8 (1914), 55.

11. Izmailov, A. and others, "Pozornyi stolb rossiiskoi kritiki," *Pervyi zhurnal russkikh futuristov,* 1-2 (1914), 104-131.

12. Kruchenykh. A. *Stikhi Maiakovskogo* (P. "EUY"), 29pp.

13. Lundberg. E. "O futurizme," *Russkaia mysl',* 3 (1914), section 4, 19-23.

14. L'vov-Rogachevskii, V. "Simvolisty i nasledniki ikh," *Sovremennik,* 6-7 (1914).

84

15. Matiushin, M "Futurizm v Peterburge," review of "Vladimir Maiakovskii. Tragediia," *Pervyi zhurnal russkikh futuristov,* 1-2 (1914), 153-57.
16. Radin, E. *Futurizm i bezumie* (P. 1914), 48pp.
17. Shershenevich, V. "Futuropitaiushchiesia," *Pervyi zhurnal russkikh futuristov,* 1-2 (1914), 86-91.
18. Shershenevich, V. *Futurizm bez maski* (M. 1914), 80-83.
19. Shklovskii, V. *Voskreshenie slova* (P. 1914), 8pp.
20. Zakrzhevskii, A. *Rytsari bezumiia* (Kiev, 1914).
21. Anon., comment on Mayakovsky's lecture in Kiev, Jan. 28, in the *Kievlianin,* 30 (Jan. 30, 1914).

1915

22. Bukhov, A. "V zashchitu Maiakovskogo" (Neobkhodimoe posleslovie k ego ispovedi), *Zhurnal zhurnalov,* 17 (1915).
23. Brik, O. "Khleba!" (review of "Oblako v shtanakh), *Vzial. Baraban futuristov* (P. 1915), 12.
24. Filosofov, D. "Razlozhenie futurizma," *Golos zhizni,* 18 (1915), 3-5.
25. Gor'kii, M. "O russkom futurizme," *Zhurnal zhurnalov,* 1 (1915), 3-4. Reprinted in his *Nesobrannye literaturno-kriticheskie stat'i* (M. 1941), 71-73.
26. Ozhigov, A. review of "Oblako v shtanakh," *Sovremennyi mir,* 3 (1915), 143.
27. Shklovskii, V. "Oblako v shtanakh," *Vzial. Baraban futuristov* (P. 1915), 10-11.
28. Shklovskii, V. "Predposylki futurizma," *Golos zhizni,* 18 (1915), 6-9.
29. Vengrov, N. "Oblako v shtanakh," *Letopis',* 12 (1915), 388.

1916

30. Aseev, N. "Porazitel'nyi uspekh! Oblako v shtanakh," *Peta,* first collection (M. 1916), 45-46.
31. Bol'shakov, K., review of "Oblako v shtanakh," *Vtoroi sbornik tsentrifugi* (M. 1916).
32. Kamenskii, V. "V. Maiakovskii. Oblako v shtanakh," *Moskovskie mastera. Zhurnal iskusstv* (M. 1916), 91-92.
33. Khovin, V. "Vetrogony, sumasbrody, letateli," *Ocharovannyi strannik,* 1916.
34. Oksenov, I. "Literaturnyi god," *Novyi zhurnal dlia vsekh,* 1 (1916), 58-59.
35. Oksenov, I., review of "Oblako v shtanakh," *Novoe vremia,* 4304 (Jan. 4, 1916).
36. Oksenov, I., revew of "Oblako v shtanakh," *Odesskii listok,* 6 (Jan. 6 (1916).
37. Oksenov. I., review of "Oblako v shtanakh," *Mlechnyi put',* 1 (1916), 20-21.

1918

38. Bessal'ko, P. "Futurizm i proletarskaia kul'tura," *Griadushchee,* 10 (1918), 10-12.
39. Eikhenbaum, B. "Trubnyi glas," *Knizhnyi ugol,* 1 (1918), 3-6. Reprinted in his *O poezii* (L. 1969), 293-96.
40. Kamenskii, V. "Chto mne nravitsia," *Gazeta futuristov,* 1 (March 15, 1918).
41. Khovin, V. "Bezotvetnye voprosy," *Knizhnyi ugol,* 5 (1918) 1-6.
42. Khovin, V. *Segodniashnemu dniu* (P. 1918), 7pp.
43. Kushner, B. "Rukopozhatie," *Nash put',* 2 (1918), 185-86.
44. Levinson, A. "Misteriia-Buff," ZI, 10 (Nov. 11, 1918).
45. Lunacharskii, A., introduction to the futurist collection *Rzhanoe slovo* (P. 1918), 1. Reprinted in his *Sob. soch.,* (M. 1964), II, 205.
46. Lunacharskii, A. *Lunacharskii ob iskusstve* (P. 1918), 32 pp. A Separate printing of his speech of Oct. 10, 1918. Reprinted as "Iskusstvo" in his *Iskusstvo i revoliutsiia* (M. 1924), 33-40; also in his *Stat'i ob iskusstve* (M. 1941), 468-82.
47. Lunacharskii, A. "Kommunisticheskii spektakl,' " *Petrogradskaia pravda,* 243 (Nov. 5, 1918), 2. Also in *Sob. soch.,* vol. 3 (M. 1964), 39-40.

48. Lunacharskii, A. "O polemike," ZI, 24 (Nov. 27, 1918), 3.
49. Lunacharskii, A. "Lozhka protivoiadiia," *Iskusstvo kommuny,* 4 (Dec. 29, 1918), 1. Reprinted in his *Stat'i ob iskusstve* (M. 1941), 466-67; and in *Stat'i o literature,* (M. 1957), 705-707. Complete text of original MS first published in *Literaturnoe nasledstvo,* vol. 65 (M. 1958), 572-74; and reprinted in his *Sob. soch.* (M. 1964), II, 206-208.
50. Orasov, " Oblako v shtanakh. Chelovek," *Gazeta futuristov,* 1 (March 15, 1918).
51. Punin, N. "O 'Misterii-Buff' VI. Maiakovskogo," *Iskusstvo kommuny,* 2 (Dec. 15, 1918), 2-3.
52. Punin, N., review of the film "Ne dlia deneg rodivshiisia," *Kinobiulleten' Kinokomiteta Narodnogo Komissariata Prosveshcheniia,* 1-2 (1918).
53. Punin, N., review of the film "Ne dlia deneg rodivshiisia," *Rampa i zhizn',* 23 (1918).
54. Punin, N. "Zaiavlenie po povodu 'Misterii-buff'," ZI, 19 (Nov. 21, 1918).

1919

55. Aseev, N. " 'Voina i mir' - Maiakovskogo," *Dal'nevostochnoe obozrenie* (June, 1919).
56. Aseev, N. "Vesti ob iskusstve," *Dal'nevostochnoe obozrenie* (June, 1919).
57. Brik , O. "Nalet na futurizm," *Iskusstvo kommuny,* 10 (Feb. 9, 1919).
58. Evgen'ev, A. "Futuristskaia Gekuba i proletariat," *Vestnik literatury,* 10 (1919), 4-5.
59. Friche, V. "Literatura za dva goda sovetskoi vlasti," *Tvorchestvo,* 10-11 (1919), 49-50.
60. Jakobson, R. "Futurism," *Iskusstvo,* 7 (Aug. 2, 1919).
61. Kalinin, F. "O futurizme," *Proletarskaia kul'tura,* 7-8 (1919), 41-43.
62. Lvov-Rogachevskii, V. *Noveishaia russkaia literatura* (M. 1919), 131-140. Reprinted in the 1922 edition, pp. 222-39; in the 1927 edition, pp. 284-92.

1920

63. Aleksandrovskii, V. "O putiakh proletarskogo tvorchestva ," *Kuznitsa,* 4 (1920), 32-5.
64. Blium, V. "Propaganda teatrom," *Vestnik teatra,* 76-77 (1920), 2.
65. Burliuk, D. "Vladimir Maiakovskii," *Tvorchestvo,* 1 (1920).
66. Burliuk, D. "Ot laboratorii k ulitse," *Tvorchestvo,* 2 (1920), 22-25.
67. Chuzhak, N. "Trinadtsatyi apostol," *Tvorchestvo,* 1 (1920). Reprinted in his *K dialektika iskusstva* (Chita, 1921), 64-71.
68. Chuzhak, N. "Osoznanie cherez iskusstvo," *Tovrchestvo,* 6 (1920). Reprinted in his *K dialektika iskusstva* (Chita, 1921), 89-94.
69. Kii. "Poeziia obrazov i ritma," KR, 6 (1920), 19-22.
70. Lunacharskii, A. "Moim opponentam," *Vestnik teatra,* 76-77 (Dec. 14, 1920), 4-5. Reprinted in his *Teatr i revoliutsiia* M.-L. 1924), 43-47; in his *Sob. soch.,* vol. 2 (M. 1964), 227-31. A shortened version is in his *Stat'i o sovetskoi literature* (M. 1958), 396-97.
71. NAV. " 'Misteriia-buff' VI. Maiakovskogo," *Okno* (Kharbin), 2 (1920), 61-63.
72. Tret'iakov, S. "Ukhom k zemle," *Tvorchestvo,* 5 (1920).
73. Ustrialov, N. "Religiia revoliutsii," *Okno,* (Kharbin), 1 (1920).

1921

74. Abr, A. "Pervomaiskaia pobeda revoliutsionnogo teatra," *Trud,* 58 (May 4, 1921), 4.
75. Abr, A. "Sovremennyi zritel' i novyi teatr," *Trud,* 94 (June 24, 1921), 4.
76. Adamovich, G., review of "150 000 000," *Al'manakh tsekha poetov* (Petrograd), 2 (1921), 72-74.
77. Aksenov, I. "Sto piat'desiat millionov. Poema," PR, 2 (1921), 205-206.
78. Aksenov, I. "K likvidatsii futurizma," PR, 3 (1921), 82-98.
79. Aksenov, I. "Pis'ma o sovremennoi poezii," KR, 12 (1921), 16-18.
80. Aleksandrovich, Iu. "Na svoiu polochku," *Vestnik literatury,* 3 (1921), 3-4.

81. Anchar. "150 000 000," KN, 2 (1921), 321-24.
82. Beskin, E. "Revoliutsiia i teatr," Vestnik rabotnikov iskusstv, 7-9 (1921), 30-35.
83. Chukovskii, K. "Akhmatova i Maiakovskii," Dom iskusstv, 1 (1921), 23-42. The parts on Mayakovsky were used in his book Futuristy (P. 1922), 61-84.
84. Chuzhak, N. "Zemlianaia misteriia. O p'ese 'Misterii-buff' VI. Maiakovskogo," Tvorchestvo, 7 (1921), 82-86. Reprinted in his K dialektike iskusstva (Chita, 1921), 104-108.
85. Chuzhak, N. "Vokrug futurizma v teatre," Tvorchesto, 7 (1921), 113-120.
86. Chuzhak, N. "Ivannoe. Kriticheskaia poema," K dialektike iskusstva (Chita, 1921), 112-120.
87. D. L-n., review of "150 000 000," Vestnik literatury, 10 (1921), 8-9.
88. Evgen'ev, A. "Dom iskusstv—v kavychkakh," Vestnik literatury, 3 (1921), 5-6.
89. Furmanov, D., on the dispute over "Misteriia-buff," Rabochii krai, June 16, 1921.
90. Gornfel'd, A. "Kul'tura i kul'turishka," Letopis' doma literatorov, 4 (1921), 4. See also his Boevye otkliki na mirnye temy .(L. 1924), 91-97.
91. Gornfel'd, A. "Novye slovechki i starye slova," in shortened form in Dom iskusstv, 2 (1921), 82-87; full text separately (P. 1922, 64pp.) and included in Muki slova (M.-L. 1927), 144-205.
92. Gusman, B. "Vladimir Maiakovskii," Po novomu ruslu (N.-Novgorod, 1921), 27-33.
93. Iurii, V. "Misteriia-Buff," Rabochii put', 127 (Nov. 12, 1921).
94. Ivanov-Razumnik, R. "Dusha futurizma," KR, 7 (1921), 16-20. Reprinted, slightly altered,in his Vladimir Maiakovskii ("Misteriia" ili "Buff"), Berlin, 1922, 5-18.
95. Ivanov-Razumnik, R. " 'Futurizm' i 'Veshch'," KR, 8-9 (1921), 22-27. Reprinted in his Vladimir Maiakovskii [see Item 94].
96. Ivanov-Razumnik, R. "Misteriia ili buff," Iskusstvo staroe i novo ` (P. 1921), 34-74. Reprinted in his Tvorchestvo i kritika (P. 1922), 220-58; and in his Vladimir Maiakovskii [see Item 94 above].
97. Jakobson, R. Noveishaia russkaia poeziia (Prague, 1921), passim.
98. Khovin, V. "Rozanov i Maiakovskii," Na odnu temu (P. 1921), 45-62. See also Aksenov's review in PR, 1 (1922), 288-89.
99. K-ov, N. "Vesti iz Moskvy," Tvorchestvo, 7 (1921).
100. Lander, K. Nasha teatral'naia politika (M. 1921).
101. Lunacharskii, A. "Dom iskusstv, No. 1," PR, 2 (1921), 224-27. Reprinted in his Sob. soch. vol. 2 (M. 1964), 238-43.
102. Lunacharskii, A., letter to the theater of the RSFSR, June 13, 1921. First published in Maiakovskii. Materialy i issledovaniia, eds. V. Pertsov and M. Serebrianskii (M.1940), 222-225.
103. L'vov-Rogachevskii, V. Imazhinizm i ego obrazonostsy (M. 1921), 24-32.
104. Margolin, S. "Vesna teatral'noi chrezmernosti," Vestnik rabotnikov iskusstv, 10-11 (1921), 122.
105. Margolin, S. "Impozantnaia feeriia," Vestnik teatrov, 93-94 (1921), 20.
106. Nes, A."Chetveronogaia kritika," Vostok (Vladivostok), 1 (1921).
107. Pavlov, K. "Misteriia-Buff," Izvestiia Tambovskogo gubernskogo ispolnitel'nogo komiteta, 189 (Aug. 24, 1921).
108. Rozhitsyn, V. " 'Misteriia-Buff' v Geroicheskom teatre," Kommunist (Khar'kov), 254 (Nov. 11, 1921).
109. Sadko, "Teatr RSFSR Pervyi. 'Misteriia-buff'," Vestnik teatra, 91-92 (1921), 10-11. Reprinted in Russkii sovetskii teatr 1917-1921 (L. 1968), 154-55.
110. Shklovskii, V. "O novom iskusstve," Iunyi proletarii, 3-4 (1921), 20.
111. Sillov, V. "Revoliutsiia dukha," "Nitsshe i Maiakovskii," Iun' (Vladivostok), 1 (1921).
112. Slonimskii, A. "Nekrasov i Maiakovskii," KR, 2 (1921), 5-10.

113. Sosnovskii, L. "Dovol'no 'maiakovshchiny'," Pr, 199 (Sept. 8, 1921), 1.

114. Tret'iakov, S. "Poet na tribune," *Tvorchestvo*, 7 (1921), 82-86.

115. Uglov, A., review of "Misteriia-Buff," *Kommunisticheskii trud*, 333 (May 7, 1921).

116. Ustinov, G. "Literatura i revoliutsiia," *Vestnik rabotnikov iskusstv*, 10-11 (1921), 23-40.

117. Val', V. "V proletarskom teatre," *Gudok*, 320 (June 8, 1921), 2-3.

118. Zhirmunskii, V. *Poeziia Bloka* (P. 1921), 151-52, 161-63.

119. Zhirmunskii, V. "Misteriia-Buff," Iz. 94 (May 4, 1921), 1.

120. Zhirmunskii, V., on the dispute over "Misteriia-Buff," *Novyi put'* (Riga), June 26, 1921.

121. Zhirmunskii, V. "Nado li stavit' 'Misteriiu-buff'," *Vestnik teatra*, 83-84 (1921), 19.

1922

122. Adamovich, G., review of Chukovskii's article, "Akhmatova i Maiakovskii," *Tsekh poetov*, vol. 3 (P. 1922).

123. Aksenov, I., review of "Maiakovskii izdevaetsia," PR, 7 (1922), 320.

124. B., review of "150 000 000," *Kazanskii bibliofil*, 3 (1922), 97.

125. Beskin, E. " 'Kofta' Maiakovskogo i 'skandaly' Esenina," *Teatral'naia Moskva*, 43 (1922), 7-9.

126. Briusov, V. "Vchera, segodnia i zavtra russkoi poezii," PR, 7 (1922), 38-67.

127. Chaadaev, N. "O psevdorevoliutsionerakh, priemliushchikh evoliutsiiu," *Utrenniki*, 2 (1922), 187-89.

128. Chuzhak, N. "Pered opasnost'iu razlozheniia," *Cherez golovy kritikov* (Chita, 1922), 26pp.

129. Chuzhak, N. *Na bol'nye temy* (Chita, 1922).

130. Dem'ianenko, A. "Zaria. Nam po doroge," *Gorskaia mysl'* (Vladikavkaz), 2 (1922), 19-30.

131. Erenburg, I. *Portrety russkikh poetov* (Berlin, 1922), 113-17. Reprinted in his *Gul zemli* (L. 1928), 88-89.

132. Gornfel'd, A. "Novye ili novshestva," *Literaturnye zapiski*, 1 (1922), 4-7.

133. Grossman-Roshchin, I. "O 'veshchnom' i 'dukhovnom' v tvorchestve V. Maiakovskogo," Iz, 166 (July 27, 1922), 5.

134. Kii. "Prevzoiti, no ne oboiti," *Gorn*, 2 (1922), 128-31.

135. Lezhnev, A. "Rassuzhdenie o pol'ze stekla," *Vestnik iskusstv*, 5 (1922), 34.

136. Lunacharskii, A. "Teatr RSFSR," PR, 4 (1922), 80-91. Reprinted in *Teatr i revoliutsiia* (M. 1924), 97-113; and in *O teatre i dramaturgii*, vol. 1 (M. 1958), 219-233.

137. Mandel'shtam, O. "Literaturnaia Moskva," *Rossiia*, 2 (1922), 23-24. Reprinted in his *Sob. soch.*, vol. 2 (New York, 1966), 368-73.

138. Polonskii, V. "Russkii revoliutsionnyi plakat," PR, 2 (1922), 56-77. Reprinted in his *Russkii revoliutsionnyi plakat* (M. 1925).

139. Pravdukhin, V. "Pis'ma o sovremennoi literature," *Sibirskie ogni*, 2 (1922), 139-51. Reprinted in his *Tvorets - Obshchestvo - Iskusstvo* (Novonikolaevsk, 1923), 142 ff., in *Literaturnaia sovremennost'* (M. 1924), 44-56, and in *Sovremennaia russkaia kritika*, ed. I. Aksenov (L. 1925), 74-83.

140. Shapirshtein—Lers, Ia. *Obshchestvennyi smysl russkogo literaturnogo futurizma* (M. 1922), 63-74.

141. Spasskii, S. "Maiakovskii. Liubliu. I v khvost i v grivu," *Gostinitsa dlia puteshestvuiushchikh v prekrasnom*, 1 (1922).

142. Zagorskii, M. "Teatr i zritel' epokhi revoliutsii," *O teatre* (Tver', 1922), 102-112.

143. Zagorskii, M. "Diadia Vania. Teatral'nyi obzor," *Iskusstvo* (Omsk), 2 (1922).

144. Zagorskii, M., review of "Misteriia-Buff," *Vlast' truda* (Irkutsk), 92 (April 26, 1922).

145. Aksenov, I., review of "255 stranits Maiakovskogo," PR, 7 (1923), 274-75.
146. Arvatov, B. "Sintaksis Maiakovskogo," PR, 1 (1923), 84-103. Reprinted in his *Sotsiologicheskaia poetika* (M. 1928), 101-126.
147. Chuzhak, N. "K zadacham dnia," *Lef,* 2 (1923), 149-51.
148. Erenburg, I. *Portrety sovremennykh poetov* (M. 1923), 53-57.
149. Gorlov, N. "Lef, preodolevaiushchiii slova, i slova, preodolevaiushchie Lef," *Lef,* 3 (1923), 17-21.
150. Gruzdev, I. "Russkaia poeziia v 1918-23. gg.," KR, 3 (1923), 31-38.
151. Gruzdev, I. *Utilitarnost' i samotsel'* (P. 1923), 172-190.
152. Gusman, B. *Sto poetov* (Tver', 1923), 168-71.
153. Jakobson, R. *O cheshkom stikhe* (Berlin, 1923), 101-112.
154. Kuzmin, M. "Parnasskie zarosli" *Zavtra,* eds. E. Zamiatin, M. Kuzmin, and M. Lozinskii (Berlin, 1923), 117-118.
155. Lebedev-Polianskii, V. "O 'levom fronte' v iskusstve," *Pod znamenem marksizma,* 4-5 (1923), 207-208.
156. Lelevich, G. "VI. Maiakovskii, " *Na postu,* 1 (1923), 133-48. Reprinted in his *Na literaturnom postu* (Tver', 1924), 102-113.
157. Levidov, M. "Organizovannoe uproshchenie kul'tury," KN, 1 (1923), 306-318.
158. Levidov, M. "O futurizme: neobkhodimaia stat'ia," *Lef,* 2 (1923), 131-37.
159. Lunacharskii, A. "Ob A. N. Ostrovskom i po povodu ego," Iz, 78 (April 11, 1923), 2; 79 (April 12, 1923), 2.
160. Lunacharskii, A. "Novoe v literature i iskusstve," *Vlast' truda* (Irkutsk), 126 (June 10, 1923), 2.
161. Lunacharskii, A. "Kak nekhorosho vykhodit!" Pr, 278 (Dec. 7, 1923), 2.
162. Lunacharskii, A. "Georg Kaizer," introduction to G. Kaizer, *Dramy* (M.-P. 1923), 3-16. Reprinted in *O teatre i dramaturgii* (M. 1958), 288-308.
163. Miturich, P. "Otkrytoe pis'mo Maiakovskomu," appendix to the collection entitled *Sobachii iashchik* (M. 1923).
164. M-v, N. "V Tsentr. Kommunisticheskom klube," Iz (Kazan'), 249 (Nov. 9, 1923).
165. Palei, A., review of "13 let raboty," KR, 11-12 (1923), 59.
166. P. S., review of "Ni znakhar', ni bog..." Kn. 22 (1923), 9.
167. Radlov, N. *O futurizme* (P. 1923), 68pp.
168. Rodov, S. "Kak Lef v pokhod sobralsia," *Na postu,* 1 (1923), 30-55.
169. Shafir, Ia. *Gazeta i derevnia* (M. 1923).
170. Simskii, M. "Misteriia-Buff," *Izvestiia TsIK Sovetov, obl. kom. RKP (b) ATSSR i Kaz SRKD,* 251 (Nov. 11, 1923).
171. Sipovskii, V. "Intelligentsia i narod," *Literaturnyi ezhenedel'nik,* 1 (1923), 9-11; 11 (1923), 10; 12 (1923), 9-10.
172. S. L., review of "Stikhi o revoliutsii," *Prizyv,* 1 (1923).
173. Sosnovskii, L. "Zheltaia kofta iz sovetskogo sittsa," Pr, 113 (May 24, 1923), 2.
174. Sosnovskii, L. "O iakoby revoliutsionnom slovotvorchestve," *Na postu,* 2-3 (1923).
175. Startsev, review of "Maiakovskii ulybaetsia," *Krasnaia niva,* 33 (1923), 30.
176. Tret'iakov, S. "Otkuda i kuda?" *Lef,* 1 (1923), 192-203.
177. Tret'iakov, S. "Tribuna Lefa," *Lef,* 3 (1923), 154-64.
178. Trotskii, L. "Futurizm," Pr, 216 (Sept. 25, 1923), 2-4; 217 (Sept, 26, 1923), 2-3. Reprinted in *Petrogradskaia Pravda,* 216, 217, 220, 229 (Sept, 25, 27, 29, 30, 1923), and in *Literatura i revoliutsiia* (M. 1923), 91-118. Second edition (M. 1924), 94-120. Section on Mayakovsky included in I. Aksenov, ed., *Sovremennaia russkaia kritika* (L. 1925), 10-19.

179. Ustinov, V. *Literatura nashikh dnei* (M. 1923).
180. Ustrialova, N. "Obmirshchenie," *Rossiia,* 9 (1923).
181. Vinokur, G. "Futuristy—stroiteli iazyka," *Lef,* 1 (1923), 204-13.
182. Vinokur, G. "Novaia literatura po poetike," *Lef,* 1 (1923), 239-43.
183. Volodin, S. "Pereputannye stroki," *Lef,* 3 (1923), 22-27.
184. Voronskii, A. "Na perevale," KN, 6 (1923), 320-21.
185. Vygodskii, D. "Iziashchnaia literatura," KR, 2 (1923), 60.
186. Zemenko, B., Rok, R., Saikov, S. "Poruganie moshchei iskusstva," *Sobachii iashchik* (M. 1923).
187. Zhirmunskii, V. *Rifma, ee istoriia i teoriia* (P. 1923), 213-221.
188. Zhukov, P. "Levyi front iskusstv," KR, 3 (1923), 39-44.
189. Zhukov, P., review of "Stikhi o revoliutsii," *Biulleten' knigi,* 7-8 (1923), 45.
190. Zhukov, P., review of "Skazka o dezertire," *Biulleten' knigi,* 9-10 (1923), 79.
191. Zhukov, P., review of "Von samogon," "Ni znakhar', ni bog..." *Biulleten' knigi,* 9-10 (1923), 81.
192. Zhukov, P., review of "Obriady," *Biulleten' knigi,* 9-10 (1923), 82.

1924

193. Bagrii, A. "Sovremennye pisateli," *Formal'nyi metod v literature* (Vladikavkaz, 1924), 219-248.
194. Blagoi, D., review of "Stikhi o Kurske," Kn, 33 (1924), 8.
195. Brik, O. "Reklama stikhom;" *Zhurnalist,* 12 (1924), 51-52.
196. Briusov, V. "O rifme," PR, 1 (1924), 114-23.
197. Chuzhak, N. *Krivoe zerkalo* (Izd. "Oktiabr' mysli," 1924).
198. Gorbachev, G. *Ocherki sovremennoi russkoi literatury* (. 1924), 97-147. In the revised, third edition (L. 1925), 113-60.
199. Gorlov, N. *Futurizm i revoliutsiia. Poeziia futuristov* (M. 1924), 87pp. See also Lezhnev's review in PR, 1 (1925), 278-81.
200. Gorlov, N. "O futurizmakh i futurizme," *Lef,* 4 (1924), 6-15.
201. Grossman-Roshchin, I. "Sotsial'nyi zamysel futurizma," *Lef,* 4 (1924), 109-124.
202. Iskona. "Poeziia i reklama," *Gostinitsa dlia puteshestvuiushchikh v prekrasnom,* 4 (1924), 15-16.
203. Kogan, P. *Literatura etikh let* (Iv.-Voznesensk, 1924), 126-45. In the fourth edition (Iv.-Voznesensk, 1925), 138-46. Section on Mayakovsky also reprinted in I. Aksenov, ed., *Sovremennaia russkaia kritika* (L. 1925), 88-97.
204. Levman, S. "O Lefe," *Trud,* 39 (Feb. 17, 1924).
205. Lirov, M. "Iz literaturnykh itogov," PR, 2 (1924), 118-24.
206. Lunacharskii, A. "Voprosy literatury i dramaturgii," *Voprosy literatury i dramaturgii* (L. 1924), 9-18, 86-94. Reprinted in his *Sob. soch.,* vol. 2 (M. 1964), 258-69. See also Lezhnev's review in PR, 2 (1925), 256-59.
207. Lunacharskii, A. "Pushkin," *Krasnaia niva,* 24 (1924), 570-72. Reprinted (as "Eshche o Pushkine") in his *Literaturnye siluety* (L. 1925), 66-71 and in his *Sob. soch.,* vol. 1 (M. 1964), 38-43.
208. Pavlov, M. "Maiakovskii. 'Pro eto'," *Krasnyi zhurnal dlia vsekh,* 6 (1924), 481.
209. Plotnikov, N. *Revoliutsionnaia literatura* (L. 1924).
210. Pravdukhin, V. "O kul'ture iskusstv," KN, 1 (1924), 290-310.
211. Pravdukhin, V. "Novoe o literature," *Krasnaia niva,* 13 (1924), 310-311.
212. Pravdukhin, V. *Literaturnaia sovremennost'* (M. 1924), 281-84. See also the review by D. Chudinov, *Sibirskie ogni,* 5 (1924), 238-43.
213. Sen'kin, S. "Lenin v kommune VKhUTEMAS," *Molodaia gvardiia,* 2-3 (1924), 107-11.
214. Shershenevich. V. "V khvost i v grivu," *Gostinitsa dlia puteshestvuiushchikh v prekrasnom,* 1 (1924), 23-24.

215. Shklovskii, V. "Sovremenniki i sinkhronisty," *Russkii sovremennik,* 3 (1924), 232-37.
216. Tynianov, Iu. "Promezhutok," *Russkii sovremennik,* 4 (1924), 209-221. Reprinted in his *Arkhaisty i novatory* (L. 1929), 541-580.
217. Zagorskii, M. "Kak reagiruet zritel'?" *Lef,* 2 (1924), 141-51.
218. ——. Review of "Ni znakhar', ni bog...", "Obriady," *Vestnik knigi,* 1-3 (1924), 102.
219. ——. Review of "Skazka o dezertire," *Vestnik knigi,* 1-3 (1924), 105.

1925

220. Aksenov, I. "O foneticheskom magistrale," *Gosplan literatury* (M.-L. 1925), 122-44.
221. Anibal, B., review of Gorbachev's *Ocherki sovremennoi literatury* (L. 1924), NM, 10 (1925), 154-56.
222. Bliumenfel'd, V. "Lirika i agitka," ZI, 32 (1925), 9-10.
223. Burliuk, D. "Pis'ma iz sovremennoi Ameriki," *Tikhookeanskaia zvezda* (Khabarovsk), 1925.
224. Evgen'ev-Maksimov, V. *Ocherki noveishei russkoi literatury* (M. 1925), 210-13.
225. Grinberg, A., review of "Skazka o Pete Tolstom i Sime," PR, 8 (1925), 256.
226. Gusman, B. *Poety* (M. 1925), 33-39.
227. Krasil'nikov, V., review of "Vladimir Il'ich Lenin," NM, 9 (1925), 150-51.
228. Krasil'nikov, V., review of "Tol'ko novoe. Parizh." Kn, 36-37 (1925), 24.
229. Kruchenykh, A. *Lef-agitki Maiakovskogo, Aseeva, Tret'iakova* (M. 1925), 3-12.
230. Lelevich, G. "Russkaia literatura za 8 let revoliutsii," *Sovremennoe iskusstvo,* 4-5 (1925).
231. Lunacharskii, A. "Puti akademicheskogo iskusstva," ZI, 39 (1925), 1-2; "Teatral'nye rabkory," ZI, 40 (1925), 3. Reprinted as "Osnovy teatral'noi politiki sovetskoi vlasti," *Sob. soch.,* vol. 3 (M. 1964), 253-78.
232. Lunacharskii, A. "O sovremennykh napravleniiakh russkoi literatury," *Krasnaia molodezh',* 2 (1925), 139-143. Reprinted in his *Sob. soch.,* vol. 2 (M., 1964), 282-286.
233. Lunacharskii, A., "O nashei poezii," introduction to *Styk* (M., 1925), 5-12. Reprinted in his *Stat'i o sovetskoi literature* (M., 1958), 430-434, and in *Sob. soch.,* vol. 2 (M., 1964), 287-291.
234. Lunacharskii, A., *Sud'by russkoi literatury* (L., 1925), 44-50.
235. Osenev, A., review of "Vladimir Il'ich Lenin," O, 3-4 (1925), 238.
236. Pel'she, R., "Lef, iskusstvo i marksizm," *Sovremennoe iskusstvo,* 8 (1925).
237. Pertsov, V., *Za novoe iskusstvo* (M., 1925).
238. Rashkovskaia, A., "Motivy proletarskoi poezii," *Vestnik znaniia,* 13 (1925), 885-890.
239. Shafir, Ia. *Ot ostroty do pamfleta. Voprosy gazetnoi kul'tury* (M. 1925), 91-100.
240. Speranskii, V. *Maiakovskii futurizm* (Izd. "Mir," 1925), 93pp.
241. Ustrialov, N. "Religiia i revoliutsiia," *Pod znakom revoliutsii* (Kharbin), 1925.
242. Voronskii, A. "V. Maiakovskii," KN, 2 (1925), 249-76. Reprinted in his *Literaturnye tipy* (M. 1925), 5-38, and *Literaturnye portrety*, vol. 1 (M. 1928), 351-400.
243. Zhirmunskii, V. *Vvedenie v metriku. Teoriia stikha* (L. 1925), 212-225.
244. Zhirmunskii, V., review of "Voina i mir," "Tol'ko novoe," *Novaia kniga,* 3-4 (1925), 34.

1926

245. Aksenov, I. "Pochti vse o Maiakovskom," *Novaia Rossiia,* 3 (1926), 83-88.
246. Ardi. "Laboratoriia poeta," VM (Aug. 25, 1926).
247. Bagrii, A. *Russkaia literatura XIX i pervoi chetverti XX v.* (Baku, 1926), 309-310.
248. Chuzhak, N. "Khudozhestvennaia detskaia knizhka," *Sovremennoe iskusstvo,* 6 (1926), 27-32.
249. Degterevskii, I "Maiakovskii," *Sovremennaia khudozhestvennaia proza i poeziia* (M. 1926), 125-38.
250. Gorbachev, G. "Na perelome," *Zvezda,* 1 (1926), 211-240.

251. Gorodetskii, S. "Tekushchii moment v poezii," *Sovetskoe iskusstvo,* 2 (1926), 16-23.
252. Gorodetskii, S. "Oktiabr' v khudozhestvennoi literature," Iz, 258 (Nov. 7, 1926), 9.
253. Ia. Sh., review of "Ispaniia," Kn, 40 (1926), 16.
254. Iurgin, N., review of "Ispaniia," KN, 11 (1926), 240-41.
255. Lelevich, G., review of "V. I. Lenin," PR, 1 (1926), 235-36.
256. Lezhnev, A. "Dialogi," KN, 1 (1926), 250-61.
257. Malakhov, S. "Russkii futurizm posle revoliutsii," *Molodaia gvardiia,* 10 (1926), 172-83.
258. Mazhbits-Verov, I., reveiw of "Tol'ko novoe," "Parizh," "V.I. Lenin," "Letaiushchii proletarii," Iz, 43 (Feb. 21, 1926), 6.
259. Nikitina, E. *Russkaia literatura ot simvolizma do nashikh dnei* (M. 1926), 114-21.
260. Smirnov-Kutacheskii, A. "Pereiom literaturnogo stilia," PR, 2 (1926), 27-40.
261. Sosnovskii, L "Poeziia i proza ekonomiki," Pr, 81 (April 9, 1926), 3.

1927

262. Aseev, N. "Na chorta nam stikhi," O, 1 (1927), 146-150.
263. Aseev, N. "Pokhod tverdolobykh," *Novyi Lef,* 5 (1927), 37-45.
264. Aseev, N. "Moskva letom," *Sovetskaia Sibir'* (Novo-Nikolaevsk), Aug. 7, 1927.
265. Baks, B. "Voprosy teatra i dramturgii," NLP, 7 (1927), 49-55.
266. Bekker, M. "Oktiabr' v khudozhestvennoi literature," *Krasnaia zvezda,* Nov. 11, 1927.
267. Berkovskii, N., review of Mayakovsky's *Sobranie sochinenii,* V, KG (Oct. 14, 1927).
268. Bespalov, I., review of "Khorosho," Pr, 297 (Dec. 28, 1927), 5.
269. Bezymenskii, A. "Nachistotu," NM, 2 (1927), 196-201.
270. Bl.--, "Pamiatka literaturnogo desiatiletiia," ZI, 45 (1927).
271. Bliumenfel'd, V. "Dvadtsat' piatoe," KG, Nov. 10, 1927.
272. Bol'shoi, Iu. "Chetyre poeta—Oktiabriu," KG, Nov. 30, 1927.
273. Brik, O. "Za novatorstvo," *Novyi Lef,* 1 (1927), 25-28.
274. Brik, O. "Ritm i sintaksis," *Novyi Lef,* 3 (1927), 15-20.
275. Bukharin, N. "O starinnykh traditsiiakh i sovremennom kul'turnom stroitel'stve," *Revoliutsiia i kul'tura,* 1 (1927).
276. Chuzhoi, M., review of Mayakovsky's *Sob. soch. V, Tverskaia pravda* (Aug. 10, 1927).
277. D-ach, N. "VI. Maiakovskii," *Krasnoe znamia* Taganrog), Nov. 25, 1927.
278. Dukor, I. "Maiakovskii—gazetchik," NLP, 22-23 (1927), 61-73.
279. Dukor, I., review of "Khorosho," *Molodaia gvardiia,* 12 (1927).
280. Dzh. D., review of "Khorosho," *Tikhookeansk* (Khabarovsk), 36 (Dec. 31, 1927).
281. Fish, G., review of Mayakovsky's *Sob. soch. V, Leningradskaia pravda,* 217 (Sept. 23, 1927).
282. Gol'din, L. "Stikhi Maiakovskogo," *Orlovskaia pravda,* July 28, 1927.
283. Golubkob, V., Dankov, B., and others, *Pisateli—sovremenniki* (M. 1927), 241-57.
284. Gorbachev, G. "Poeticheskoe masterstvo sovremennogo Maiakovskogo," Iz (Saratov), July 31, 1927.
285. Grossman-Roshchin, I. "Otvet: otkrytoe pis'mo N. Aseevu," O, 1 (1927), 156-57.
286. Ikarskii, N. "Maiakovskii v Saratove," Iz (Saratov), Jan. 28, 1927.
287. Iuzovskii, Iu. "Kartonnaia poema," *Sovetskii iug* (Rostov n/D), Nov. 27, 1927.
288. Kassil', L. "Kak zhivem?—Khorosho," *Sovetskaia Sibir'* (Novo-Nikolaevsk), Oct. 30.
289. Kogan, P. "Poeziia," KN, 11 (1927), 193-208.
290. Kogan, P. *Literatura velikogo desiatiletiia* (M.-L. 1927), 144-56.
291. Kogan, P. *Istoriia russkoi literatury s drevneishikh vremen do nashikh dnei* (M.-L. 1927), 218-225.
292. Krasil'nikov, V., review of "Khorosho," *Molodaia gvardiia,* 12 (1927), 217-20.
293. Krasil'nikov, V., review of "Khorosho," *Nasha gazeta,* 268 (1927).
294. Krupskaia, N. "Chto nravilos' Il'ichu iz khudozhestvennoi literatury," VM, Jan. 23, 1927.

295. Larin, B. "O lirike kak raznovidnosti khudozhestvennoi rechi," *Russkaia rech'.*
Novaia seriia (L. 1927), 42-73.
296. Lelevich, G. "O formal'nykh vliianiiakh v proletarskoi poezii," PR, 5 (1927), 124-29.
297. Lezhnev, A. "Delo o trupe," KN, 5 (1927), 218-35. Reprinted in his *Sovremenniki*
(M. 1927), 5-31.
298. Lezhnev, A. "Khudozhestvennaia literatura," PR, 7 (1927), 81-118.
299. Liberman, G. "Vl. Maiakovskii," *Bakinskii rabochii,* Dec. 4, 1927.
300. Lunacharskii, A. "Nashi poety," VM, 18 (Jan. 24, 1927), 3. Reprinted in his *Sob.*
soch., vol. 2 (M. 1964), 336-41.
301. Lunacharskii, A. "Etapy rosta sovetskoi literatury," NLP, 22-23 (1927), 16-20. Reprinted in *Sob. soch.,* vol. 2 (M. 1964), 362-67.
302. Lunacharskii, A. *10 let kul'turnogo stroitel'stva* (M. 1927).
303. Lunacharskii, A. "Desiat' knig za desiat' let revoliutsii," *Smena,* 9 (1927), 1.
304. L'vov-Rogachevskii, V. *Khudozhestvennaia literatura revoliutsionnogo desiatiletiia*
(M. "Mir," 1927).
305. L'vov-Rogachevskii, V. "Futurizm," *Literaturnaia entsiklopediia* (1927), 1047-58.
306. Mar, I., review of Mayakovsky's *Sob. soch.,* V, *Krasnaia Tatariia* (Kazan'), 168 (1927).
307. Mazhbits-Verov, I. "Novyi Maiakovskii," VM, Sept. 23 (1927).
308. Meis-an, review of "Khorosho," *Zhurnal iskusstva* (Leningrad), Dec. 31, 1927.
309. N. N., review of chaps. 2-8 of "Khorosho," NLP, 17-18 (1927), 85.
310. Novich, I. "V. Maiakovskii," *Ural'skii rabochii* (Sverdlovsk), Nov. 21, 1927.
311. Ol'shevets, M. "Pochemu 'Lef'?" Iz, 22 (Jan. 28, 1927), 5.
312. Palei, A. "Novyi lef," *Segodnia,* almanac 2 (M. 1927).
313. Polianskii, V. *Voprosy sovremennoi kritiki* (M.-L. 1927), 170-72.
314. Polonskii, V. "Lef ili blef?" Iz, 46 (Feb. 25, 1927), 5; 48 (Feb. 27, 1927), 3. Reprinted
in his *Ocherki sovremennoi literatury* (M.-L., 3rd ed., enlarged, 1930), 314-331.
315. Polonskii, V. "Blef prodolzhaetsia," NM, 5 (1927), 147-59. Reprinted with No. 314
in his *Na literaturnye temy* (M. 1928), 17-45.
316. Polonskii, V. "Literaturnoe dvizhenie oktiabr'skogo desiatiletiia," PR, 7 (1927), 15-80.
317. P. T. "Maiakovskii sredi rabochikh," *Bakinskii rabochii,* Dec. 7, 1927.
318. Rozanov, I. "Sovremennye liriki," *Rodnoi iazyk v shkole,* 5 (1927), 123-29.
319. Shengeli, G. *Maiakovskii vo ves' rost* (M. 1927), 51pp.
320. Shibanov, V., review of "Moe otkrytie Ameriki," PR, 2 (1927), 198-200.
321. Shklovskii, V. *Tekhnika pisatel'skogo remesla* (M.-L. 1927), 64-70.
322. Sov., review of "Khorosho," *Sovetskaia Sibir'* (Novosibirsk), Dec. 6, 1927.
323. Tarasov, P., review of Mayakovsky's *Sob. soch. V, Bakinskii rabochii,* Nov. 4, 1927.
324. T. M. "Vl. Maiakovskii," *Zaria Vostoka* (Tiflis), Dec. 9, 1927.
325. Trifonov, N. "O Maiakovskom," *Uchitel'skaia gazeta,* Nov. 7, 1927.
326. V., review of "Khorosho," *Rabochaia pravda* (Tiflis), Nov. 10, 1927.
327. V. N., review of "Khorosho," *Rabochaia Moskva,* Oct. 20, 1927.
328. V. N., review of "Khorosho," *Rabochii put'* (Smolensk), Nov. 26, 1927.
329. Voronskii, A. "Nasha literatura," *Oktiabr' v iskusstve* (L. 1927), 23-26.
330. Zaitsevskii, G. "Kuban' i chernomor'e v sovremennoi khudozhestvennoi literature,"
Sbornik statei po ekonomike i kul'ture, vol. 1 (Krasnodar, 1927), 37-55.
331. ——. "Protokol o Polonskom," *Novyi Lef,* 3(1927), 39-46.
332. ——. Note on the dispute "Lef ili Blef," NLP, 7 (1927), 72-73.

1928

333. Afonin, M., review of "Khorosho," *Komsomol'skaia Pravda,* 15 (Jan. 18, 1928).
334. Aseev, N. "Stradaniia molodogo Vertera," *Novyi Lef,* 4 (1928), 1-5.
335. Bekker, M. "Khorosho li 'Khorosho'," NLP, 2 (1928), 21-25.
336. Chuzhak, N. "Literatura zhiznestroeniia," *Novyi Lef,* 10 (1928),2-17.
337. Druzin, V. "Zadachi proletarskogo poeticheskogo molodniaka," NLP, 8 (1928), 42-46.

338. Gorbachev, G. *Sovremennaia russkaia literatura* (L. 1928), Chapter 8: "Futurizm." In the third edition (L. 1931), 61-72.

339. Gorbov, D. *U nas i za rubezhom: literaturnye ocherki* (M. 1928), 191, 200.

340. Iuzovskii, Iu. "Kartonnaia poema," NLP, 13-14 (1928), 92-93.

341. Kassil', L. "Izustnyi period v g. Pokrovske," *Novyi Lef,* 1 (1928), 42-45.

342. Kogan, P. "Kakoi stil' nam nuzhen?" VM, 1928.

343. Kruchenykh, A. "Krasnoustyi," *Turnir poetov* (M. 1928).

344. Kruchenykh, A. *15 let russkogo futurizma* (M. 1928), 7-13.

345. Lezhnev, A. "Dve poemy," *Pereval,* 6 (1928), 353-64.

346. Manfred, A. "Tvorcheskii put' Maiakovskogo," Iz (Saratov), Feb. 12, 1928.

347. Markov, P. "Pis'ma o moskovskikh teatrakh," *Zaria Vostoka* (Tiflis), Apr. 10, 1928.

348. Mendelevskii. "Maiakovskii i Sendberg," *Vestnik inostrannoi literatury,* 11 (1928), 141-144.

349. Pokrovskii, V. "Maiakovskii," *Smychka* (Orenburg), Feb. 23, 1928.

350. Polonskii, V. "Listki iz bloknota," PR, 1 (1928), 108-112.

351. Polonskii, V. *Ocherki literaturnogo dvizheniia epokhi* (M. 1928), chapter 2: "Ot futurizma do Kuznitsa," chapter 6: "Lef." In the 2nd ed., expanded (M.-L. 1929), 25-34, 143-49.

352. Rozanov, I. *Literaturnye reputatsii* (M. 1928), 5-22.

353. Saianov, V. *Sovremennye literaturnye gruppirovki* (L. 1928), chapter 3: "Lef." In the 2nd ed. (L. 1930), 44-54.

354. Shklovskii, V. *Gamburgskii schet* (L. 1928), 87, 118-21, 171.

355. Shugaeva, N. "Chistka poetov," *Chitatel' i pisatel',* 3 (1928).

356. Si-Eks. "Maiakovskii," *Chitatel' i pisatel',* 18 (1928), 2.

357. Tal'nikov, D. "Literaturnye zametki," KN, 8 (1928), 259-81; 11 (1928), 213-44.

358. Voronskii, A. "Desiatiletie Oktiabria i sovetskaia literatura," *Iskusstvo videt' mir* (M. 1928), 170-82.

359. Zelinskii, K. "Itti li nam s Maiakovskim," NLP, 5 (1928), 49-54. Reprinted in his *Poeziia kak smysl* (M. 1929), 300-310.

360. ——. "Chetyre prem'ery v teatre im. Meierkhol'da. Novaia p'esa Maiakovskogo," a conversation with Meyerhold, VM, 299 (Dec. 27, 1928).

361. ——. "Literaturnyi kommentarii k pervomu tomu," in Maiakovskii, *Sochineniia,* (M.-L. 1928), I, 31-56.

1929

362. Alpers, B. "Klop," *Komsomol'skaia pravda,* 48 (Feb. 27, 1929).

363. Al'tsest. " 'Klop' Maiakovskogo," *Chernomors'ka komuna* (Odessa), Sept. 11, 1929.

364. Al'tsest. "Teatr im. Meierkhol'da v Odesi," *Shkval* (Odessa), Sept. 14, 1929.

365. Andreevich, V. "Maiakovskii u Meierkhol'da," *Vechernii Kiev,* Aug. 19, 1929.

366. Aseev, N. "Stikhotvornyi fel'eton," *Rabota nad stikhom* (L. 1929), 42-50.

367. Bachelis, I. "Novaia p'esa VI. Maiakovskogo 'Klop'," *Komsomol'skaia pravda,* 1 (Jan. 1, 1929).

368. Baian, V. "Otkrytoe pis'mo V. V. Maiakovskomu," LG, 14 (July 22, 1929), 4.

369. Berezark, I. " 'Klop' Maiakovskogo v postanovke Meierkhol'da," *Gudok,* Feb. 16, 1929.

370. Berezark, I. "Veshch' na stsene," *Novyi zritel',* 32-33 (Aug. 18, 1929).

371. Berkovskii, N. "Zametki o dramaturgakh," O, 12 (1929), 171-84.

372. Beskin, O. " 'Klop' Maiakovskogo," KN, 5 (1929), 241-46.

373. Chuzhak, N. *Literatura fakta* (M. 1929), 49-50.

374. D. S. "Interesnye p'esy," *Zavodskaia pravda* (Leningrad), 9 (Nov. 28, 1929).

375. Dreiden, S. " 'Klop' (Filial BDT)," ZI, 49 (Dec. 8, 1929), 6-7.

376. Druzin, V. "Vmesto Lef'a—Ref," ZI, 42 (1929), 12.

377. Dukor, I. "Bor'ba za poeziiu," PR, 8 (1929), 29-49.

378. Eidel'man, Ia. "Teatr Meierkhol'da zhivet. 'Klop'," *Smena* (L.) Feb. 24, 1929.

379.. Eidel's, L. "Sredi knig i zhurnalov," *Molodoi kommunar* (Voronezh), July 6, 1929.

380. Elin, S. " 'Klop' v teatre imeni Meierkhol'da," *Trud,* Feb. 22, 1929.

381. Evenlev, M. " 'Klop' u teatri Meierkhol'da," *Komsomolets' Ukraini* (Khar'kov), July 18, 1929.

382. Evgen'ev, " 'Klop' Maiakovskogo. Gastroli teatr im. Meierkhol'da," *Molodaia gvardiia* (Odessa), Sept. 14, 1929.

383. Fel'dman, K. "Klop," *Rabochaia Moskva,* 42 (Feb. 20, 1929).

384. Fevral'skii, A. " 'Bania' VI. Maiakovskogo," Pr, 244 (Oct. 22, 1929), 5.

385. Flit. "Nashestvie klopov," *Revizor* (L.), 39 (1929).

386. G., V. "Gastroli teatra im. Meierkhol'da," KG, 278 (evening, Dec. 4, 1929).

387. G., V. "Klop," *Smena* (L.), 278 (Dec. 4, 1929).

388. Gel'fand, M. "Literaturnye zametki," Pr, 112 (May 19, 1929), 5.

389. Gorbov, D. *Poiski galatei* (M. 1929), 259-73.

390. Gorelov, A. "Komediia o 'Serzhe,' 'Klop' V. Maiakovskogo," *Krasnaia panorama* (L.), 17-18 (April 26, 1929).

391. Gorodinskii, V. " 'Klop' v teatre im. Meierkhol'da. Pis'mo iz Moskvy," *Rabochii i teatr,* 10 (1929), March 3.

392. G-ov. " 'Klop' Maiakovskogo," ZI, 7 (Feb. 10, 1929), 16.

393. Iankovskii, M. " 'Klop' Maiakovskogo na stsene," *Rabochii i teatr,* 48 (Dec. 1, 1929).

394. K., K. "Teatr im. Meierkhol'da. 'Les,' 'Klop'," *Proletarska pravda* (Kiev), Aug. 17, 1929.

395. K-ii. "Rabochie 'Krasnoi zari' o 'Klope.' Posle takogo spektaklia protivno pit'," *Golos tekstilei* (M.), 41 (Feb. 19, 1929).

396. K-ii. " 'Klop.' Novaia p'esa VI. Maiakovskogo," VM, 1 (Jan. 2, 1929).

397. Kin-gei. "Obsuzhdaem p'esu 'Klop'," *Komsomolets Vostoka* (Tashkent), 49 (May 1, 1929).

398. Konovalov, A. " 'Klop' v Bol'shom dramaticheskom," *Rabochii i teatr,* 49 (Dec. 8, 1929).

399. Korenev, G. "Klop," *Krasnaia zvezda,* 41 (February 19, 1929).

400. Koroteev. "O 'Bane'. Vecher 'Daesh'.' Mnenie slushatelei," *Daesh',* 12 (1929).

401. Kruti, I. " 'Klop' Maiakovskogo v teatre Meierkhol'da. (Pis'mo iz Moskvy)," *Srednevolzhskaia kommuna* (Kuibyshev), Feb. 27, 1929.

402. Kurella, A. "Prem'era u Meierkhol'da. 'Klop'. P'esa Maiakovskogo," *Nasha gazeta,* 39 (Feb. 16, 1929).

403. Levidov, M. "Literatura v teatre," ZI, 19 (May 12, 1929), 2-3.

404. Lezhnev, A. *Literaturnye budni* (M. 1929), 222-32.

405. Lezhnev, A., Gorbov, D. *Literatura revoliutsionnogo desiatiletiia 1917-1927* (Khar'kov, 1929), 15-27.

406. Lorentso, B. "Moskovskie pis'ma. Prokhodnoi sezon," *Vechernie izvestiia* (Odessa) March 3, 1929.

407. Lukhmanov, N. "Bez slov," ZI, 22 (June 2, 1929), 4.

408. Lunacharskii, A. "Molodaia rabochaia literatura," *Iskusstvo i molodezh'* (M. 1929). Reprinted in *Sob. soch.* vol. 2 (M. 1964), 390-407.

409. Lunacharskii, A. "Literaturnyi god," *Krasnaia panorama,* 1 (1929), 5-6. Reprinted in *Sob. soch.* vol. 2 (1964), 408-11.

410. M. "Gastroli teatra im. Meierkhol'da. Pervoe predstavlenie 'Klopa'," *Vechernyi Kiev,* August 26, 1929.

411. M., N. "K postanovke komedii 'Klop'," *Kievskii proletarii,* Aug. 16, 1929.

412. Malakhov, S. "Bor'ba za poeziiu," PR, 10 (1929), 32-40.

413. Manukhin, V. "Dve novykh postanovki. 'Klop'," *Ekran,* March 24, 1929.

414. Mashirov, A. "Dve postanovki 'Klopa'," KG, evening, 300 (Nov. 29, 1929).

415. Mokul'skii, S. "Eshche o 'Klope'," ZI, 13 (March 24, 1929), 10.

416. Morskoi, V. " 'Klop'. Gastroli teatr im. Meierkhol'da," *Proletarii* (Khar'kov), July 19, 1929.

417. Novitskii, P. "Klop," *Repetuarnyi biulleten',* 1 (1929).

418. Novitskii, P. "Metkii udar," *Daesh',* 1 (1929).

419. Novitskii, P. "O kul'turnoi zrelosti sovremennogo teatra," PR, 4 (1929), 97-109.

420. Novskii, B. " 'Klop' v teatre im. Vs. Meierkhol'da," *Novyi zritel'*, March 3, 1929.
421. Obolenskii, L. "Klop," KG, evening, 48 (Feb. 22, 1929).
422. Oksenov, I. "V. Maiakovskii. 'Klop.' Feericheskaia komediia," KG, evening, 263 (Oct. 19, 1929).
423. Ol'khovyi, B. "O peregruppirovke sil na literaturnom fronte," Iz. 240 (Oct. 17, 1929), 3.
424. Osinskii, N. " 'Klop' v teatre Meierkhol'da," Iz, 47 (Feb. 26, 1929), 5.
425. P. " 'Klop' v teatre Vs. Meierkhol'da," *Prozhektor*, 10 (1929).
426. P., M. " 'Klop' VI. Maiakovskogo v teatre im. Meierkhol'da," *Smena*, Dec. 1 (1929).
427. P., N. " 'Klop' Maiakovskogo u Meierkhol'da," *Nizhegorodskaia kommuna* (Gor'kii), Feb. 24, 1929.
428. Pel'she, R. " 'Klop'. Analiz spektaklia," *Sovremennyi teatr*, 15 (April 9, 1929).
429. Pervomai, Plenumov. "Teatral'nye ekspromty. Klop, klopa, klopu, o klope," VM, 41 (Feb. 19, 1929).
430. Postupal'skii, I., review of "Novye stikhi," PR, 1 (1929), 135-36.
431. Pozdniakov, P. "Pis'mo iz Moskvy. 'Bania.' Novaia p'esa Maiakovskogo," *Krasnoarmeets* (Kuibyshev), Nov. 30, 1929.
432. P-skii, L. "Novaia p'esa Maiakovskogo," *Golos tekstilei*, 2 (Jan. 3, 1929).
433. Rezhissura spektaklia, " 'Klop' V. Maiakovskogo. K postanovke v filiale Bol'shogo dramaticheskogo teatr," *Rabochii i teatr*, 47 (Dec. 24, 1929).
434. Rogov, V. "O 'Klope'," *Kievskii proletarii*, Aug. 18, 1929.
435. Roi, N. " 'Klop' V. Maiakovskogo na klubnoi stsene," *Ural'skii rabochii* (Sverdlovsk) Feb. 27, 1929.
436. Romanovskii, M. " 'Klop'. Gastroli im. Vs.Meierkhol'da," *Khar'kovskii proletarii*, 163 (July 16, 1929).
437. S. " 'Klop' - novaia p'esa Maiakovskogo," *Kommuna*, (Voronezh), Feb. 10, 1929.
438. Saianov, V. *Ocherki po istorii russkoi poezii XX veka* (L. 1929), 89-103.
439. Sh. " 'Klop.' V khudsovete teatra im. Meierkhol'da," *Novyi zritel'*, 2 (Jan. 6, 1929).
440. Sheko, I. "Klop," *Proletar* (Khar'kov), July 18, 1929.
441. Shevchenko, I. "Klop," *Visti* (Khar'kov), July 18, 1929.
442. Shin, A., and Per-ov, N. "Klop," *Rabochaia gazeta*, 44 (Feb. 22, 1929).
443. Shplatov, Z. "Razobrali 'Klopa' Maiakovskogo," *Kolotushka* (Orekhovo-Zuevo), March 23, 1929.
444. Stankevich, O. "Gastroli teatru im. Vs. Meierkhol'da. 'Klop'," *Vecherne radio* (Khar'kov), July 17, 1929.
445. Tal'nikov, D. *Gul vremeni. Literatura i sovremennost'* (M. 1929).
446. Tal'nikov, D. "Novye postanovki. I. 'Klop'," ZI, 11 (March 10, 1929), 10.
447. Tanin, S. "Negr i klop," *Zvezda* (Perm'), March 24, 1929.
448. Tasin, L. "Teatral'naia nedelia," KG, evening, 277 (Dec. 3, 1929).
449. Tikhonov, V. "Opyt literaturnoi poezdki po rabochim raionam," NLP, 6 (1929), 71-76.
450. Turkel'taub, I. " 'Klop' v teatre im. Meierkhol'da," ZI, 12 (March 17, 1929), 7.
451. Uriel', " 'Klop' v teatre imeni vs. Meierkhol'da," VM, Feb. 19, 1929.
452. V., V. "Bania," *Chudak*, 39 (1929).
453. V. D. "Klop," Pr, 46 (Feb. 24, 1929), 5.
454. V-K. "Dobrodushnyi 'Klop'," *Rabochaia gazeta*, 10 (Jan. 12, 1929).
455. Verkhoturskii, A. " 'Klop' Maiakovskogo," KG, evening, 8 (Jan. 10, 1929).
456. Vinokur, G. "Rechevaia praktika futuristov," *Kul'tura iazyka*, 2nd ed., corrected and enlarged (M. 1929), 304-318.
457. Volkov, N. " 'Klop' v teatre Meierkhol'da v Moskve," *Krasnaia panorama* (L.), 12 (March 22, 1929).
458. Zagorskii, M. "Tol'ko ob akterakh," *Sovremennyi teatr*, 14 (April 2, 1929).
459. Zaslavskii, D. "Udar po meshchanstvu," *Molodaia gvardiia*, 2 (1929), 86-87.
460. Zonin, A. "V. Maiakovskii," KR, 7 (1929), 14-21.

461. ——. "Rabochie o p'ese Maiakovskogo. Smychka pisatelia s chitatelem," *Rabochaia gazeta,* 11 (Jan. 13, 1929).

462. ——. "Golos rabochego zritelia," *Rabochaia gazeta,* 44 (Feb. 22, 1929).

463. ——. "Rabochie Leningrada, Khar'kova, Kazani i Ivanovo-Voznesenska o 'Klope',' *Rabochaia gazeta,* 51 (March 2, 1929).

464. ——. "Klop," *Sovremennyi teatr,* 2 (Jan. 8, 1929).

465. ——. " 'Klop' Maiakovskogo v GosTIM,e. Chto govoriat khudozhniki. I. Kukryniksy (epizody 1-4), II. A. Rodchenko (epizody 5-9), *Sovremennyi teatr,* 7 (Feb. 12, 1929).

466. ——. "Rabkory o 'Klope'," *Sovremennyi teatr,* 10 (March 5, 1929).

467. ——. "Novoe v teatre Meierkhol'da," *Shkval* (Odessa), 2 (Jan. 12, 1929).

468. ——. " 'Klop' u teatri Meierkhol'da," *Shkval* (Odessa), March 17, 1929.

469. ——. "Govorit rabochii zritel' - 'Klop'," *Novyi zritel',* 14 (March 31, 1929).

470. ——. "Klop," *Trud,* 2 (Jan. 3, 1929).

471. ——. "Klop," *Radioslushatel',* 4 (1929).

472. ——. "V. Meierkhol'd o 'Klope'," *VM,* 34 (Feb. 11, 1929).

473. ——. "Rabochie zavoda 'Dinamo' o 'Klope'," *Rabochaia Moskva,* 46 (Feb. 24, 1929).

474. ——. " 'Klop' v teatre Meierkhol'da," *Smena,* Feb. 17, 1929.

475. ——. " 'Klop,' feericheskaia komediia V. Maiakovskogo. Gusudarstvennyi bol'shoi dramaticheskii teatr, filial," (L. 1929). [brochure]

476. ——. "Gastroli derzhteatru im. Vs. Meierkhol'da, 'Klop'," *Proletars'ka pravda* (Kiev) Aug. 16, 1929.

477. ——. "K postanovke 'Klopa' Maiakovskogo," *Kievskii proletarii,* Aug. 15, 1929.

478. ——. " 'Klop' v teatre Meierkhol'da," *Vlast' truda* (Minusinsk), Feb. 27, 1929.

479. ——. "Novoe v teatre Meierkhol'da," *Vechernie isvestiia* (Odessa), Jan. 3, 1929.

480. ——. "Klop," *Krasnyi Oktiabr'* (Syzran'), March 6, 1929.

481. ——. " 'Klop'. Novaia p'esa VI. Maiakovskogo. Po telefonu iz Moskvy," *Vechernee radio* (Khar'kov), Jan. 2, 1929.

482. ——. "Novaia p'esa Maiakovskogo" (comments by Meyerhold), LG, 29 (Nov. 4, 1929), 3.

483. ——. "Novaia p'esa Maiakovskogo," *Tverskaia pravda,* Nov. 5, 1929.

484. ——. "Vs. Meierkhol'd o 'Bane' V. Maiakovskogo," *Brianskii rabochii,* Dec. 1, 1929.

485. ——. "Novaia p'esa Maiakovskogo," *Rabochii klich* (Riazan'), Dec. 14, 1929.

1930

486. A., L. "Maiakovskii v teatre i na estrade. Na vystavke '20 let Maiakovskogo'," *Rabochii teatr* (L.), 14 (March 12, 1930).

487. Andreev, N. "Rabochie o 'Bane'," *Rabochii teatr* (L.), 9 (Feb. 16, 1930).

488. Anisimov, I. "Puti razvitiia Maiakovskogo," *Literatura i marksizm,* 3 (1930), 3-23.

489. Aramilev, V. "O Vladimire Maiakovskom," *Russkii iazyk v sovetskoi shkole,* 3 (1930), 196-202.

490. Aristov-Litvak. "Biurakratizm pod 'udarami' kartonnogo mecha. ('Bania' v dramatich. teatre Nardoma)," *Leningradskaia pravda,* 33 (Feb. 3, 1930).

491. Aristov-Litvak. "Kritika nashei kritiki," *Leningradskaia pravda,* March 25, 1930.

492. Aseev, N. "Kak chitat' Maiakovskogo," *Izbrannye proizvedeniia* (M.-L. 1930), 12-23.

493. Averbakh, L. "Pamiati Maiakovskogo," NLP, 9 (1930), 5-13. Reprinted as a separate brochure (M. 1930), 32 pp; in an enlarged second ed. (M.-L. 1931), 48pp; and in *Bor'ba za metod* (M.-L. 1931), 179-95.

494. B., V. " 'Bania' v teatre im. Meierkhol'da," *Rabochii i teatr* (L.), 18 (April 1, 1930).

495. Bek. "Vystuplenie obyvatelia," *Molodoi leninets* (Saratov), 143 (June 29, 1930).

496. Berezark, I. "Maiakovskii na stsene," *Pioner,* 19 (1930).

497. Beskin, O. "Rannii Maiakovskii," *Literatura i iskusstvo,* 1 (1930), 68-90. Reprinted in his *Tvorcheskii put' Maiakovskogo* (Voronezh, 1931), 3-47.

498. Bespalov, I. "Put' Maiakovskogo," PR, 3 (1930), 5-7.

499. Bespalov, I. "Iz temy o Maiakovskom," KN, 7 (1930), 185-95. Reprinted in his *Stat'i o literature* (M. 1959), 36-59.

500. Bespalov, I. "Put' Maiakovskogo," KN, 9-10 (1930), 190-202.

501. Bromberg, A. "Obrazy goroda u Maiakovskogo," Russkii iazyk v sovetskoi shkole, 3 (1930), 134-43.

502. Bukhshtab, B., review of "Slony v komsomole," Zvezda, 1 (1930).

503. Charov, A. " 'Bania'. Teatr imeni Meierkhol'da," Komsomol'skaia pravda, 66 (March 22, 1930), 4.

504. Chereiskii, L. "Iz rabkorskikh otzyvov. 'Bania' Maiakovskogo," KG, evening, April 3.

505. Chumandrin, M. "Neskol'ko slov o Maiakovskom," Vladimir Maiakovskii (Odnodnevnaia gazeta), April 24, 1930.

506. Dankman, A. "Za poslednei rabotoi," Rabochii i iskusstvo, 22 (April 20, 1930).

507. Dinamov, S. "Tvorcheskii metod Maiakovskogo," O, 12 (1930), 187-200.

508. Dreiden, S. " 'Bania' V. Maiakovskogo v teatre Gos. Nardoma," Rabochii i teatr, 7 (1930).

509. Dukor, I. "Magistrali Maiakovskogo," O, 9 (1930), 183-199.

510. Embe. "Udar po obyvateliu. 'Klop,' teatr im. Karla Marksa," Molodoi leninets (Saratov), 142 (June 27, 1930).

511. Ermilov, V. "O nastroeniiakh melkoburzhuaznoi 'levizny' v khudozhestvennoi literature," Pr, 67 (March 9, 1930). 4.

512. Ermilov, V. "O trekh oshibkakh tov. Meierkhol'da," VM, 62 (March 17, 1930).

513. Ermilov, V. "O V. Maiakovskom," NLP, 8 (1930), 2-3.

514. Fel'dman, K. " 'Moskva gorit' (I Gostsirk)," Rabochaia Moskva, May 7, 1930.

515. Fevral'skii, A. "Maiakovskii i teatr," Sovetskii teatr, 2 (1930).

516. Fevral'skii, A. "Bania," Revoliutsiia i kul'tura, 9-10 (1930), 117.

517. F. K. V. "Maiakovskii i kino," VM, 88 (April 17, 1930).

518. F-skii, A. " '1905 god' Maiakovskogo," Rabochii i iskusstvo, 25 (May 5, 1930).

519. Gel'fand, M. "Glavnoe v oblike Maiakovskogo," PR, 3 (1930), 7-9.

520. Gets, S. "Znamenonosets revoliutsionnogo teatra," Proletarii (Khar'kov), Apr. 20, 1930.

521. Goncharova, N. " 'Bania' V. Maiakovskogo," Rabochaia gazeta, 65 (March 21, 1930).

522. Goncharova, N. "S legkim parom," Ekran, April 5, 1930.

523. Gor'kii, M. "O solitere," Nashi dostizheniia, 6 (1930). Reprinted in his Sob. soch., vol. 25 (M. 1953), 182-83.

524. Gr., K. "Teatr im. Meierkhol'da, 'Bania'," Bor'ba (Volgograd), 158 (July 12, 1930).

525. Grinval'd, Ia. "Klop," Povolzhskaia pravda (Saratov), 143 (June 27, 1930).

526. Grossman-Roshchin, I. "Tezisy i tvorchestvo Vl. Maiakovskogo," O, 5-6 (1930), 243-256; and in NLP, 11 (1930), 20-34.

527. Gvozdev, A. "Maiakovskii i teatr," KG, evening, 92 (April 19, 1930).

528. Gvozdev, A. " 'Moskva gorit' v moskovskom Gostsirke," Rabochii i teatr, 27 (May 16, 1930), 10-11.

529. Iankovskii, M. "Dve prem'ery," Rabochii i teatr, 18 (April 1, 1930).

530. Is. "Maiakovskii i tsirk," LG-Komsomol'skaia pravda, evening, April 17, 1930.

531. Khrapchenko, M. "Vl. Maiakovskii," Russkii iazyk v sovetskoi shkole, 4 (1930), 28-44.

532. Kon, F. "O Maiakovskom," Komsomol'skaia pravda, 86 (April 15, 1930).

533. Kostrov, T. " 'Bania' v teatre Meierkhol'da," Rabochii i iskusstvo, 16 (March 20, 1930).

534. Kuznetsov, E. " 'Bania' i Narodnyi dom," KG, evening, 26 (Feb. 31. 1930).

535. Kuznetsov, E. "Vtorichno o 'Bane'," KG, evening, 65 (March 19, 1930).

536. Linev, Iu. "Bania," Nasha gazeta, March 28, 1930.

537. Litovskii, O. "Dognat'! (Teatral'naia zima 1930)," Molodaia gvardiia, 9 (1930).

538. Liutse, V. " V. V. Maiakovskii i teatr," Stroika (L.), 7 (1930) May 5.

539. Lunacharskii, A. "Zhizn' i smert'," Komsomol'skaia pravda, 91 (April 20, 1930), 3. Reprinted in his Sob. soch., vol. 2 (M. 1964), 477-83.

540. Mamontov, R. "Shliakh entuziastiv," Zoria (Dnepropetrovsk), 9 (1930).

541. Meierkhol'd, V. "O 'Bane' V. Maiakovskogo," VM, 59 (March 13, 1930).

542. Meierkhol'd, V. "O postanovke 'Bani' V. Maiakovskogo," *Rabochii i iskusstvo,* 15 (March 15, 1930).

543. Meierkhol'd, V. "Slovo o Maiakovskom," *Sovetskoe iskusstvo,* April 11, 1930.

544. Mokul'skii, S. "Maiakovskii-dramaturg," *Stroika* (L.), 7 (1930), May 5.

545. Ol'khovyi, B. "Poet sotsial'noi napravlennosti," *Molodaia gvardiia,* April, 1930, 67-70.

546. P., M. " 'Bania.' Prem'era v Nardome," *Smena,* 29 (Feb. 5, 1930).

547. Pavlov, G. "Poet revoliutsii," *Sibirskie ogni,* 4 (1930), 106-108.

548. Polevoi, K. " 'Moskva gorit' (v I Moskovskom Gostsirke)," KG, evening, May 23, 1930.

549. Polonskii, V. "Maiakovskii," NM, 6 (1930), 173-98. Reprinted in his *O Maiakovskom* (M.-L. 1931).

550. Popov, A. "Maiakovskii v Pervoi obraztsovoi tipografii," *Pechatnik,* 10-11 (1930).

551. Popov-Dubovskii, V. "V poiskakh putei," Pr, 97 (April 8, 1930), 4.

552. Popov-Dubovskii, V. "Maiakovskii i teatr," *LG-Komsomol'skaia pravda,* special edition, April 17, 1930.

553. Popov-Dubovskii, V. "Maiakovskii i teatr," *Rabochii i teatr* (L.) 22 (April 21, 1930).

554. Rabkor, D. " '1905 god' (pantomima v I Gostsirke)," *Tsirk i estrada,* 12 (1930).

555. Radlov, S. "Maiakovskii v tsirke," *Rabochii i teatr* (L.) 22 (April 21, 1930).

556. Radlov, S. "O postanovke pantomimy Maiakovskogo 'Moskva gorit.' Pis'ma," LG, 19 (May 12, 1930), 4.

557. RAPP. "Somknem tesnee riady," NLP, 8 (1930), 1-2.

558. S., A. "Zadanie teatru im. Meierkhol'da i t. Maiakovskomu: 'Baniu' dorabotat'," VM, 73 (March 31, 1930).

559. S., G. "Klop (1 Gosdramteatr)," *Kommunist* (Astrakhan'), 106 (May 15, 1930).

560. Saianov, V. *Nachala stikha* (L. 1930), 71-84.

561. Selivanovskii, A. "Svintsovo-tiazhelye stikhi," NLP, 9 (1930), 16-18.

562. Severnyi, G. "Shag vpered. 'Klop' v klube pishchevikov," *Na smenu* (Sverdlovsk), Feb. 14, 1930.

563. Sharo, Iu. "Desiati tysiach revoliutsionnykh proklamatsii (posmertynye stikhi VI. Maiakovskogo," KG, evening, 93 (April 21, 1930).

564. Tanin, B. "O Maiakovskom," *Iunyi kommunist,* 9-10 (1930), 89-94.

565. Tasin, L. "Tri novykh postanovki," KG, evening, March 26, 1930.

566. Temp, E. "Bania," *Leninskaia smena* (Gor'kii), May 28, 1930.

567. Urazov, I. " 'Moskva gorit' v tsirke," *Tsirk i estrada,* 12 (1930).

568. Usievich, E., introduction to Mayakovsky's selected works (M.-L. 1930), 5-11.

569. V., review of "Tuda i obratno," *Plamia,* 2 (1930), 131.

570. Veisbrem, P. "Maiakovskii kak dramaturg-lirik," *Vladimir Maiakovskii* (L.), odnodnevnaia gazeta. April 24, 1930.

571. Verkhovskii, N. "Opiat' neudacha. 'Bania' v dramaticheskom teatre Nardoma," KG, morning, 27 (Feb. 2, 1930).

572. Vishenevsky, V. "Maiakovskii i kino," *Kino,* 24 (April 25, 1930).

573. Vitin, N. "O Maiakovskom" *Literaturnaia ucheba,* 3 (1930), 88-106.

574. V. S. "Maiakovskii i tsirk. ('Moskva gorit' v I Gostsirke)," VM, 95 (April 25, 1930).

575. Zagorskii, M. "Dialog o 'Bane,' " LG, March 31, 1930, p. 3.

576. Zagorskii, M. "Dramaturgiia Maiakovskogo," *Rabis,* 18 (1930).

577. Zagorskii, M. "Maiakovskii v Gostsirke. 'Moskva gorit'," LG, 17 (April 28, 1930), 4.

578. Zemenkov, B. *Udarnoe iskusstvo Okon Satiry* (M. 1930).

579. Zonin, A. "Dialektika tvorchestva V. Maiakovskogo," *Obrazy i deistvitel'nost'* (M. 1930), 51-61.

580. Zonin, A. "Dovol'no groshevykh istin," PR, 3 (1930), 9-11.

581. ——. "Peredovaia," PR, 3 (1930), 3.

582. ——. "Poet revoliutsii," PR, 3 (1930), 4-5.

583. ——. "Pisateli o Maiakovskom," KG, April 15, 1930.

584. ——. "Bania. Filial Gosudarstvennogo Bol'shogo dramaticheskogo teatra," (L. 1930), 15pp.

585. ——. "Maiakovskii v teatre," *Rabochiii zritel'* (Baku), 16 (April 20, 1930).

586. ——. "K priezdu teatra im. Meierkhol'da," *Nizhegorodskaia kommuna,* 102 (May 5, 1930).

587. ——. "K priezdu teatra im. Meierkhol'da," interview with Meyerhold, *Severnyi rabochii* (Iaroslavl'), April 16, 1930.

588. ——. " 'Bania' neponiatna. Teatr Meierkhol'da dolzhen prisposobit' p'esu dlia massovogo zritelia," *Gudok,* 82 (April 10, 1930).

589. ——. "Zapiski podannye na chitke 'Bani' v klube 'Proletarii'," *Sovetskii teatr,* 1 (1930).

590. ——. "Teatr, sluzhi kommunisticheskoi propagande," *Smena,* 13 (1930).

591. ——. "Moskovskie rabochie o 'Bane'," *Rabochii i teatr,* 19 (April 6, 1930).

592. ——. "Maiakovskii i tsirk," *Tsirk i estrada,* 12 (1930).

593. ——. "Chto govoriat rabochie o pantomime 'Moskva gorit'," VM, 95 (April 25, 1930).

594. ——. " 'Moskva gorit' (posmertnoe proizvedenie Maiakovskogo)," KG, evening, 89 (April 16, 1930).

595. ——. "V. V. Maiakovskii. Poet, grazhdanin, boets," *Kino,* 23 (April 20, 1930).

596. ——. "Maiakovskii i kino," *Kinofront* (L.), 16 (April 21, 1930).

ADDENDA - 1923-1930

597. Abikh, R. "Agitator Maiakovskii," LG, 16 (April 21, 1930), 2.

598. Ben, E. "Komakademiia pristupaet k izucheniiu Maiakovskogo," LG, 17 (April 28, 1930), 2.

599. Iurin, M. "Chelovek shirokogo golosa," LG, 17 (April 28, 1930), 2.

600. Kolosov, P. " 'Levyi marsh' Maiakovskogo" (Metodicheskii kommentarii), *Vestnik prosveshcheniia,* 3 (1927), 43-48.

601. Krasil'nikov, V. "Vladimir Maiakovskii," *Zemlia sovetskaia,* 4 (1930), 251.

602. Mandel'shtam, O. "Buria i natisk," *Russkoe iskusstvo,* 1 (1923), 75-82.

603. Popov-Dubovskii, V. "Bol'shoi poet velikogo vremeni," Pr, 170 (June 22, 1930), 5-6.

604. Shukher, V. "Vladimir Maiakovskii," *Rezets,* 13 (1930), 8-10.

605. Zorich, A. "Ob odnom 'intsidente'," NM, 12 (1928), 221-226.

INDEX OF AUTHORS

INDEX OF WORKS

A SELECTED BIBLIOGRAPHY OF WORKS BY AND ABOUT
ALEXANDER GRIN (1880-1932)

Compiled by

Nicholas J. L. Luker

INTRODUCTION

There is no published bibliography of Grin in Russian or in any other alnguage. However, the Lenin State Library in Moscow does hold an unpublished bibliography in Russian which is available for general reference. This is a 54-page document in type-script, entitled, "Grin, A. Bibliograficheskii ukazatel' " (Moscow, March 1960), privately compiled by A.M. Gurvich and Vl. M. Rossels. Though admirably full, it is not complete; it omits many of Grin's more obscure works and those discovered since 1960, as well as the numerous critical articles published during the last ten years.

The chief difficulty involved in compiling a bibliography of Grin is that he himself never kept any reliable record of either the titles or the places of publication of his works. Consequently many hitherto unknown tales and poems have been discovered by chance during the last decade in lesser known journals, many of them published only for a short time during the First World War.

This bibliography does not include: (i) critical articles which are of little value to the student of Grin, (ii) literary works (e.g., poems) about or dedicated to Grin, and (iii) articles and reviews relating to productions of Grin's work on stage and screen.

The most accessible and easily the most complete edition of Grin's work at present is the SOBRANIE SOCHINENII V SHESTI TOMAKH, Moscow: "Pravda," 1965. This contains a representative selection of Grin's prose work, including five of his six novels, a brief commentary on each story, useful essays by V. Vokhrov and Vl. Ros-sel's in Vol. 1 (see section 3 [iii] below), and an index in Volume 6.

In the lists below, places of publication of books are given in full, except for Moscow, St. Petersburg, Petrograd and Leningrad, which are indicated respectively by M., SPb., Pgd., and L.

1. COLLECTIONS OF GRIN'S WORK

1908   SHAPKA-NEVIDIMKA. (Rasskazy o revoliutsionerakh.) SPb.: "Nasha Zhizn'."
1910   RASSKAZY. Tom 1. SPb.: "Zemlia."
1913   SOB. SOCH. V 3-KH TOMAKH. SPb.: "Prometei."
        Tom 1. SHTURMAN "CHETYREKH VETROV."
        Tom 2. PROLIV BUR'.
        Tom 3. POZORNYI STOLB.
1915   ZAGADOCHNYE ISTORII. (Rasskazy.) SPb., Izd-vo zhurnala "Otechestvo."
       ZNAMENITAIA KNIGA. (Rasskazy.) SPb.: "Pechat'."
       PROISHESTVIE V ULITSE PSA. (Rasskazy.) SPb.: "Novyi satirikon."
1916   ISKATEL' PRIKLIUCHENII. (Rasskazy.) M.: "Severnie dni."
1922   BELYI OGON'. (Rasskazy.) Pgd.: "Poliarnaia zvezda."
1923   RASSKAZY. M.-Pgd.: GIZ.
1924   SERDTSE PUSTYNI. Sbornik rasskazov. M.: "Zemlia i fabrika."

1925 GLADIATORY. (Rasskazy.) M.: "Nedra."
NA OBLACHNOM BEREGU. (Rasskazy.) L.-M.: GIZ.
NA SKLONE KHOLMOV; PREDATEL'SKOE PIATNO. (Rasskazy.) M.: "Krasnaia zvezda."
1926 ZOLOTOI PRUD. (Rasskazy.) M.-L.: "Krasnyi proletarii."
ISTORIIA ODNOGO UBIISTVA. (Rasskazy.— M.-L.: "Zemlia i fabrika."
SHTURMAN "CHETYREKH VETROV." (Rasskazy.) M.-L.: "Zemlia i fabrika."
1927 BRAK AVGUSTA ESBORNA. (Rasskazy.) L.: "Priboi."
ZOLOTOI PRUD. (Rasskazy.) (2nd. ed.) M.-L.: "Krasnyi proletarii."
PO ZAKONU. (Rasskazy.) M.-L.: "Molodaia gvardia."
SHTURMAN "CHETYREKH VETROV." (Rasskazy.) 2nd ed. M.-L.: "Zemlia i fabrika."
POLNOE SOBRANIE SOCHINENII. V 15-ti tomakh. L.: "Mysl'." Vols. 1, 3, 4, 7, 9, 10, and 15 never published.
Tom 2. ZOLOTAIA TSEP'. (Roman.)
Tom 5. SHEST' SPICHEK. (Rasskazy.)
ISTORIIA ODNOGO UBIISTVA. (Rasskazy.) 2nd ed. M.-L.: "Zemlia i fabrika."
1928 VOKRUG SVETA. (Rasskazy.) M.: "Ogonek."
POLNOE SOBRANIE SOCHINENII. V 15-ti tomakh. L.: "Mysl'."
Tom 6. CHERNYI ALMAZ. (Rasskazy.)
Tom 11. VESELYI POPUTCHIK. (Rasskazy.)
1929 NA OBLACHNOM BEREGU. (Rasskazy.) M.: "Ogonek."
POLNOE SOBRANIE SOCHINENII. V 15-ti tomakh. L.: "Mysl'."
Tom 8. OKNO V LESU. (Rasskazy.)
Tom 12. KORABLI V LISSE. (Povesti i rasskazy.)
Tom 13. KOLONIIA LANFIER. (Rasskazy.)
Tom 14. Prikliucheniia Gincha. (Rasskazy.)
1930 OGON' I VODA. (Rasskazy.) M.: "Federatsiia."
1934 FANTASTICHESKIE NOVELLY. M.: "Sovetskii pisatel'."
1935 RASSKAZY. L.: "Izd-vo pisatelei v Leningrade."
1937 RASSKAZY, 1880-1932. M.: "Sovetskii pisatel'."
1940 RASSKAZY. M.-L.: "Detizdat."
1941 IZBRANNOE. M.: "Sovetskii pisatel'."
1956 IZRANNOE. M.: "Goslitizdat."
RASSKAZY. Sverdlovsk: "Knizhnoe izd-vo."
1957 IZBRANNOE. M.: "Pravda."
1958 ALYE PARUSA; IZBRANNYE PROIZVEDENIIA. Barnau: "Altaiskoe knizhnoe izd-vo."
1959 IZBRANNOE. Somferopol': "Krymizdat."
1965 SOBRANIE SOCHINENII V SHESTI TOMAKH. M.: "Pravda."
ALYE PARUSA; BEGUSHCHAIA PO VOLNAM; ZOLOTAIA TSEP'. M.: "Detskaia literatura."
1966 FANDANGO. (Roman. Povesti i rasskazy. Avtobiograficheskie ocherki.) Simferopol': Izd-vo "Krym."
DZHESSI I MORGIANA. (Oovest', novelly, roman.) L': "Lenizdat."
BELYI SHAR. (Rasskazy i povesti.) M.: "Molodaia gvardiia."
1969 IZBRANNOE. BEGUSHCHAIA PO VOLNAM; BLISTAIUSHCHII MIR; RASSKAZY. Simferopol': Izd-vo "Krym."

2. INDIVIDUAL WORKS BY GRIN

The list below comprises, in Russian alphabetical order, all Grin's known works, both in prose and verse, with the place of first publication wherever known. Exact page numbers are given whenever possible. Also included are tht titles of works which Grin is known to have written but which were either not found in the publications where they were first believed printed, or which still remain undiscovered in unspecified journals and periodicals, e.g. the tale ARESTNAIA PALATKA.

(N) after a title indicates a novel; (P) is a poem; and an asterisk before a title that the work so marked is also to be found in the most comprehensive collection of Grin's work published—A.S. Grin, SOBRANIE SOCHINENII V SHESTI TOMAKH, Biblioteka "Ogonek," Izd-vo "Pravda," Moscow, 1965. A question mark before a title indicated that there is some doubt as to whetner Grin wrote the work, while a question mark after a year, E.G. 1927?, shows that the year is inaccurate as a search failed to find the work in question. The word SBORNIK is abbreviated to sb., and PRILOZHENIE to prilozh.

The titles of the more common newspapers and periodicals in qhich Grin's work appeared have been abbreviated in accordance with the system below.

A	ARGUS
B	BICH
BV	BIRZHEVYE VEDOMOSTI
ChP	CHERTOVAIA PERECHNITSA
ChS	CHESTNOE SLOVO
DV	DVADTSATYI VEK
GER	GERKULES
Kr.N	KRASNAIA NIVA
Kr.Nov'	KRASNAIA NOV'
KM.	KRASNYI MILITSIONER
MUKH	MUKHOMOR
N	NIVA
NM	NOVYI MIR
NS	NOVYI SATIRIKON
NSS	NEDELIA SOVREMENNOGO SLOVA
NZh	NOVYI ZHURNAL DLIA VSEKH
OG	OGONEK
PE	PETROGRADSKOE EKHO
PL	PLAMIA
PLI	PETROGRADSKII LISTOK
SR	SOLNTSE ROSSII
SZ	SINII ZHURNAL
SZh	SVOBODNYI ZHURNAL
VP	VSEMIRNAIA PANORAMA

AVIATOR-LUNATIK, DV, No. 37 (1915), p. 12
AVTOBIOGRAFICHESKAIA POVEST', ZVEZDA, Nos. 2, 3, 4, 9 (1931).
AKVAREL', Kr.N, No. 26 (1928), pp. 4-5.
AKULA, DV, No. 40 (1915), pp. 11-12.
ALMAZY, DV, No. 25 (1915), pp. 12-13.
*ALYE PARUSA (N), M.-Pgd.: "Izd-vo L.D. Frenkel'," 1923.
*APEL'SINY, BV (24 June 1907).
ARESTNAIA PALATKA. Not found. Believed written between 1908 and 1912.
ARMIANIN TINTOS, DV, No. 47 (1915), p. 7.
ARKHIMED. MS. of this believed to be in archive of Pul'kin.
ASSAKRIFAKS. Believed published in PLAMIA, 1919. Not found in numbers for that

year.
*ATAKA, DV, No. 28 (1915), p. 13.
ATU EGO! (P), B, No. 5 (1918), p. 2.
BALKON, SR, No. 25 (1913), pp. 13-16.
BARKA NA ZELENOM KANALE, VP, No. 27 (1909), pp. 1-7.
*BARKHATNAIA PORT'ERA, Kr.Nov', No. 5 (1933), pp. 177-82.
*BATALIST SHUAN, OG, No. 37 (1915), pp. 6-7, 10-15.
*BEGUSHCHAIA PO VOLNAM (N), M.-L.: "Zemlia i fabrika," 1928.
BEZ VESTI PROPAVSHII, VOINA, No. 38 (1915), p. 11.
*BEZNOGI, OG, No. 7 (1924), pp. 4, 6-8.
BEZ PUBLIKI, GER, No. 6 (1914), pp. 12-13.
*BELYI SHAR, TOVARISHCH TERENTII, (Sverdlovsk), No. 8 (1924), p. 9.
BITVA V VOZDUKHE, DV, No. 10 (1915), pp. 5-6.
*BLISTAIUSHCHII MIR (N), Kr.N, Nos. 20-30 (1923).
BLONDINKA, DV, No. 26 (1915), pp. 12-13.
BLOKHA I EE TEN' (P), NS, No. 4 (1915), p. 6.
?BOI BYKOV, DV, No. 44, p. 13. Signed Grinevich.
*BOI NA SHTYKAKH, DV, No. 6 (1915), p. 10.
BOL'NOI VOLK (P), PL, No. 64 (1919), p. 2.
BOL'SHOE SCHAST'E MALEN'KAGO BORTSA, GER, Nos. 2-3 (1916), pp. 9-10.
BOR'BA S PULEMETOM, ZHENSHCHINA, No. 4 (1915), pp. 9-10.
BOCHKA PRESNOI VODY' ZNANIE-SILA, No. 7 (1930), pp. 7-8.
*BRAK AVGUSTA ESBORNA, Kr.N, No. 13 (1926), pp. 4-6.
BRAT I SESTRA (P), DV, No. 4 (1915), p. 12.
BRODIAGA (P), OBRAZOVANIE, No. 6 (1908), p. 80.
BRODIAGA, ZHENSHCHINA, No. 24 (1914), pp. 11-12.
*BRODIAGA I NACHAL'NIK TIUR'MY, in sb. SERDTSE PUSTYNI, M.-L': 1928.
BUDUSHCHIE DACHNIKI (P), NS, No. 11 (1915), p. 8
BUKA-NEVEZHA, NS, No. 16 (1918), p. 15.
VANIA RAZSERDILSIA NO CHELOVECHESTVO, ChP, No. 4 (1918), p. 3.
V GOSTIAKH U PRIIATELIA, NUKH, No. 4 (1922), p. 3.
VESELAIA BABOCHKA, PLI (19 September 1916).
VESELYI MERTVETS, VMESTO KNIGI, No. 1 (1918), p. 3.
*VESELYI POPUTCHIK, LENINGRAD, No. 4 (1924), pp. 19-24.
*VETKA OMELY, Kr.N, No. 21 (1929), pp. 4-5.
VECHER (Eskiz), VP, No. 33 (1912), pp. 1-2.
VECHNAIA PULIA, DV, No. 26 (1915), p. 10.
*V ITALIIU, BV (5 December 1906).
VOENNAIA KHRONIKA (P), NS, No. 8 (1915), p. 10.
VOENNYI LETCHIK (P), NS, No. 35 (1914), p. 7.
VOENNYI UZOR (P), VOINA I GEROI, No. 4 (1914), pp. 10-12.
VOZVRASHCHENIE, RESPUBLIKANETS, Nos. 37-8 (1917), pp. 6-8.
*VOZVRASHCHENIE, Kr.N, No. 49 (1924), pp. 176-8.
*VOZVRASHCHENNYI "CHAIKI," (as SEREBRO IUGA), VES' MIR, No. 22 (1910).
*VOZVRASHCHENNYI AD, SOVREMENNYI MIR, No. 12 (1915).
*VOZDUSHNYI KORABL', VP, No. 2 (1909).
VOKRUG RAZVALIN, NS, No. 18 (1917), pp. 10-11.
*VOKRUG SVETA, RUSSKAIA VOLIA, (31 December 1916).
VOKRUG TSENTRAL'NYKH OZER, M.-L.: "Molodaia gvardiia," 1927.
VOLDYR', ILI DOBRYI PAPA, ESHAFOT, No. 3 (1917), p. 5.
VOLCHEK, NIVA, No. 39 (1915), pp. 721-22, 724.
VOLSHEBNOE BEZOBRAZIE, PL, No. 52 (1919), pp. 13-14.
VOLSHEBNYI EKRAN, SEVERNAIA ZVEZDA, No. 3 (1915), p. 54.

*VOR V LESU, Kr. N, No. 52 (1929), pp. 2-3.
VOSPIMINANIIA NA EKRANE, DV, No. 46 (1914), pp. 5-7.
VOSSTANIE, VOL'NOST', (SPb.), No. 3 (1917), p. 2.
*VPERED I NAZAD, ChS (1 and 2 August 1918).
VRAGI, SVOBODNAIA ROSSIIA, No. 33 (1917), p. 3.
*VRAGI, OG, No. 14 (1917), pp. 216-19.
V RAZLIVE, MIR, No. 5 (1910), pp. 344-46.
*VSADNIK BEZ GOLOVY (As RUKOPIS' XVIII STOLETIIA), SZ, No. 26 (1913).
*V SNEGU, VP, No. 62 (1910).
*VSTRECHA, DV, No. 47 (1914), pp. 3-4.
VSTRECHA (P), NS, No. 12 (1915), p. 7.
*VSTRECHI I PRIKLIUCHENIIA. Place of first publication unknown. Varian VSTRE-
    CHI I ZAKLIUCHENIIA published in NEVA, No. 8 (1960), pp. 144-50.
VYDUMKA EPITRAMA, DV, No. 42 (1915), p. 14.
VYDUMKA PARIKMAKHERA, ChS, No. 5 (1918), pp. 3-5.
VYSOKAIA TEKHNIKA, BV, Nos. 15850, 15852, 15854, 15856, 15858 (1916).
VYSTUP SKALY, OG, No. 8 (1917), pp. 117-19.
GAREM KHAKI-BEIA, DV, No. 44 (1915), p. 12.
*GATT, VITT I REDOTT, in AL'MANAKH DLIA DETEI I IUNOSHESTVA, (prilozh.
    k kr.n (1924), pp. 55-64.
*GENIAL'NYI IGROK, KRASNAIA GAZETA (8 March 1917), pp. 7-8.
GLAVNYI VINOVNIK, DV, No. 19 (1917), pp. 7-8.
*GLADIATORY, PETROGRAD, No. 1 (1923), pp. 11-12.
*GLUKHAIA TROPA (as GLUKHAIA TREVOGA), SR, No. 28 (1913).
*GNEV OTSA, Kr.N, No. 41 (1928), pp. 2-3.
GOLOSA I ZVUKI, ZHENSHCHINA, No. 1 (1915), p. 12.
*GOLOS I GLAZ, OG, No. 25 (1923).
GOLOS SIRENY. Place of first publication unknown. In Sb. PO ZAKONU. M.-L., 1927.
GORBUN, OG, No. 32 (1908), pp. 6-7.
GOSTINITSA VECHERNIKH OGNEI, SZ, No. 47 (1912), pp. 2-4.
*GOST'. Written not later than 1907. Believed first published in sb. SHAPKA-NEVI-
    DIMKA, SPb., 1908.
*GRAN'KA I EGO SYN, NSS, No. 260 (1913).
*GRIF, KM, No. 1 (1921), pp. 10-12.
GROZNOE PORUCHENIE, SZ, No. 14 (1918), pp. 4-5.
DAITE! (P), NS, No. 36 (1917), p. 3.
*DALEKII PUT', (as GORNYE PASTUKHI V ANDAKH), in lit. appendix to journal
    NIVA, for September, 1913.
DACHA BOL'SHOGO OZERA, BV morning edition (15, 16, 17, 18 November 1909).
DVA BRATA, DV, No. 14 (1915), pp. 6-7.
DVA MUZHIKA (P), Maiak (26 September 1908), p. 4.
DVA OBESHCHANIIA, Kr.N, No. 17 (1927), pp. 5-7.
DVOINIK PLEREZA, DV, No. 41 (1915), p. 14.
DELO S BELOI PTITSEI ILI BELAIA PTITSA I RAZRUSHENNYI KOSTEL, ZHEN-
    SHCHINA, No. 1 (1914), p. 11.
DZHESSI I MORGIANA (N), L.: "Priboi," 1929.
*DIKAIA MEL'NITSA, DV, No. 31 (1915), p. 10.
DIPLOMATICHESKAIA SEKRETNAIA PEREPISKA, B, No. 3 (1918), p. 10.
DON-KIKHOT (P), NS, No. 6 (1915), p. 7.
*DOROGA NIKUDA (N), M.: "Federatsiia," 1930.
DRUG CHELOVEKA, DV, No. 30 (1915), pp. 11-12.
*DUEL', DV, No. 28 (1915), p. 7.
DUKHOVNAIA VANNA, NS, No. 5 (1918).

*D'IABOL ORANZHEVYKH VOD, PERVYI AL'MANAKH IZD-VA "SOIUS'," SPb. 1913.
*EROSHKA, MAIAK (2 October 1908).
ZHELEZNAIA PTITSA, ZHENSHCHINA, No. 1 (1915), pp. 7-8.
*ZHELTYI GOROD, DV, No. 16 (1915), p. 6.
?ZHENSKAIA TAINA (P), DV, No. 45 (1915), p. 10. Signed Sasha Grigor'ev.
*ZHIZNEOPISANIIA VELIKIKH LIUDEI, SR, No. 51 (1913).
*ZHIZN' GNORA, NZ, No. 10 (1912).
ZHURNALIST V BEDE (Basnia), NS, No. 42 (1914), p. 10.
*ZABYTOE, BV (11 October 1914).
ZAVESHCHANIE PESSIMISTA, VP, No. 126 (1911), pp. 14-15.
ZA GAZETOI (P), NS, No. 15 (1918), p. 6.
*ZAGADKA PREDVIDENNOI SMERTI, SZ, No. 9 (1914).
*ZAKOLOCHENNYI DOM, EKRAN, No. 23 (1924), pp. 2-4.
ZAPUTANNYI KRUG. Place of first publication unknown. In sb. SHEST' SPICHEK, I., 1927.
ZA REKOI, V RUMIANOM SVETE. . . , (P), NZ, No. 16 (1910), cols. 3-4.
ZA RESHETKAMI, PLI, No. 265 (1916), p. 9.
ZARIA (P), PE, No. 17 (1918).
*ZASLUGA RIADOVOGO PANTELEEVA. First publication almost all destroyed. In SOB. SOCH. V SHESTI TOMAKH, M., 1965, Vol 1, pp. 431-45.
ZAKHVAT ZNAMENI, DV, No. 50 (1914), p. 6.
ZVERI O VOINE (P), NS, No. 2 (1915), p. 10.
ZVER' ROSHFORA, DV, No. 22 (1915), pp. 6-7.
*ZELENAIA LAMPA, Kr.N, Nos. 23-24 (1930), p. 11.
ZEMLIA I VODA, A, No. 14 (1914).
*ZIMNIAIA SKAZKA, SR, No. 47 (1912).
*ZMEIA, Kr.N, No. 42 (1926), pp. 3-5.
ZNAI NASHIKH (Basnia), NS, No. 40 (1914), p. 3.
*ZOLOTOI PRUD, Place of first publication unknown. In sb. ZAGADOCHNYE ISTO-RII, SPb., 1915.
*ZURBAGANSKII STRELOK, N, Nos. 43, 44, 45, 46 (1913), pp. 853-54, 872-74, 890-91, 911-13 respectively.
*IVA, PETROGRAD, No. 11 (1923), pp. 1-7, 10-13.
IGRA, ZHENSHCHINA, No. 2 (1915), p. 10.
*IGRUSHKA, NSS, No. 14 (1908).
*IGRUSHKI, DV, No. 9 (1915), pp. 11-12.
IDIOT, B, No. 17 (1916), p. 3.
I DLIA MENIA PRIDET VESNA, GER, No. 9 (1914), p. 19.
IZ DNEVNIKA (P), DEN' POEZII V KRYMU, Simferopol': "Krym," 1964. pp. 120-22.
IZ ZAPISNOI KNIZHKI KHIMIKA (P), MUKH, No. 1 (1922), p. 5.
IZ ZAPISOK AMNISTIROVANNOGO. Written 1906. Perhaps never published.
IZMENA, Kr.N, No. 2 (1929).
IZ PAMIATNOI KNIZHKI SYSHCHIKA, VP, No. 29 (1912), p. 8.
*IMENIE KHONSA, VES' MIR, No. 8 (1910).
INTERESNAIA FOTOGRAFIIA, DV, No. 39 (1915), p. 7.
ISKAZHENIIA (P), ChP, No. 8 (1918), p. 2.
*ISKATEL' PRIKLIUCHENII, SOVREMENNYI MIR, No. 1 (1915), pp. 1-26.
ISPORCHENNYI APPETIT (P), GER, No. 16 (1914), pp. 10-11.
ISTERIKA (P), ZHURNAL DLIA VSEKH, No. 3 (1918), p. 3.
*ISTORIIA ODNOGO UBIISTVA. In sb. RASSKAZY, Tom 1, SPb., 1910.
ISTORIIA ODNOGO IASTREBA, VSEMIRNYI SLEDOPYT, No. 2 (1930), pp. 146-52.
ISTORIIA TAURENA, SZ, No. 6 (1913).

*ISTREBITEL', PL, No. 60 (1919), pp. 4-7.
KAZHDYI SAM MILLIONER, DV, No. 19 (1917), pp. 12-14.
*KAK BY TAM NE BYLO, OG, No. 31 (1923).
KAK MY RABOTAEM? SO SVEZHEI GOLOVOI, ZHURNAL ZHURNALOV, No. 5
    (1915), p. 8.
KAK SILACH RYZHII DZHON BOROLSIA S KOROLEM, GER, No. 13 (1914), p. 12.
KAK IA BYL TSAREM, B, No. 4 (1918), p. 4.
*KAK IA UMIRAL NA EKRANE, PLI (9 and 10 August 1916).
*KANAT. In Sb. BELYI OGON', Pgd., 1922.
KAPITAN, OG, No. 43 (1908), pp. 6-7.
*KAPITAN DIUK, SOVREMENNYI MIR, No. 8 (1915).
KAPRICHCHIO, NS, No. 22 (1915), p. 12.
*RARANTIN. In Sb. SHAPKA-NEVIDIMKA, Spb., 1908.
KARNAVAL' OG, No. 15 (1918), pp. 9-12.
*KACHAIUSHCHAIASIA SKALA, DV, No. 25 (1915), p. 7.
KINZHAL I MASKA, DV, No. 30 (1915), p. 7.
*KIRPICH I MUZYKA. In sb. SHAPKA-NEVIDIMKA, SPb., 1908.
*KLUBNYI ARAP, OG, No. 1 (1918), pp. 10, 12-16.
KNIAZ BIULOV (P), NS, No. 13 (1915), p. 10.
KOLOKOLA, DV, No. 13 (1917), p. 3.
*KOLONIIA LANFIER, NZ, No. 15 (1910), pp. 25-84.
KOLOS'IA, ChS, No. 4 (1918).
*KOMENDANT PORTA, Kr.Nov', No. 5 (1933), pp. 182-6.
*KORABLI V LISSE. In sb. BELYI OGON', Pgd., 1922.
KOROL'NA VOINE (P), OG, No. 4 (1915), p. 12.
*KOSHMAR, SLOVO (1 and 8 March 1909).
KOSHMARNYI SLUCHAI, DV, No. 8 (1915), p. 5.
KRASNYE BRYZGI. Exact date and place of first (and only) publication unknown.
    Probably autumn, 1917.
*KRYSOLOV, ROSSIIA, No. 3 (1924).
*KSENIIA TURPANOVA, RUSSKOE BOGATSTVO, No. 3 (1912).
LABIRINT, BV, No. 15424 (1916), morning edition.
LAKEI PLIUNUL V KUSHAN'E, ChP, No. 1 (1918), p. 2.
*LEAL' U SEBIA DOMA, DV, No. 52 (1915), pp. 12-14.
*LEBED', NSS, No. 7 (1908).
LEGENDA VOINY, ZHENSHCHINA, No. 23 (1914), pp. 3-5.
*LEGENDA O FERGIUSONE, SMENA, No. 7 (1928), pp. 6-7.
LEGCHE STALO, ChP, No. 3 (1918), p. 1.
LESNAIA DRAMA, VP, No. 31 (1911), pp. 1-6.
LETAIUSHCHII NOZH, DV, No. 11 (1915), pp. 6-7.
LI, SVOBODNAIA ROSSIIA, No. 19 (1917), pp. 2-3.
*LICHNYI PRIEM, SMENA, No. 20 (1926), pp. 8-9.
*LOSHADINAIA GOLOVA, Kr.N, No. 18 (1923).
*LUZHA BORODATOI SVIN'I, NSS, No. 247 (1912).
*LUNNYI SVET, NP, No. 95 (1911).
*LIUBIMYI, BV (18 November 1907).
LIUBOVNITSA PRISTAVA, DV, No. 17 (1917), pp. 3-4.
L'VINYI UDAR, OG, No. 2 (1916), pp. 5, 8-12.
*MALEN'KII ZAGOVOR (as ISTORIIA ODNOGO ZAGOVORA), NZ, No. 4 (1909).
*MALEN'KII KOMITET, NSS, No. 20 (1908).
*MALINNIK IAKOBSONA, VP, No. 73 (1910).
MAN'IAK. In sb. CHERNYI ALMAZ, L., 1928.
*MARAT, TRUDOVOI PUT', No. 5 (1907).

MARIONETKA, NOVOE SLOVO, No. 9 (1910), pp. 57-60.
*MAT V TRI KHODA, BODROE SLOVO, No. 4 (1908), cols. 39-48.
MAIATNIK VESY, SVOBODNAIA ROSSIIA, No. 15 (1917), p. 3.
MAIATNIK DUSHI (as VOZVRASHCHENIE), in RESPUBLIKANETS, Nos. 37-8
    (1917), p. 6.
MEBLIROVANNYI DOM (as ROMANTICHESKOE UBIISTOVO), VSEMIRNAIA
    NOV', No. 9 (1916), p. 2.
MEDVED' I NEMETS, DV, No. 17 (1915), p. 6.
*MEDVEZH'YA OKHOTA, OG, No. 48 (1915).
MELODIIA (P), SR, No. 386 (1917), p. 14.
MERTVYE ZA ZHIVYKH, SZ, No. 3 (1913), p. 2.
MOLODAIA SMERT' (P), AL'MANAKH 17, SPb., (Izd-vo "Russkaia skoropechatnia."),
    1909, p. 74.
MOLCHANIE ,' VOKRUG SVETA, No. 30 (1930), pp. 21-23.
MONOLOG, NS, No. 30 (1917), p. 6.
MONTE-KRISTO, MUKH, No. 5 (1922), p. 3.
MORSKOI BOI, DV, No. 47 (1915), p. 12.
MOTYGA (P), NZ, No. 10 (1909), pp. 15-16.
MRAK, PLI, No. 79 (1916).
NA BIRZHE, RUSSKII FIGARO, (Prilozh. k PROBUZHDENIE) in PROBUZHDENIE,
    No. 20 (1907), p. 31.
NAD BEZDNOI, DV, No. 21 (1915), p. 6.
*NA DOSUGE, TOVARISHCH (20 July 1907).
NAEMNYI UBIITSA, DV, No. 37 (1915), p. 13.
NAIVNYI TUSSALETTO, A, No. 8 (1913), pp. 71-76.
*NAKAZANIE, in literary appendix, No. 100 to PLI (from 15 December 1916).
NAKHODKA, VP, No. 45 (1910), pp. 4-10.
*NA OBLACHNOM BEREGU, Kr.N, No. 28 (1924), pp. 666-72.
NA OSTROVE, VP, No. 66 (1910), pp. 1-2.
*NA SKLONE KHOLMOV, PROBUZHDENIE, No. 11 (1910).
*NASLEDSTVO PIK-MIKA, in sb. ZAGADOCHNYE ISTORII, SPb. (1915).
NEDOTROGA (unfinished novel), (extract: ISTORIIA DEGZHA), TRIDTSAT' DNEI,
    No. 3 (1935), pp. 17-28.
NEDOTROGA (extract, different from above), OG, Nos. 2-3 (1936), p. 10.
NEDOTROGA (extracts from second chapter), LITERATURNOE NASLEDSTVO, No.
    74, (M. 1965), pp. 654-67.
NEZHNYI ROMAN, MUKH, No. 7 (1922), p. 3.
NEZAMERZAIUSHCHII KLIUCH (P), SR, No. 385 (1917), p. 15.
NEPOBEDIMYI, GER, Nos. 4-5 (1916), p. 5.
NEPROBIVAEMYI PANTSYR', DV, No. 5 (1915), p. 6.
NE SOVSEM UIASNIL, ChP, No. 5 (1918), p. 4.
NECHTO IZ DNEVNIKA, UTRO ROSSII, No. 65 (1916), p. 5.
NOVOGODNYI PRAZDNIK OTSA I MALEN'KOI DOCHERI, RASNAIA GAZETA
    (from 30 December 1922).
NOVYI TSIRK, SZ, No. 47 (1913).
NOCHLEG, VP, No. 21 (1909).
NOCHNYE GOSTI, NZ. Believed first published in 1917, but not found in numbers for
    that year.
NOCHNOE DEZHURSTVO, VP. Believed first published in 1918, but not found in
    numbers of VP for that year.
*NOCH', TRUDOVOI PUT', No. 6 (1907).
NOCH'IU, ZHENSHCHINA, No. 4 (1915), pp. 11-12.
*NOCH'IU I DNEM (as BOL'NAIA DUSHA), in NOVAIA ZHIZN', No. 3 (1915).

*NIAN'KA GLENAU, SMENA, No. 17 (1926), pp. 4-5.
OBEZ'IANA (P), NS, No. 32 (1917), p. 6.
OBEZ'IANA-SOPUN, in sb. BRAK AVGUSTA ESBORNA, L., 1927, pp. 127-34.
OGNENNAIA VODA, STREKOZA, No. 18 (1917), pp. 4-5.
*OGNENNAIA VODA, in sb. PO ZAKONU, M.-L., 1927.
*OGON' I VODA, SZ, No. 9 (1916).
ODIN' DEN' (autobiographical sketch), TRIDTSAT' DNEI, No. 10 (1927), p. 13.
ODIN IZ MNOGIKH, DV, No. 51 (1914), pp. 5-6.
OKNO V LESU, SLOVO (11 May 1909).
*"ONA" (as IGRA SVETA) in NASH DEN' (18 February 1908), shortened version.
     First full version in LITERATURNO-KHUDOZHESTVENNYI AL'MANAKH,
     No. 1, SPb., "Priboi," 1909.
OPASNYI PRYZHOK, DV, No. 38 (1915), p. 7.
ORGIIA, SVOBODNAIA ROSSIIA, No. 27 (1917), p. 1.
ORIGINAL'NYI SHPION, DV, No. 28 (1915), pp. 12-13.
O SPORTE, GER, No. 19 (1914), p. 10.
OSTROV, VOINA, No. 33 (1915), pp. 3-4.
*OSTROV RENO, NZ, No. 6 (1909).
OTKRYVATEL' ZAMKOV, OG, No. 34 (1929), pp. 6-7.
OTRAVLENNYI OSTROV (as SKAZKA DELKOGO OKEANA), OG, No. 36 (1916).
OTRYVOK IS FAUSTA, NS, No. 38 (1914), p. 6.
OTSTAVSHII VZVOD (P), PL, No. 41 (1919), p. 16.
*OTSHEL'NIK VINOGRADNOGO PIKA, BV (from 2 May 1916).
OTIAGOTENIE K UBIISTVU (as PRIZVANIE?), PLI (1916?).
OKHOTA V VOZDUKHE, DV, No. 18 (1915), pp. 6-7.
*OKHOTA NA MARBRUNA, DV, No. 29 (1915), pp. 6-7.
OKHOTA NA KHULIGANA, A, No. 6 (1915), pp. 23-30.
OKHOTNIK ZA MINAMI, DV, No. 5 (1915), p. 7.
O CHEM PELA LASTOCHKA (P), DV, No. 8 (1915), p. 10.
PAMIATI LEITENANTA SHMIDTA, NA VAKHTE (28 November 1928).
*PARI, Kr.Nov', No. 5 (1933), pp. 174-77.
*PASSAZHIR PYZHIKOV (as ZAIATS), VP, No. 2 (1912).
PASKHA NA PAROKHODE, UTRO SIBIRI, No. 142 (1910), p. 3.
PASYNKAM PRIRODY (P), ChP, No. 9 (1918), p. 2.
PAKHUCHII KUSTARNIK, SOVETSKAIA UKRAINA, No. 8 (1960), pp. 103-04.
PERVYI SNEG (P), NSS, No. 240 (1912), p. 3.
PETROGRAD OSEN'IU 1917, SR, No. 380 (1917), p. 10.
PESHKOM NA REVOLIUTSIIU, in Al'manakh REVOLIUTSIIA V PETROGRADE,
     Pgd., Izd-vo Delopol'skogo) 1917, pp. 15-24.
PIS'MO LITERATORA KHARITONOVA K DIADE V TAMBOV (P), BV (7 May 1915),
     p. 4, evening edition.
*PLEMIA SIURG, in book EZHEMESIACHNYE LITERATURNYE I POPILIARNO-
     NAUCHNYE PRILOZHENIIA K ZHURNALU NIVA NA 1913 G., No. 1 (SPb.,
     1913), cols 97-112.
PLIASKA SMERTI, DV, No. 9 (1915), pp. 6-7.
*POBEDITEL', Kr.N. No. 13 (1925), pp. 296-98.
PO BRACHNOMU OB' IAVLENIIU, LISTOK-KOPEIKA (SPb.), No. 1 (1909), p. 4.
*POVEST', OKONCHENNAIA BLAGODARIA PULE, OTECHESTVO, No. 5 (1914),
     short version. First full version in sb. ISKATEL' PRIKLIUCHENII (M., 1916).
*PODARENNAIA ZHIZN', (as IGROK), BV (from 18 December 1915).
POEDINOK, DV, No. 48 (1914), pp. 10-11.
*POEDINOK PREDVODITELEI, DV, No. 41 (1915).
*POZORNYI STOLB, BSEOBSHCHII ZHURNAL LITERATURY, Nos. 7-8 (1911).

'POKAIANNAIA RUKOPIS', (as KAK SILACH GANS PIKHGOL'TS SOKHRANIL ALMAZY GERTSOGA POMMERSI), GER, No. 11 (1914), p. 17.

POKOI, SOVREMENNYI MIR, No. 1 (1917), pp. 47-60.

PORYV (P), NS, No. 21 (1915), p. 8.

POSIDELI NA BEREGU, SOVETSKAIA UKRAINA, No. 8 (1960), pp. 101-03.

POSLEDNIE MINUTY RIABININA, SR, No. 4 (1913), pp. 2241-42.

POSHLOST', ZHURNAL DLIA VSEKH, No. 4 (1918), p. 3.

POETY IAPONTSY V PETROGRADE, NS, No. 29 (1917), pp. 6-7.

PREDSMERTNAIA ZAPISKA, DV, No. 13 (1915), pp. 6-7.

*PRESTUPLENIE OTPAVSHEGO LISTA, OG, No. 3 (1918), pp. 13-15.

PRIDESH' TY—I SCHAST'EM POVEET (P), in sb. PERED LITSOM ZHIZNI, M., Tipografiia "Zemlia," 1913, p. 153.

PRIZVANIE, RODINA, Nos. 21 and 22 (1916), pp. 245-58 and 257-60.

*PRIKAZ PO ARMII, KRASNAIA PANORAMA, No. 1 (1923), pp. 1-2.

PRIKLIUCHENIE, OG, No. 41 (1908), pp. 6-7.

PRIKLIUCHENIIA GINCHA, NOVAIA ZHIZN', Nos. 3 and 4 (1912), pp. 16-46 and 59-83.

*PRISHEL I USHEL (as POROKHOVOI POGREB), VES' MIR, No. 37 (1910).

*PRODAVETS SCHAST'IA, A, No. 9 (1913).

"PRODOLZHENIE SLEDUET," SZ, No. 5 (1917).

PROISHESTVIE V KVARTIRE G-ZHI SERIZ, A, No. 22 (1914), pp. 81-87.

*PROISHESTVIEW V ULITSE PSA, SLOVO (from 21 June 1909).

PROISHESTVIEW S CHASOVYM, DV, No. 16, p. 12.

*PROLIV BUR', NZ, No. 20 (1910).

*PROPAVSHEE SOLNTSE, DRASNAIA GAZETA (from 29 January 1923).

*PROKHODNOI DVOR, NSS, No. 232 (1912).

PRUSSKII RAZ' 'ESD, DV, No. 4 (1915), pp. 6-7. Version of SLUCHAI (see below).

*PTITSA KAM-BU, SEVERNAIA ZVEZDA, No. 10 (1915).

PUSTIAKI, NS, No. 15 (1918), p. 3.

*PUTESHESTVENNIK UI-F'IU-EOI, RASNAIA GAZETA, No. 105 (1923).

*PUT', A, No. 8 (1915), pp. 30-35.

P'ER I SURINE, SZ, No. 47 (1916), p. 12.

PIATNADTSATOE IIULIA, OTECHESTVO, Nos. 5-6 (1915), pp. 98-101.

RABOTA (P), NS, No. 47 (1915), p. 8.

RAZVEDCHIK, ZHENSHCHINA, No. 2 (1915), pp. 11-12.

RAZGOVOR, NS, No. 5 (1918), pp. 11 and 13.

RAI, ZVUKI ZHIZHNI, (Lit.-khudozh. al.manakh sovremennykh pisatelei), SPb., Izd-vo "Pushkinskaia skoropechatnia," 1909, pp. 65-88.

RANCHO "KAMENNYI STOLB," in sb. IANTARNAIA KOMNATA, L., "Detskaia literatura," 1961.

RAPSODIIA, ChP, No. 3 (1918), p. 2.

*RASSKAZ BIRKA (as RASSKAZ BIRKA O SVOEM PRIKLIUCHENII), MIR, No. 4, 1910.

RASSKAZ O STRANNOI SUD'BE, NSS, No 243 (1912), pp. 1-2.

RASSKAZ O KHRONOMETRE, VECHERNIAIA KRASNAIA GAZETA (1923).

REVNOST' I SHPAGA, DV, No. 44 (1915), p. 10.

REDAKTOR I PISATEL', NOVYI SATIRIKON, No. 45 (1914).

*REDKII FOTOGRAFICHESKII APPARAT (as OGNENNAIA STRELA), GER, No. 10 (1914).

*REKA, in sb. KNIGA RASSKAZOV, prilozh. k VES' MIR for 1910, SPb., Sipografiia Gaevskogo, 1910, pp. 167-73.

REKVIEM (P), NS, No. 2 (1918), p. 6.

*RENE, in sb. NA OBLACHNOM BEREGU, N.-M., 1925. WM (P), NS, No. 2 (1918), p. 6.

ROZHDENIE GROMA, VSEMIRNAIA NOV', No. 18 (1917, pp. 3-7.
ROZHDESTVENSKII LED (P), SR, No. 386 (1917), p. 10.
ROZOVYI PAVIL'ON, VECHERNIAIA KRASNAIA GAZETA (1923).
ROKOVOE MEST, ZHENSHCHINA, No. 5 (1915), p. 6.
*RUKA, BV (from 3 February 1908).
RUSALKI VOZDUKHA, PETROGRAD, No. 4 (1923), pp. 9, 11-12.
RYTSAR' MAL'IAR, OTECHESTVO, No. 15 (1915), pp. 2-5.
SAMOUBIISTVO, SVOBODNAIA ROSSIIA, No. 27 (1917), p. 1.
SAPOGI, VOROBEI? (1908?).
SARYN' NO KICHKU, MUKH, No. 3 (1922), p. 4.
SVAD'BA MASHI, ZHENSHCHINA, No. 9 (1915), pp. 3-4.
SVOEGO RODA—ANKETA (P), NS, No. 1 (1915), p. 6.
SDELAITE BABUSHKU! ChP, No. 7 (1918), p. 2.
*SERDTSE PUSTYNI, Kr.N, No. 14 (1923), pp. 12-13.
SERYI AVTOMOBIL', in sb. NA OBLACHNOM BEREGU, N.-M., 1925.
SER'EZNYI PLENNIK, DV, No. 19 (1915), p. 13.
*SILA NEPOSTIZHIMOGO, OG, No. 8 (1918), pp. 11-13.
SILA SLOVA, OTECHESTVO, No. 11 (1915), p. 10.
SINII VOLCHEK, DV, No. 2 (1915), p. 6.
*SINII KASKAD TELLURI, NZ, No. 1 (1912).
*SISTEMA MNEMONIKI ATLEIA, PROBUZHDENIE, No. 9 (1911).
SKROMNOE O VELIKOM, MIR, No. 32 (1918), p. 2.
SLABAIA RUKA ZHENSHCHINY, DV, No. 49 (1914), p. 6.
*SLABOST' DANIELIA KHORTONA, Kr.N, No. 29 (1927), pp. 6-7.
*SLADKII IAD GORODA, A, No. 10 (1913).
*SLEPOI DEI KANET, VECHERNIE IZVESTIIA (M.)(from 2 March 1916).
SLOVA, VP, No. 40 (1911), pp. 2-4.
SLOVA, PLI, No. 125 (1917).
*SLOVOOKHOTLIVYI DOMOVOI, LITERATURNYI LISTOK (part of KRASNAIA
    GAZETA) (from 29 March 1923).
SLOVO-UBIITSA, DV, No. 17 (1915), p. 7.
SLON I MOS'KA, in sb. BELYI SHAR, M., 1966, pp. 47-80.
*SLUCHAI, TOVARISHCH (from 25 March 1907).
SLUCHAINYI DOKHOD, NA VAKHTE, No. 126 (1924).
SMERTEL'NYI DEKOKHT, NA VAKHTE (1929?)
SMERT' ALAMBERA, DV, No. 27 (1915), p. 7.
SMERT' DEVUSHKI (P), ZVUKI ZHIZHNI, Al'manakh sovremennykh pisatelei, SPb.,
    1910, p. 22.
*SMERT' ROMELINKA (as SMERT'), VP, No. 58 (1910), pp. 3-6.
SOBYTIE MORIAKA (as SOBYTIE), VP, No. 25 (1909), pp. 1-3.
SOVEST' ZAGOVORILA, Malen'KAIA GAZETA, No. 2 (1914), p. 4.
*SOZDANIE ASPERA, OG, No. 25 (1917), pp. 6-11.
SOKROVISHCHE AFRIKANSKIKH GOR, M.-L.: "Zemlia i fabrika," 1925.
SON (P), PL, No. 56 (1919), p. 15.
SOREVNOVANIE, PLI (1917).
SO STUPEN'KI NO STUPEN'KU, NS, No. 49 (1914), p. 6.
*SOSTIAZANIE V LISSE, KRASNYI MILITSIONER, Nos. 2-3 (1921), pp. 27-30.
SOTSIAL'NYI REFLEKS, in sb. CHERNYI ALMAZ, L., 1928, pp. 147-54.
*SOCHINITEL'STVO VSEGDA BYLO VNESHNEI MOEI PROFESSIEI. . . . (as RA-
    ZMYSHLENIE NAD ALYMI PARUSAMI), SOVETSKAIA UKRAINA, No. 8
    (1960).
SPOKOINAIA DUSHA, VOINA, No. 54 (1915), p. 2.
SSORA V GOSTINITSE, OG, No. 22 (1929), pp. 12-13. Extract from novel DOROGA

NIKUDA.

STARIK KHODIT PO KRUGU, ChP, No. 2 (1918), p. 3.

*STO VERST PO REKE, SOVREMENNYI MIR, No.s 7-8 (1916).

STORONNEE SOOBSHCHENIE (P), ChP, No. 5 (1918), p. 2.

STRADALETS, NS, No. 51 (1914), pp. 4-5.

STRANNOE ORUZHIE, DV, No. 13 (1915), pp. 5-6.

STRANNOE PIS'MO, ChP, No. 9 (1918), p. 4.

STRANNOE PROISHESTVIE NA MASKARADE, DV, No. 52 (1914), p. 6.

STRANNYI VECHER, OG, No. 1 (1927). Chapter one of collective novel BOL'SHIE POZHARY.

STRASHNAIA POSYLKA, VOINA, No. 36 (1915), p. 7.

STRASHNAIA TAINA AVTOMOBILIA, DV, No. 34 (1915), pp. 11-12.

STRUIA (as SKAZKA O SLEPOI RYBE), DLIA DETEI, prilozh. k NIVA, No. 12 (1917), pp. 370-74.

*SUD'BA, VZIATAIA ZA ROGA, OTECHESTVO, No. 7 (1914).

*SUD'BA PERVAGO VZVODA, DV, No. 6 (1915), p. 12.

SCHAST'E TORGOVTSA, VSEMIRNAIA NOV', Nos 16-17 (1917), pp. 5-6.

TABU, A, No. 7 (1913), pp. 51-60.

*TAINSTVENNAIA PLASTINKA, PLI (from 24 July 1916).

TAINSTVENNYI APEL'SIN, B (1917).

TAINSTVENNYI LES, NIVA, Nos 19, 20, 21 and 22 (1913), pp. 361-68, 382-89, 402-49, 401-27 respectively.

TAINA DIEGO (P), DV, No. 27 (1915), p. 14.

TAINA DOMA, NO. 41, BV, Nos. 15574, 15576, 15578, 15580, 15582, 15584 (1916), evening edition.

*TAINA LESA (as V LESU), in VSELENNAIA, No. 2 (1910).

*TAINA LUNNOI NOCHI, DV, No. 15 (1915), pp. 10-11.

TAINY RUKI (P), VOINA, No. 17 (1914), pp. 10-11.

TALANT, DLIA DETEI, prilozh. k NIVA, No. 6 (1917), pp. 183-92.

*TAM ILI TAM, DV, No. 19 (1915), p. 6.

TANETS, DV, No. 38 (1917), pp. 11-13.

"TELEGRAFIST" IZ MEDIANSKOGO BORA, RUSSKAIA MYSL', No. 12 (1908), pp. 39-74.

TIFOZNYI PUNKTIR, LITERATURNAIA ROSSIIA (21 January 1972), pp. 18-19.

*TIKHIE BUDNI, SOVREMENNIK, No. 10 (1913).

TORGOVTSY, SVOBODNAIA ROSSIIA, No. 33 (1917), p. 3.

*TRAGEDIIA PLOSKOGOR'IA SUAN, RUSSKAIA MYSL', No. 7 (1912).

TRAMVAINAIA BOLEZN', B, No. 17 (1916), p. 6.

TRETII GLAZ, MS. probably lost in late twenties in Tiflis. (See article in Russian by Sukiasova, I., below.)

*TRETII ETAZH, NSS, No. 1 (1908).

TRI BRATA, SZh, No. 2 (1914), pp. 51-70.

TRI VSTRECHI, DV, No. 7 (1915), p. 11.

*TRI POKHOZHDENIIA EKHMY, SZ, No. 36 (1913).

TRI PULI, DV, No. 42 (1915), pp. 13-14.

TRI SVECHI, PETROGRADSKII GOLOS, No. 84 (1918?).

TRUPKA-NEVIDIMKA, PLI (4 May 1917), pp. 6-7.

TRUPY. Exact date and place of first (and only) publication unknown. Probably Autumn 1917.

?TRUS, VES' MIR, No. 10 (1913), pp. 13-14. Signed V. Grin.

TRIUM I PALUBA, BODROE SLOVO, No. 1 (1908), cols. 27-46.

TIUREMNAIA STARINA, TRIDTSAT' DNEI, No. 7 (1933), pp. 69-70.

*TIAZHELYI VOZDUKH (as LETCHIK KIRSHIN), VES' MIR, No. 26 (1912), p. 9.

*UBIISTVO V KUNST-FISHE, KRASNAIA GAZETA (from 15 January 1923).
*UBIISTVO V RYBNOI LAVKE, SEVERNAIA ZVEZDA, No. 1 (1916).
UBIISTVO ROMANTIKA, SEVERNAIA ZVEZDA, No. 6 (1915), pp. 63-64.
UBIITSA, OG, No. 45 (1908), p. 6.
UDUSHLIVYI GAZ, DV, No. 29 (1915), pp. 5-6.
*UZHASNOE ZRENIE, DV, No. 20 (1915), pp. 11-12.
*UZNIK "KRESTOV," DV, No. 17 (1917), p. 7.
URBAN GRATS PRINIMAET GOSTEI, DV, No. 44 (1914), pp. 10-12.
UCHENIK CHARODEIA, OG, No. 17 (1917), pp. 258-67.
FABRIKA DROZDA I ZHAVORONKA (P), PL, No. 36 (1919), pp. 11-15.
*FANDANGO. Place of first publication unknown. In VOINA ZOLOTOM, Al'manakh
    prikliuchenii, M., 1927.
FANTAZERY, PLI, No. 275 (1916).
FLIUGER (P), NS, No. 9 (1915), p. 7.
KHOZIAIN IZ LODZI, DV, No. 11 (1915), pp. 5-6.
KHRUSTAL'NAIA VAZA. . . . (P), PL, No. 46 (1919).
TSENZURNO-NETSENZURNYI ANEKDOT, B, No. 31 (1917), p. 11.
*TSIKLON V RAVNINE DOZHDEI (as TSIKLON) in VP, No. 36 (1909).
CHELOVEK V TOMANE, VP (1908?).
CHELOVEK, KOTORYI PLACHET, in sb. ZNAMENITAIA KNIGA, SPb., 1915.
CHELOVEK S DACHI DURNOVO, SVOBODNAIA ROSSIIA, No. 33 (1917), p. 3.
*CHELOVEK S CHELOVEKOM, RANNEE UTRO, No. 298 (1913).
CHERNOE I BELOE, EKHO (1918).
CHERNYE TSVETY, DV, No. 45 (1915), p. 10.
CHERNYI AVTOMOBIL', DV, No. 18 (1917), p. 8.
*CHERNYI ALMAZ, OG, No. 16 (1916), pp. 5-8.
CHERNYI GRAVER, OG (1927?).
CHERNYI ROMAN, DV, No. 24 (1915), pp. 6-7.
CHERNYI KHRUSTAL' SIPAIA, DV, No. 52 (1914), p. 7.
*CHETVERTYI ZA VSEKH, SR, No. 32 (1912).
CHETYRE GINEI, NA DOSUGE, No. 4 (1929), pp. 5-7.
*CHETYRNADTSAT' FUTOV, ZARIA VOSTOKA (Tbilisi, 5 September 1924).
CHTO BUDET CHEREZ 200 LET?, SZ, No. 1 (1914), p. 11.
CHUDESNYI PROVAL, DV, No. 43 (1915), p. 7.
*CHUZHAIA VINA, in sb. PO ZAKONU, N.-L., 1927.
SHEDEVR, SVOBODNAIA ROSSIIA, No. 33 (1917), p. 3.
*SHEST' SPICHEK, Kr.N, No. 45 (1925), pp. 1085-89.
*SHTURMAN "CHETYREKH VETROV," SLOVO (from 31 May 1909).
ELDA I ANGOTEIA, TRIDTSAT' DNEI, No. 8 (1928), pp. 34-39.
ELEGIIA (P), SEGODNIA (SPb., 13 March 1907).
*EPIZOD PRI VZIATII FORTA "TSIKLOP" (as EPIZOD IZ VZIATIIA. . . .), SZ, No.
    29 (1914).
ERNA, VSEVIDIASHCHEE OKO, No. 1 (1918), pp. 3-4.
ESPERANTO, NS, No. 32 (1917), pp. 11, 13 and 14.
ESTET I SHCHI (Basnia), NS, No. 14 (1915), p. 10.
IASHCHIK S MYLOM, VP, No. 65 (1910), p. 1.

3. CRITICAL WORKS ON GRIN

(i) Books in Russian

Kovskii, V.E., PREOBRAZHENIE DEISTVITEL'NOSTI. Frunze: "Ilim," 1966.

115

Kovskii, V.E., ROMANTICHESKII MIR ALEKSANDRA GRINA. M.: "Nauka," 1969.
PROKHOROV, E.I., ALEKSANDR GRIN. M.: "Prosveshchenie," 1970.

(ii) Selected Articles in Russian

Aliev, E.A., "Ob esteticheskom ideale A.S. Grina posle velikoi Oktiabr'skoi Revoliutsii,"
    UCHENYE ZAPISKI AZERBAIDZHANSKOGO PEDAGOGICHESKOGO IN-
    STITUTA IAZYKOV, Seriia XII, Iazy i literatura, No. 1 (1966), pp. 3-15.
Aliev, E.A., "K voprosu o romanticheskom geroe A. Grina v romane BLISTAIUSHCHII
    MIR," UCHENYE ZAPISKI AZERBAIDZHANSKOGO PEDAGOGICHESKOGO
    INSTITUTA IAZYKOV, Seriia XII, Iazyk i literatura, No. 4 (1967), pp. 3-12.
Arnoldi, E., "Belletrist Grin. Vstrechi s pisatelem," ZVEZDA, No. 12 (1963), pp. 176-
    82.
Borisov, L., "Aleksandr Grin i ego tvorchestvo," in A.S. Grin, BEGUSHCHAIA PO VOL-
    NAM, M.-L., 1945, pp. 3-8.
Vazhdaev, V., "Propovednik kosmopolitizma. Nechistyi smysl 'chistogo iskusstva' A.
    Grina," NOVYI MIR, No. 1 (1950), pp. 257-72.
Verzhbitskii, N., "Svetlaia dusha," NASH SOVREMENNIK, No. 8 (1964), pp. 103-06.
Vikhrov, V., "Ob Aleksandre Grine," in A. Grin, IZBRANNOE, Simferopol, 1959, pp.
    543-59.
Vikhrov, V., "Rytsar' mechty," foreword to A.S. Grin, SOB. SOCH. V SHESTI TO-
    MAKH, M., 1965, Vol. !, pp. 3-36.
Vol'pe, Ts., "Ob avantiurno-psikhologicheskikh novellakh A. Grina," in A. Grin, RASS-
    KAZY, L., 1935, pp. 5-22.
Voronova, O., "Poeziia mechty i nravstvennykh poiskov," NEVA, No. 8 (1960), pp.
    144-50.
Voronova, O., "Sto verst po zhizhni," BAIKAL, No. 4 (1967), pp. 144-49.
Gornfel'd, A.G., "A. Grin. RASSKAZY, Tom I, 1910," RUSSKOE BOGATSTVO, No. 3
    (1910), pp. 145-47.
Gornfel'd, A.G., "A. G. ISKATEL' PRIKLIUCHENII. RASSKAZY, M., 1916," RUSS-
    KOE BOGATSTVO, Nos. 6-7 (1917), pp. 279-82.
Dmitrevskii, VI., "V chem volshebstvo Aleksandra Grina?", afterword to A.S. Grin, ZO-
    LOTAIA TSEP'; DOROGA NIKUDA, I., 1957, pp. 377-89.
Zavalishin, V., "Fantast ne pokidavshii rodiny," MOSTY (New York), No. 1 (1958), pp.
    228-38.
Zelinskii, K., "Grin," KRASNAIA NOV', No. 4 (1934), pp. 199-206.
Zelinskii, K., "Grin," in Zelinskii, K., V IZMENIAIUSHCHEMSIA MIRE, M., 1969, pp.
    183-201.
Izergina, N.P., "A.S. Grin i A.M. Gor'kii," UCHENYE ZAPISKI. Kafedra literatury.
    Kirovskii gosudarstvennyi pedagogicheskii institut im. Lenina, Vol. XX, Kirov,
    1965, pp. 78-108.
Kovskii, V.E., "Aleksandr Grin o literature i iskusstve," KIROVSKAIA PRAVDA (3
    March 1966), p. 4.
Kovskii, V.E., "Vospitanie romantikoi," LITERATURA V SHKOLE, No. 1 (1966), pp.
    6-12.
Kudievskii, K., "Iz neizdannykh i zabytykh rukopisei." Foreword to Grin's RAZMYSH-
    LENIE NAD ALYMI PARUSAMI and other short works. SOVETSKAIA UKRAI-
    NA, No. 8 (1960), pp. 96-97.
Levidov, M., "Inostranets russkoi literatury," ZHURNAL ZHURNALOV, No. 4 (1915),
    pp. 3-5.
Levina, Ia. B., "Romantika i osobennosti ee voploshcheniia v ALYKH PARUSAKH A.S.
    Grina," TRUDY BATUMSKOGO GOSUDARSTVENNOGO PEDAGOGICHES-

KOGO INSTITUTA IM. SH. RUSTAVELI, Vol XIII (1966), pp. 290-7. (Published 1968.)

Lidin, VI., "Aleksandr Grin," MOSKVA, No. 10 (1963), pp. 164-65.

Mikhailova, L., "Grin i vremia," NEDELIA, No. 42 (1969), pp. 14-15.

Myl'tsyna, I.V., i Tolstaia, A. V., "O mere uslovnosti v rannikh rasskazakh Grina," NAUCHNYE DOKLADY VYSSHEI SHKOLY. FILOLOGICHESKIE NAUKI, No. 6 (1968), pp. 96-103.

Olesha, Iu., "Aleksandr Grin," in Olesha, Iu., IZBRANNYE SOCHINENIIA, M., 1956, pp. 463-67.

Paustovskii, K., "Aleksandr Grin," GOD XXII, Al'manakh 15 (M., 1939), pp. 410-30.

Paustovskii, K., "Zhizn' Grina," foreword to Grin's ZOLOTAIA TSEP'; AVTOBIOGRA-FICHESKAIA POVEST', M., 1939, pp. 3-24. The first of many subsequent very similar introductory essays.

Roskin, A., "Sud'ba pisatelia-fabulista," KHUDOZHESTVENNAIA LITERATURA, No. 4 (1935), pp. 4-9.

Roskin, A., "Puteshestview iz strany Grina," LITERATURNYI KRITIK, No. 5 (1938), pp. 167-87.

Roskin, A., "Zolotaia tsep'," in Roskin, A., STAT'I O LITERATURE I TEATRE, M., 1959, pp. 87-91.

Rossel's, VL., "Dorevoliutsionnaia proza Grina," in A.S. Grin, SOB. SOCH. V SHESTI TOMAKH, M., 1965, pp. 629-48.

Rossel's, VI., "A. Grin. Iz neizdannogo i zabytogo," LITERATURNOE NASLEDSTVO, No. 74 (m., 1965), pp. 629-48.

Rossel's, VI., "A.S. Grin," ISTORIIA RUSSKOI SOVETSKOI LITERATURY, Tom I, 1917-1929, M., 1967, pp. 370-91.

Samoilova, V.D., "Nekotorye osobennosti tvorchestva A.S. Grina," UCHENYE ZAPISKI MOSKOVSKOGO OBLASTNOGO PEDAGOGICHESKOGO INSTITUTA, Vol CXVI (1963), pp. 103-14.

Sandler, VI., "Shel po zemle mechtatel'," foreword to A.S. Grin, DZHESSI I MOR-GIANA, L., 1966, pp. 3-20.

Sandler, VII, "O cheloveke is pisatele," foreword to A.S. Grin, BELYI SHAR, M., 1966, pp. 3-25.

Sandler, VI., "Chetyre goda za Grinom," Al'manakh PROMETEI, Vol V (M., 1968), pp. 190-207.

Slonimskii, M., "Aleksandr Grin," ZVEZDA, No. 4 (1939), pp. 159-67.

Slonimskii, M., "A.S. Grin," foreword to Grin's ZOLOTAIA TSEP'; AVTOBIOGRAFI-CHESKAIA POVEST', M., 1939, pp. 24-35.

Sukiasova, I., "Novoe ob Aleksandre Grine," LITERATURNAIA GRUZIIA, No. 12 (1968), pp. 67-76.

Tarasenkov, A., "O natsional'nykh traditsiiakh i burzhuaznom kosmopolitizme," ZNA-MIA, No. 1 (1950), pp. 152-64.

Kharchev, V., "Khudozhestvennye printsipy romantiki A.S. Grina," UCHENYE ZAPIS-KI, Gor'kovskii gosudarstvennyi pedagogicheskii institut, Tom 54, 1966, Seriia literatury, pp. 22-50.

Kharchev, V., "M. Gor'kii i A. Grin," UCHENYE ZAPISKI, For'kovskii gosudarstvennyi pedagogicheskii institut, Tom 110, 1968, Seriia filologicheskikh nauk, pp. 196-206.

Khokhlov, E., "Sud'ba Aleksandra Grina," RUSSKIE NOVOSTI (Paris, 5 June 1964), pp. 2-3.

Shaginian, M., "A.S. Grin," KRASNAIA NOV', No. 5 (1933), pp. 171-73.

Shevchenko, V., "A.S. Grin v sovetskoi kritike," VOPROSY RUSSKOI I ZARUBEZH-NOI LITERATURY, Rostov-on-Don, 1967, pp. 159-74.

Shcheglov, M., "Korabli Aleksandra Grina," NOVYI MIR, No. 10 (1956), pp. 220-23.

(iii) Selected articles in languages other than Russian.

Castaing, P., "Le thème du conflit chez Aleksandr Grin," CAHIERS DU MONDE
 RUSSE ET SOVIÉTIQUE, Vol XII-3 (July-September 1971), pp. 217-46.
Croise, J., "Alexandre Grine et l'Irréel," LA REVUE DES DEUX MONDES (December
 1959), pp. 707-11.
Frioux, C., "Alexandre Grin," REVUE DES ETUDES SLAVES, Vol 38 (Paris 1961),
 pp. 87-87.
Frioux, C., "Sur deux romans d'Alexandr Grin," CAHIERS DU MONDE RUSSE ET
 SOVIÉTIQUE, Vol. III-4 (October-December 1962), pp. 546-63.
Kobzev, M., "O. Grin. BIBLISKUIUCHII SVIT," RADIANS'KE LITERATUROZNAV-
 STVO, Institut literatury im. T.G. Shevchenko, Akad. Nauk URSR, Kiev, No. 5
 (1969), pp. 63-74. IUkrainian.
Pollak, S., "Geograf krajow urojonych," in Pollack, S., WYPRAWY ZA TRZY MORZA
 (Warsaw, 1962), pp. 180-96. Polish.
Sukiasova, I., "Za tvorchestvo na A.S. Grin," YEZIK I LITERATURA (sofia), No. 5
 (1964), pp. 9-20. Bulgarian.

4. ENGLISH TRANSLATIONS OF GRIN'S WORK

THE MAKING OF ASPER, in DISSONANT VOICES IN SOVIET LITERATURE, ed.
 Patricia Blake and Max Hayward. London: Allen and Unwin, 1964, pp. 61-72.
SCARLET SAILS, tr. T. Whitney. New York: Charles Scribner's Sons, 1967.
THE WATERCOLOUR, tr. M. Wheeler, in SOVIET SHORT STORIES, NO. 2. London:
 Penguin, 1968. pp. 95-107.

ADDENDA

Critical works on Grin

Luker, N.J.L., ALEXANDER GRIN. Letchworth: Bradda, 1973.
Mikhailova, L. ALEKSANDR GRIN. M.: "Khud. lit.," 1972.

Selected articles in languages other than Russian.

Luker, N.J.L., "Alexander Grin's last novel THE ROAD TO NOWHERE (DOROGA
 NIKUDA), NEW ZEALAND SLAVONIC JOURNAL, No. 11 (1973), pp. 51-75.
Luker, N.J.L., "Alexander Grin: A Survey," RLT, No. 8 (1974), pp. 341-61.

English translations

PEACE, tr. N.J.L. Luker, NEW ZEALAND SLAVONIC JOURNAL, No. 1 (1974), pp.
 87-99.
THE SNAKE, THE VOICE OF THE SIREN, THE WINDOW IN THE FOREST, tr. N.J.
 L. Luker, RLT, No. 8 (1974), pp. 177-88.
THE GARRULOUS GREMLIN, tr. R.W. Rotsel, RLT, No. 8 (1974), pp. 188-91.
THE CORPSES and RED SPLASHES OF BLOOD, tr. N.J.L. Luker, RLT, No. 11 (1975)
 pp. 88-94.

A BIBLIOGRAPHY OF WORKS BY AND ABOUT
VASILII PAVLOVICH AKSENOV

Compiled by

Priscilla Meyer

I. Original Works in Russian by Aksenov

2. APEL'SINY IZ MAROKKO, IUNOST', No. 1, 1963.

4. "Dikoi," IUNOST'-IZBRANNOE (M. Pravda, 1965), 10-36.
5. "Duet—rasskaz byvalogo cheloveka," LR (Oct. 9, 1970), 12-13.
6. "Dvor v fonarnom pereulke," LG (July 31, 1966), 3.
7. "Fenomen 'Puzyria'," LG (Nov. 19, 1969), 16.
8. "Gebrarii," [ocherk], LG (Feb. 18, 1961), 2.
9. "Golubie morskie pushki," TRUD (April 14, 1967), 4.
10. "Goriachii sneg v rukakh," [stat'ia], LG (Dec. 1, 1960), 3.

12. "Kardiogramma pisatel'skogo serdtsa," SOVETSKAIA BELORUSSIIA (Aug. 22, 1963).
13. "Katapul'ta," NEDELIA (Jan. 28-Feb. 3, 1962), 10-11.
14. KATAPUL'TA. M. Sovietskii pisatel', 1964. Contains: "S utra do temnoty," "Samson i Samsonikha," "Poltory vrachebnykh edinitsy," "Siurprizy," "Katapul'ta," "Peremena obraza zhizni," "Zavtraki sorok pervogo goda," "Papa, slozhi!" APEL'SINY IZ MAROKKO.

16. KOLLEGI, IUNOST' (June-July, 1960).
17. KOLLEGI, M. Sovetskii pisatel', 1961.

19. "Kto ty, syn Gippokrata" [retsenziia], KO (Nov. 25, 1967), 10-11.
20. [Literatura i iazyk] (otvet na anketu), VLit, No. 6 (1967), 89-90.
21. "Literaturnaia zhizn'—pisateli za rabotoi," VLit, No. 3 (1964), 240.
22. "Liubiteliam basketbola," LG (March 29, 1967), 8.
23. LIUBOV' K ELEKTRICHESTVU, ROMAN-KHRONIKA [zhurnal'nyi variant], IUNOST', Nos. 3-5 (1971).
24. LIUBOV' K ELEKTRICHESTVU. M. Politizdat, 1971.

26. MECHTA TAKSISTA (ironicheskaia proza), LG (August 26, 1970), 16.
27. "Mne dorogi sud'by romana," LG (Aug. 27, 1963), 3.
28. "Mnogotochie nadezhdy," [retsenziia], LG (April 10, 1962), 4.
29. "Moi dedushka—pamiatnik" [povest'], KOSTER, 1970, No. 7, pp. 38-50; No. 8, pp. 22-36; No. 9-10. pp. 44-56.
30. "Na ploshchadi i za rekoi," Iu. No. 5 (1966), 40-44.
31. "Na polputi k lune," NM, No. 7 (1962).
32. NA POLPUTI K LUNE, M. 1965. Contains: "Dikoi," "Zavtraki 41-go goda," "Mestnyi khuligan Abramashvili," "Katapul'ta," "Peremena obraza zhizni," "Iaponskie zametki," "Papa, slozhi!" "Tovarishch Krasivyi Furazhkin," "Na polputi k lune," "Malen'kii Kit, lakirovshchik deistvitel'nosti."
33. "Na polputi v redaktsiiu," LG (Sept. 1, 1962), 3.

35. "Nasha anketa, molodye o sebe," VLit, No. 9 (1962), 117-119.
36. "Nasha Vera Ivanovna," and "Asfal'tovye dorogi," Iu., No. 7 (1959), 50-63.

37. "Neobyknovennyi amerikanets," INOSTRANNAIA LITERATURA, No. 3 (1966). [retsenziia].
38. "Ne otstavaia ot bystronogogo" [stat'ia], LG (June 15, pp. 1,3.
39. "Novye rasskazy," Iu. No. 12 (1964).
40. "Opyt zapisi letnego sna," KODRY (Kishinev), No 2 (1970).
41. "Otvetstvennost' pered narodom" [stat'ia], Iu. No. 4 (1963), 5; and in PRAVDA (April 3, 1963), 4.
42. "Papa, slozhi!" NM, No. 7, 1962.
43. "Pobeda," Iu, No. 6, 1965.
44. "Pod nebom znoinoi Argentiny," LR (May 13, 1966), 21-24.
45. "Poema ekstaza," LG (Jan. 1, 1968), 5.
46. "Poltory vrachebnykh edinitsy," and "Na ploshchadi i za rekoi," in BIBLIOTEKA SOVREMENNOI MOLODEZHNOI PROZY I POEZII, M. "Molodaia gvardiia," 1967. Vol. 1, pp. 59-94.
47. PORA, MOI DRUG, PORA! MG, Nos. 4-5, 1964.
48. PORA, MOI DRUG, PORA! M. "Molodaia gvardiia," 1965.
49. "Preds"ezdovskaia tribuna" [anketa], VLit, No. 5 (1966), 12-13.
50. "Printsy, nishchie dukhom" [ocherk], LG (Sept. 17, 1960), 2.
51. "Promezhutochnaia posada v Saigone," TRUD, No. 111 (May 14, 1969), 3.
52. "Prostak v mire dzhaza," Iu., No. 8, 1967, pp. 94-99.
52. "Punktir progressa," LG (Feb. 8, 1966), 1.
53. "Puteshestvie v Meskhetiiu," SEL'SKAIA MOLODEZH', No. 1 (1965), 26-28.
54. "Puteshestviia Levy Ermolaeva," PIONER, No. 10 (1968), 31-32.
55. "Ranimaia lichnost'," LG (Jan. 21, 1970), 16.
56. "Razgovory v sochel'nik" [retsenziia], NM, No. 1 (1961), 258-61.
57. "Randevu" [povest'], AVRORA, No. 5 (May 1971), 26-35.
58. "Ryzhii s togo dvora," LR (Aug. 20, 1966), 12-14.
59. "Riadom s nami" [seminar], LENINGRADSKAIA PRAVDA (Oct. 22, 1970).
60. "Semisvetnaia raduga" [retsenziia], LG (Nov. 21, 1964), 3.
61. "Shkola prozy (masterstvo pisatelia. Rasskaz o segodnia)," VLit, No. 7 (1969), 84-85.
62. "Smeetsia tot, kto smeetsia. Kollektivnyi roman," Glava 5, NEDELIA (May 24-30), 1964, pp. 6, 16.
63. "S utra do temnoty," LG (Sept. 24, 1960), 3,5.
64. "S pervym aprelia," LG (Feb. 1 1967), 16.

66. "Schast'e na beregu zagriaznennogo okeana," LG (Sept. 23, 1970), 16.
67. "Tam, gde rastut rododendrony," NEDELIA, No. 20 (1967).

69. "Tovarishch krasivyi Furazhkin," Iu. No. 12, 1964.
70. "Tovarishch krasivyi Furazhkin," SOVETSKAIA ESTONIA (Oct. 11, 1964).

72. "Tuchi nashego detstva" [retsenziia], LR (April 22, 1965), 10-11.
73. "U pisatelei Rossii" [zametka], LR (Dec. 22, 1967), 4.
74. "Vsegda v prodazhe" [p'esa], unpublished manuscript.
75. "V svete podgotovki k predstoiashchei vesne. Rasskaz bez edinogo svoego slova," Iu. No. 4 (1969), 110.
76. "Vyvod nezhelatel'nogo gostia iz doma," LG, No. 41 (Oct. 8, 1969), 16.
77. "Zhal', chto vas ne bylo s nami," MOSKVA, No. 6, 1965.
78. ZHAL', CHTO VAS NE BYLO S NAME. M. "Sovetskii pisatel'," 1969. Contains: KOLLEGI, "Malen'kii Kit, lakirovshchik deistvitel'nosti," "Mestnyi khuligan Abramashvili," "Iaponskie zametki," "Pod nebom znoinoi Argentiny," "Tovarishch Krasivyi Furazhkin," "Pobeda," "Ryzhyi s togo dvora," "Na ploshchadi i za rekoi," "Zhal', chto vas ne bylo s nami."

79. "Zametka k povesti Viacheslava Shugaeva, 'Begu i vozvrashchaiu'," Iu., No. 11 (1965), 6.
80. ZATOVARENNAIA BOCHKOTARA, Iu. No. 3 (1968), 37-63.
81. "Zavtraki sorok pervogo goda," NEDELIA (Sept. 16-22, 1962), pp. 8,9.
82. "Zemnaia solnechnaia krov' (iz bloknota pisatelia)," LG (Oct. 13, 1962), 2,3.
83. ZVEZDNYI BILET, Iu. (June-July, 1961), Nos. 6-7.

II. Works by Aksenov Translated into English

84. "An Unusual American," trans. Carl R. Proffer, in SOVIET CRITICISM OF AMERI-
    CAN LITERATURE IN THE SIXTIES, ed. C. Proffer. Ann Arbor: Ardis, 1972.
    pp. 12-14.
85. COLLEAGUES, trans. A. Brown. London: Putnam, 1962.
86. COLLEAGUES, trans. M. Wettlin. Moscow: Progress. n.d.
87. COLLEAGUES, trans. M. Wettlin. SOVIET LITERATURE MONTHLY, No. 4 (1961).
88. "Halfway to the Moon," HALFWAY TO THE MOON, eds. M. Hayward & P. Blake. New
    York: Doubleday, 1965.
89. "Halfway to the Moon," trans. Ronald Hingley, ENCOUNTER (April, 1963).
90. "Halfway to the Moon," FOUR SOVIET MASTERPIECES, trans. Andrew MacAndrew.
    New York: Bantam, 1965.
91. "Halfway to the Moon," THE NEW WRITING IN RUSSIA, trans. Thomas Whitney.
    Ann Arbor: University of Michigan Press, 1964.
92. IT'S TIME, MY LOVE, IT'S TIME. trans. Olive Stevens. London: Macmillan, 1969.
93. "On the Square and Across the River," SOVIET LITERATURE (Moscow), No. 4, 1967.
94. "Papa, What Does it Spell?" THE NEW WRITING IN RUSSIA, ed. T. Whitney. Ann
    Arbor: University of Michigan Press, 1964.
95. A STARRY TICKET, trans. A. Brown. London: Putnam, 1962.
96. "Thoughts of a Prose Writer," SOVIET LITERATURE, No. 5 (1966).
97. A TICKET TO THE STARS, trans. Andrew MacAndrew. New York: Signet, 1963.

III. Critical Works about Aksenov in Russian

KOLLEGI

98. Anninskii, L. "Ot prostoty do mudrosti," LG (May 27, 1961), 2,3.
99. Blinkova, M. "Sasha Zelenin i ego druz'ia," NM, No. 11 (1960),248-53.
100. Borisov, S. "Sverstniki," LG (June 11, 1960), 3.
101. Fomenko, L. "Vremia zovet," NASH SOVREMENNIK, No. 2 (1961), 194-211.
102. Girvich, A. "Chelovek uchitsia zhit'," Iu., No 2 (1961), 69-74.
103. Kadran, V. "Vechnye voprosy—novye otvety," VLit, No. 3 (1961), 25-48.
104. Kuznetsov, F. "Chetvertoe pokolenie," LG (July 29, 1961), pp. 1,2,3.
105. — — — —, "Geroi nashei zhizni," SMENA (April 2, 1963), 3.
106. — — — —,"Kakim byt'?" LG (July 14, 1960), 3.
107.— — — —, "Otsu Serafimu," KP (July 13, 1964).
108. — — — —, "V mire boets," Iu., No. 4 (1966), 83-90.
109. — — — —, "Vozmuzhanie geroia," VL (Dec. 13, 1963), 3.
110. Kuznetsov, M. "Spor reshit zhizn'," NM, No. 9 (1960), 236-50.
111. Makarov, A. "Ser'eznaia zhizn'," ZNAMIA, No. 1 (1961), 188-211.
112. Maslin, N. "Krasivaia molodost'," MOSKVA, No. 2 (1961), 200-201.
113. Mikhailov, O. "Liudi truda i mysli," ZNAMIA, No. 4 (1961), 195-208.
114. — — — — , "Nashei molodosti spory," Iu., No. 10 (1964), 52-57.
115. Ozerov, V. "Novyi chelovek v tsentre vnimaniia," VLit. No. 12 (1960), 3-26.
116. Podopulo, G. "Partiinost'—iskhodnaia pozitsiia molodogo khudozhnika," MK, No. 11
    (1960), 248-53.

117. Rassadin, S. "Shestidesiatniki," Iu. No. 12 (1960), 58-62.
118. Savel'ev, I. "Sosed po obshchezhitiiu," KP (Dec. 9, 1964).
119. Solov'ev, B. "Istoricheskoe i povsednevnoe," NEVA, No. 3 (1961), 187-201.
120. Trifonova, T. "S liubov'iu k cheloveku," KZ, No. 1 (1961), 20-22.

ZVEZDNYI BILET

121. Bertse, V. "Karta i marshruty," LG (Aug. 24, 1961), 2.
122. Bondarev, Iu. "Poiski semnadtsatiletnikh," LG (July 29, 1961), 1,2,3.
123. Brovman, G. "Pafos zhizneutverzhdeniia ili zhupel' lakirovki?" VLit. No. 12 (1963), 3-24.
124. Bryl', Ia. "Chto pishut o tebe, liubov'?" LG (Sept. 30, 1966), 2,3.
125. Charnyi, M. "O svobode liubvi," ZVEZDA, No. 10 (1962), 193-99.
126. Ivashchenko, V. "Zemskaia statistika," VLit, No. 2 (1966), 38-41.
127. Kholopov, G. "Liniia razvitiia—sovremennost'," VLen. (Sept. 26, 1961). 3.
128. Lavlinskii, L. "Bilet, no kuda?" KP (Sept. 15, 1961).
129. Panova, V. "Prochtite, chto interesno!" NEDELIA (Sept. 3-9, 1966), 18.
130. Shishkina, A. "Moral' i moralisty," NEVA, No. 1 (1963), 163-170.

NA POLPUTI K LUNE

131. Aleksandrova, T. "Skvoz' okno restorana," ZVEZDA, February 12, 1963.
132. Antopol'skii, L. "Korni cheloveka," Iu., No. 1 (1969), 67-70.
133. Brovman, G. "Dialog o geroe," LR, No. 6 (1964), 6-7.
134. – – – – , "Pravda istoricheskogo optimizma," MOSKVA, No. 1 (1964).
135. – – – – , "Sut'—v ideinoi pozitsii," OKTIABR', No. 5 (1963), 180-90.
136. Chalmaev, V. "Pervoe slagaemoe," LG (Aug. 24, 1963), 1, 4.
137. Chudakov, A. and Chudakova, M. "Isskusstvo slova," NM. No. 2 (1963), 239-54.
138. Kriachko, L. "Puti, zabluzhdeniia i nakhodki," OKTIABR', No. 3 (1963), 200-209.
139. – – – – , " 'V kadre' i 'za kadrom'," LG (June 27, 1964), 3.
140. Kuznetsov, M. "Chelovechnost'," V MIRE KNIG, No. 1 (1963), 22-27.
141. Ianovskii, N. "V romanticheskom kliuche," OKTIABR', No. 1 (1963), 188-95.
142. Maksimov, N. "Snezhnyi chelovek," SOVETSKII SAKHALIN (Oct. 14, 1962).
143. Rekemchuk, A. "Da ne oskudeet," VLit, No. 7 (1969), 90-93.
144. Volynskii, K. "Zhivaia voda," LG (Jan. 11, 1964), 1.
145. Khovanskaia, A. "S kogo oni portrety pishut?" SOVETSKII SAKHALIN (Oct. 21, 1962).

PAPA, SLOZHI!

146. Gorlovskii, A. "Chtoby byli schastlivy," SMENA, No. 15 (1965), 13-15.
147. Kriachko, L. "Zhit' dlia bor'by," MOSKVA, No. 10 (1966), 194-203.
148. Solov'eva, I. "Nachalo puti," NM, No. 9 (1959).

APELSINY IZ MAROKKO

149. Baturina, T. "Zrelost' romantikov," MG, No. 6 (1965), 306-312.
150. Chaikovskii, B. "A dal'she chto?" UCHITEL'SKAIA GAZETA (March 21, 1963), 4.
151. Chalmaev, V. "K novym pobedam kommunisticheskoi ideologii," DN, No. 8 (1963), 3-10.
152. Dymshits, A. "Rasskazy o rasskazakh," OGONEK, No. 13 (1963), 30-1.
153. El'iashevich, Arkadii. "Nerushimoe edinstvo," ZVEZDA, No. 8 (1963), 185-202.
154. Fedorov, V. "Dorozhit' pravdoi" [speech at the Fourth Plenum of the Union of Soviet Writers], LG (April 2, 1963), 1.
155. Fomenko, L. "Gde oni, zavtrashnye zaboty?" MOSKOVSKAIA PRAVDA (Feb. 16, 1963), 3.
156. Gagarin, Iurii. "Slovo k pisateliam," LR, No. 16 (1963), 2-3.

157. Kedrina, Z. "Chelovek-sovremennik-grazhdanin," VLit. No. 8 (1963), 27-50.
158. Kozhemiako, V. "Imenem revoliutsii," KP (Mar. 27, 1963).
159. Kuznetsov, F. "Molodoi pisatel' i zhizn'," IU. No. 5 (1963), 73-80.
160. Lomidze, G. "Sila realizma," VLit, No. 5 (1963), 47-68.
161. Makarov, A. "Chitaia pis'ma," LG (Dec. 19, 1963), 1, 3.
162. Markov, Georgii. "Velikaia pravda nashikh dnei," LG (Mar. 30, 1963), 3.
163. Novgorodov, A. "Tsena apel'siny," MK, No. 4 (1963), 119-22.
164. Novikov, V. "Geroicheskomu vremeni—geroicheskoe iskusstvo," ZNAMIA, No. 10 (1963), 187-96.
165. Osetrov, E. "Darovanie i igra," LG (Feb. 9, 1963), 3.
166. Pankin, B. "Ni slovechka v prostote," KP (Feb. 17, 1963).
167. PLENUM TSENTRAL'NOGO KOMITETA KPSS, LG (June 20, 1963), 2.
168. Raskin, Aleksei. "Moroka s bananami," [parodiia] , KROKODIL', No. 6 (1963), 12-13.
169. Riurikov, Iurii. "Tri vlecheniia," VLit., No. 8 (1965), 25-47.
170. Shamota, N. "Chem bogat chelovek," LG (June 15, 1963), 1-2.
171. Sinel'nikov, M. "Geroi truda—geroi literatury," TRUD, No. 14, 1963.
172. — — — —, "Videt' 'strezhen' '!" LR (April, 1963), 14-15.
173. Slobodian, D. "O spornom i besspornom," LG (Oct. 1, 1963), 3.
174. Titov, V. "Pust' kniga uchit zhit'," VLit. (April , 1963), 1, and PRAVDA (April 11, 1963), 4.
175. Verchenko, Iu. "Gde zhe obeshchanie Korchagina?" SMENA, No. 8 (1963), 10-11.

PORA, MOI DRUG, PORA

176. Anen'eva, A. "Preuvelichenie chuvstv," SO, No. 2 (1966), 169-76.
177. Bocharov, A. "Potok i pisatel'," KP (Nov. 21, 1964).
178. — — — —, "Utverzhdaia tsel'nost'," VLit., No. 1 (1965), 26-32.
179. Brovman, G. "Dykhanie zhizni," IZVESTIIA (Feb. 26, 1965), 3.
180. — — — —, "Pora vozmuzhaniia," TRUD (July 3, 1965), 5.
181. Geideko, V. "pered sleduiushchim shagom," LG (June 6, 1964), 3.
182. Glinkin, P. "Proza dlia molodezhi," SO, No. 10 (1964), 180.
183. — — — —, "Chemu pora?" SMENA, July 2, 1964.
184. Golyshev, G. "Staromodnye klassiki i urbanist Kovrigin," DAL'NII VOSTOK, No. 5 (1966).
185. Gregoriev, V. "Pora slov i pora deistvii," KP (August 4, 1964).
186. Kireeva, A. "Letiat za dniami dni..." SMENA, No. 1 (1965), 26-27.
187. Khvatov, A. "Dukhovnyi mir cheloveka i koordinaty vremeni," ZVEZDA, No. 4 (1968), 192-208.
188. Kriachko, L. "Poistine—pora!" MOSKVA, No. 9 (1964), 213.
189. Kuznetsov, F. "Grazhdanin ili meshchanin?" Iu. No. 12 (1964), 75-80.
190. Lugovskoi, V. "Vroven' s vekom," TRUD (July 12, 1964), 2.
191. Maksimov, N. "Ob istorizme podlinnom i mnimom," VOLGA, No. 9 (1966).
192. Mitin, G. "Ishchu sebia v knige," MK, No. 7 (1964), 122-27.
193. Motiashov, I. "K bor'be zovushchaia," UCHITEL'SKAIA GAZETA (June 20, 1964), 4.
194. Nechaeva, L. "Ten' geroia," MK, No. 4, (1965), 118-23.
195. Ozerov, V. "Proza 1964-ogo goda," VLit, No. 1 (1965), 18-26.
196. Popov, N. "V poiskakh geroia," LENINSKII PUT', (Aug. 30, 1964).
197. Zhak, L. "Pokoia ne budet," ZNAMIA, No. 1 (1965), 229-31.

POBEDA

198. Khotimskii, Boris. "Myslit' i chuvstvovat'," UCHITEL'SKAIA GAZETA (Dec. 11, 1964), p. 4.
197. Motiashov, I. "Logika bor'by," MOSKVA, No. 3 (1967), 201-209.

VSEGDA V PRODAZHE

198. Anninskii, L. "Idei i liudi," Iu. No. 11 (1965), 72-74.
199. Farbshtein, A. [Review of "Vsegda v prodazhe"], VECHERNII LENINGRAD (June 28, 1966), 3.
200. Georgievskii, G. "Kak ia okazalsia na lestnitse," TEATR, No. 9 (1965), 3-13.
201. Goldobin, V. "V luchshikh traditsiiakh," TEATR, No. 2 (1966), 3-8.
202. Kagarlitskii, Iu. "Simpatii u nas obshchie," TEATR, No. 9 (1965), 35-43.
203. Mitin, G. "Pomogi sebe sam!" VLit, No. 4 (1966), 12-17.
204. Shcherbanov, K. "V spore o zhizni," KP (June 19, 1965), 3.
205. Solodovnikov, A. "Puti obnovleniia," SOVETSKAIA KUL'TURA (Mar. 24, 1966), 3-4.
206. Velekova, N. "Stol ne kruglyi," TEATR, No. 12 (1965), 23-33.
207. "Vsegda v prodazhe", [review], VERCHERNIAIA MOSKVA (June 2, 1965), 3.
208. " 'Sovremennike'," SOVETSKAIA KUL'TURA (June 5, 1965), 1.

ZATOVARENNAIA BOCHKOTARA

209. Brovman, G. "Voploshchenie zhizni, ili literaturnaia igra?" LR (May 24, 1965), 8-9.
210. Elkin, A. "O 'khoroshem cheloveke' i ZATOVARENNOI BOCHKOTARE," VECHER-NIAIA MOSKVA (Aug. 1, 1968), 3.
211. – – – –, "Pered kem snimet shliapu Shekspir?" MOSKVA, No. 10 (1968), 190-210.
212. Lokonov, V. "Posleslovie k obsuzhdeniiu," UCHITEL'SKAIA GAZETA (Sept. 21, 1968), 4.
213. Ognev, Gr. "Kuda spisat' bochkotaru?" KP (April 30, 1968), 2.
214. Rassadin, St. "Shestero v kuzove, ne shchitaia bochkotara," VLit. No. 10 (1968), 93-115.
215. Solov'eva, I. "S preuvelicheniiami i snovideniiami," LG (May 1, 1968), 6.
216. Vladin, V. L. "Zabochkotarennyi tovar," LG (Oct. 2, 1968), 16.

LIUBOV' K ELEKTRICHESTVU

217. Pankov, Viktor, "Brilliantiny dlia literatury," OGONEK, No. 42 (1971), 26-27.
218. – – – –, "Gody-desiatiletiia-epokha..." ZNAMIA, Vol. 2 (1972), 217-32.
219. Riabikova, T. "Vo imia revoliutsii," TUVINSKAIA PRAVDA (July 28, 1971).
220. Rosliakov, V. "Dorogoi revoliutsii," LG (May 26, 1971), 6.
221. Tsurikova, G. and Kuzimichev, I. "Chelovek i vremia," NEVA, No. 3 (1972), 162-70.
222. Veshniakov, V. "Odna, no plamennaia strast'," KRASNOE ZNAMIA (Feb. 22, 1972).

GENERAL STUDIES

223. Anninskii, L. "Posledniaia kniga Makarova," DN, No. 10 (1968), 268-70.
224. – – – –, "Realnost' prozy," DON, No. 3 (1964), 152-58.
225. Antol'skii, Pavel. "Otsy i deti," LG (Dec. 11, 1962), 3.
226. Baigusev, A. "Schast'e?" VECHERNIAIA MOSKVA (Sept. 2, 1963).
227. Baranov, V. "V glub' okeana!" URAL, No. 5 , pp. 163-79.
228. Belash, Iu. "Na sashu Zelenina oni ne pokhozhi," MG, No. 4 (1961).
229. Borisov, S. and Sorin, S. "Malaia entsiklopediia Iunosti," Iu., No. 10 (1962), 11-51.
230. Borshchagovskii, A. "Krovnaia sviaz' pokolenii," LG (Sept. 29, 1962), 1, 2.
231. – – – –, "Poiski molodoi prozy," MOSKVA, No. 12 (1962).
232. Brovman, G. "Grazhdanskoe chuvstvo i kharakter sovremennika," MOSKVA, No. 4 (1966), 197-203.
233. – – – –, "Grazhdanstvennost' geroia," MOSKVA, No. 6 (1963), 197-203.
234. – – – –, "Obraz sovremennika," NASH SOVREMENNIK, No. 1 (1965), 110-14.
235. – – – –, "Voploshchenie zhizni ili literaturnaia igra?" LR (May 24, 1968), 8-9.
236. Bursov, B. "Literatura nashego veka," PRAVDA (Nov. 27, 1967).
237. Bushin, V. "Shtampy byvaiut raznye," LZ (Aug. 19, 1959).
238. Bukhanov, V. "Ne tol'ko pisatel'," MK (Aug. 27, 1964), 4.

239. Chernov, A. "Schast'e mnimoe," ZNAMIA, No. 1 (1964), 248.

240. Chukovskaia, Lidiia. "Zerkalo, kotoroe ne otrazhaet," NM, No. 2 (1965), 241-49.

241. Chukovskii, Kornei. "Nechto o labude," LG (Aug. 12, 1961), 4.

242. Dalada, N. "Pered novoi vstrechi," LZ (May 10, 1961).

243. Dymshits, A. "I vpriam'—pora!" LR (Aug. 20, 1965), 10-11.

244. Elkin, A. "Sovremenniki," MG, No. 10 (1961), 294-305.

245. Ermachenko, V. "Tsvet liubvi," IUZHNYI KAZAKHSTAN (Mar. 26, 1964).

246. Favorin, V. "Grazhdane bol'shogo mira," URAL, No. 10 (1962), 171-80.

247. Filippov, Iu. "Vot takim Makarom," LG (April 8, 1970), 5.

248. Fomenko, L. "Naslediia klassikov," LG (Dec. 5, 1963).

249. – – – –, "Proza dlia iunoshestva," PRAVDA (Sept. 2, 1967), 3.

250. Frolov, V. "Sovremennost'," OKTIABR', No. 10 (1959).

251. Golubev, P. "Zvuchal li 'zvon bregeta'?" SMENA, No. 19 (1964), 24.

252. Idashkin, Iu. "Istoki podviga," OKTIABR', No. 12 (1962), 182-87.

253. Ivanova, L. "Nartsiss ne iz legendy," MG, No. 9 (1963).

254. Kamianov, V. "Ispytanie krasotoi," LITERATURA V SHKOLE, No. 4 (1966), 15-21.

255. – – – –, "Tak nazyvaemyi zhanr..." LG (June 23, 1964).

256. Karetnikova, M. "Ostanovlenie mgnoveniia," MG, No. 5 (1964).

257. Kassil', Lev. "Moi mladshii brat," PRAVDA (Nov. 18, 1962), 6.

258. Kedrina, Z. "Glavnoe—chelovek," DN, No. 3 (1963), 246-62.

259. Klepikova, E. and Solovev, V. "Traditsii i pisateli," NEVA, No. 8 (1960), 172-78.

260. Kogan, A. "Venets delu," LR (Oct. 2, 1964), 14.

261. – – – –, "Odin rasskaz," SO, No. 9 (1964), 183-86.

262. Kozhevnikov, V. "Molodost' sovetskoi literatury," SMENA (Oct. 20, 1962), 1, 3.

263. Kozlov, I. "Chutkaia dusha khudozhnika," OGONEK, No. 20 (1966), 23.

264. Kriachko, L. "Geroi ne khochet vzroslet'," LG (Mar. 19, 1963), 2-3.

265. – – – –, "Pogovorim o geroe," MG, No. 12 (1964), 292-306.

266. Kuz'lichev, I. "Puti i pereput'ia," OKTIABR', No. 5 (1966), 183-200.

267. Levin, F. "Spor s Nestorom," VLit. No. 11 (1965), 37-49.

268. Lobanov, M. "Feierverk..." LG (Dec. 17, 1964).

269. – – – –, "Vnutrennii i vneshnii chelovek," MG, No. 5 (1966), 286-302.

270. Makarov, A. "Cherez piat' let," ZNAMIA, No. 7 (1966), 201-219; No. 8, 217-27; No. 9, 207-225.

271. – – – –, POKOLENIIA I SUB'BY. M. "Sovetskii pisatel'," 1967. [Contains No. 270.]

272. Mitin, G. "Truba zovet," LR (Dec. 3, 1965), 17.

273. Mikhailova, L. "Grubaia plot' i gore ot uma," ZNAMIA, No. 11 (1963), 203-216.

274. Nagibin, Iurii. "Svoe i chuzhoe," DN, No. 7 (1959).

275. Nechaeva, L. "O chuvstve pravdy," MG, No. 4 (1965), 313-316.

276. Nikolin, E. "Polnoi dushoi," NEVA, No. 7 (1963), 171-76.

277. Ninov, A. "Gde nachinaetsia gorizont?" NEVA, No. 10. (1966), 171-78.

278. – – – –, "Iazyk rasskaza," DN, No. 4 (1966), 257-66.

279. Ozerov, V. "Na boevykh pozitsiiakh," VLit, No. 3 (1963), 3-9.

280. Permitin i Smirnov, "Liubiashchim vzgliadom," LR (June 12, 1964), 19.

281. Pertsovskii, V. "Sila dobra," VLit, No. 11 (1963) 21-44.

282. – – – –, "Osmyslenie zhizni," VLit, No. 2 (1964), 27-44.

283. Portnov, V. i drugie, "S kogo vy pishete portrety?" [pis'mo] IZVESTIIA (Aug. 14, 1965), 5.

284. Povarov, S. "Poeziia prozy," OMSKAIA PRAVDA (Dec. 17, 1964).

285. Radlov, D. "Liubliu i nenavizhu," OKTIABR', No. 10 (1969), 197-202.

286. Rassadin, St. "Sila i slabost' molodosti," VECHERNII LENINGRAD (Oct. 2, 1962), 3.

287. Rybakov, Iu. "Kistochkin i drugie," Lg (June 15, 1965), 3.

288. Sarnov, V. "Eto bylo nevozmozhno desiat' let nazad," VLit, No. 7 (1964), 31-36.

289. Shcherbakov, "Geroi, kotoromu segodnia 20," TEATR, No. 24, 1, 1963, p. 58.

29

290. Shcherbatova, G. A., ed., OB ISKUSSTVE CHTETSA. M. "Iskusstvo," 1960.
291. Semenov, G. "Pochti iz zapisnoi knigi," ZNAMIA, No. 9 (1962).
292. Shim, Eduard, "Voprosy k samomu sebe," ZNAMIA, No. 9 (1962).
293. Smoliakov, S. "O geroiakh vydumannykh," DAL'NII VOSTOK, No. 3 (1963), 177-82.
294. Sokolov, V. "Chitatel' i literaturnyi protsess," VLit, No. 1 (1965), 44-47.
295. Solov'eva, I. "Nachalo puti'" NM, No. 9 (1959).
296. Svetov, F. "Detali i sut'," NM, No. 4 (1966), 262-65.
297. ————, "Geroi rasskaza," VLit, No. 12 (1962), 17-35.
298. —— ——, "O molodom geroe," NM, No. 5 (1967), 218-32.
299. Trifonova, T. "Dlia cheloveka i chelovechestva," VLit, No. 6 (1961), 12-35.
300. Velengurin, N. "Velikoe i prostoe," KUBAN', No. 2 (1963), 47-51.
301. Vinogradov, V. V. i drugie [pochta Redaktora], LG (June 7, 1967), 5.
302. Vlasenko, A. "Pisateli o literaturnom masterstve," NASH SOVREMENNIK, No. 7 (1965), 108-110.
303. — — — —, "Siuzhet i geroi," NEVA, No. 8 (1963), 171-80.
304. — — — —, "Trud—poeziia!" OKTIABR', No. 12 (1964), 193-203.
305. Voronov, V. "Chelovek—riadom s toboi," LG (Oct. 20, 1962).

IV. Critical Studies in Foreign Languages or Published Outside the USSR

306. Brown, Deming. "Vasily Aksenov at 33," TRIQUARTERLY, No. 3 (1965), 75-83.
307. Burg, David. "Molodoe pokolenie," MOSTY, No. 11 (1965), 211-29.
308. Erlich, V. "Post-Stalin Trends in Russian Literature," SLAVIC REVIEW, XXIII, 3 (1964), 405-419.
309. Esmein, Isabelle. "Polemique autour des oeuvres d'Axionov et de Tendriakov," TABLE RONDE, No. 215 (1965), 175-79.
310. Ireland, Rosh. "A Note on Aksenov," MEANJIN QUARTERLY, XXIII, 117 (1964).
311. Kariakin, Iurii. "An Episode in the Current Battle of Ideas," NM, No. 9 (1964), translated in THE SOVIET REVIEW, No. 3 (1965), 21-31.
312. "The Old and Young in Literature," SURVEY (January 1963, pp. 23-30), translated from answers to a questionnaire in VLit, No. 9 (1962).
313. Piskunov, Vladimir. CONFERENCE OF PROBLEMS OF SOCIALIST REALISM, A SURVEY. In SOVIET LITERATURE, No. 7 (1967), 143-51.
314. Samarin, R. "The Provocateurs of SURVEY," LG April 18, 1963, translated in SURVEY (July 1963).
315. Slonim, Marc. "European Notebook," NEW YORK TIMES BOOK REVIEW (May 19, 1968). [On "Zatovarennaia bochkotara"]
316. Whitney, T., ed., THE NEW WRITING IN RUSSIA. Ann Arbor, 1964.
317. Zelinskii, Kornelii. RUSSIAN POETRY TODAY, in SURVEY (January 1962).

ADDENDA

318. Vasily Aksenov, "Kruglye sutki non-stop," NOVYI MIR 8 (August 1976), pp. 51-122.
319. Vasily Aksenov, "Victory," RLT 5 (Winter 1973), pp. 191-95.
320. Priscilla Meyer, "Aksenov and Soviet Literature of the 1960s," RLT 6 (Spring 1973), pp. 447-60.
321. Priscilla Meyer, "Interview with Vasily Pavlovich Aksenov," RLT 6 (Spring 1973), pp. 569-94.

A BIBLIOGRAPHY OF SOVIET PUBLICATIONS ON
RUSSIAN VERSIFICATION, 1958-1972

Compiled by G.S. Smith

I. Introduction

The efflorescence of Russian studies of versification that followed Andrei Bely's essays in *Simvolizm* (1910) and closed with Boris Tomashevsky's *O stikhe* (1929) is documented in M. P. Shtokmar's still indispensable bibliography[1] and its supplements.[2] For nearly thirty years after the appearance of Tomashevsky's collection of essays, the publication of versification studies ceased almost entirely in the Soviet Union, and the tradition was continued abroad, notably in Czechoslovakia, Poland, the United States, and Yugoslavia. K. F. Taranovski's *Ruski dvodelni ritmovi* (Belgrade 1953) can be seen as the culminating point of the statistical studies of Russian verse rhythms that had formed one of the most innovative elements in Russian work published before 1929; and this book, with its formulation, on the basis of unprecedentedly extensive material, of general laws that describe the rhythmic norms of certain Russian meters, can also be seen as the starting point of a significant proportion of the works listed below. These works began to appear in the Soviet Union in 1957-58, one aspect of a general revitalization of Soviet literary criticism; and the revival of studies of versification has continued to gain momentum, despite some harsh criticism directed against its earlier phases.[3] The collection *Teoriia stikha* (1968) was a milestone in the history of the new movement, bringing together the work of the major figures involved up to this date. There is a wide variety of approaches and an equally wide range in quality within the works listed below, but certain areas of achievement can be singled out:

(a) A. N. Kolmogorov's refinement (44, 156, 159, 161) of the statistical techniques pioneered by Bely, Shengeli and Tomashevsky.

(b) The subsequent application of this technique in exhaustive studies of specific meters within the work of individual poets (114, 117, 128, 160) and historical periods (113, 116, 118, 119, 200), with attention being focussed on subjects previously neglected, such as the *dol'nik,* the versification of Mayakovsky, and folk verse.

(c) The compilation of exhaustive "metrical handbooks" to the versification of individual poets (94, 175, 207, 214, 224, 254) and historical periods (109, 127, 183, 200, 207); a scheme has now been established to combine such studies in a collective history of Russian versification (78).

(d) Studies of the semantic function and linguistic associations of particular meters (171, 172, 173, 185, 198, 206, 207).

(e) V. E. Kholshevnikov's re-examination of the types of intonation in Russian lyric poetry.(219).

(f) The statistical study of rhyme (48, 62).

(g) Studies of syllabic verse that have undermined the heretofore dominant "evolutionary" view of its development (125, 242).

(h) The publication and discussion of archival materials (247, 249, 253, 256) that shed new light on the history of Russian studies of versification.

There remain several notable areas of controversy. L. I. Timofeev's long-dominant view of verse as essentially a language-determined phenomenon (76, 308) is opposed by those who would assert the old Jakobsonian view of meter as "violence done to language." The music-oriented theories of A. P. Kviatkovsky and S. V. Shervinsky have been widely attacked. An idiosyncratic terminology, that reflects the general lack of an accepted terminology especially in marginal areas of versification, has hampered the effectiveness of S. Bobrov's remarkable articles. In general, the newer work has reinstated rather than superseded the now classic textbooks of the earlier period,[4] but despite continual complaint only two such works have been reprinted in the Soviet Union (257, 258). However, at the present time the study of Russian versification by native scholars is in a significantly more active state than are versification studies in other modern languages, with the possible exception of Polish; the application to the verse of other languages of the techniques developed in the study of Russian verse,[5] and the resultant opportunities for comparative and typological studies, constitute an extremely promising field for future research.

NOTES

1. M. P. Shtokmar, *Bibliografiia rabot po stikhoslozheniiu* (M. 1933). Reviewed and supplemented by Roman Jakobson, *Slavia*, XIII (1934-35), 416-31.

2. *Literaturnyi kritik*, 8 (1936), 194-205, and 9 (1936), 235-53.

3. The beginnings of the revival are discussed by K. Taranovski in T. Sebeok (ed.), *Current Trends in Linguistics,* I (The Hague, 1963), 192-201, and by I. I. Revzin and V. N. Toporov, "Novoe issledovanie po stikhovedeniiu," *Voprosy iazykoznaniia,* 3 (1962), 126-31. For hostile criticism see below, 296, 301, 302, 307, 308.

4. For example, B. V. Tomashevskii, *Russkoe stikhoslozhenie* (P. 1923) and *O stikhe* (L. 1929); V. M. Zhirmunskii, *Rifma, ee istoriia i teoriia* (L. 1923), and *Vvedenie v metriku, Teoriia stikha* (L. 1925); Roman Jakobson, *O cheshskom stikhe, preimushchestvenno v sopostavlenii s russkim* (Berlin, 1923).

5. In a series of pioneering works, M. G. Tarlinskaia has applied Russian statistical methods to the study of English versification: "Aktsentnye osobennosti angliiskogo sillabo-tonicheskogo stikha," *Voprosy iazykoznaniia,* 3 (1967), 81-91; "Metr i ritm dochoserov-skogo rifmovannogo stikha," *Voprosy iazykoznaniia,* 3 (1971), 73-88; "Nekotorye aspekty teorii i rezul'taty analiza angliiskogo stikha," in Z. Kopczynska and L. Pszczolowska (eds.), *Metryka slowianska* (Wroclaw-Warsaw-Krakow-Gdansk, 1971),   119-40; "Aktsentnaia struktura i metr angliiskogo stikha," *Voprosy iazykoznaniia,* 4 (1972), 100-11; see also Section IV of the bibliography below, and also A. I. Mamonov, *Svobodnyi stikh v iaponskoi poezii* (M. 1971).

II. Bibliography

The bibliography below lists only works specifically devoted to versification, ignoring the extensive material on the subject published in wider contexts such as the introductory articles to editions of poetry and general histories of literature; an exception has been made, however, for textbooks of literary theory.

Those works which are of outstanding importance either from the point of view of methodology or of the factual material they contain are marked by asterisks.

The compiler would like to acknowledge the generous and invaluable help of K. D. Vishnevskii, M. L. Gasparov, S. I. Gindin, and V. E. Kholshevnikov. A shorter version of this bibliography was circulated in connection with a paper read at the third meeting of the Neo-Formalist Circle, held in the University of Bristol, December 1971; thanks are due to the participants in the discussion following this paper.

Abbreviations

Vop Lit - **Voprosy literatury** (Moscow)

VRL - **Voprosy russkoi literatury** (Lvov)

Vop Iaz - **Voprosy iazykoznaniia** (Moscow)

ISSh - L. E. Timofeev (ed.), **Izuchenie stikhoslozheniia v shkole** (M. 1960).

KLE - **Kratkaia literaturnaia entsiklopediia** (Moscow, 1964-   ).

L - Leningrad

M - Moscow

M-LPTL - F. A. Steklova (chief ed.), **Marksizm-leninizm i problemy teorii literatury (Tezisy dokladov nauchnoi konferentsii, posviashchennoi 100-letiiu so dnia rozhdeniia V. I. Lenina)** (Alma-Ata, 1969), (Kazakhskii gos. un-t imeni S. M. Kirova)

MS - Z. Kopczynska, L. Pszczolowska (eds.), **Metryka slowianska** (Wroclaw-Warsaw..., 1971).

NRL - V. A. Sapogov (chief ed.),N. A. Nekrasov i russkaia literatura. Tezisy dekladov i soobshchenii mezhvuzovskoi nauchnoi konferentsii, posviashchennoi 150-letiiu so dnia rozhdeniia N. A. Nekrasova, Kostromskii gos. ped. inst. imeni N. A. Nekrasova (Kostroma, 1971).

PSRL - M. P. Alekseev (chief ed.), Poetika i stilistika russkoi literatury. Pamiati akademika Viktora V. Vinogradova (L. 1971).

Rus Lit - Russkaia literatura (Leningrad)

RSPiS - K. G. Petrosov (chief ed.), Russkaia sovetskaia poeziia i stikhoslozhenie, Materialy mezhvuzovskoi konferentsii, Moskovskii ob. ped. inst. imeni N. K. Krupskoi, (Moscow 1969).

TGU - Tartuskii gosudarstvennyi universitet

TS - V. M. Zhirmunskii, D. S. Likhachev, V. E. Kholshevnikov (eds.), Teoriia stikha (L. 1968).

UZ - Uchenye zapiski

I. BIBLIOGRAPHICAL ARTICLES

1. Goncharov, B. P. "Annotirovannaia bibliografiia noveishikh stikhovedcheskikh rabot," ISSh, 209-17. Discusses, among other things, Nos 280, 282, 82, 226, 83, 76 below.

2. Kozhinov, V. V. "Poetika za 50 let," IZVESTIIA AKADEMII NAUK SSSR, Seriia literatury i iazyka, XXVI, vyp. 5 (1967), 432-44. Interesting mainly for listing and positive assessment of works of the 1920s.

3. Leont'ev, A. A. "Issledovaniia poeticheskoi rechi," in F. P. Filin (ed.), TEORE-TICHESKIE PROBLEMY SOVETSKOGO IAZYKOZNANIIA (M. 1968), 143-53. A brief survey of publications 1917-67.

*4. Rudnev, P. A. "O nekotorykh problemakh sovremennogo sovetskogo stikho-vedeniia," in S. I. Kaufman (ed.), VOPROSY ROMANO-GERMANSKOGO IAZYKO-ZNANIIA (Kolomna, 1966), 83-102 (UZ, Kolomenskii ped. inst.). Concise, informative survey, with bibliography of Soviet and other publications.

5. Kholshevnikov, V. E. "Stikhoslozhenie," in B. P. Gorodetskii, N. V. Izmailov, B. S. Meilakh (eds.), PUSHKIN. ITOGI I PROBLEMY IZUCHENIIA (M-L. 1966), 535-54. Deals with studies in Pushkin's versification since 1910.

II. STUDIES OF THE THEORY OF VERSIFICATION

6. Antoshchenkov, G. N. "Dol'niki v sisteme russkogo stikhoslozheniia," RSPiS, 185-91.

7. Baevskii, V. S. "O chislovoi otsenke sily slogov v stikhe al'terniruiushchego ritma," Vop Iaz, 2 (1966), 84-89.

8. ———, "Chislovye znacheniia sily slogov v stikhe al'terniruiushchego ritma," NAUCHNYE DOKLADY VYSSHEI SHKOLY. FILOLOGICHESKIE NAUKI, 3 (1967), 50-5.

9. ———, "Stikh al'terniruiushchego ritma v svete auditorskogo eksperimenta," RSPiS, 244-50.

10. ———, "O sootnoshenii metricheskikh sistem russkoi poeticheskoi rechi," NRL, 109-10.

11. Bobrov, S. "Tesnota stikhovogo riada (Opyt statisticheskogo analiza literaturo-vedcheskogo poniatiia, vvedennogo Iu. N. Tynianovym)," Rus Lit 3 (1965), 109-24.

12. ———, "Sintagmy, slovorazdely i litavridy (Poniatie o ritme soderzhatel'no-effektivnom i o estestvennoi ritmizatsii rechi)," (1) Rus Lit 4 (1965), 80-101; (2) Rus Lit 1 (1966), 79-97.

13. ———, "Russkii tonicheskii stikh s ritmom neopredelennoi chetnosti i var'iruiushchei sillabikoi," (1) Rus Lit 1 (1967), 42-64; (2) Rus Lit 2 (1968), 61-87.

14. Burina, L. Zhovtis, A. "Eksperimental'naia proverka izokhronnykh teorii russkoi stikha," M-LPTL, 68-70.

15. Bukhshtab, B. "Ob osnovakh i tipakh russkogo stikha," M-LPTL, 56-57.

16. Bukhshtab, B. "O strukture russkogo klassicheskogo stikha," UZ TGU, vypusk 236, TRUDY PO ZNAKOVYM SISTEMAM IV (1969), 386-408.

17. Vasiutochkin, G. S. "O respredelenii form chetyrekhstopnogo iamba v stikhotvornykh tekstakh," TS, 202-10.

18. Gindin, S. I. "Vnutrenniaia semantika ritma i ee matematicheskoe modelirovanie," PROBLEMY PRIKLADNOI LINGVISTIKI. Tezisy mezhvuzovskoi konferentsii 16-19 dekabria 1969 g., Chast' I (M. 1969), 92-96.

19. _____, "Puti modelirovaniia ritmicheskoi organizatsii teksta," in STRUKTURNO-MATEMATICHESKIE METODY MODELIROVANIIA IAZYKA. Tezisy dokladov i soobshchenii vsesoiuznoi nauchnoi konferentsii, Chast' I (Kiev, 1970), 33-35.

20. _____, "K osnovaniiam deskriptivnoi metriki," in MATERIALY V VSESOIUZNOGO SIMPOZIUMA PO KIBERNETIKE (Tbilisi, 1970), 343-44.

21. Girshman, M. M. "Stikhotvornaia rech'," in TEORIIA LITERATURY. OSNOVNYE PROBLEMY V ISTORICHEKOM OSVESHCHENII (M. 1965), 317-92.

22. _____, "Stikh i smysl ili stikh kak smysl? (Eshche raz o smyslovoi vyrazitel'nosti stikha)," Vop Lit 6 (1971), 198-202.

23. Golenishchev-Kutuzov, I. N. "Slovorazdel v russkom stikhoslozhenii," Vop Iaz 4 (1959), 20-34.

24. Goncharov, B. P. "Rifma i ee smyslovaia vyrazitel'nost'," ISSh, 59-95.

25. _____, "K probleme smyslovoi vyrazitel'nosti stikha," IZVESTIIA AKAD. NAUK SSSR, seriia literatury i iazyka, Tom XXIX, vyp. 1 (1970), 23-32.

26. Derkachev, I. Z. "O stikhotvornom ritme kak iazykovom iavlenii," UZ UL'IANOVSKOGO PED. INST., Tom 17, Vyp. 5 (1962), 112-22.

27. Ermilova, E. "Osnovy russkogo stikhoslozheniia," Vop Lit, 6 (1959).

28. Zhirmunskii, V. M. "O ritmicheskoi proze," Rus Lit 4 (1966), 103-14; translation, "On Rhythmic Prose," in TO HONOR ROMAN JAKOBSON, III (The Hague—Paris, 1967), 2376-88.

29. _____, "Vorrede," in reprint of RIFMA, EE ISTORIIA I TEORIIA (Munich, 1970), v-xi (Slavische Propylaen, Band 71).

30. Zhovtis, A. L. "Granitsy svobodnogo stikha," Vop Lit 5 (1966), 105-23.

31. _____, "Chto takoe svobodnyi stikh?" PROSTOR 8 (1966).

32. _____, "V rassypanom stroiu... (Grafika sovremennogo russkogo stikha)," Rus Lit 1 (1968), 123-34. Reprinted in No. 33 below.

33. _____, STIKHI NUZHNY. STAT'I (Alma-Ata, 1968). Review: M. L. Gasparov, "Stikhovedenie nuzhno..." Vop Lit 4 (1969), 203-207.

34. _____, "O sposobakh rifmovaniia v russkoi poezii," Vop Iaz 2 (1969), 64-75.

35. _____, "Otnosheniia banal'nosti-original'nosti v strukture stikha," RUSSKOE I ZARUBEZHNOE IAZYKOZNANIE, vyp. 3 (Alma-Ata, 1970), 280-94.

36. _____, "O kriteriiakh tipologicheskoi kharakteristiki svobodnogo stikha," Vop Iaz 2 (1970), 63-77.

37. Zivel'chinskaia, L. "Ritm," Vop Lit 3 (1963), 174-81.

38. Karpov, A. "Ritmicheskaia organizatsiia stikha," ISSh, 21-58.

39. _____, STIKH I VREMIA (M. 1966). Review: B. Goncharov, Rus Lit 4 (1967), 253-57.

40. Kviatkovskii, A. P. "Russkoe stikhoslozhenie," Rus Lit 1 (1960), 78-104.

41. _____, "Ritmologiia narodnoi chastushki," Rus Lit 2 (1962), 92-116.

42. _____, "Russkii svobodnyi stikh," Vop Lit 12 (1963), 60-77.

43. Kovalenkov, A. "Ritm i metricheskie kanony. Zametki pisatelia," Vop Lit 10 (1967), 171-77.

44. Kolmogorov, A. N., Prokhorov, A. V., "Statistika i teoriia veroiatnostei v issledovanii russkogo stikhoslozheniia," SIMPOZIUM PO KOMPLEKSNOMU IZUCHENIIU KHUDOZHESTVENNOGO TVORCHESTVA. Tezisy i annotatsii (L. 1963), 23-24.

*45. _____, "K osnovam russkoi klassicheskoi metriki," in B. Meilakh (ed.),
SODRUZHESTVO NAUK I TAINY TVORCHESTVA (M. 1968), 397-432.

46. Kondratov, A. M. "Teoriia informatsii i poetika," in SIMPOZIUM PO STRUK-
TURNOMU IZUCHENIIU ZNAKOVYKH SISTEM. Tezisy dokladov (M. 1962).

47. _____, "Teoriia informatsii i poetika (Entropiia ritma russkoi rechi),"
PROBLEMY KIBERNETIKI (1963), 279-86.

48. _____, "Statistika tipov russkoi rifmy," Vop Iaz 6 (1963), 96-106.

49. Korman, B. "K opredeleniiu perenosa (enjambement)," Rus Lit 3 (1963), 165.

50. Kotrelev, N. "K voprosu o vzaimootnoshenii ritma i metra," TGU, MATERIALY
XXII NAUCHNOI STUDENCHESKOI KONFERENTSII. Poetika, istoriia literatury,
lingvistika (Tartu, 1967), 4-9.

51. Krasnoperova, M. A. "Ob ispol'zovanii EVM (elektronno-vychislitel'nykh
mashin) dlia izucheniia metra i ritma stikhotvornykh tekstov," in MATERIALY V
VSESOIUZNOGO SIMPOZIUMA PO KIBERNETIKE (Tbilisi, 1970), 345-47.

52. Levin, Iu. I. "O nekotorykh chertakh plana soderzhaniia v poeticheskikh
tekstakh," in STRUKTURNAIA TIPOLOGIIA IAZYKOV (M. 1966), 199-215.

53. Lotman, M., Reifman, S. "Opyt funktsional'nogo opisaniia strofiki," TGU.
MATERIALY XXVII NAUCHNOI STUDENCEHSKOI KONFERENTSII. Literaturovedenie, lingvistika (Tartu, 1972), 131-35.

54. Lotman, Iu. M. LEKTSII PO STRUKTURAL'NOI POETIKE. VVEDENIE,
TEORIIA STIKHA (Tartu, 1964), (UZ TGU, vypusk TRUDY PO ZNAKOVYM SISTE-
MAM, I). Reprinted, Brown University Press Slavic Reprint No. 5 (Providence, 1968).
Translation: VORLESUNGEN ZU EINER STRUKTURALEN POETIK (Munich, 1971)

55. Maimin, E. "Stikh i metr," Rus Lit 3, (1964), 108-18.

*56. Nikonov, V. A. "Strofika," ISSh, 96-149.

57. _____, "Mesto udareniia v russkom slove," INTERNATIONAL JOURNAL
OF SLAVIC LINGUISTICS AND POETICS, VI (1963), 1-8.

58. "Ot chego ne svoboden svobodnyi stikh," Vop Lit 1 (1972), 124-60. A sym-
posium with contributions from Arvo Mets, Sergei Narovchatov, Vlad. Burin, Rasul Rza,
Oiar Vatsietis, Boris Slutskii, Arsenii Tarkovskii, Viach. Kupriianov, David Samoilov, and
editorial summary.

59. Pavlova, V. I. "Issledovanie stikha metodami eksperimental'noi fonetiki," TS,
211-17.

60. Panchenko. A. M. "O rifme i deklamatsionnykh normakh sillabicheskoi
poezii XVII v. " TS, 280-93.

61. Peisakhovich, M. A. "Taktometricheskaia teoriia i stikhotvornaia praktika,"
VRL 2 (1969), 80-83.

62. Petrov. V. M. Melamid, L. A. "O kharaktere izmeneniia nekotorykh parametrov
khudozhestvennykh proizvedenii (Osnovnye tendentsii evoliutsii rifmy v sovremennom
russkom stikhoslozhenii)," VRL 3 (1968), 31-38.

63. Prokhorov, A. "Teoria prawdopodobienstwa w badaniach rytmu wiersza,"
PAMIETNIK LITERACKI, LXI, zeszyt. 3 (1970), 113-27.

64. Poldmae, J. "O primenenii znakovoi modeli pri opisanii rifmy," M-LPTL 73-74.
Expanded version, but without examples from Russian: Viitso T-R., Poldmae, J. "K
aksiomatike i transkriptsii rifmy," TGU. TEZISY DOKLADOV IV LETNEI SHKOLY
PO VTORICHNYM MODELIRUIUSHCHIM SISTEMAM (1970), 155-58.

65. Rodnianskaia, I. B. "Slovo i 'muzyka' v liricheskom stikhotvorenii," in V. V.
Kozhevnikova (ed.), SLOVO I OBRAZ. SBORNIK STATEI (M. 1964), 195-233.

66. _____, "Zamechaniia k ritmologii A. P. Kviatkovskogo," VRL 2 (1971),
68-74.

67. Rudnev, P. A. "Ritm-metr-ritmicheskaia forma. (K voprosu ob utochnenii
stikhovedcheskoi terminologii)," TGU. TEZISY DOKLADOV IV LETNEI SHKOLY PO
VTORICHNYM MODELIRUIUSHCHIM SISTEMAM (1970), 151-4.

68. _____, "Metr i smysl," MS, 77-88.

69. Samoilov, D. "Nabliudeniia nad rifmoi," Vop Lit 6 (1970), 160-77.

70. Sapogov, V. " 'Ritm-obraz' v stikhoslozhenii XX veka," M-LPTL, 72-73.

71. _____, "Opyt eksplikatsii poniatiia 'stikhotvornyi ritm'," TGU, TEZISY DOKLADOV IV LETNEI SHKOLY PO VTORICHNYM MODELIRUIUSHCHIM SISTEMAM (1970), 142-44.

72. Sel'vinskii, I. STUDIIA STIKHA (M. 1962).

73. Semenov, A. A. "Proza i stikh (Obzor problemy)," DOKLADY NA NAUCH-NYKH KONFERENTSIIAKH (UZ; Iaroslavskii gos. ped. inst., Tom 3, Vyp. 2), 1964, 50-59.

74. Sidorenko, G. "Voprosy metodologii i metodiki v izuchenii stikhoslozheniia," M-LPTL, 53-45.

75. Tarlinskaia, M. G. "Aktsentnaia differentsiatsiia odnoslozhnykh slov i ikh strukturnaia funktsiia v russkom iambe," NRL, 118-21.

*76. Timofeev, L. I. OCHERKI TEORII I ISTORII RUSSKOGO STIKHA (M. 1958). Reviews: *M. L. Gasparov, "Tsel' i put' sovetskogo stikhovedeniia," Vop Lit 8 (1958), 208-213; L. Dolgopolov, Rus Lit 2 (1960), 232-36.

77. Timofeev, L. I., Girshman, M. "Podgotovka kollektivnoi istorii russkogo stikha," Vop Lit 12 (1968), 138-43.

*78. _____, "Na puti k istorii russkogo stikhoslozheniia," IZVESTIIA AKAD. NAUK SSSR, Seriia literatury i iazyka, Tom XXIX (1970), 442-46.

79. Tolstaia, S. M. "O fonologii rifmy," UZ TGU. TRUDY PO ZNAKOVYM SIS-TEMAM II (1965), 300-305.

80. Tomashevskii, B. V. Review of B. O. Unbegaun, RUSSIAN VERSIFICATION, Vop Iaz 3 (1957), 127-34.

81. _____, STIKH I IAZYK (M. 1958). Reprinted in No. 83 below.

*82. _____, STILISTIKA I STIKHOSLOZHENIIA (L. 1959)

83. _____, STIKH I IAZYK. FILOLOGICHESKIE OCHERKI (M-L. 1959). Reviews: L. Ginzburg, Rus Lit 2 (1960), 226-31; (with No. 82) V. E. Kholshevnikov, VESTNIK LENINGRADSKOGO UNIVERSITETA, 2 (1960), Seriia istorii, iazyka i liter-atury, 1, 163-64.

84. Kharlap, M. O STIKHE (M. 1966). Review: B. Goncharov, "Stikh i ego zakony," Vop Lit 9 (1967), 199-203.

85. Kholshevnikov, V. E. "Izuchenie stikha metodami eksperimental'noi fonetiki," SIMPOZIUM PO KOMPLEKSNOMU IZUCHENIIU KHUDOZHESTVENNOGO TVOR-CHESTVA. Tezisy i annotatsii (L. 1963).

86. _____, "Pereboi ritma," RSPiS, 173-84.

87. Shakhverdov, S. "Strofika," TGU. MATERIALY XXVII NAUCHNOI STU-DENCHESKOI KONFERENTSII. LITERATUROVEDENIE, LINGVISTIKA (1972), 135-37.

88. Shervinskii, S.V. "Vremennye kompensatsii v stikhe," IZVESTIIA AKAD. NAUK SSSR, Seriia literatury i iazyka, Tom XIX, 6 (1960), 471-78. Incorporated in No. 225 below.

89. _____, "Smyslovoe udarenie kak stikhologicheskii element," in SLAVIAN-SKOE IAZYKOZNANIE. DOKLADY SOVETSKOI DELEGATSII, V MEZHDUNAROD-NYI S"EZD SLAVISTOV (M. 1963), 399-420.

III. STUDIES OF THE VERSIFICATION OF SPECIFIC POETS AND PERIODS

90. Afonnikov, G. "K voprosu o pauzakh v stikhakh Maiakovskogo," in PROBLEMY NARODNOSTI, REALIZMA, I KHUDOZHESTVENNOGO MASTERSTVA (Chardzhou, 1963), 43-58. (UZ Turkmenskogo gos. Ped. Inst.)

91. Baevskii, V. S. "Tipy stroficheskoi organizatsii stikhotvorenii Nekrasova," in A. M. Garkavi (ed.), NEKRASOVSKII SBORNIK (Kaliningrad, 1972), 106-109.

92. _____, "Pesennye struktury v nekrasovskom stikhe," Ibid. 114-117.

93. Belza, M. "Ritmika poemy 'Egipetskie nochi' A. S. Pushkina, dopisannoi V. Ia. Briusovym," in T. Gamkrelidze (ed.), PLAN RABOTY I TEZISY DOKLADOV II MEZHVUZOVSKOI STUDENCHESKOI NAUCHNOI KONFERENTSII PO PROBLEM-AM STRUKTURNOI I PRIKLADNOI LINGVISTIKI (Tbilisi, 1966), 9-10.

94. Belousov, A. "O metricheskom repertuare poezii I. A. Bunina," TGU. RUSSKAIA FILOLOGIIA. 3 SBORNIK NAUCHNYKH STUDENCHESKIKH RABOT (Tartu, 1971), 48-61.

95. Bel'skaia, L. "Iz nabliudenii nad ritmami S. Esenina," in FILOLOGICHESKII SBORNIK, Vypusk 4 (Alma-Ata, 1965), 102-110.

96. _____, " 'Eseninskii tip' russkogo dol'nika," M—LPTL, 74-77.

97. Berkov, P. N. "K sporam o printsipakh chteniia sillabicheskikh stikhov XVII-nachala XVIII v.," TS , 294-316.

98. _____, "Stikhotvornoe akademicheskoe privetstvie 1727 goda (K istorii russ-kogo tonicheskogo stikhoslozheniia)," in F. Ia. Priima (chief ed.), OT "SLOVA O POLKU IGOREVE" DO "TIKHOGO DONA," (L. 1969), 282-90.

99. Birzhishko, A. "O ritmiko-smyslovykh otnosheniiakh v stikhotvorenii Lermon-tova 'Kak chasto, pestroiu tolpoiu okruzhen...' , " M-LPTL, 61-63.

100. Bobrov, S. P. "Opyt izucheniia vol'nogo stikha pushkinskikh 'Pesen zapadnykh slavian'," TEORIIA VEROIATNOSTI I EE PRIMENENIIA, Tom IX, Vyp. 2 (1964), 262-72.

101. _____, "K voprosu o podlinnom stikhotvornom razmere pushkinskikh 'Pesen zapadnykh slavian'," Rus Lit 3 (1964), 119-37.

102. Burtin, Iu. "Iz nabliudenii nad stikhom Tvardovskogo," Vop Lit 6 (1960), 177-200.

103. Bychkov, V. V. "Iz nabliudenii nad osobennostiami kompozitsii i iazyka poemy S. Esenina 'Anna Snegina'," RSPiS, 258-65.

104. Vishnevskii, K. D. "Strofika Lermontova," in TVORCHESTVO LERMONTOVA (Penza, 1965), 3-131 (UZ Penzenskogo gos. ped. inst., seriia filolgicheskaia, vyp.14).

105. _____, "Strofa i zhanr (Tezisy doklada)" in PROBLEMY MASTERSTVA V IZUCHENII I PREPODAVANII KHUDOZHESTVENNOI LITERATURY (M. 1967), 12-13.

106. _____, "Zhanrovaia i stilisticheskaia rol' strofy desiatistishiia v russkoi poezii XVIII veka (Tezisy doklada)," in MATERIALY IX NAUCHNOI KONFERENTSII LITERA-TUROVEDOV POVOLZH'IA (Penza, 1969), 14-17.

107. _____, "Stanovlenie trekhslozhnykh razmerov v russkoi poezii," RSPiS, 207-15.

108. _____, "Traditsii i novatorstvo v stikhotvornoi tekhnike M. Iu. Lermontova," in IAZYK I STIL' PROIZVEDENII M. Iu. LERMONTOVA (Penza, 1969), 78-88 (UZ Penzenskogo gos. ped. inst., Tom 78).

*109. _____, "Vvedenie v stikhotvornuiu tekhniku XVIII veka," in VOPROSY METODA I STILIA V RUSSKOI I ZARUBEZHNOI LITERATURE (Penza, 1969), 3-15 (UZ Penzenskogo gos. ped. inst., Tom 81).

110. _____, "Ob istokakh stikha poemy Nekrasova 'Komu na Rusi zhit' khorosho?'," NRL, 101-103.

111. Vrazovskaia, L. V. "Mesto narodnogo stikha v poemakh N. A. Nekrasova i sovremennoi russkoi poeme," *Ibid.* 132-34.

112. Gasparov, M. L. "O ritmike russkogo trekhudarnogo dol'nika," in SIMPOZIUM PO STRUKTURNOMU IZUCHENIIU ZNAKOVYKH SISTEM. Tezisy dokladov (M. 1962), Superseded by No. 118 below.

113. _____, "Statisticheskoe obsledovanie russkogo trekhudarnogo dol'nika," TEORIIA VEROIATNOSTI I EE PRIMENENIIA, Tom 8, Vyp. 1 (1963), 102-108. Super-seded by No. 118 below.

114. _____, "Vol'nyi khorei i vol'nyi iamb Maiakovskogo", Vop Iaz 3 (1965), 76-88.

115. _____, Review of Robin Kemball, ALEXANDER BLOK, A STUDY IN RHYTHM AND METRE, in Vop Iaz 6 (1966), 137-39.

*116. _____, "Iamb i khorei sovetskikh poetov i problema evoliutsii russkogo stikha," Vop Iaz 3 (1967), 59-67.

117. _____, "Aktsentnyi stikh rannego Maiakovskogo," UZ TGU, Vypusk 198, TRUDY PO ZNAKOVYM SISTEMAM III (1967), 324-60.

*118. Gasparov, M. L. "Russkii trekhudarnyi dol'nik XX veka," TS, 59-106.

119. _____, "Taktovik v russkom stikhoslozhenii XX v.," Vop Iaz 5 (1968), 79-90.

120. _____, "Tsepnye strofy v russkoi poezii nachala XX v.," RSPiS, 251-56.

121. _____, "Statisticheskoe obsledovanie russkogo bylinnogo stikha," in PRO-BLEMY PRIKLADNOI LINGVISTIKI. Tezisy mezhvuzovskoi konf. 16-19 dek 1969g., (M. 1969), Chast' I, 82-86.

122. _____, "Elementy strofiki v russkom nestroficheskom iambe XIX v.," M-LPTL, 57-59.

123. _____, "Oppozitsiia 'stikh-proza' v stanovlenii russkogo stikhoslozheniia," TGU. Tezisy dokladov IV letnei shkoly po vtorichnym modeliruiushchim sistemam (1970), 140-41.

124. _____, "Ritmika trekhslozhnykh razmerov v russkoi poezii," NRL, 86-88.

*125. _____, "Russkii sillabicheskii trinadtsatislozhnik," MS, 39-64.

126. _____, "Narodnyi stikh A. Vostokova," PSRL, 437-43.

*127. _____, "Metricheskii repertuar russkoi liriki XVIII-XX vv.," Vop Iaz 1 (1972), 54-67.

128. _____, Tarlinskaia, M. G. "Ritmika trekhslozhnykh razmerov Nekrasova," in A. M. Garkavi (ed.), NEKRASOVSKII SBORNIK (Kaliningrad, 1972), 110-13.

129. Gvozdikovskaia, G. "Dvuslozhnye razmery i stilevye iskaniia v sovremennoi liricheskoi poezii," NAUCHNYE TRUDY FIL. FAK. KIRGIZSKOGO UNIVERSITETA, Vypusk 16 (1970), 106-112.

130. Gindin, S. I. "Ritmika i kompozitsiia poemy V. A. Lugovskogo 'Kak chelovek plyl s Odiseem'," TGU. MATERIALY XXII NAUCHNOI STUDENCHESKOI KONFERE-NTSII. POETIKA, ISTORIIA, LITERATURY, LINGVISTIKA (1967), 124-27.

131. Girshman, M. M. "Stikh N. A. Nekrasova i problema ritmicheskoi evoliutsii dvuslozhnykh razmerov v russkoi poezii," NRL, 95-96.

132. Golenishchev-Kutuzov, I. N. "Aleksandricheskii stikh v Rossii XVIII v.," in P. N. Berkov, A. Bushmin, V. Zhirmunskii (eds.), RUSSKO-EVROPEISKIE LITERATURNYE SVIAZI. Sbornik statei k 70-letiiu so dnia rozhdeniia akademika M. P. Alekseeva (M-L. 1966), 415-22.

133. Goncharov, B. P. "O pauzakh v stikhe Maiakovskogo," Rus Lit 2 (1970), 47-61.

134. _____, "Nekrasov i Maiakovskii (k probleme traditsii i novatorstva v stikhe)," NRL, 130-31.

135. _____, "Ob izuchenii stikha Maiakovskogo," in L. A. Evstigneeva and others (eds.), POET I SOTSIALIZM. K ESTETIKE V. V. MAIAKOVSKOGO (M. 1971), 233-98.

136. _____, "Intonatsionnaia organizatsiia stikha Maiakovskogo," Rus Lit 2 (1972), 77-97.

137. Ermilova, E. "O ritmicheskom novatorstve sovetskoi poezii," Vop Lit 5 (1961), 74-88.

138. _____, "Maiakovskii i sovremennyi stikh," in MAIAKOVSKII I SOVET-SKAIA LITERATURA (M. 1964), 231-56.

*139. Zhirmunskii, V. M. "Stikhoslozhenie Maiakovskogo," Rus Lit 4 (1964), 3-26. Translation: "The Versification of Majakovski," in POETICS. POETYKA. POETIKA II, (Warsaw, 1966), 211-42.

140. _____, "Russkii narodnyi stikh v 'Skazke o rybake i rybke'," in PROBLEMY SOVREMENNOI FILOLOGII. SBORNIK STATEI K 70-letiiu V. V. VINOGRADOVA (M. 1965), 129-35.

141. _____, "O russkoi rifme XVIII v.," in D. S. Likhachev, G. Makogonenko, I. Serman (eds.), ROL' I ZNACHENIE LITERATURY XVIII VEKA V ISTORII RUSSKOI KUL'TURY. K 70-letiiu SO DNIA ROZHDENIIA CHLENA-KORRESPONDENTA AN SSSR P. N. BERKOVA (M-L. 1966), 419-27.

142. Zhovtis, A. L. "V poiskakh 'vozmozhnogo raznoobraziia' (Avtor otveta na 'Poslanie v Sibir' ' v istorii russkogo stikha)," in his STIKHI NUZHNY (Alma-Ata, 1968), 227-44.

143. Zhovtis, A. L. "K voprosu o zvukovoi organizatsii sovremennoi russkoi poezii," M-LPTL, 59-61.

144. _____, "Svobodnyi stikh Feta," in RUSSKOE I ZARUBEZHNOE IAZYKO-ZNANIE, Vypusk 3 (Alma-Ata, 1970), 294-306.

145. _____, "Osvobozhdennyi stikh Maiakovskogo. Predlagaemye printsipy klassifikatsii," Rus Lit 2 (1971), 53-75.

146. Zapadov, V. A. "Derzhavin i russkaia rifma XVIII v., " in XVIII VEK. SBOR-NIK 8. DERZHAVIN I KARAMZIN V LITERATURNOM DVIZHENII KONTSA XVIII NACHALA XIX VEKA (L. 1969), 54-91.

147. _____, "Russkii shestistopnyi iamb XVIII - pervoi treti XIX veka," in A. L. Grigor'ev (ed.), LITERATUROVEDENIE. XXV GERTSENOVSKIE CHTENIIA. KRATKOE SODERZHANIE DOKLADOV 1972 g (L. 1972), 9-11.

148. Ivanov, V. V. "Ritmicheskoe stroenie 'Ballady o tsirke' A. Mezhirova," in SIMPOZIUM PO STRUKTURNOMU IZUCHENIIU ZNAKOVYKH SISTEM. Tezisy dokladov (M. 1962), 157. Superseded by No. 150.

149. _____"Ritm poemy Maiakovskogo 'Chelovek'," in POETICS. POETYKA. POETIKA II (Warsaw, 1966), 243-46.

*150. _____, "Ritmicheskoe stroenie 'Ballady o tsirke' Mezhirova," *Ibid.*, 277-300.

*151. _____, "Metr i ritm v 'Poeme kontsa' M. Tsvetaevoi," TS, 168-201.

152. _____, "Ritmicheskoe stroenie ody Lomonosova (Oda 1747 g.), in V. Iu. Rozentsveig (chief ed.), PROBLEMY PRIKLADNOI LINGVISTIKI,Chast' I (M. 1969), 131-33.

153. Izmailov, N. V. "Iz istorii russkoi oktavy," PSRL, 102-10.

154. Karpov, A. S. O STIKHE MAIAKOVSKOGO (Kaluga, 1960).

155. Kozhinov, V. V., Kozhinova, L. A., "O stikhe Maiakovskogo," in MAIAKOV-SKII V SHKOLE. SBORNIK STATEI (M. 1961), 424-54.

*156. Kolmogorov, A. N."K izucheniiu ritmiki Maiakovskogo," Vop Iaz 4 (1963), 64-71.

157. _____, "Zamechaniia po povodu analiza ritma 'Stikhov o sovetskom pasporte' Maiakovskogo," Vop Iaz 3 (1965), 70-75.

158. _____, "O metre pushkinskikh 'Pesen zapadnykh slavian'," Rus Lit 1 (1966), 98-111.

159. _____, "Primer izucheniia metra i ego ritmicheskikh variantov," TS, 145-67. (On Tsvetaeva's "Stol" and "Poema kontsa".)

160. _____, Kondratov, A. M. "Ritmika poem Maiakovskogo," Vop Iaz 3 (1962), 62-74.

*161. _____Prokhorov, A. V. "O dol'nike sovremennoi russkoi poezii," Vop Iaz 6 (1963), 84-95.

162. _____ _____, "O dol'nike sovremennoi russkoi poezii (Statisticheskaia kharakteristika dol'nika Maiakovskogo, Bagritskogo, Akhmatovoi)," Vop Iaz 1 (1964), 75-94.

163. Kondratov, A. M. "Evoliutsiia ritmika Maiakovskogo," Vop Iaz 5 (1962), 101-108.

164. _____, "Czterostopowy jamb N. Zabolockiego i niektore zagadnienia statystyki wiersza," in R. Mayenowa (ed.), POETYKA I MATEMATYKA (Warsaw, 1965), 97-111.

165. Krasnova, L. V. "Poeticheskii stroi 'Skifov' A. Bloka," VRL 2 (1968), 104-110.

166. Krasnoperova, M. "Zamechaniia o ritme strofy 'Evgeniia Onegina'," TGU. MATERIALY XXV NAUCHNOI STUD. KONFERENTSII. LITERATUROVEDENIE, LINGVISTIKA (1970), 59-63, 66-67.

167. Kriukova, N. "Nekotorye nabliudeniia nad ritmikoi stikha Pavla Vasil'eva," M-LPTL, 63-64.

168. Lotman, M. "Sposoby metricheskoi organizatsii stikha v russkoi poezii XVIII-XX v.," TGU. MATERIALY XXVI NAUCHNOI STUDENCHESKOI KONFERENTSII. LITERATUROVEDENIE. LINGVISTIKA (1972), 149-52.

169. Maimin, E. "Zametki o russkom stikhe," ANNALI SEZIONE SLAVA

INSTITUTO UNIVERSITARIO ORIENTALE, IX (1965), 21-43.

170. Maksimov, D. E. "O stikhe Briusova," UZ ped. inst. im. Gertsena, Tom 198 (1959), 265-69.

171. Maller, L. "Ekspressivno-tematicheskii oreol trekhstopnogo amfibrakhiia," TGU. MATERIALY XXV NAUCHNOI STUD. KONF. LITERATUROVEDENIE, LINGVISTIKA (1970), 55-9.

172. _____, "Semantika trekhslozhnykh razmerov v poezii Nekrasova," NRL, 89-91.

173. _____, "O vzaimodeistvii strukturnykh urovnei stikha v poezii A. Bloka," TGU. MATERIALY XXVI NAUCHNOI STUD. KONF. LITERATUROVEDENIE, LINGVISTIKA (1971), 84-87.

174. Markov, N. V. "Lomonosov i russkaia strofika," in his OCHERKI PO ISTORII RUSSKOGO IAZYKA I LITERATURY XVIII VEKA (Lomonosovskie chteniia), Vyp. 1 (Kazan', 1967), 135-58.

175. Matiash, S. "Metrika Zhukovskogo," TGU. MATERIALY XXVII NAUCHNOI STUD. KONF. LITERATUROVEDENIE (1972), 144-48.

176. Meus, Kh. "Metricheskii repertuar A. K. Tolstogo," TGU. MATERIALY XXVI NAUCHNOI STU. KONF. LITERATUROVEDENIE (1971), 82-84.

177. Mikhailov, V. "K voprosu o ritme i intonatsii v stikhakh G. R. Derzhavina," TRUDY TBILISSKOGO UNIVER., Tom 83, Vyp. 2 (1959), 147-60.

178. Neiman, B. V. "Stikh Nekrasova," in NEKRASOV V SHKOLE. SBORNIK STATEI (M. 1960), 224-58.

179. Nikonov, V. "Ritmika Maiakovskogo," Vop Lit 7 (1958), 89-108.

180. Novinskaia, L. P. "Rol' Tiutcheva v istorii russkoi metriki XIX - nachala XX vv.," RSPiS, 218-26.

181. Ognev, Vladimir. KNIGA PRO STIKHI (M. 1963).

182. Ozmitel', E., Gvozdikovskaia, T. "Metricheskii repertuar sovremennoi liriki i traditsii russkogo stikha," M-LPTL, 64-66.

183. _____, "Materialy k metricheskomu repertuaru russkoi liricheskoi poezii (1957-68 gg.)," NAUCHNYE TRUDY FIL. FAKUL'TETA KIRGIZSKOGO UNIVERSITETA. Vypusk 16 (1970), 113-21.

184. Orlova, O. A. "Osobennosti trekhslozhnykh razmerov v poezii Nekrasova i Polonskogo," NRL, 94-94.

*185. Papaian, R. A. "K voprosu o sootnoshenii stikhotvornykh razmerov i intensivnosti tropov v lirike A. Bloka," in BLOKOVSKII SBORNIK II (Tartu, 1972), 238-90.

186. Peisakhovich, M. A. "Strofika Lermontova," in TVORCHESTVO M. Iu. LERMONTOVA (M. 1964), 417-91.

187. _____, "Stroficheskaia organizatsiia poem Lermontova," VRL 3 (1966), 72-9.

188. _____, "Stikhovaia kompozitsiia poemy Lermontova 'Mtsyri'," VRL 2 (1967), 97-104.

189. _____, "Stroficheskoe stroenie poemy Lermontova 'Demon'," VRL 2 (1968), 92-103.

190. _____, "Oneginskaia strofa v poemakh Lermontova," NAUCHNYE DOKLADY VYSSHEI SHKOLY. FILOL. NAUKI, 1 (1969), 25-38.

191. _____, "Stikh iunosheskikh poem Lermontova (Dvustishnie formy)," VRL 1 (1971), 72-77.

192. _____, "Dvustishnye formy v poezii Nekrasova," NAUCHNYE DOKLADY VYSSHEI SHKOLY. FILOL. NAUKI, 6 (1971), 13-27.

193. _____, "Dvustishnye formy i ikh mesto v poezii Nekrasova," NRL, 104-106.

194. Pozdneev, A. V. "Die tonische Elemente im russischen syllabischen Vers," ZEITSCHRIFT FUR SLAVISCHE PHILOLOGIE, XXVII (1960), 405-12.

195. _____, "Stikhoslozhenie drevnei russkoi poezii," SCANDO-SLAVICA, XI (1965), 5-24.

196. _____, "Iz istorii russkogo stikha XV-XVII vekov," in J. Levy (ed.), TEORIE VERSE I (Brno, 1966), 95-108.

197. Reiser, S. A. "Strofa v poeme Nekrasova 'Komu na Rusi zhit' khorosho?'," RSPiS, 192-206.

198. ———, "Slovar' trekhstopnogo iamba poemy Nekrasova 'Komu na Rusi zhit' khorosho?'," UZ TGU, Vyp. 236, TRUDY PO ZNAKOVYM SISTEMAM IV (1969), 368-85.

199. Rudnev, P. A. "Metricheskaia kompozitsiia stikhotvornykh dram A. Bloka i V. Briusova," in PROBLEMY KHUDOZHESTVENNOGO MASTERSTVA. Tezisy dokladov mezhvuzovskoi nauchno-teoreticheskoi konferentsii (Alma-Ata, 1967), 71-73.

200. ———, "Iz istorii metricheskogo repertuara russkikh poetov XIX-Nachala XX v.," TS, 107-44.

201. ———, "O stikhe poemy A. Bloka 'Dvenadtsat'," in RUSSKAIA LITERATURA XX v. (dooktiabr'skii period). SBORNIK STATEI (Kaluga, 1968), 227-38. Superseded by No. 206 below.

202. ———, "Metricheskaia kompozitsiia i stikhovaia stilistika poemy A. Bloka 'Ee pribytie'," M-LPTL, 66-68.

203. ———, "O sootnoshenii monometricheskikh i polimetricheskikh konstruktsii v sisteme stikhotvornykh razmerov A. Bloka," RSPiS, 227-36.

204. ———, "O stikhe dramy A. Bloka 'Roza i krest'," UZ TGU, Vyp 251, Trudy po russkoi i slavianskoi filologii, Tom 15 (1970), 294-334.

205. ———, "Stikhotvorenie A. Bloka 'Vse tikho na svetlom litse...' (Opyt semanticheskoi interpretatsii metra i ritma)," PSRL, 450-55.

*206. ———, "Opyt opisaniia i semanticheskoi interpretatsii polimetricheskoi struktury poemy A. Bloka 'Dvenadtsat'," UZ TGU, Vyp 266, Trudy po russkoi i slavianskoi filologii, 18 (1971), 195-221.

*207. ———, "Metricheskii repertuar A. Bloka," in BLOKOVSKII SBORNIK II (Tartu, 1972), 218-67.

208. Sapogov, V. A. "'Snezhnaia maska' Aleksandra Bloka," UZ MOSKOVSKOGO GOS. PED. INSTITUTA IMENI V LENINA, 255 (1966).

209. ———, "O nekotorykh strukturnykh osobennostiakh liricheskogo tsikla A. Bloka," in IAZYK I STIL' KHUDOZHESTVENNOGO PROIZVEDENIIA (M. 1966), 90-91.

210. ———, "Liricheskii tsikl i liricheskaia poema v tvorchestve A. Bloka," in RUSSKAIA LITERATURA XX VEKA (Dooktiabr'skii period). Sbornik statei (Kaluga, 1968).

211. ———, "K probleme stikhotvornoi stilistiki liricheskogo tsikla," RSPiS, 237-43.

212. ———, "O polimetricheskikh kompozitsiiakh Karoliny Pavlovoi," in XXIII GERTSENOVSKIE CHTENIIA. Kratkoe soderzhanie dokladov (L. 1970), 60-61.

213. ———, "K tipologii polimetricheskikh kompozitsii (O polimetrii u N. A. Nekrasova i K. K. Pavlovoi)," NRL, 97-100.

214. Speranskaia, L. "Sistema stikhotvornykh razmerov P. A. Katenina," TGU. MATERIALY XXVI NAUCHNOI STUD. KONF. LITERATUROVEDENIE (1971), 79-81.

215. Stelletskii, V. "K voprosu o ritmicheskom stroe 'Slova o polku Igoreve'," Rus Lit 4 (1964), 27-40.

216. Timofeev, L. I. "Ritmika 'Slova o polku Igoreve'," Rus Lit 1 (1963), 88-104.

*217. Tomashevskii, B. V. "Strofika Pushkina," in M. P. Alekseev (ed.), PUSHKIN. ISSLEDOVANIIA I MATERIALY II (M-L. 1958), 49-184.

218. Kholshevnikov, V. E. "O tipakh intonatsii russkogo klassicheskogo stikha," UZ LENINGRADSKOGO GOS. UNIV-A, 295, Seriia filol. nauk, Vyp. 58 (1960), 3-34. Superseded by No. 219 below.

*219. ———, "Tipy intonatsii russkoi klassicheskogo stikha," in V. V. Kozhevnikova (ed.), SLOVO I OBRAZ. Sbornik statei (M. 1964), 125-63.

220. ———, "Russkii sillabicheskii vos'mislozhnik," MS, 21-24.

221. ———, "Logaedicheskie razmery v russkoi poezii," PSRL, 429-36.

222. Tsetliak, S. I. "...Stseplenniai gvozdiami bezoshibochnykh rifm...", VRL 3 (1969), 63-70. (On Maiakovskii's rhyme.)

223. Shakhverdov, S. "Sistema stikhotvornykh razmerov E. A. Baratynskogo,"

224. _____, "Metricheskii repertuar E. A. Baratynskogo (Materialy k metricheskomu spravochniku)," in QUINQUAGENARIO. Sbornik statei molodykh filologov k 50-letiiu prof. Iu. M. Lotmana (Tartu, 1972), 223-44.

225. Shervinskii, S. V. RITM I SMYSL. K IZUCHENIIU POETIKI PUSHKINA (M. 1961). Reviews: A. Kviatkovskii, "Strannaia teoriia," Vop Lit 8 (1962), 203-205; A. Zhovtis, Rus Lit 1 (1964), 216-20; M. Chudakov, Novyi mir 4 (1962), 284.

226. Shtokmar, M. RIFMA MAIAKOVSKOGO (M. 1958). Reprinted, Letchworth, 1972 (Russian Titles for the Specialist).

IV. COMPARATIVE STUDIES

227. Gasparov, M. L. "Antichnyi trimetr i russkii iamb," in M. Gasparov, M. Grabar'-Passek, F. Petrovskii (eds.),VOPROSY ANTICHNOI LITERATURY I KLASSICHESKOI FILOLOGII (M. 1966), 393-410.

228. Zhirmunskii, V. M. "Stikh i perevod (iz istorii romanticheskoi poemy)," in P. N. Berkov, A. Bushmin, V. Zhirmunskii (eds.), RUSSKO-EVROPEISKIE LITERATURNYE SVIAZI. Sbornik statei k 70-letiiu akademika M. P. Alekseeva (M-L. 1966), 423-34.

229. _____, "O natsional'nykh formakh iambicheskogo stikha," TS, 7-23. Translation: "Der russische und der deutsche Jambus. (Lomonosov und Gunther)," in SLAVISCHE-DEUTSCHE WECHSELBEZIEHUNGEN IN SPRACHE, LITERATUR, UND KULTUR (Berlin, 1969), 436-45.

230. Zhovtis, A. "Pul's stikhotvornogo perevoda," in MASTERSTVO PEREVODA 1963 (M. 1964), 107-23.

231. _____, "U istokov russkogo verlibra (stikh 'Severnogo moria' Geine v perevodakh M. L. Mikhailova)," in MASTERSTVO PEREVODA 7 (M. 1970). 386-404.

232. _____, "Nemetskie freie Rhythmen v rannikh russkikh interpretatsiiakh (20-ie-nachalo 40-kh gg. XIX veka)," in RUSSKOE IAZYKOZNANIE, 1 (Alma-Ata, 1970), 89-105.

233. Kovalevskii, V. "...razmerom podlinnika..." in MASTERSTVO PEREVODA 1962 (M. 1963), 179-202.

234. Lekomtseva, M. I. "K sootnosheniiu fonologicheskikh struktur sloga i metricheskikh sistem sootvetstvuiushchikh iazykov," TGU. Tezisy dokladov 2 letnei shkoly po vtorichnym modeliruiushchim sistemam (1966), 75-79.

235. _____, "O sootnoshenii edinits metricheskoi i fonologicheskoi sistem iazyka (v sillabicheskom stikhoslozhenii)," UZ TGU, Vyp. 236, TRUDY PO ZNAKOVYM SISTEMAM 4 (1969), 336-44.

236. Papaian, R. "K voprosu o metricheskikh transformatsiiakh russkogo i armianskogo stikha v sovetskoi poezii," TGU. MATERIALY XXVI NAUCH. STUD. KONFERENTSII. LITERATUROVEDENIE, LINGVISTIKA (1971), 69-71.

237. Poldmae, J. "O primenenii znakovoi modeli pri opisanii rifmy," M-LPTL, 73-74.

238. _____, "Eshche raz o kriteriiakh tipologicheskoi kharakteristiki verlibra," TGU. Tezisy dokladov IV letnei shkoly po vtorichnym modeliruiushchim sistemam (1970), 148-49.

239. _____, "O tipologii sistem stikhoslozheniia," *Ibid.*, 145-47.

240. Timofeev, L. I. "Sistemy stikhoslozheniia," in his OSNOVY TEORII LITERATURY, 3rd ed. (M. 1966), 300-36.

241. Toporov, V. N. " 'Istochnik' Batiushkova v sviazi s 'Le Torrent' Parny (1. K probleme perevoda. 2. Analiz struktury)," UZ TGU, Vyp. 236. TRUDY PO ZNAKOVYM SISTEMAM 4 (1969), 306-334.

*242. Kholshevnikov, V. E. "Russkaia i pol'skaia sillabika i sillabo-tonika," TS, 24-58.

243. Etkind, E. "Metr. Ritm. Intonatsiia," in his POEZIIA I PEREVOD (M-L. 1963), 266-316.

V. PUBLICATIONS AND DISCUSSIONS OF ARCHIVE MATERIALS.
HISTORY OF RUSSIAN METRICS. REPRINTS.

244. Gindin, S. I. "O vozmozhnostiakh veroiatnostnogo stikhovedeniia i odnoi zabytoi modeli Andreia Belogo," in PLAN RABOTY I TEZISY DOKLADOV II MEZH-VUZOVSKOI STUD. NAUCH. KONF. PO PROBLEMAM STRUKTURNOI I PRI-KLADNOI LINGVISTIKI (Tbilisi, 1966), 13-14.

245. _____, "Teoreticheskie osnovy metriki i ritmiki V. Briusova v svete ponia-tiia ekstensional'nogo metra i teorii prozhdaiushchikh grammatik," TEZISY DOKLADOV VI NAUCH. STUD. KONF. 22-26 APRELIA 1968 g. OBSHCHESTVENNYE NAUKI (Novosibirsk, 1968), 44-45.

246. _____, "V. Ia. Briusov o rechevoi prirode stikha i stikhotvornogo ritma i o russkikh ekvivalentakh antichnykh stikhotvornykh razmerov," Vop Iaz 6 (1968), 124-29.

247. _____, "Vzgliady V. Ia. Briusova na iazykovuiu priemlemost' stikhovykh sistem i sud'by russkoi sillabiki (po rukopisiam 90-kh gg.)," Vop Iaz 2 (1970), 99-109.

248. _____, "Briusovskaia semanticheskaia teoriia narodnogo stikha i razvitie literaturnogo stikha na rubezhe XIX-XX stoletii," TGU. MATERIALY XXV NAUCH. STUD. KONF. Literaturovedenie, Lingvistika (1970), 64.

*249. _____, "Transformatsionnyi analiz i metrika (iz istorii problemy)," MASHINNYI PEREVOD I PRIKLADNAIA LINGVISTIKA, 13 (1970), 177-200. (On Briusov's OSNOVY STIKHOVEDENIIA [1924]).

250. _____, "Briusov o poetike Nekrasova," NRL, 128-29.

251. _____, Commentary to the translation of J. Levy, "Znachenie formy i formy znachenii," in Iu. Lotman (ed.), SEMIOTIKA I ISKUSSTVOMETRIIA (M. 1972), 335-39.

252. Girshman, M. M. "M. V. Lomonosov o strukturnykh razlichiiakh stikha i prozy," in A. N. Markov (ed.), OCHERKI PO ISTORII RUSSKOGO IAZYKA I LITERA-TURY XVIII VEKA (Lomonosovskie chteniia), Vyp. 2-3 (Kazan', 1969), 42-50.

253. Grechishkin, S. S., Lavrov, A. V. "O stikhovedcheskom nasledii Andreia Belogo," TGU. MATERIALY XXVI NAUCH. STUD. KONF. Literaturovedenie. Lingvistika (1971), 67-68.

254. Lapshina, N. V., Romanovich, I. K., Iarkho, B. I. "Iz materialov METRICHESKOGO SPRAVOCHNIKA K STIKHOTVORENIIAM M. IU. LERMON-TOVA"(publikatsiia M. L. Gasparova), Vop Iaz 2 (1966), 125-37.

255. Maimin, E. "Pushkin o russkom stikhe," Rus Lit 3 (1966), 65-75.

256. (Tomashevskii, B. V.) "Pis'ma B. V. Tomashevskogo V. Ia. Briusovu (pub-likatsiia L. S. Fleishmana)," UZ TGU. TRUDY PO ZNAKOVYM SISTEMAM V (1971), 532-44.

257. Tynianov, Iu. PROBLEMA STIKHOTVORNOGO IAZYKA (M. 1965).

258. Eikhenbaum, B. "Melodika liricheskogo stikha," in his O POEZII (L. 1969), 327-511.

VI. REFERENCE WORKS

259. Beliaev, V. F. "Osnovnaia terminologiia metriki i poetiki," in O. S. Akhmanova, SLOVAR' LINGVISTICHESKIKH TERMINOV (M. 1966), 573-605.

260. Gasparov, M. L. "Pauza," "Pauznik," KLE 5 (M. 1968), col. 627.

261. Ermilova, E. "Dol'nik," KLE, 2 (M. 1964), cols. 734-35.

262. Kviatkovskii, A. P. POETICHESKII SLOVAR' (M. 1966). Reviews: I. Smir-nov, "Stikhi i terminy," Rus Lit 2 (1967), 205-209; K. Zelinskii, "Poeticheskii slovar' A. P. Kviatkovskogo," Vop Lit 1 (1968), 194-98; *V. E. Kholshevnikov, "Kakim dol-zhen byt' slovar'?" Vop Lit 1 (1968), 198-203; Tsetliak, S. I. "Beskonechnost' ritmi-cheskikh modifikatsii stikha," VRL 2 (1969), 75-79; V. E. Fedorishchev, "Taktome-tricheskaia teoriia v svete poetiki, muzyki i iazykoznaniia," VRL 3 (1970), 98-102; M.

A. Peisakhovich, "Taktometricheskaia teoriia i stikhotvornaia praktika," VRL, 80-83.
263. Timofeev, L. I., Vengrov, N. KRATKII SLOVAR' LITERATUROVED-
CHESKIKH TERMINOV, 4th ed. (M. 1963).
264. Kharlap, M. G. "Metr," KLE, 4 (M. 1967), cols. 807-809.
265. _____, "Metrika," KLE, 4 (M. 1967), cols. 809-810.
266. Kholshevnikov, V. E. "Intonatsionno-sintaksicheskaia organizatsiia stikha,"
KLE, 3 (M. 1966). cols. 153-54.
267. _____, "Napevnyi stikh," KLE, 5 (M. 1968), cols. 98-99.
268. _____, "Rifma," KLE, 6 (M. 1971), cols. 306-309.
269. _____, "Sillabicheskoe stikhoslozhenie," KLE, 6, cols. 819-820.
270. _____, "Sillabo-tonicheskoe stikhoslozhenie," KLE, cols. 820-22.

VII. PRIMERS

271. Gutorov, I.V. "Osnovnye sistemy stikhoslozheniia," "Rifma i strofika," in his
OSNOVY SOVETSKOGO LITERATUROVEDENIIA, 3rd ed. (Minsk, 1967).
272. Kalacheva, S. V. "Stikhoslozhenie," in her VVEDENIE V LITERATURO-
VEDENIE (M. 1970).
273. Kovalenkov, A. PRAKTIKA SOVREMENNOGO STIKHOSLOZHENIIA
(M. 1960). 2nd ed., revised and augmented, M. 1962.
274. _____, POEZIIA PROSTYKH SLOV (M. 1965).
275. _____, PROSTOE I NEPROSTOE. OSNOVY STIKHOSLOZHENIE, (M. 1970).
276. Kondratov. A. M. MATEMATIKA I POEZIIA (M. 1962). (Novoe v zhizni, nauke,
tekhnike, IX seriia, fizika i khimiia, No. 20.)
277. Lotman, Iu. M. ANALIZ POETICHESKOGO TEKSTA. STRUKTURA
STIKHA (L. 1972).
278. Timofeev, L. I. "Ob izuchenii stikhoslozheniia v shkole," ISSh, 3-20.
279. Kharchevnikov, V. OSNOVY RUSSKOGO SILLABO-TONICHESKOGO
STIKHOSLOZHENIIA (Groznyi, 1962). Review: A. Karpov, "O pol'ze gramotnosti," Vop
Lit 9 (1963), 218-21.
280. Kholshevnikov, V. E. OSNOVY RUSSKOGO STIKHOSLOZHENIIA (L. 1958).
2nd ed. L. 1959.
*281. _____, OSNOVY STIKHOVEDENIIA. RUSSKOE STIKHOSLOZHENIIA,
1st ed. (L. 1962). 2nd revised edition, L. 1972.
282. Shengeli, G. TEKHNIKA STIKHA (M. 1960). Review: A. Kviatkovskii,
SIBIRSKIE OGNI 8 (1961), 187.
283. Shchepilova, L. V. VVEDENIE V LITERATUROVEDENIE (M. 1968).
284. Etkind, E. "Ritm," in his RAZGOVOR O STIKHAKH (M. 1970), 58-118.

VIII. SURVEY ARTICLES. POLEMIC.

285. Gal'di, L. 'Lichnost' poeta i tekhnika stikha," Vop Iaz 3 (1967), 53-58.
286. Gasparov, M. L. "K 60-letiiu K. F. Taranovskogo," UZ TGU, 284, TRUDY
PO ZNAKOVYM SISTEMAM V (1971), 545-46.
287. Gindin, S. I. "Soveshchanie stikhovedov," Vop Lit 5 (1970), 249-50. (On
conference at Institute of Foreign Languages, Moscow, April 1969).
288. Goncharov, B. "Soveshchanie stikhovedov," Vop Lit 5 (1970), 250-51. (On
conference at Institute of World Literature, Moscow, February 1970.)
289. _____, Timofeev, L. I. "Obogashchenie ili obednenie? (K sporam o soderzhatel'noi prirode stikha)," LITERATURNAIA GAZETA (May 17, 1972), 4.
290. Ermilova, E. "Poeziia i matematika," Vop Lit 3 (1962), 71-82. (Discussion
of the conference on mathematics and the language of literature held in Gorky, September 1961.)
291. Zaretskii, V. M. "Vremia obratit'sia k novoi tseli..." Vop Lit 10 (1967), 126-36.

292. Zhirmunskii, V. M. "Konferentsiia po teorii stikha v Varshave," IZVESTIIA AKADEMII NAUK SSSR, Otdelenie literatury i iazyka, 2 (1965).

293. Zholkovskii, A. K. "Soveshchanie po izucheniiu poeticheskogo iazyka (g. Gorky, Sept.1961) (Obzor dokladov)" MASHINNYI PEREVOD I PRIKLADNAIA LINGVISTIKA, 7 (1962), 88-101.

294. Ivanov, V. V. "O primenenii tochnykh metodov v literaturovedenii, " Vop Lit, 10 (1967), 115-26.

295. Karpov, A. S. "Ob"ektivnost' issledovaniia (O primenenii teorii informatsii v literaturovedcheskom issledovanii)," NAUCHNYE DOKLADY VYSSHEI SHKOLY, FILOLOGICHESKIE NAUKI, 2 (1965), 3-13.

296. Kozhinov, V. V. "Vozmozhna li strukturnaia poetika?" Vop Lit, 6 (1965), 88-107.

297. Kondratov, A. M. "Bity, bukvy, poeziia (K probleme primeneniia 'teorii informatsiia' v linvistike i poetike," ZNANIE—SILA, 11 (1961), 18-21.

298. _____, "Rozhdenie odnoi idei (O matematicheskikh metodakh issledovaniia stikha)," TEKHNIKA—MOLODEZHI, 5 (1962), 28-30.

299. Meilakh, B. "Sodruzhestvo nauk i tainy tvorchestva," LITERATURNAIA GAZETA (October 11, 1962).

*300. _____, "Sodruzhestvo nauk—trebovanie vremeni," Vop Lit, 11 (1963), 61-85.

301. Palievskii, P. V. "O strukturalizme v literaturovedenii," ZNAMIA, 12 (1963), 139-98.

302. _____, "Mera nauchnosti (K problemam strukturnogo izucheniia literaturnogo tvorchestva)," ZNAMIA, 4 (1966), 133-37.

303. Prokhorov, A. V. "Matematicheskii analiz stikha," NAUKA I ZHIZN', 6 (1964).

304. Revzin, I.I. "Soveshchanie v g. Gor'kom, posviashchennoe primeneniiu matematicheskikh metodov k izucheniiu iazyka khudozhestvennoi literatury (23-27 sent. 1961g.)," Vop Iaz, 1 (1962), 161-65; reprinted in STRUKTURNO-TIPOLOGICHESKIE ISSLEDO-VANIIA (M. 1962), 285-93.

305. _____, "O tseliakh strukturnogo izucheniia khudozhestvennogo proizvedeniia," Vop Lit, 6 (1965), 73-87.

306. Timofeev, L. I. "Zvuk i stikh," LITERATURA I ZHIZN' (August 26, 1959).

307. _____, "Stikh—slovo—obraz," Vop Lit, 6 (1962).

*308. _____, "Sorok let spustia... (chislo i chuvstvo mery v izuchenii poetiki)," Vop Lit, 4 (1963), 62-80. Reprinted in V. Kozhevnikova (ed.), SLOVO I OBRAZ (M. 1964), 270-87.

309. Kholshevnikov, V. E. "Stikhovedenie i matematika," in B. S. Meilakh (ed.), SODRUZHESTVO NAUK I TAINY TVORCHESTVA. Sbornik statei (M. 1968), 384-96.

310. Khrapchenko, M. B. "O razrabotke problem poetiki i stilistike," IZVESTIIA AKADEMII NAUK SSSR, Otdelenie literatury i iazyka, 5 (1961), 398-401.

311. Shklovskii, V. "Na Vorob'evykh gorakh," LITERATURNAIA GAZETA (May 15, 1962). (Interview with A. N. Kolmogorov.)

IX. CONCISE SUBJECT INDEX

Isochronic theory: 14, 59, 61, 66, 85, 88, 225, 262.
Logaoedic verse: 221.
Meter-rhythm relationship: 50, 55, 67, *151, 245, *249.
Metric typology: 10, 15, 16, 27, *45, 168, 238, 239.
Phonetics and meter: 6, 7, 8, 9, 14, 57, 59, 75, 85, 89, 143, 234, 235.
Polymetric verse: 201, 203, *206, 212, 213.
Prose-verse relationship: 28, 73, 123, 252.
Rhyme: 24, 29, 34, 48, 60, 62, 69, 79, 141, 146, 222, 226, 237, 268.
Semantics and meter: 18, 22, 25, 52, 65, 68, 70, 99, 171, 172, *206, 225.
Stanza: 53, 87, 91, 104, 105, 106, 120, 122, 153, 166, 174, 186, 187, 188, 189, 190,
    191, 192, 193, 197, *217.
Syllabic verse: 60, 97, 98, *125, 194, 195, 196, 220, *242, 247, 269.
Ternary meters: 107, 124, 128, 171, 172, 184.
Word boundary and meter: 12, 23.

X. CONCISE INDEX OF POETS

Akhmatova: 162.
Bagritskii: 162.
Baratynskii: 223, 224.
Batiushkov: 241.
Belyi (as theorist): 244, 253.
Blok: 115, 165, 173, *185, 199, 201, 202, 203, 204, 205, *206, *207, 208, 209, 210, 211.
Briusov (as poet): 93, 170, 199; (as theorist): 245, 246, 247, 248, *249, 250, 256.
Bunin: 94.
Vasil'ev: 167.
Vostokov: 126.
Derzhavin: 146, 177.
Esenin: 95, 96, 103.
Zhukovskii: 175.
Zabolotskii: 164.
Katenin: 214.
Lermontov: 99, 104, 108, 186, 187, 188, 189, 190, 191, 254.
Lomonosov: 152, 174, 229, 252.
Lugovskoi: 130.
Maiakovskii: 90, 114, 117, 133, 134, 135, 136, 138, *139, 145, 149, 154, 155, *156, 157,
    160, 162, 163, 179, 222, 226.
Mezhirov: 148, *150.
Mikhailov: 231.
Nekrasov: 91, 92, 110, 111, 128, 131, 134, 172, 178, 184, 192, 193, 197, 198, 213, 250.
Odoevskii, A. I: 142.
Pavlova: 212, 213.
Polonskii: 184.
Pushkin: 5, 93, 100, 101, 140, 158, 166, *217, 225, 255, 256.
Slovo o polku Igoreve: 215, 216.
Tvardovskii: 102.
Tolstoi, A. K.: 176.
Tiutchev: 180.
Fet: 144.
Tsvetaeva: *151, 159.

NOTE ON ABBREVIATIONS - The system of abbreviations used here is the same as in
previous RLT bibliographies. See for example No. 4 (1972), the bibliography of works
on Blok's "The Twelve."

A BIBLIOGRAPHY OF WORKS BY AND ABOUT BELLA AKHMADULINA

Compiled by Christine Rydel

I. Original Works by Akhmadulina.

A. BOOKS

Struna. Moscow, 1962.

Contents: Svetofory, "Ty govorish'," Moloko, Iz tselinnoi tetradi, Iz sibirskoi tretradi [Drevnie risunki v Khakassii, Novaia domna na KMK, Kemerovo, Gora Burluk na stroitel'stve dorogi, Abakan-Taishet] , Gruzinskikh zhenshchin imena, Abkhazskie pokhorony, Bars, Tsvety, Kon', Den' poezii, Chuzhoe remeslo, Novaia tetrad', "I snova, kak ogni martenov," Starinnyi portret, Mazurka Shopena, Kheminguei, Vulkany, Sadovnik, Lunatiki, "O, slovo tochnoe—podonki!...", "Chelovek v chistoe pole vykhodit.", Zimnii den', "Vlechet menia starinnyi slog...", Snegurochka, "Zhivut na ulitse Peschanoi...", Nevesta, Koroleva, Beg, "Vot zvuk dozhdia...", "Ia dumala, chto ty moi vrag...", "Zhilos' mne veselo i shibko...", "Smeias', likuia i buntuia...", "Glubokim golosom proroka..." Zhaleika, Lodka, Tvoi dom, Avgust, Aprel', Nezhnost', Nesmeiana, "V tot mesiats mai...", "Ne udelai mne mnogo vremeni...", "O, eshche s toboi sluchitsia...", Avtomat s gaziro-vannoi vodoi, "Nas odurachil nyneshnii sentiabr'...", Sentiabr', Dekabr', "My rasstaem-sia—i odnovremenno...", "Opiat' v prirode peremena...", Motoroller.

Oznob. Frankfurt, 1968.

Contents: 1955: Chernyi ruchei, Noch'iu. 1957: Zhaleika. Until 1960: Beg, "On prigotovil pistolet...", Piatnadtsat' mal'chikov, "Chem otlichaius' ia ot zhenshchiny s tsvetkom...", Gorod nauki pod Novosibirskom, "Zhilos' mne veselo i shibko...", "Ia du-mala, chto ty moi vrag..." 1960-61: "V rubashke beloi i steril'noi...", "Zhila v pozore okaiannom...", "Nu, predali. Nu, predali, Potom...", "Kak koril ty menia za zhestokost'..." "—Vse eto nado pereshit'...", "O, moi zastenchivyi geroi...", "Smotriu na zhenshchin, kak smotreli vstar'...", "Tvoe okno na storonu vostochnuiu...", "Tak i zhivem—naprasno maias'...", "Iz glubiny moikh nevzgod...", "Predat' menia? No dlia chego zhe?...", Ada, "O bol' ty—mudrost'. Sut' reshenii...", Vulkany, "O zhest zimy ko mne..." Until 1962: "Glubokim golosom proroka...", Nevesta, Abkhazkie pokhorony, Moloko, Lunatiki, Gruzinskikh zhenshchin imena, "Vlechet menia starinnyi slog...", Aprel' Tsvety, "My rasstaemsia—i odnovremenno...", Bars, Svetofory, Kon', Den' poezii,

Chuzhoe remeslo, Novaia tetrad', Starinnyi portret, Kheminguei, Sadovnik, "O, slovo
tochnoe—podonki!...", "Chelovek v chistoe pole vykhodit...", Zimnii den', Snegurochka,
"Zhivut na ulitse Peschanoi...", Koroleva, "Vot zvuk dozhdia, kak budto zvuk dombry...",
"Smeias', likuia i buntuia...", Tvoi dom, Drevnie risunki v Khakassii, Nezhnost', Nesmeiana, "O, eshche s toboi sluchitsia...", "Nas odurachil nyneshnii sentiabr'...", Sentiabr',
"Opiat' v prirode peremena...", Motoroller, Mazurka Shopena, Avgust, Avtomat s gazi-
rovannoi vodoi.   1962: Duel', "V tot mesiats mai...", "Ne udelai mne mnogo vremeni...",
Vstuplenie v prostudu, Svecha, Peizazh, Magnitofon, "Po ulitse moei kotoryi god...", Glavy iz poemy (o Pasternake), Voskresnyi den'. 1963: Malen'kie samolety, Oznob, Uroki
muzyki,   Moia rodoslovnaia (poema), V metro na ostanovke "Sokol", Son, Moi
tovarishchi.   1964: Skazka o dozhde (v neskol'kikh epizodakh, s dialogami i khorom
detei) [N.B. This poem was first published in 1963. C.R.]   1965: Proshchanie, V opustevshem dome otdykha, Kto znaet—vechnost' ili mig, Noch', Simonu Chikovani, Slovo.
1966: Nemota, Drugoe, Toska po Lermontovu.   1967: Prikliuchenie v antikvarnom
magazine, Sumerki, "Sny o Gruzii—vot radost'!...", Spat', Plokhaia vesna, "Sluchilos'
tak, chto dvadtsati semi...", "Ia dumaiu: kak ia byla glupa...", "Kak dolgo ia ne vysypalas'..."   1968: "Tak durno zhit', kak ia vchera zhila...", Varfolomeevskaia noch',
Gostit' u khudozhnika, Smert' Akhmatovoi, Zaklinanie, Klianus'
    PROSE: Na sibirskikh dorogakh; Pushkin. Lermontov...; Vospominanie o Gruzii.
    TRANSLATIONS OF GEORGIAN POETRY: M. Kvlividze: Tiino, Sledy na
snegu.   Simon Chikovani: Marskaia rakovina, Skazannoe vo vremia bombezhki, Byki
Oleni na gumne, Gremskaia kolokol'nia, Na naberezhnoi, Prekratim eti rechi na mig...,
Po puti v Svetaniiu, Zadumannoe povedai oblakam, Ot etogo poroga..., Deviat' dubov,
Nachalo.   Otar Chiladze: "Ia poprosil podat' vina i pil...", "V byt stola, sostoia-
shchii iz iastv i gostei..."

Uroki muzyki. Moscow, 1969.

    Contents: Motoroller, Noch', Gazirovannaia voda, Magnitofon, Malen'kie samo-
lety, Vstuplenie v prostudu, Bolezn', Son, Moi tovarishchi, Po ulitse moei kotoryi god...,
Drugoe, Nemota, Osen', Toska po Lermontovu, Stikhotvorenie, napisannoe vo vremia bessonnitsy v Tbilisi; Uroki muzyki, Svecha, Peizazh, Voskresnyi den', Sumerki,
V opustevshem dome otdykha, Gruzinskikh zhenshchin imena, Zima, Zimniaia zamknutost', "Ia dumaiu: kak ia byla glupa...", "Sluchilos' tak, chto dvadtsati semi...", Gostit' u khudozhnika, Plokhaia vesna, "On utverzhdal—Mezhdu teplits...",Prikliucheniia v
antikvarnom magazine, Oznob, Skazka o dozhde, Moia rodoslovnaia.

POEMS IN PERIODICALS
Listed Chronologically by Year

"Rodina," *Komsomol'skaia pravda.* May 5, 1955.
"El'," "Noch'iu," "Chernyi ruchei," *Oktiabr',* XXXII, 5 (1955).
"V voiny," *Komsomol'skaia pravda.* January 7, 1956.
"Tsvety," *Den' poezii.* M. 1957.
"Zhaleika," "Kon'," *Molodaia gvardiia,* 2 (1957), 156-57.
"El'," *Grani,* No. 38 (1958).
"Chuzhoe remeslo," *Literaturnaia gazeta,* March 8, 1960.
"Gorod nauki pod Novosibirskom," "Mne nevterpezh ot vlazhnosti, ot polnoluniia,"
    "Iodki," "Zhilos' mne veselo i shibko," "Ia dumala, chto ty moi vrag," *Iunost'*
    (May, 1960), 72-73.
"Mazurka Shopena," "My sobliudaem pravila zimy," "Bog," "Avgust," "Avtomat s gazi-
    rovannoi vodoi," *Znamia,* 8 (1961), 91-94.
"Stikhi o Gruzii—Gruzinskikh zhenshchin imena...", Skazannoe vo vremia bombezhki,
    Literaturnaia gruzia, No. 5 (1962), 45-50.
"Duel'," *Iunost',* (Feb., 1962), p. 72.
"Malen'kie samolety," *Literaturnaia gazeta.* November 20, 1962.
"Po ulitse moei, kotoryi god..." *Literaturnaia gazeta.* September 22, 1962.

"Vstuplenie v prostudu," "Svecha," "Peizazh," "Magnitofon," "Po ulitse moei, kotoryi god," *Den' poezii* (Moscow, 1962).

"Dozhd'," glavy iz poemy, *Literaturnaia gruziia,* 12 (1963), 9-11.

"Voskresnyi den'," "Osen'," *Literaturnaia gazeta.* December 1, 1963.

Moia rodoslovnaia (otryvok), Den' poezii (M. 1963).

Moia rodoslovnaia (poema). *Iunost',* 1 (1964), 39-46.

"Moi tovarishchi," *Molodaia gvardiia,* 8 (1964), 19-21.

"V metro, na ostanovke Sokol," *Nash sovremennik,* 3 (1964), 43.

"Mart," *Smena,* 3 (1964), 2.

"Zima," "Uroki muzyki," "Son," *Molodaia gvardiia,* 3 (1964), 18-21.

"Simonu Chikovani," *Literaturnaia gruziia,* 1 (1965), 32.

"Proshchanie," "V opustevshem dome otdykha," "Kto znaet—vechnost' ili mig," *Iunost',* 6 (June, 1965), 63.

"Bog," "Sara Bernar," "On prigotovil pistolet," "Piatnadtsat' mal'chikov," "Chem otlichaius' ia ot zhenshchiny s tsvetkom," *Sintaksis,* in *Grani,* 58 (1965), 137.

"Slovo," *Literaturnaia gazeta.* November 27, 1965.

"Simonu Chikovani," *Literaturnaia Rossiia.* January 22, 1965. 19.

"Noch'," "Nemota," *Iunost'* (June, 1966), 59.

"Toska po Lermontovu," *Molodaia gvardiia,* 12 (1966), 125-28.

"Oznob," *Zvezda vostoka,* 3 (1967), 71-74.

"Istoriia odnogo obeda," *Literaturnaia Rossiia.* July 14, 1967. 22.

"Prikliuchenie v antikvarnom magazine," *Moskva,* 2 (1967), 30-31.

"Plokhaia vesna," "Sluchilos' tak, chto dvadtsati semi...", "Ia dumaiu, kak ia byla glupa," *Iunost'* (September, 1967), 34-35.

"Snegopad," "Metel'," *Novyi mir,* 5 (1968), 74-75.

"Gostit' u khudozhnika," "Tak durno zhit', kak ia vchera zhila," "Varfolomeevskaia noch'," *Literaturnaia gruziia,* 1 (1968), 26-27.

"Dozhd' i sad," *Den' poezii.* (M. 1968).

"Ne pisat' o groze," "Proshchai, proshchai! So lba sotru," *Iunost'* (May, 1969), 50.

"Zaklinanie," "Vesnoi, vesnoi, v ee nachale," "Bolezn'," "Tak durno zhit' , kak ia vchera zhila," "Zima na iuge," *Den' poezii.* (M. 1969).

"Zimnaia zamknutost'," "Chetvert veka, Marina tomu..." *Literaturnaia gruziia,* 1 (1970), 9-10.

"Opisanie nochi," "Opisanie komnaty," "Opisanie boli v solnechnom spletenii," "Opisanie udoda dlia docheri Ani," *Iunost'* (August, 1970), 71-72.

"Poslednii den' zhivu ia v strannom dome," "Odnazhdy, pokachnuvshis' na kraiu," *Den' poezii* (M. 1970).

C. POEMS IN ANTHOLOGIES

Milner-Gulland, R. R. *Soviet Russian Verse.* New York, 1963.
    Contents: "Gazirovannaia voda," "Vstuplenie v prostudu," "Po ulitse moei, kotoryi god," "Peizazh," "Skazannoe vo vremia bombeshki" (pp. 241-45).

Obolensky, Dmitri, ed. *Penguin Book of Russian Verse.* Baltimore, 1965.
    "Novaia domna na KMK " (pp. 460-61).

Vo ves' golos. Moscow, n.d.
    Contents: "Kheminguei," "Ia dumala, chto ty moi vrag," "Tvoi dom," "Sentiabr'," "Mazurka Shopena"

D. OTHER WORKS

"Stikhotvorenie, podlezhashchee perevodu," "K diskussii po povodu stat'i L. Khikhadze, "Perevodchik ili avtor?", *Literaturnaia gruziia,* 1 (1960) , in *Literaturnaia gruziia,* 4 (1960), 104-105.

Chistye prudy. Stsenariia po libretto Iu. Nagibina. *Iskusstvo kino,* 1 (1962), 18-67.
"Vstrecha," *Literaturnaia gazeta.* February 3, 1962. p. 3. [article on Pushkin]
"Na sibirskikh dorogakh"—ocherk. *Iunost'* (December 1963), 30-42.
Chistye prudy—otryvok iz kinostsenarii, *Moskovskaia pravda.* December 1, 1963.
"Dlia tvoei zemli i moei (OAR Putevye zametki), *Literaturnaia gazeta.* Jan. 1, 1963.
"Ia polon vse' mechtami o budushchem" (Stat'i i zametki), *Literaturnaia gazeta.* October 15, 1964.
Chistye prudy—otryvok iz konstsenarii, *Moskovskii komsomolets.* January 26, 1964.
"Mig ego zreniia," *Literaturnaia gazeta.* August 27, 1964. [article on Lermontov]
"Pushkin," "Lermontov," Vospominanie o Gruzii, *Literaturnaia Gruziia,* 7 (1965), 73-76.
"K 130-letiiu so dnia gibeli A. S. Pushkina," *Literaturnaia gazeta.* February 8, 1967. p. 3.
"Pushkinskii prazdnik," *Literaturnaia gazeta.* June 4, 1969. p. 2.

II. TRANSLATIONS BY AKHMADULINA

ABKHAZIAN
Shinkuba, Bagrat. "Son," *Novyi mir,* 3 (1965), 65.
Tarba, Ivan. "Tebe," "Otpravliaias' v Sukhumi, voz'mu li s soboi," *Druzhba narodov,* 4 (1968), 108.

ARMENIAN
Tumanian, Ovanes. "Parvana," *Literaturnaia Armenia,* 12 (1968), 59-62.
"   " . "Ne prosi menia pet'. Ia nemnogo nemoi...", "Iavilsia iz snegov, izda-leka...", *Literaturnaia Armenia,* 7 (1968), 34-36.

CHUVASH
Aigi, Gennadii. "Moi sestry," "Poezda," "Otdykh," "Skazka o shlagbaume i o storozhevoi budke," *Literaturnaia gazeta.* September 26, 1961.
"   " . "Khudozhnik" "Kuet," *Znamia,* 9 (1962), 132-33.

GEORGIAN

Abashidze, Iraklii
"Khvamli," *Literaturnaia gazeta.* May 1, 1961.
"Khvamli," *Literaturnyi azerbaidzhan,* 5 (1961), 80-81.
"Korni," "Khvamli," "Opustevshaia dacha," "Pamiati nevyskazannykh stikhotvorenii," tr. with V. Tur, *Literaturnaia Gruziia,* 5 (1961), 26-30.
"Kamen'," "Ty uvidel? Zametil? Vgliadelsia?", "Zhazhdesh' uzret'—eto neobkhodimo," "Dalekaia Shkhelda," "Vesna," "Pamiati Baratashvili," tr. with Iu. Riashentsev, *Literaturnaia gazeta.* January 15, 1969), p. 6.
"Ia knigochei, ia temen' knig gliadel," "Al'pany," "Georgiiu Leonidze," "Rustaveli u Gollofy," "Malen'komu i bol'shomu," tr. with V. Leonovich, Iu. Riashentsev, A. Tarkovskii, *Literaturnaia Gruziia,* 4 (1969), 26-29.

Baratashvili, N.
"Merani," tr. with V. Lugovoi, V. Lipko, E. Vinokurov, Iu. Riashchentsev, *Zaria vostoka.* September 14, 1968.

Chikovani, Simon
"Na naberezhnoi," "Po puti v Svanettiiu," "Byki," "Zadumannoe povedai oblakam," "Oleni v gumne," "Deviat' dubov," "Rakovina," "Ot etogo poroga," *Literaturnaia Gruziia,* 2 (1960), 5-11.
"Prekratim eti rechi," "Gremskaia kolokol'nia," "Metekli," *Literaturnaia Gruziia,* 11 (1960), 30-32.
"Nachalo," "Prekrati eti rechi," "Gremskaia kolokol'nia," *Literaturnaia gazeta.* December 15, 1960.
"Rakovina," *Literaturnaia gazeta.* March 5, 1960.
"Na naberezhnoi," *Zaria vostoka.* June 18, 1961.
"Teleti i Tskhneti," "Liubliu ia starinnye eti stradaniia," "I nyne pomniu etot samolet," *Literaturnaia Gruziia,* 11 (1964), 3-4.

"Dve okruglykh ulybki," "Teleti i Tskhneti," "V teni platana," *Literaturnaia gazeta.*
January 26, 1965.
"Razdum'ia o Serafite," "Zovu Serafitu," "Granatovoe derevo u grobnitsy Serafity,"
Literaturnaia Gruziia, 12 (1965), 3-5.
"V lignakhi, na gore," *Znamia,* 2 (1967), 5.
"I nyne pomniu etot samolet," *Smena,* 3 (1968), 5.

Chiladze, Otar
"Sneg," *Znamia,* 2 (1967), 10-11.
"Ia poprosil podat' vina i pil," "V byt stola, sostoiashchii iz iastv i gostei," *Literaturnaia
Gruziia,* 6 (1967), 40-41.
"Ia poprosil podat' vina i pil," "V byt stola, sostoiashchii iz iastv i gostei," *Moskovskii
komsomolets.* June 9, 1967.
"Shel dozhd'," *Smena,* 3 (1968), 5.

Chiladze, Tamaz
"Nichego eshche net," "O, kak pokhozhe more na bessonitsy," "Otrazheniia zvezd,"
"Amirani," "Ippodrom," "Uleshsia veter," "Most Vaterloo," "Shekspir," "Drev-
nii Tallin," "Kolokola zvoniat," tr. with E. Evtushenko, *Literaturnaia Gruziia,* 11
(1960), 58-64.
"Solnechnyi zimnii den'," "Da ne uslyshish' ty," "Petergof," *Literaturnaia Gruziia,* 12
(1962), 54-55.
"Solnechnyi zimnii den'," *Literaturnaia Armeniia,* 2 (1964), 75.
"Zimnii den'," *Znamia,* 2 (1967), 13.
"Petergof," *Smena,* 3 (1968), 5.

Kalandadze, Anna
"Mravalzhamier," "Prekrasnaia Gruziia," "Razgovor s chiamaiei v Den' Pobedy," "Takaia
li byla pogoda," "Chto tebe bol'she nravitsia?", "Ty takoe glubokoe, nebo gruzin-
skoe," "Sneg adzharo-guriiskikh doch'...", "Vkhodila v Guriiu Kalanda," "Kogda
nastupit noch'," "Ia slishu, siren?" "Ne ia, a serdtse khokhochet moe," "Ia sovsem malen'kaia vetochka," "Chto delaet vesna s vladeniiami roz...", "O ty, chinara,
vzmysvshaia vysoko," "Tuta," "Skazhi mne, chiamaniia," "Chto za noch'—po
reke i po roshcham!", "Zvezdy," "Ia tebia uvenchaiu koronoi," "Lado Asatiani,"
"Oblaka," *Literaturnaia Gruziia,* 4 (1958), 20-30.
Iz chekhoslovatskoi tetradi: "Vltava," "Na vystavke meksikanskikh khudozhnikov v Bratislave," "Zlata ulichka," "Iulius Fuchik v Prage," *Literaturnaia Gruziia,* 4 (1959),
31-33.

Kvlividze, Mikhail
"O uezzhai, igrai v ot"ezd," *Novyi mir,* 12 (1959), 82-83.
"Speshu na stantsiiu," "Kogda ia tseluiu tebia," *Literaturnaia gazeta.* July 30, 1960.
"Berezu v Klebnikove," "S tekh por," "Begstvo ot tebia vo Mtskheta," tr. with V. Vino-
kurov, *Literaturnaia Gruziia,* 2 (1961), 32-33.
"Tiino," *Novyi mir,* 7 (1962), 108-109.
"Sledy na snegu," *Novyi mir,* 4 (1966), 111-112.
"Sledy na snegu," *Literaturnaia Gruziia,* 5 (1966), 27-28.
"Masshtaby zhizni," "Domik okolo moria," "Na smert' E. K. Khemingueia," *Smena,* 3
(1968), 5.
"Prodolzhenie sleduet," "Liricheskii reportazh s prospekta Rustaveli," "Nostalgiia," "On
zhdal voznikonoven'ia svoego," "Kogda b ia ne liubil tebia—ugriumym," "Stikhot-
vorenie s propushchennoi strokoi," "V nochi neprokhodimoi besprosvetnoi,"
"Pesnia," "Kogda by ia, ne vedaia styda," "Sobliudaiushchii tishinu," *Literaturnaia
Gruziia,* 12 (1968), 19-20.
"Chola," "Fotografiia," "Mol'bo," "Pesnia," "On zhdal vozniknoven'ia," *Iunost'* (Febru-
ary, 1969), 20.
"Prodolzhenie sleduet," "Ia govoriu vam: nauchites' zhdat'," "Kogda by ia ne liubil tebia—
ugriumym," "Severnyi etiud," *Novyi mir,* 12 (1968), 29-30.
"Ona vse-taki vertitsia!", "Kogda rozhdaetsia poet," "31 dekabria," *Moskva,* 5 (1969), 50-51.
"Slovno milost'," "Vse koncheno," "Ochki," tr. with E. Nikolaevskaia, *Literaturnaia Gru-
ziia,* 7-8 (1969), 30.

Tabidze, Galaktion

"Iz rasskazannogo lunoi," *Literaturnaia Gruziia,* 2 (1961), 22-23.

"Mir sostoit iz gor," "Platany Shindisi," *Literaturnaia gazeta.* May 11, 1961.

"Poeziia—prezhde vsego" "Tebe trinadtsat' let," "Sneg," "Orly usnuli, "Meri" "Persi-kovoe derevo," "Natela iz Tsinandali," *Literaturnaia Gruziia,* 4 (1962), 3-6.

"Poeziia—prezhde vsego," "Orly usnuli," *Literaturnaia Armeniia,* 2 (1964), 7-8.

"Poeziia—prezhde vsego," "Lish' by zhit'," "Natela iz Tsinandali," *Znamia,* 2(1967), 3-5.

"Tebe trinadtsat' let," *Smena,* 3 (1968), 5.

KAZAKHSTANI

Maulenov, Syrbai. "Podpisal sam Lenin," "Vozle zimovki," tr. with M. Lukozhin, *Zvezda vostoka,* 12 (1959), 10-11.

Seitkhazin, Sattar. "Devushka, ukhazhivaiushchaia za iagniatami," *Ashkhabad,* 4-5(1960),17.

KIRGHIZ

Moldokmatov, Abdykalyi. "Vecher na beregu," *Znamia,*12 (1967), 8.

" " . "Na beregu Issyk," "Kulia," *Pravda vostoka.* September 15,1969.

SOUTH VIETNAMESE

An' Tkho. "Kukushka," "Devushki pletut seti," *Inostrannaia literatura,* 6 (1966), 83-85.

TATAR

Erikeev, Akhmed. "Ne gasnut iunye poryvy," "Ia pomniu, ia znaiu—da," tr. with V. Zviachintseva, *Literatura i zhizn'.* October 21, 1962.

III. WORKS BY AKHMADULINA TRANSLATED INTO OTHER LANGUAGES.

A. BOOKS

BULGARIAN

Izbrani stihotvorenija. Tr. Stanka Penčeva. Sofija, 1968.

CZECH

Môj rodokomeň. Tr. Ján Majernik. Bratislava, 1966.

Struna. Tr. Václav Daněk. Praha, 1966.

ENGLISH

Fever and Other New Poems. Tr. Geoffrey Dutton and Igor Mezhakoff-Koriakin. Intro-duction by E. Evtushenko. New York, 1969.

Contents: Invocation, I Swear, Remembering Siberia, The Word, Longing for Ler-montov, To Sleep, Verses about Georgia, In the Deserted Resthouse, Fever, Motor Scooter, The Waitress, Autumn, Winter, Small Aircraft, Pages from a Poem, The Night before the Seventh of October, *A Tale about the Rain in Several Episodes,* What Has Happened to Me?, To A. N. Korsakova, Marina, Adventure in an Antique Shop, Farewell.

GEORGIAN

Stihi. Tbilisi, 1962. [translator not cited].

SERBO-CROATIAN

Moj Rodoslav. Tr. Sava Penčić. Kruševac, 1966.

Groznitsa. Beograd, 1968. [translator not cited].

B. POEMS IN PERIODICALS AND ANTHOLOGIES

CZECH

"Lunatici," tr. Václav Daněk, *Dvacáte století—1963-1964,* L963, 375.

"Kuň," tr. Václav Daněk, *Praha-Moskva,* r.14, č.6 (1964), 351.

"Pardál," tr. Václav Daněk, *Kulturni tvorba,* r.2, č.1 (1964), 1.

"Na cestach Sibiri," tr. Ludmila Dušková, *Tvar,* r.1, c. 9-10 (1964), 44-49.

ENGLISH

"Volcanoes," tr. W. H. Auden, in P. Blake (ed.), *Halfway to the Moon* (London, 1964), pp. 42-43.

"Winter Day," tr. R. A. D. Ford, *Tamarack Review,* vol. 37 (Autumn, 1965), 44-45.

"Bride," *Harpers,* 232 (June, 1966), 50. [no translator cited].

"Fifteen Boys," "Sara Bernhardt," "He got his pistol ready," "God," "How am I

different?," tr. G. Reavey, *Problems of Communism,* 17 (May 1968), 104-106.
"I thought you were my enemy," tr. Daniel Weissbort, *New Measure,* 8 (1968), 43.
"Farewell," tr. Geoffrey Dutton and Igor Mezhakoff-Koriakin, *Poetry Australia,* 20
    (February 1968), 38.
"Word," tr. G. Dutton and I. Mezhakoff-Koriakin, *Poetry Australia,* 20 (1968), 37-38.
"God," "Sara Bernhardt," "Click, the bullet was engaged," "Fifteen boys," "What Makes
    me Different?", tr. D. Pospielovsky, Janis Sopiets, Keith Bosley, *Russia's Other
    Poets* (London, 1968).
"Lunatics," tr. D. Weissbort, *New Measure,* 8 (1968), 44.
"Different Smile," tr. A. Hollo, *Nation,* 209 (December 15, 1969), 666-667.
"Fir-tree," tr. C. C. Kurylo, *Literary Review,* 13 (Spring 1970), 397.
A Fairytale about the Rain, tr. Christine Rydel, *RLT* No. 1 (1971), 129-37.

NORWEGIAN
"Lengael etter Lermontov," tr. Martin Nag, *Ord och Bild,* 76 (1967), 119-22.
"Et eventyr i antikvariatet," tr. Martin Nag, *Ord och Bild,* 77 (1968), 39-44.
"Akhmadulinas duell," tr. Martin Nag, *Ord och Bild,* 77 (1968), 38.

RUMANIAN
"N-am mai dormit deatita vreme," "Nu-ti pierde veaucri," "Sa dorm! Eu-dansatore a
    lunii, care pling," *Secolul 20,* 12 (Bucharest, 1967), 125-28, tr. M.Fortunescu.
"Despre Okudjava," *Secolul 20,* 6 (1968), 167-70, tr. Tatiana Nicolescu of a work
    written especially for this journal.

SLOVAK
"Tvoj dom," tr. Jań Turan, *Slovenka,* r.16, č.49 (1963), 9.
"Mòj rodokomeń," tr. Milan Fenko, *Kultúrny Život,* r.19, c.8 (1964), 3.
"Šalmoj," *Umelecké slovo, č. 8 (1964), 2.*
"Snehulienka," "Leopard," tr. Jan Majerńik, *Smena,* 7-11 (1964), 4.
"Snehulienka," tr. Jań Majerńik, *Slovenka,* r.20, č.3 (1967), 9.
"Neha," tr. Jan Majerńik, *L'udový Kalendár,* 1967, 64.
"Ešte sa ti do života...", tr. Jań Majerńík, *Malý repertoar, č.* 9 (1967), 352-353.

C. BILINGUAL PUBLICATIONS OF POEMS

ENGLISH-RUSSIAN
Carlisle, Olga. *Poets on Street Corners.* New York, 1968.   [Commentary and poems,
    pp. 365-73.] Contents: "Stikhi o Gruzii," "Skazannoe vo vremia bombezhki"
    (adapted by Stanley Noyes), "V toi davnosti," "Glavy iz poemy," "V opustevshem
    dome otdykha," "Nemota," "Son" (adapted by Jean Valentine).
Markov, Vladimir and M. Sparks. *Modern Russian Poetry.* New York, 1967. "Akh, malo
    mne drugoi zaboty," pp. 798-801.
Reavey, George. *New Russian Poets.* New York, 1967. Contains: "Piat'nadtsat' mal'chi-
    kov," "Vulkany," "Lodka," "V tot mesiats mai," "Ne udeliai mne mnogo vreme-
    ni," "Dekabr'," pp. 131-43.
FRENCH-RUSSIAN
Triolet, Elsa. *La Poesie russe.* Paris, 1965. *"Moia rodoslovnaia"*—otryvok. pp. 533-37.
GERMAN-RUSSIAN
Baumann, Hans von. *Russische Lyrik 1185-1963.* "Auf meiner Strasse," 248.

IV. CRITICAL ARTICLES ABOUT AKHMADULINA

ENGLISH
Rydel, Christine. "The Metapoetical World of Bella Akhmadulina," *Russian Literature
    Triquarterly* No. 1 (1971).

RUSSIAN
Annenskii, L. "Real'nost' skazki i prizrachnost' byli," (O poemakh B. Akhmadulinoi
    Skazka o dozhde i Moia rodoslovnaia), Don, 3 (1965), 166-68.
Benediktov, S. "Tsikl pro mototsikl," parodiia, *Voprosy literatury,* 9 (1962),   235-36.
Evseev, B. "Uroki *Chistykh prudov,"* (Instsenirovka Belly Akhmadulinoi *Chistye prudy*
    po rasskazom Iu. Nagibina v molodezhnom teatre MEI), *Moskovskii komsomolets,*
    July 2, 1965.

441

Geoletsian, S. "Poeticheskie struny," (O perevodakh na armianskii iazyk *Metakse* sbornika stikhov Akhmadulinoi), *Kommunist.* May 27, 1969.
Guliev, A. "O *Chistykh prudakh,*" *Iskusstvo kino,* 10 (1964), 73-74.
Neimirok, Aleksandr. "Bella Akhmadulina," *Grani,* 55 (1964), 169-77.
Pertsov, V. "Replika dobrozhelatelia," *Literaturnaia Rossiia.* February 7, 1964. pp.14-15.
Rzhevskii, Leonid. "Zvuk struny: o tvorchestve Belly Akhmadulinoi," *Vozdushnye puti,* V (1967), 257-78. Reprinted in his *Prochten'e tvorcheskogo slova* (New York, 1970), 253-75.
Shanin, Iurii. "Vvedenie v nasmork," (parodiia), *Voprosy literatury,* 7 (1963), 241.
Sargina, Ludmilla. "Akhmadulina," *Filologiia,* 146 (1967), 399-409.
Turevich, L. "Vysokoparnyi ekran," (O khudozhestvennom fil'me, *Chistye prudy), Iskusstvo kino,* 10 (1966), 35-40.

SERBO-CROATIAN
Nikolić, Milica. "Izlomljena realnost Bele Ahmaduljine," *Delo,* 14 (1968), 556-83.
Review of "Groznitza," *Književnost,* 11 (1968), 501.

SLOVAK
Beňo, Jań. "Talent pôvabnej Belly Achmadulinovej, sovietsky poetky," *Smena,* July 21, 1966, p. 4.
Chomová, Tatiana. "Bella Achmadulinová," *L'udové kurzy ruštiny,* r.13, c.10 (1965), 308-309.
Thorez, Paul. "Politika srdca," (O Andrejovi Voznesenskom a Belle Achmadulinovej), *Sloboda,* r.21, č.44 (1966), 8.
Wagnerová, Dagmeer. "S Bellou Achmadulinou v dači Negibina," *Slovenka,* r.20, č.3 (1967), 8-9.

ADDENDA

1. Original works by Akhmadulina.

A. BOOKS

STIKHI. Moscow, 1975.
Contents: Svetofory, Den' poezii, Chuzhoe remeslo, "Ne udeliai mne mnogo vremeni. . . ," Nevesta, Lunatiki, Gruzinskikh zhenshchin imena. . . , "Chelovek v chisto pole vykhodit. . . ," Avgust, "Zhivut na ulitse peschanoi. . . ," Tvoi dom, Sentiabr', Gazirovannaia voda, Motoroller, "Vlechet menia starinnyi slog. . . ," Bolezn'. Magnitofon, Zima, Svecha, Simonu Chikovani, Gostit' u khudozhnika, Moi tovarishchi, Oznob, Malen'kie samolety, Toska po Lermontovu, Uroki muzyki, Slovo, Nemota, Drugoe, Zimniaia zamknutost', Son, Sluchilos' tak, chto dvadtsati semi. . . ," Noch', Plokhaia vesna, Snegopad, Metel', Dozhd' i sad, "Zima na iuge. Daleko zashlo. . . ," "Ia dumaiu: kak ia byla glupa. . . ," "Tak durno zhit', kak ia vchera zhila. . . ," "Kak dolgo ia ne vysypalas'. . . ," Opisanie nochi, Medlitel'nost', "Chto za mgnoven'e! Rodnoe ditia. . . ," "V toi toske, na kakuiu sposoben. . . ," Snimok, "Opiat' sentiabr', kak t'mu vremen nazad. . . ," Eto ia. . . , Lermontov i ditia, Moia rodoslovnaia, Skazka o dozhde, Prikliuchenie v antikvarnom magazine.

B. Poems in Periodicals
Listed Chronologically by Year

"Mne vspominat' spodruchnei, chem imet'. . . ," LITERATURNAIA GAZETA. January 1, 1971, p. 6.

Vospominaniia o lalte, "Sperva ditia iavilos' iz potomok. . . ," Osen', LITERATURNAIA GAZETA. October 13, 1971, p. 7.

Iz novoi knigi. Stikhi. "I otstoiav za upokoi. . . ," Medlitel'nost', "Remeslo nashi dushi svelo. . . ," NOVYI MIR 5 (1972), pp. 24-25.

Medlitel'nost'. Stikhi, KODRY 6 (1972), p. 23.

Gruzinskikh zhenshchin imena, ZARIA VOSTOKA. October 1, 1972.

"Moroz i solntse, Den' chudesnyi, LITERATURNAIA ROSSIIA. February 9, 1973, p. 13.

"Prekratim eti rechi na mig"—K 70 letiiu so dnia rozhdeniiaS.Chikovani, LITERATUR-NAIA GAZETA. May 23, 1973, p. 7.

Snimok—"Opiat' sentiabr' kak t'mu vremen nazad. . . ," Eto ia, LITERATURNAIA GA-ZETA. October 17, 1973, p. 7.

Zhdet menia neskazannyi idol, Chto za mgnoven'e!; Rodnoe ditia, "V toi toske, na kakuiu sposoben. . . ," LITERATURNAIA ROSSIIA. October 26, 1973, p. 6.

Lermontov i ditia, LITERATURNAIA GAZETA. January 1, 1974, p. 7.

Metel'. Stikhi: Ozhidanie elki; Ada, "Zhila v pokoe okaiannom," "On popravliaet pisto-let," Metel', NOVYI MIR 6 (1974), pp. 145-48.

"Sobralis', zaveli razgovor. . . ," LITERATURNAIA ROSSIIA. August 16, 1974, p. 10.

Dachnyi roman, LITERATURNAIA GAZETA. January 1, 1974, p. 7.

Novye stikhi: Son, Dom i les, "Ia zaviduiu ei—molodoi. . . ," ZNAMIA. Book 1, 1975, pp. 122-24.

"Kak nikogda, bespechna i dobra. . . ," LITERATURNAIA GAZETA. February 12, 1975, p. 7.

Iz tsikla "Zhenshchina i poety." Stikhi: "Tak znachit, kak vy delaete, drugi?"; "Teper' o tekh, ch'i detskie portrety," Noch' pered vystupleniem, "Ni slova o liubvi! . . ," OKTIABR' 3 (1975), pp. 25-27.

Otryvok iz malen'koi poemy o Pushkine. Vzoiti na stsenu, Dom, Dva geparda!; "Kakoe blazhenstvo, chto bleshchut snega. . . ," "Prokhozhii, mal'chik, chto ty? . . ."; Vospominanie, Fevral' bez snega, OKTIABR' 6 (1975), pp. 3-12.

"Prishla. Stoit. Ei vosemnadtsat' let. . . ," "Sad eshche ne obletel. . . ," LITERATUR-NAIA GAZETA. November 12, 1975, p. 7.

C. Other Works

"Schastlivyi dar dobroty," LITERATURNAIA ROSSIIA. January 6, 1967, p. 15. This is a review of Korinets, Iu. I. SUBBOTA V PONEDEL'NIK. STIKHI I SKAZKI. Moscow, 1966.

"Dobryi i iasnyi svet," LITERATURNAIA GAZETA. March 8, 1967, p. 15. A review of IZBRANNAIA LIRIKA, tr. from the Japanese of Fukao Sumako by E. Vinoku-rov. Moscow, 1966.

". . . k taine pervonachal'nogo zvuchaniia." [Problemy literaturnogo perevoda] . LITE-RATURNAIA GAZETA. September 2, 1970, pp. 4-5.

"Chudo tantsa" [Balet R. Shchedrina ANNA KARENINA v Bol'shom teatre SSSR] . LITERATURNAIA GAZETA. June 5, 1972, p. 8.

"Poeziia—prezhde vsego." K 80 letiiu so dnia rozhdeniia G. Tabidze. KOMSOMOL-SKAIA PRAVDA. November 7, 1973.

B.A. and Pozdneeva, L.D. NARODY AZII I AFRIKI 5 (1973), pp. 196-200.
Map"ëciu "Sob. miriad list'ev" B 3-x T. Per. s iapon. A.E. Gluskinnoi, Moscow,

1971-72.

SLOVO O PUSHKINE [Stat'i i zametki] . "Chudnaia vechnost'," LITERATURNAIA GAZETA. June 5, 1974, pp. 6-7.

"Iskusstvo razbudilo v nikh tvortsov" [Zametki s vystavki samodeiatel'nosti khudozh-nikov SLAVA TRUDU. Moskva. Beseda s poetessoi B. Akhmadulinoi. Zapisal S. Liknitskii]. LITERATURNAIA ROSSIIA. June 21, 1974, p. 9.

"Samyi strogii sud'ia. Shtrikhi k portr. chitatelia." [Vyskazyvaniia s komment. otd. rus. literatury: gaz.:] A. Ivanov; S. Narochatov; D. Granin; Bella Akhmadulina; D. Kugul'tinov. LITERATURNAIA GAZETA. January 1, 1976, p. 5.

"Predislovie" Tushnova, Veronika. "Stikhi o liubvi," LITERATURNAIA ROSSIIA. March 26, 1976, p. 16.

II. Translations by Akhmadulina.

ABKHAZIAN

Shinkuba, Bagrat. "Slovo," "Dlia vygody brennogo tela. . . ," "Zaveshchanie," "Kak ia zhelal osilit' pereval! . . ."; "Slyshu golos. . . ," "Zhazhda," LITERATURNAIA GAZETA. July 22, 1970, p. 7.

ARMENIAN

Emin, Gevork. "Osen'," NOVYI MIR 6 (1972), p. 6.

Isaakian, Avetik. MOEI RODINE—"Vzdykhaiut veter i volna," "Izmucheno more, i pena," "Vidish', Chernyi orel," "Mne snilos' more, bedniaky," "Ia govoriu vam," "O golubka moia, slovno my ne znakomy," "Shelestit veterok," tr. B.A. and others. LITERATURNAIA GAZETA. October 29, 1975, p. 6.

Khachatrian, Agvan. "Mat' matrosa," "Ty govorish': rasskazhi ob Armenii. . ."; "Chut' vylupivshiisia ptenets. . . ," "Ty volosy moi laskaesh' nezhno. . . ." [Stikhi. Per. V. Zvialintseva i B.A.] LITERATURNAIA ARMENIIA 12 (1974), pp. 62-63.

BALKAR

        Kuliev, Kaisyn

"Kukushka," "Stikhotvorenie, napisannoe v bol'nitse"; "Vecher v gorakh," "Govoriu v puti," "Govoriu samom u sebe," "Govoriu odinokomu derevu u dorogi," "Voly pod dozhdem," "Kolybel'naia teni dereva." LITERATURNAIA GAZETA. August 23, 1972, p. 6.

"Lunnyi svet," "Prislushaisia k slovam," "My slushali muzyku," "Belizna zimnei nochi, "Dvornik moei materi," "Son zimnei noch'iu," "Zima prishla," "Chokka." LITERATURNAIA ROSSIIA. September 22, 1972, p. 11.

"Veselye liudi," "Kak mnogo v gorode liudei!" "Derev'ia vy—brat'ia moi. . . ," LITERATURNAIA GAZETA. August 28, 1974, p. 7.

"Pis'mo Rasulu Gamzatovu." TRUD. January 18, 1976.

GEORGIAN

Chikovani, Simon. "Prekratim eti rechi na mig," "Nachalo," "Morskaia rakovina," ZARIA VOSTOKA. June 3, 1973.

Chiladze, Otar. "Sneg," KOMSOMOLSKAIA PRAVDA. August 15, 1972.

        Kaladze, Karlo

"Stikhi: Russkomu poetu—moemu drugu"—"S gor i kholmov, ni v chem ne vinova-tykh. . . ," "Na beregu to l' nochi, to li dnia. . . ," "Eti sklony odela trava. . . ," "Zvezdy," "Morskaia volna." [with V. Sokolov] . DRUZHBA NARODOV 3 (1971), pp. 8-11.

"Zhizn' lozy" [Poema] , LITERATURNAIA GAZETA. February 4, 1976, p. 7.

        Kalandadze, Anna

LETITE, LIST'IA, Tbilisi, 1959, 70 p.
"Vazha, " "Zvoni v kolokola, Loreta!" ZARIA VOSTOKA, March 8, 1972.
"Mravalzhamier. Stikhi," LITERATURNYI AZERBAIDZHAN 11 (1972), p. 8.
          Kvlividze, Mikhail
"Ochki," IUNOST' 5 (1971), p. 21.
"Liricheskii reportazh s prospekta Rustaveli," IUNOST' 8 (1973), p. 78.
Tabidze, Galaktion. "Meri," Zakhod solntsa," [and O. Ivinskaia] , ZARIA VOSTOKA,
      October 14, 1973.

III. Works by Akhmadulina Translated into Other Languages.

A. Books

ARMENIAN
STIKHI. tr. Metakse. Erevan, "Aiastan," 1968. Translation of Struna.

CZECH
MLADÁ SOVĚTSKÁ POEZIE. Olomouc, 1971. Translations of poems of Akhmadulina
      and other Soviet Russian poets.

SLOVAK
JODINA HUDBY, tr. Jan Majerník, Bratislava, 1972.

YUGOSLAVIA
MOJ RODOSLOV, tr. Sava Penčić, Kruševac, 1966.
GROZNICA. tr. Milica Nikolić, Beograd, 1968. Contents: Odlomci iz poeme "Moj rodo-
     slov," "Uverenje o njigovoj bolesti," "Slobodno prepričana totarska pesma," "Pri-
     govor Ipsilona," "Varto lo mejska noc," "Kunem se."

B. Poems in Periodicals and Anthologies

BULGARIAN
"Avtomat za gaziran sok," "Lunatitsi," tr. Gr. Lenkov and L. Prangov, LITERATUREN
     FRONT. Br. 24, June 9, 1966.
"Bez kraen oni prostor. . . ," tr. Iordan Iankov, Br. 135, NARODNA MLADEZH. June
     10, 1967.
"Ne biva—kazbash—nedei plaka!" "Vulkany," tr. St. Pencheva, LITERATUREN
     FRONT. Br. 25, June 15, 1967.
"Ecen," tr. Grigor Lenkov and Liuben Prangov, RODNA RECH. Kn. 9, 1967, pp. 10-14.
"Otk"s ot Poemata," "Prikaza za d'zhda," tr. Stank Pencheva, SENTEMVRI. Kn. 7,
     1967, pp. 22-39.
"Ne mi otdeliai vreme," ZHENATA DNES. Kn. 9, 1967, p. 8.
"Tsvetia," tr. T. Mitskov, LITERATUREN FRONT. br. 50, December 5, 1968.
"Ne mi otdeliai veche vreme," tr. Georgi Mitskov, PULS, 24 (November 20, 1973), p. 7.
"Koi shche vi v'zdee," tr. Dim. Vasilev, LITERATUREN FRONT, 10 (March 6, 1975),
     p. 8.
"Bezgrizhna i dobra izliazakh pak," tr. Dimit"r Vasilev, LITERATUREN FRONT, 37
     (September 11, 1975), p. 7.
"Avgust," "Poleka," "Magnitofon," tr. Ivan Nikolov, PLAM"K, 1 (1976), p. 8.
"Dachen roman," tr. Dimit"r Vasilen, LITERATUREN FRONT, 35 (August 26, 1976),
     p. 8.

CZECH

"Nezaklínej se, dobře vim. . . ," tr. Václav Daněk, HOST DO DOMU, r. 13. 1966, č 11. 5. 43. 1 obr.

ENGLISH

"The Chills," tr. Sam Driver, RUSSIAN LITERATURE TRIQUARTERLY, 5 (Winter 1973), pp. 47-50. Reprinted in THE ARDIS ANTHOLOGY OF RECENT RUS-SIAN LITERATUARE. Ann Arbor, 1974.

"Don't Write About the Storm," A Description of the Night," tr. Christine Rydel, RUSSIAN LITERATURE TRIQUARTERLY, 5 (Winter 1973), pp. 51-52. Re-printed in THE ARDIS ANTHOLOGY OF RECENT RUSSIAN LITERATURE!

"I Swear," tr. Joseph Lanland, Tamas Aczel, and Laszlo Tikos, PARTISAN REVIEW 40:2 (1973), p. 259.

"I Swear," tr. Paul Schmidt, NEW YORK REVIEW OF BOOKS 20:7 (May 1973), p. 20.

"Silence," tr. Daniel Halpern and Albert Todd, NEW YORK REVIEW OF BOOKS 20:16 (18 October 1973), p. 4.

"Though I've lived in contempt and discrace," "For how many years along this street of mine have I," "Music Lessons," "Winter," "Some lyrics from RAIN," "Night," "I Swear," tr. Elaine Feinstein, POST-WAR RUSSIAN POETRY, ed. Daniel Weissbort, Baltimore, 1974, pp. 229-40.

"The New Blast Furnace in the Kemerovo Matallurgical Combine," tr. Daniel Halpern, ATLANTIC (234:6) December 1974, p. 81.

"Winter," "Sleepwalkers," "Autumn," "Goodbye," tr. Barbara Einzig, RUSSIAN LIT-ERATURE TRIQUARTERLY 9 (Spring 1974), pp. 41-44.

"How am I distinguished from a woman," "Fifteen Boys," "I am drawn to the old style," "Your House," tr. Nancy Condee, RUSSIAN LITERATURE TRIQUAR-TERLY 11 (Winter 1975), pp. 309-13.

POLISH

"Lunatycy," tr. Andzej Drawicz, WSPÓŁCZESNOŚĆ. 22 (1966), p. 4.

"Nie potrzeba mi nic," "Jak długo wody nie zmącona toń," "Pamięć wojny," tr. Wiktor Woroszylski, MATERIAŁY REPERTUAROWE ZARZĄD KULTURY I OŚWIA-ŁY GŁOWNEGO ZARZĄDU POLITYCZENEGO WP, 4 (1967), pp. 124-27.

"Mazurek szopena," tr. Andrzej Tchórzewski, KIERUNKI, 42 (1967), p. 6.

"Kto wie, przez chwilę czy przez wieczność," tr. Andrzej Boszkowski, POMORZE, 21 (1967), p. 11.

"Mazurek Szopena," tr. Wiktor Woroszylski, TYGODNIK POWSZECHNY 5 (1972), p. 6.

*For additional Polish entries, see BIBLIOGRAFIA ZAWARTOSCI CZASOPSIM, 1962, entry numbers 51408, 63831, 72424. These volumes were unavailable at the time of the compilation of this bibliography.

SLOVAK

"Šalmaj," tr. Ján Majerník, L'UD. June 14, 1973, p. 8.

YUGOSLAVIA

"Mislila sam da si neprijaleli," tr. Radaje Kavedžić, STUDENT, 19, V, 1964, XXVIII, p. 17-18.

"Mjesčari," tr. Stijepo Mijović, REPUBLIKA, 1964, XX, 5, p. 209.

"Mislila sam," "Dušman simoj. . . ," "Nesnosno mil 11," tr. Božo Bulatović, ODJEK, 15, VI, 1964, XVIII, p. 12.

"Mislila sam. . . ," "Nesnosno mi. . . ," tr. Božo Bulatović, LETOPIS MATICE SRPSKE, 1964, CXL, Knj CCCXCIV, p. 78.

"Pejsaž," tr. Dragan Janevski, MISLA I, 1966, I, p. 1.

"Mesečari," tr. Georgi Arsovski, STUDENTSKI ZBOR, VII-VIII, 1967, XVIII, p. 20.

"Ulica ta se peščana zone. . . ," tr. Sava Penčić, BORBAS, 24, IX, 1967, XXXII, p. 263.

"Hemingveij," "Odlamsk," "Šopenova Mazurka," tr. Slobodanska Jentovič, BAGDULA, X, 1967, IX, p. 103.

"Cviječe," tr. Vladimir Gerić, MOGUĆNOSTI, 1968, XV, 9-10, p. 1107-07.

"Hemingvey," "Mleko," "Panter," tr. Dragolub Rajič, USTVARI, 1968, X, 33, p. 47-50.

"Ne gubi samnom suvišno vreme," "Mene privlači reč starinska," NAŠE STVARANJE, 1969, XVI, 4-5, pp. 209-10.

"Kunem se," POLJA, 1970, XVI, 136, p. 13.

"Verglaševa pesmica," tr. Lav Zaharov, ODJEK, 1970, XXIII, 5-6, p. 24.

"O prevodjenju," tr. Milorad Luketić, OVDJE, 1971, III, 22, p. 23.

"Bez naslov," tr. Dragan Janevski, BESEDA, 1973, I, 3, pp. 257-58.

"Ne gubi za mnom vreme. . . ," tr. Mirko Zarkević, GRADINA, IX, 7-8, p. 98.

IV. Critical Works about Akhmadulina.

BULGARIAN

Gerova, Darina. "Goliama poeziia na goliam narod," [Beseda s Bela A. za poet. tvorchest-vo] , NARODNA MLADEZH, br. 135, June 10, 1967.

Vasileva, Khristiana. "Vazhnoto e tia de deti," RODNA RECH, kn. 9, 1967.

CZECH

Arnautová, Maita. "Křídla a závaží tradice," HOST DO DOMU, r. 14, 1967, č 4. p. 48-9.

Arnautová, Maita. "Achmadulinová a Ajgi—dvě pojeti moderni poezie," ČESKOSLOVEN-SKÁ RUSSISTIKA, r. 12. 1967. č. 4. pp. 246-48.

Mathauser, Zdenek. "Baśníŕčina struna," RUDÉ PRÁVO, January 14, 1967, p. 5.

"Pout života." Disk, Praha, režie Fr. Štěpánek Ciprová Inka: Poetický Disk. =MF., 3.1. 1968, p. 5.

RUSSIAN

Neymirok, A. "Bella Akhmadulina," GRANI, 55 (1964), pp. 169-77.

Tsurikova, G. "Poeziia, igra, zhizn'," LITERATURNAIA GAZETA, 33 (March 7, 1964).

Vladimirov, Iu. "Spiriticheskii seans v poezii," OKTIABR', 4 (1964), pp. 190-91.

SLOVAK

Hivešová, Daniela. "Polokamih pri človeku. [B.A. HODINA HUDBY, poézia] , NOVÉ SLOVO, r. 15, 1973, c. 11, p. 15.

I.S. "V tichu poézie," ROMBOID, r. 8. 1973, č 3, p. 74-75.

Klátik, Zlatko. "Bella Achmadulinová HODINA HUDBY," SLOVENSKÉ POHLADY, r. 88. 1972. č 12, p. 131-34.

Spíra, Vladimir. "Hrdinom tohto príbehu je človek," [B.A. "Môj rodokmeň" pásmo poé-zie] . PRAVDA, February 26, 1974, p. 5.

Urbkova, Veronika. "Báseň je hudba," SMENA NA NEDEL'U, r. 8 (26) 1973, č 13, p. 7. 1 obr.

Vegin, Peter. "Bella, ako sa máš," [Rozhovor so sovietskou poetkou.] , REVUE SVETO-VEJ LITERATURY, r. 7, 1971, č 6, pp. 180-81.

Vopálenská, Eva, "Bella Achmadulinová," TELEVÍZIA, r. 6. 1970, č. 47, p. 7.

YUGOSLAVIA

Danojlič, Miča, "Groznica," BORBA, 31, VIII, 1968, XXXIII, p. 240.

Nikolič, Milica, "Izlomljena Realnost Bele Ahmaduljine," DELO, 1968, XIV, 5, pp. 556-83.

Nikolić, Milica, "Izlomljena realnost (Bela Ahmaduljina)," in RUSKE POETSKE TEME. Beograd, 1972.

B. REVIEWS

STRUNA:
CZECH
Honzik, Jiři, "Básnicka struna," LITERÁRNÍ NOVINY, r. 16. 1967. č. 9. p. 9.

RUSSIAN
Anninskii, L. "Bezzashchitnoe vseoruzh'e," MOSKOVSKII KOMSOMOLETS, October 27, 1962.
Elkin, A. "Glubina nashei vspashki," SMENA, 18 (1962), pp. 30-31.
Foniakov, N. "Dobyvaite, rebiata, opyt," LITERATURNAIA GAZETA, Dec. 20, 1962.
Lesnevskii, S., "Ne zria slova poetov oseniaiut. . . ," LITERATURNAIA GAZETA, September 4, 1962.
Levin, M., "V unison s vekom," SOVETSKAIA ESTONIIA, August 8, 1962.
Ognev, V., LITERATURNAIA GAZETA, September 20, 1962.
Smeliakov, Ia., MOLODAIA POEZIIA NOVOGO VREMENI, No. 12, Moscow 1962, pp. 212-20.
Solov'ev, B. "Poeziia i ee kritiki," OKTIABR', 2 (1963), pp. 193-209.
Urban, A. "Slovo-poisk" (Poeziia 1962 goda), VOPROSY LITERATURY, 1 (1963), pp. 50-55.
Zaitsev, V. and Krasukhin, G. "Pervye knigi poetov," OKTIABR', 2 (1963), pp. 205-13.

SLOVAK
Mathauser, Z. "Poetkina struna," RUDE PRAVO, January 14, 1967, p. 5.

UROKI MUZYKI:
Antokol'skii, P. "Darovanie sil'noe dobroe" and Osetrov, E. "Kapronovye dva kryla," KOMSOMOL'SKAIA PRAVDA, August 6, 1970.
Evtushenko, Evgenii. "Liubvi i pechali poryv tsentrobezhnyi," DRUZHBA NARODOV, 6 (1970), pp. 279-82.
Gusev, V. "Muzyka, zhizn', poeziia," POD"EM, 3 (1971), pp. 136-37.
Kubat'ian, G. "Ne vedai nemoty. . . ," LITERATURNAIA ARMENIIA, 9 (1970), pp. 85-88. This review also discusses the Armenian translation.
Sarnov, B. "Privychka stavit' slovo posle slovo. . . ," NOVYI MIR, 12 (1970), p. 257-62.
Shaginian, M. "Chitaia UROKI MYZYKI," LITERATURNAIA ROSSIIA, June 26, 1970, p. 17.
"Voskresnyi den'":
Mikhailov, A. Na srednem urovne," ZNAMIA, 10 (1964), p. 229-40.
"Moi tovarishchi":
Protagin, V. "V ozhidanii sleduiushchego shaga," MOSKOVSKII KOMSOMOLETS, December 9, 1964.
CHISTYE PRUDY:
Orlov, V. "A chto budet na ekrane?" LITERATURNAIA GAZETA, Nov. 24, 1964.
MOIA RODOSLOVNAIA:
Abramov, A. "Rabotat' ser'ezno," VOPROSY LITERATURY, 2 (1965), pp. 42-47.
Osetrov, E. "Sintez sovremennosti," (Poeziia 1964 g.), VOPROSY LITERATURY, 2 (1965), pp. 19-29.

C. Books and Articles Containing Sections About Akhmadulina

ENGLISH

Forgues, Pierre, "Russian poetry 1963-65," SURVEY, (July 1965), pp. 54-70. Comments on "Rain."

Forgues, Pierre, " The Young Poets," SURVEY (January 1963), pp. 31-52.

RUSSIAN

Kovalenkov, Aleksandr. "Do pervoi knigi," in KHOROSHIE, RAZNYE . . . LITERA-
TURNYE PORTRETY, Moscow, 1966.

Rhevsky, L. PROCHTEN'E TVORCHESKOGO SLOVA, New York, 1970.

D. Other

Smirnov, Sergei. "Bela Belle—Rozn'," in DRUGI—ODNOPOLCHANE, Moscow, 1975, p.
32. Literary parody.

A BIBLIOGRAPHY OF THE PUBLISHED WORKS OF
IOSIF ALEKSANDROVICH BRODSKY

Compiled by George L. Kline

PART I: TEXTS*

A. *POETRY*

  1. Books

1965

    Iosif Brodskii, *Stikhotvoreniia i poemy*. Washington-New York: Inter-Language Literary Associates, 1965. 239pp. Foreword by Georgii Stukov.

    Contents: "Khudozhnik" (The Artist), "Slava" (Fame), "Stikhi pod epigrafom" (Verses beneath an Epigraph), "Ryby zimoi" (Fish in Winter), "Petukhi" (Roosters),

---

    *Russian titles are translated only when they first appear. Titles and first lines of short poems are enclosed in quotation marks (except in the first translation); titles of longer poems (three or more pages) are italicized. Main words in translated titles are capitalized. An attempt has been made to list all of Brodsky's poetry and poetic translations published in the Soviet Union. However, in the case of poems published in Russian-language journals abroad, only those works are listed which are not included in either of the two volumes of Brodsky's poetry: *Stikhotvoreniia i poemy* (1965) and *Ostanovka v pustyne* (1970).

"I vechnyi boi" (And endless battle), "Gladiatory" (Gladiators), "Pamiatŋik Pushkinu" (The Pushkin Monument), "Proshchai" (Farewell), "Pesenka o Fede Dobrovol'skom" (Song about Fedya Dobrovolsky), "Pamiati Fedi Dobrovol'skogo" (In Memory of Fedya Dobrovolsky), "Sonet: Perezhivi vsekh" (Sonnet: Outlive them all), "Sonet k Glebu Gorbovskomu" (Sonnet for Gleb Gorbovsky), "Posviashchenie Glebu Gorbovskomu" (To Gleb Gorbovsky), "Stikhi o slepykh muzykantakh" (Verses about Blind Musicians), "Pamiatnik" (The Monument), "Zachem opiat' meniaemsia mestami" (Why are we changing places again), "Teper' ia uezzhaiu iz Moskvy" (I now am leaving Moscow), "Prikhodit vremia sozhalenii" (The time for regret has come), "Zatem, chtob pustym razgovortsem" (In order that an empty talker), "Evreiskoe kladbishche okolo Leningrada" (The Jewish Cemetery near Leningrad), "Prikhodit mart. Ia syznova sluzhu" (March is coming. Once again I serve), "Vorotish'sia na rodinu. Nu chto zh" (You're coming home again. What does that mean?) "Nastupaet vesna" (Spring is Here), "Teper' vse chashche chuvstvuiu ustalost' " (Exhaustion now is a more frequent guest), "Stansy" (Stanzas), "Sad" (The Park), "Piligrimy" (Pilgrims), "Da, my ne stali glushe ili starshe" (We have not grown older or more deaf), "Stansy gorodu" (Stanzas to the City), "Vospominaniia" (Memories), "Glagoly" (Verbs), "Kniga" (The Book), "Rozhdestvenskii romans" (A Christmas Ballad), "Proplyvaiut oblaka" (The Clouds are Sailing), *Vot ia vnov' posetil (Once More I Have Visited),* "Ty poskachesh' vo mrake po beskrainim kholodnym kholmam" (You gallop in the dark on the endless cold hills), "Opredelenie poezii" (Definition of Poetry), "Romans" (A Ballad), "Pis'mo k A. D." (A Letter to A. D.), "V tot vecher vozle nashego ognia"* (That evening, sprawling by an open fire), "Ia obnial eti plechi i vzglianul" (I bent to kiss your shoulders, and I saw), "Ia kak Uliss" (I, like Ulysses), *Tri glavy (Three Chapters),* "Mne govoriat, chto nuzhno uezzhat' "(They say that I must leave), "Sonet: Velikii Gektor strelami ubit" (Sonnet: Great-hearted Hector has been speared to death), "Sonet: My snova prozhivaem u zaliva" (Sonnet: Once more we're living as by Naples Bay), "Dialog" (Dialogue), "Kogda podoidet k izgolov'iu" (When at the head of your bed), "Ne zhazhdal iavliat'sia do sroka" (He did not want to be too early), "Dorogomu D. B." (To Dear D. B.), "Pod vecher on vidit, zastyvshi v dveriakh" (At evening he watches, immobile in the doorway), "Pustaia doroga pod sosnami spit" (The empty road slumbers beneath the pines), "Iiul'skoiu noch'iu v poselke temno" (On a July night it's dark in the village), "Dva vsadnika skachut v prostranstve nochnom" (Two riders gallop in the vastness of the night), "Sonet: Ia snova slyshu golos tvoi tosklivyi" (Sonnet: Once more I hear your melancholy voice), *Gost' (The Guest), Kholmy (The Hills), Bol'shaia elegiia Dzhonu Donnu (Elegy for John Donne), Isaak i Avraam (Isaac and Abraham), Shestvie (The Procession),* "Sadovnik v vatnike, kak drozd" (Quilt-jacketed, a tree-surgeon), "S grust'iu i s nezhnost'iu" (Sadly and Tenderly), "K sadovoi ograde" (Toward the Park Fence), "Okna" (Windows), "Vse chuzhdo v dome novomu zhil'tsu" (New tenants find their houses wholly strange), "Topilas' pech'. Ogon' drozhal vo t'me" (The stove was lit. Flames trembled in the dark), "Oboz" (Wagon Train), "Kolesnik umer, bondar' "(The wheelwright's dead, the cooper), "Zagadka angelu" (Enigma for an Angel).

1970

Iosif Brodskii, *Ostanovka v pustyne: Stikhotvoreniia i poemy.* New York: Izdatel'stvo imeni Chekhova, 1970. 231pp. Biographical Note. Foreword by "N. N." Index of titles and first lines.

Contents: "Rozhdestvenskii romans," *Bol'shaia elegiia Dzhonu Donnu,* "Vorotish'sia na rodinu. Nu chto zh," *Ot okrainy k tsentru (From the Outskirts to the Center),* ** "V tot vecher vozle nashego ognia,"*** "Teper' vse chashche chuvstvuiu ustalost'," "Iz 'Starykh angliiskikh pesen': Zimniaia svad'ba" (From 'Old English Songs': Winter Wedding), "Vse chuzhdo v dome novomu zhil'tsu," *Kholmy,* "Ty poskachesh' vo mrake po beskrainim kholodnym kholmam," "Sonet: Velikii Gektor strelami ubit," "Sonet: My snova prozhivaem u zaliva," *Isaak i Avraam,* "Pod vecher on vidit, zastyvshi v dveriakh," "Pustaia doroga pod sosnami spit," "Iiul'skoiu noch'iu v poselke temno," "Dva vsadnika skachut v prostranstve nochnom," "Ogon', ty slyshish', nachal ugasat' " (The fire, as you

---

*"Byl chernyi nebosvod svetlei tekh nog" (The night-black sky was brighter than his legs) —which is printed as the first line of this poem—is in fact the first line of a two-line epigraph. The text of the poem begins with the third line: "V tot vecher..."

**In the 1965 edition this poem is untitled and identified by its first line: *Vot ia vnov' posetil.*

***See the first note on this page.

can hear, is dying down), "Glagoly," "Stikhi pod epigrafom," "Pesenka o Fede Dobrovol'-skom," "Proplyvaiut oblaka," "A. A. Akhmatovoi" (To A. A. Akhmatova), "Sonet: Pro-shel ianvar' za oknami tiur'my" (Sonnet: The month of January has flown past the prison windows), "Ia obnial eti plechi i vzglianul," "Zagadka angelu," "Lomtik medovogo mes-iatsa" (A Slice of Honeymoon), "Ty vyporkhnesh', malinovka, iz trekh" (You'll flutter, robin redbreast, from those three), "Pesni schastlivoi zimy" (Songs of a Happy Winter), "Odna vorona (ikh byla gur'ba" (One crow—there was a swarm of them), "Dlia shkol'no-go vozrasta" (For the School Age), "Prorochestvo" (A Prophecy), "Otkazom ot skorbno-go perechnia—zhest" (Refusing to catalogue all of men's woes), Anno Domini, "K Liko-medu, na Skiros" (To Lycomedes on Scyros), "Elegiia" (Elegy), Strofy (Stanzas), "Sonet: Kak zhal', chto tem, chem stalo dlia menia" (Sonnet: How sad that my life has not come to mean), "Enei i Didona" (Aeneas and Dido), "Sem' let spustia" (Seven Years Later), "Sadovnik v vatnike, kak drozd," "Oboz," "S grust'iu i s nezhnost'iu," "V rasputitsu" (Spring Season of Muddy Roads), "K severnomu kraiu" (To the Northland), "V derevne Bog zhivet ne po uglam" (In villages God lives not just in ikon corners), "Dni begut nado mnoi" (The days glide over me), "Derev'ia v moem okne, v dereviannom okne" (The trees in my window, in my wooden-framed window), "Topilas' pech'. Ogon' drozhal vo t'me," "Orfei i Artemida" (Orpheus and Artemis), "Pervoe ianvaria 1965 goda" (January 1, 1965), "Vecherom" (Evening), "Podsvechnik" (The Candlestick), Iz "Shkol'noi antologii" (From "The School Anthology"), "Sumev otgorodit'sia ot liudei" (Now that I've walled myself off from the world), "Pervoe sentiabria" (September First), "Poslanie k stikham" (Message to my Verses), "Fontan" (The Fountain), "Na Prachechnom mostu, gde my s toboi" (On Washerwoman Bridge, where you and I), "Pochti elegiia" (Almost an Ele-gy), "Zimnim vecherom v Ialte" (A Winter Evening in Yalta), "Stikhi v Aprele" (Verses in April), Stikhi na smert' T. S. Eliota (Verses on the Death of T. S. Eliot), Odnoi poetesse (To a Certain Poetess), Einem alten Architekten in Rom, Pis'mo v butylke (A Letter in a Bottle), Novye stansy k Avguste (New Stanzas to Augusta), Dva chasa v rezervuare (Two Hours by the Reservoir), Ostanovka v pustyne (Halt in the Wilderness); Proshchaite, madmuazel' Veronika (Adieu, Mademoiselle Véronique); Gorbunov i Gorchakov (Gorbunov and Gorchakov).*

2. Periodicals

1965

"Stikhi o priniatii mira" (Verses on Accepting the World), "Zemlia" (The Earth), "Doiti ne tomom, ne domom" (To get there not by book or by building), Grani, 58 (1965), 168-70.

1966

"Ia obnial eti plechi i vzglianul," "Oboz," Molodoi Leningrad 1966. Moscow-Leningrad: Sovetskii pisatel', 1966. pp. 120-121.

1967

Stikhi na smert' T. S. Eliota (here titled Pamiati T. S. Eliota), "V derevne Bog zhivet ne po uglam" (here written "V derevne bog..."), Den' poezii 1967. Leningrad: Sovetskii pisatel', 1967. pp. 134-135.

"Kak tiuremnyi zasov" (Like a prison bolt), "V tvoikh chasakh ne tol'ko khod, no tish' " (Your hours know calm as well as movement), "Instruktsiia zakliuchennomu" (Instructions to the Prisoner), "V fevrale daleko do vesny" (In February it's a long way to Spring), "V odinochke zhelanie spat' " (In solitary one wants to sleep), "Pered progulkoi po kamere" (Before Taking a Walk in One's Cell), "Pesenka" (Song), Vozdushnye Puti: Al'manakh, V (New York, 1967), 67-68, 70-73.

1968

"Stuk" (Knocking), "Iiul'skoe intermetstso" (Intermezzo in July), Grani, 68 (1968), 5-6.

---

*Those texts which were included in the 1965 volume but are not retained in the 1970 volume have been omitted at Brodsky's request. Most of the omitted poems date from 1961 or earlier.

1969

"Stikhi ob Ispantse—Miguele Servete, eretike sozhennom kal'vinistami" (Verses on the Spaniard Michael Servetus, a Heretic Burned by the Calvinists), *Grani,* 70 (1969), 111-112.

1970

"Odinochestvo" (Solitude), *Novyi Zhurnal,* 98 (New York, 1970), 103.

1971

Pen'e bez muzyki (Song Without Music), Russian Literature, 1 (1971), 415-20.

B. POETIC TRANSLATIONS BY BRODSKY

1. In Books

1963

Milan Rakić's "Češnja" and Tin Ujević's "Visoki jablani" in Boris Slutskii, ed., *Poety Iugoslavii XIX-XX vv.,* Moscow: Khudozhestvennaia literatura, 1963. pp. 195, 302-303.

A poem by Hernandez, *Zaria nad Kuboi.* Moscow, 1963.

1966

John Donne's "The Apparition" in B. R. Vipper and T. N. Livanova, eds., *Renessans. Barokko. Klassitsizm: Problema stilei v zapadno-evropeiskom iskusstve XV-XVII vekov.* Moscow: Nauka, 1966. p. 226.

1970

John Donne's "The Flea," "To Mr. Christopher Brooke: The Storm," "A Valediction: Forbidding Mourning," "The Apparition," in Iosif Brodskii, *Ostanovka v pustyne.* New York, 1970. pp. 221-226.

1971

Translations of Polish lyrics in *Sovremennaia pol'skaia poeziia.* Moscow, 1971 (?).

2. In Periodicals

1968

An untitled 18-line poem by Cassius Clay (Muhammed Ali), beginning "Etot rasskaz, ni na chto ne pokhozhii," *Koster,* 7 (Leningrad, 1968), 45.

PART II: TRANSLATIONS OF BRODSKY'S POETRY*

A. BOOKS

1966

George Reavey, ed. & tr., *The New Russian Poets: 1953-1966* (New York: October House, 1966), pp. 255-69. With facing Russian texts and an introductory note. Contents: "Ryby zimoi," "Pamiatnik Pushkinu," "V tot vecher vozle nashego ognia," "Ia obnial eti plechi i vzglianul," "Sadovnik v vatnike, kak drozd," "Vse chuzhdo v dome novomu zhil'tsu," "Kolesnik umer, bondar'."

Iossip [sic] *Brodski: Collines et autres poèmes.* Paris: Editions du Seuil, 1966. 110pp. Preface by Pierre Emmanuel. Translations by Jean-Jacques Marie. Contents: "Opredelenie poezii," "V tot vecher vozle nashego ognia," "A. A. Akhmatovoi," "Piligrimy," "Pamiatnik Pushkinu," "Stikhi o slepykh muzykantakh," "Khudozhnik," "Gladiatory," "I vechnyi boi," "Glagoly," *Kholmy,* "Zemlia," "Pamiatnik," "Kniga," "Da,

---

*Arranged chronologically by year and, within a given year, alphabetically by language: Czech, English, French, German, Hebrew, Italian, Norwegian, Polish, Serbo-Croatian.

my ne stali glushe ili starshe," "Doiti ne tomom, ne domom," "Stikhi pod epigrafom," "Proshchai," "Pamiati Fedi Dobrovol'skogo," "Posviashchenie Glebu Gorbovskomu," *Bol'shaia elegiia Dzhonu Donnu,* "Proplyvaiut oblaka," "Sonet: Velikii Gektor strelami ubit," "Sonet: My snova prozhivaem u zaliva," "Sonet: Ia snova slyshu golos tvoi tosklivyi," "Vospominaniia," "Pesenka o Fede Dobrovol'skom," "Sad," "Nastupaet vesna," "Oboz," "Ia kak Uliss," "Zachem opiat' meniaemsia mestami," "Prikhodit vremia sozhalenii," "Topilas' pech'. Ogon' drozhal vo t'me," "Ty poskachesh' vo mrake po beskrainim kholodnym kholmam," "Pod vecher on vidit, zastyvshi v dveriakh," "Rozhdestvenskii romans," "Evreiskoe kladbishche okolo Leningrada.

Jossif Brodskij, *Ausgewählte Gedichte* [n. p.] Bechtle Verlag, 1966. 58pp. Afterword by Alexander Kaempfe. Translations by Heinrich Ost and Alexander Kaempfe. Contents: "Opredelenie poezii," "Posviashchenie Glebu Gorbovskomu," "Glagoly," "Evreiskoe kladbishche okolo Leningrada," "Kniga," "S grust'iu," "Ty poskachesh' vo mrake po beskrainym kholodnym kholmam," "Sadovnik v vatnike, kak drozd," "Pamiatnik", *Kholmy,* "Sonet: My snova prozhivaem u zaliva," "Vospominaniia," "Nastupaet vesna," "Iiul'skoiu noch'iu v poselke temno," "Sad," "Ryby zimoi," "Plach" (Sec. 28 of *Shestvie), Bol'shaia elegiia Dzhonu Donnu,* "Dorogomu D. B.," "Pamiati Fedi Dobrovol'skogo."

Nicola Sorin, ed., *Da riviste clandestine dell' URSS* (Milan: Jaca Book, 1966), 72-77. Introductory note. The translation of "Zemlia" has facing Russian text. Translations by Jean Ibsen. Contents: "Evreiskoe kladbishche okolo Leningrada, " "Piligrimy," "Doiti ne tomom, ne domom," "Zemlia."

1967

Joseph Brodsky, *Elegy to John Donne and Other Poems.* London: Longmans, 1967. 77pp. Translator's introduction. Translations by Nicholas Bethell. Contents: "Khudozhnik," "Petukhi," "I vechnyi boi," "Gladiatory," "Proshchai," "Stikhi o slepykh muzykantakh," "Pamiatnik," "Zachem opiat' meniaemsia mestami," "Evreiskoe kladbishche okolo Leningrad," "Vorotish'sia na rodinu. Nu chto zh," "Sad," "Piligrimy," "Doiti ne tomom, ne domom" [erroneously printed as part of "Piligrimy"] , "Rozhdestvenskii romans," *Vot ia vnov' posetil,* "V tot vecher vozle nashego ognia," "Ia obnial eti plechi i vzglianul," "Mne govoriat, chto nuzhno uezzhat'," "Dialog," "Pamiatnik Pushkinu," "Ryby zimoi," "Stikhi pod epigrafom," "Zemlia," "Kogda podoidet k izgolov'iu," "Ne zhazhdal iavliat'sia do sroka," *Kholmy, Bol'shaia elegiia Dzhonu Donnu,* "Sadovnik v vatnike, kak drozd," "K sadovoi ograde," "Okna," "Vse chuzhdo v dome novomu zhil'tsu," "Kolesnik umer, bondar'," "Zagadka angelu."

Poesia russa contemporanea: Da Evtušenko a Brodskij. (Milan: Dall'Oglio, 1967), pp. 161-73. Introductory note. Translations by Giovanni Buttafava. Contents: "Stikhi o priniatii mira," "Sonet: Ia snova slyshu golos tvoi tosklivyi," "Zagadka angelu," "Vecherom."

1968

Josif Brodskij, *Velka elegie.* Paris: Edice Svědectví, 1968. 63pp. Introductory note. Czech translations by Jiří Kovtun. Contents: "Khudozhnik," "Opredelenie poezii," "Pamiatnik Pushkinu," "Kniga," "Glagoly," "Pamiati Fedi Dobrovol'skogo," "Pamiatnik," "Ia obnial eti plechi i vzglianul," "Nastupaet vesna," "Iiul'skoiu noch'iu v poselke temno," "Sad," "Ryby zimoi," "Sonet: Ia snova slyshu golos tvoi tosklivyi," "Sonet: My snova prozhivaem u zaliva," "Sonet: Velikii Gektor strelami ubit," "Gladiatory," "I vechnyi boi," "Evreiskoe kladbishche okolo Leningrada," "V tot vecher vozle nashego ognia," "Mne govoriat, chto nuzhno uezzhat'," "Proshchai," *Kholmy,* "Romans dlia krysolova i khor" (Sec. 39 of *Shestvie), Bol'shaia elegiia Dzhonu Donnu.*

Olga Carlisle, ed., *Poets on Street Corners: Portraits of Fifteen Russian Poets.* (New York: Random House, 1968), pp. 400, 402-421. Contents: an abridged English adaptation by Rose Styron of *Bol'shaia elegiia Dzhonu Donnu* (the last 56 lines are omitted); English adaptations by W. S. Merwin of "Da, my ne stali glushe ili starshe," "Stikhi o slepykh muzykantakh," "Glagoly," "Vospominaniia," "Pamiatnik," and

163

"Evreiskoe kladbishche okolo Leningrada." All except "Da, my ne stali glushe ili starshe" have facing Russian texts.

New Underground Russian Poets (Calcutta, 1968?), 4. George Reavey, tr. "Evreiskoe kladbishche okolo Leningrada."

La Protesta intellettuale nell'URSS (Supplement No. 5 of "Documentazione sui paesi dell'Est"), Milan, 1968. pp. 93-94. Italian translations of "Pamiatnik" and "Piligrimy."

1969

Keith Bosley, ed., *Russia's Underground Poets* (New York: Praeger, 1969), 18-23. Translations by Keith Bosley with Dimitri Pospielovsky and Janis Sapiets. Contents: "Evreiskoe kladbishche okolo Leningrada," "Piligrimy," "Stikhi o priniatii mira," "Doiti ne tomom, ne domom," "Ia obnial eti plechi i vzglianul," "Pamiatnik Pushkinu," "Ryby zimoi."

Joseph Brodsky, *'Akedat Yisak* [The Binding of Isaac] . Tel Aviv: Eqed, 1969. 127pp. Introduction and Hebrew translations by Ezra Zusman. Contents: "Stikhi pod epigrafom," "Ryby zimoi," "I vechnyi boi," Gladiatory," "Pamiatnik Pushkinu," "Pamiati Fedi Dobrovol'skogo," "Stikhi o slepykh muzykantakh," "Pamiatnik," "Evreiskoe kladbishche okolo Leningrada," "Sad," "Piligrimy," "Da, my ne stali glushe ili starshe," "Iiul'skoe intermetstso," "Romans Printsa Gamleta" (Sec. 40 of *Shestvie), "*Kniga," "Proplyvaiut oblaka," *Vot ia vnov' posetil,* "Ty poskachesh' vo mrake po beskrainim kholodnym kholmam," "Opredelenie poezii," "V tot vecher vozle nashego ognia," "Sonet: My snova prozhivaem u zaliva," "Dialog," "Kogda pododidet k izgolov'iu," *Kholmy,* "V odinochke zhelanie spat'," "V fevrale daleko do vesny," *Bol'shaia elegiia Dzhonu Donnu, Isaak i Avraam,* "Prorochestvo," *Stikhi na smert' T. S. Eliota* (Part I only), "V derevne Bog zhivet ne po uglam," *Ostanovka v pustyne,* and one unidentified 46-line poem.

1970

Leopold Tyrmand, ed., *Explorations in Freedom: Prose, Narrative, and Poetry from Kultura* (New York: The Free Press in cooperation with SUNY at Albany, 1970), 265-70. Translations by George L. Kline of "Prorochestvo" and *Dva chasa v rezervuare.*

1971

La Preghiera di Solženitsin e le voci clandestine in Russia (Milan, 1971), 21-24. Italian translations of "V derevne Bog zhivet ne po uglam" and *Ostanovka v pustyne.*

Poesia sovietica degli anni 60 (Milan: Mondadori, 1971), 348-403. With facing Russian texts. Introductory note by C. G. De Michelis. Translations by Gigliola Venturi. Contents: "Proshchai," "Stikhi o slepykh muzykantakh," "Proplyvaiut oblaka," "Pis'mo k A. D.," an unidentified poem which begins: *"All'oscuro, dal letto mi levo,"* *Bol'shaia elegiia Dzhonu Donnu,* "K severnomu kraiu," "V odinochke zhelanie spat'," an unidentified poem entitled *"Senza lampione,"* "V derevne Bog zhivet ne po uglam," *Stikhi na smert' T. S. Eliota.*

Josif Brodski, *Stanica u pustinji* [Halt in the Wilderness] . Belgrade: Nolit (Biblioteka "Orfej"), 1971 [in press] . Preface by Milica Nikolić. Serbo-Croatian translations by Milovan Danojlić. Contents: "Ty poskachesh' vo mrake po beskrainym kholodnym kholmam," "Glagoly," *Ostanovka v pustyne,* "V pustom, zakrytom na prosushku parke," "Podsvechnik," "Prishel son iz semi sel," "Pochti elegiia," "K sadovoi ograde," "Okna," "Teper' vse chashche chuvstvuiu ustalost'," "Dialog," *Kholmy,* "Pesenka o Fede Dobrovol'skom," "Evreiskoe kladbishche okolo Leningrada," "Sonet: Perezhivi vsekh," *Dva chasa v rezervuare,* "Ryby zimoi," *Stikhi na smert' T. S. Eliota,* "Odna vorona (ikh byla gur'ba," "Romans liubovnika" (first of the two "Romansy liubovnikov"—Sec. 35 of *Shestvie),* "Romans Kolumbiny" (Sec. 5 of *Shestvie,* third stanza only), "Plach" (Sec. 28 of *Shestvie), Einem alten Architekten in Rom, Tri glavy,* "Proplyvaiut oblaka," "Kak tiuremnyi zasov," *Bol'shaia elegiia Dzhonu Donnu,* "V tot vecher vozle nashego ognia," "Zagadka angelu," "K severnomu kraiu," *Pen'e bez muzyki, Isaak i Avraam.*

B. PERIODICALS

1964

"Pamiatnik Pushkinu," tr. Collyer Bowen, *The New Leader*, XLVII, 13 (June 22, 1964), 11. With facing Russian text. Introductory essay by Andrew Field.

"Pamiatnik," tr. Giovanni Buttafava, *La Fiera Letteraria* (Rome), Nov. 1, 1964, 1.

"Ia kak Uliss," "Stikhi o priniatii mira," and two unidentified poems (first lines: "*In campagna nessuno esce di senno," "Pietre della terra,"* tr. G. Buttafava, *La Fiera Letteraria,* Nov. 29, 1964, 5.

1965

Bol'shaia elegiia Dzhonu Donnu (abridged adaptation by Jean Garrigue), English adaptations by Stephen Stepanchev of "Zagadka angelu" (erroneously divided into two separate poems), "Topilas' pech'. Ogon' drozhal vo t'me," "Oboz," "Vse chuzhdo v dome novomu zhil'tsu," "Sadovnik v vatnike, kak drozd", *The New Leader*, XLVIII, 10 (May 10, 1965), 11-15.

Bol'shaia elegiia Dzhonu Donnu, "Rozhdestvenskii romans," "V tot vecher vozle nashego ognia," "Odinochestvo," "S grust'iu i s nezhnost'iu," *TriQuarterly,* 3 (Spring 1965), 85-96. Introductory note. Translations by Goerge L. Kline.

Bol'shaia elegiia Dzhonu Donnu, tr. George L. Kline (a revised translation), *Russian Review,* vol. 24 (1965), 341-53. With introductory essay.

Bol'shaia elegiia Dzhonu Donnu, tr. Giovanni Buttafava, *La Fiera Letteraria,* March 14, 1965. 3-4. Introductory note by Arthur Channing.

"S grust'iu i s nezhnost'iu," "Kolesnik umer, bondar'," "Okna," "Topilas' pech'. Ogon' drozhal vo t'me," tr. Jósef Łobodowski, *Kultura* (Paris), No. 1/207-2/208 (1965), 156-60. Introductory note. Polish.

Bol'shaia elegiia Dzhonu Donnu, tr. Józef Łobodowski, *Kultura,* No. 3/209 (1965), 30-35.

"Ia obnial eti plechi i vzglianul," "Sadovnik v vatnike, kak drozd," "K sadovoi ograde," "Oboz," tr. Józef Łobodowski, *Kultura,* No. 7/213-8/214 (1965), 106-108.

1966

"Kniga," tr. Jan Zábrana, *Literární Noviny* (Prague), 47 (1966), 7.

"Pamiatnik Pushkinu," "Piligrimy," "Posviashchenie Glebu Gorbovskomu," tr. George L. Kline, *Russian Review,* vol. 25 (1966), 131-134.

1967

"Khudozhnik," tr. Jiří Franek, *Literární Noviny,* 36 (1967), 7.

"Pamiatnik Pushkinu," tr. Jiří Franek, *Literární Noviny,* 38 (1967), 3.

"Sonet: Velikii Gektor strelami ubit," "Sonet: My snova prozhivaem u zaliva," "Opredelenie poezii," "Pamiatnik," "Glagoly," "Evreiskoe kladbishche okolo Leningrada," "Pamiati Fedi Dobrovol'skogo," "Vospominaniia," "Sonet: Ia snova slyshu golos tvoi tosk-livyi," tr. Jan Zábrana, *Sešity* (Prague), II, 15 (1967), 14-18.

"Iiul'skoi noch'iu v poselke temno," "Kniga," and the last eight stanzas of *Kholmy,* tr. Jiří Kovtun, *Švědectví* (Paris), 31 (1967), 379-81. Introductory note. Czech.

"Stikhi pod epigrafom," tr. Anton S. Beliajeff, *Paroles* (Dartmouth College), Spring 1967. English.

"Pamiatnik," "Ryby zimoi," "Evreiskoe kladbishche okolo Leningrada," "Gladia-tory," and an abridged translation of "Piligrimy," Norwegian translations by Martin Nag, *Ord och Bild* (Stockholm), LXXVI, 2 (1967), 116-119. Introductory note in Swedish by Lars Bäckström.

"Prorochestvo," "V derevne Bog zhivet ne po uglam," "Pesenka," *Kultura,* No. 4/ 234 (1967), 69-71.

1968

Stikhi na smert' T. S. Eliot, tr. George L. Kline, *Russian Review,* vol. 27 (1968), 195-98. Introductory note.

"K Likomedu, na Skiros," "Na Prachechnom mostu, gde my s toboi," "Sonet: Kak zhal', chto tem, chem stalo dlia menia," "Fontan," *Stikhi na smert' T. S. Eliota,*

Ostanovka v pustyne, tr. George L. Kline, *Unicorn Journal* (Santa Barbara, Calif.), 2 (1968), 20-30. Introductory note.

"V derevne Bog zhivet ne po uglam," *Russia Cristiana* (Rome), May 1968, 25.

"Pamiatnik," and "Glagoly," Italian adaptations in G. de Sanctis and A. Azzaroni, eds., *L'Altra protesta,* Quaderno No. 10 dell'UIPC (Rome), 1968, 22.

1969

Ostanovka v pustyne, Bol'shaia elegiia Dzhonu Donnu, Stikhi na smert' T. S. Eliota, "Prorochestvo," "V tot vecher vozle nashego ognia," *Proshchaite, madmuazel' Veronika,* tr. Václav Daněk, *Světová Literatura* (Prague), 5-6 (1969), 290-309. With introductory note and photograph of Brodsky. *N.B.* These six translations, plus a translation of "Pamiatnik," were included in *Světová Literatura,* 3 (1969), of which only a few copies were distributed before it was withdrawn from circulation. That issue was replaced by an entirely new issue No. 3 in which there were *no* Brodsky translations.

"Vorotish'sia na rodinu. Nu chto zh," tr. Rolf-Dietrich Keil, *Die Zeit* (Hamburg), 1969?.

1970

"Zimnim vecherom v lalte," tr. George L. Kline, *Observer Review* (London), January 11, 1970, 29.

"Sumev otgorodit'sia ot liudei," tr. George L. Kline, *The Third Hour* (New York), 9 (1970), 10.

"Pochti elegiia," "Zagadka angelu," *Strofy,* "Ty vyporkhnesh', malinovka, iz trekh," "Podsvechnik," tr. George L. Kline, *TriQuarterly,* 18 (Spring 1970), 175-83.

"Proplyvaiut oblaka," tr. Mateja Matejič, *The Literary Review* (Fairleigh Dickinson University), XIII, 3 (1970), 402-403.

Novye stansy k Avguste, tr. Jean-Marc Bordier, *Nouvelle Revue Française,* vol. 18, no. 210 (June 1970), 895-900. Introductory note.

"Romans liubovnika" (first of the two "Romansy liubovnikov" in section 35 of *Shestvie),* "K severnomu kraiu," tr. Milovan Danojlić, *Književne Novine* (Belgrade), No. 365 (May 23, 1970), 9. With introductory note and a photograph of Brodsky and Danojlić (taken in Leningrad).

Isaak i Avraam, tr. Milovan Danojlić, *Knjizevnost* (Belgrade), L, 6 (1970), 542-52. Introductory essay by Milica Nikolić.

"Zagadka angelu," *Stikhi na smert' T. S. Eliota,* "K severnomu kraiu," "Romans Kolumbiny" (Sec. 5 of *Shestvie,* 3rd stanza only), "Plach" (Sec. 28 of *Shestvie),* "V tot vecher vozle nashego ognia," tr. Milovan Danojlić, *Letopis Matice Srpske* (Belgrade), vol. 146, no. 406 (July 1970), 52-59.

"Romans dlia krysolova i khor" (Sec. 39 of *Shestvie),* tr. Milovan Danojlić, *Ježe* (Belgrade), No. 1627 (Sept. 4-9, 1970), 14-15. [Brodsky's name is not given; the poem is identified only as "translated from the Russian".]

Pen'e bez muzyki, tr. Milovan Danojlić, *Vidici* (University of Belgrade), August (?), 1970. Introductory note.

1971

Proshchaite, madmuazel' Veronika, tr. George L. Kline, *Russian Review,* vol. 30 (January 1971), 27-32. Introductory note.

"Stikhi v Aprele," "Pervoe sentiabria," "Sonet: My snova prozhivaem u zaliva," tr. George L. Kline, *Arroy* (Bryn Mawr College), May 1971, 2-4.

Pis'mo v butylke, "Enei i Didona," "Ogon', ty slyshish', nachal ugasat'," "Derev'ia v moem okne, v dereviannom okne," "Pervoe ianvaria 1965 goda," *Russian Literature,* 1 (1971), 77-90.

Ostanovka v pustyne, "Zimnim vecherom v lalte," "Stikhi v Aprele," excerpts from *Gorbunov i Gorchakov,* tr. Jamie Fuller, *Russian Literature,* 1 (1971), 66-76.

Gorbunov i Gorchakov, tr. Carl R. Proffer with Assya Humesky, *Russian Literature,* 1 (1971), 91-127.

"Ty poskachesh' vo mrake po beskrainim kholodnym kholmam," "Pochti elegiia," "V pustom, zakrytom na prosushku parke," "Prishel son iz semi sel," tr. Milovan Danojlić, *Spone* (Nikšić), II, 5-6 (May 1971), 79-8I. This includes Danojlić's translation of W. H. Auden's unpublished essay on Brodsky (which will appear as the foreword to the forthcoming Brodsky volume, translated by George L. Kline, in the series of Modern European Poets, Penguin Books, 1972).

PART III: ALPHABETICAL LISTING BY TITLE OR FIRST LINE

Note: References by roman numeral, capital letter, arabic numeral and date are to the sections of this Bibliography. Thus: "Enei i Didona" (Aeneas and Dido) I.A.1 1970; II.B 1971 indicates that the text of the poem is listed in the section on Brodsky's poetry published in book form in the year 1970, and that a translation (or translations) is listed in the section of translations of his poetry published in periodicals in the year 1971.

"A. A. Akhmatovoi" (To A. A. Akhmatova) I.A.1 1970; II.A 1966.
"A dream has come from seven villages" (Prishel son iz semi sel) II.A 1971; B 1971.
Adieu, Mademoiselle Véronique (Proshchaite, madmuazel' Veronika) I.A.1 1970; II.B 1969, 1971.
"Aeneas and Dido" (Enei i Didona) I.A.1 1970; II.B 1971.
"Almost an Elegy" (Pochti elegiia) I.A.1 1970; II.A 1971; B 1970, 1971.
"And endless battle" (I vechnyi boi) I.A.1 1965; II.A 1966, 1967, 1968, 1969.
Anno Domini I.A.1 1970.
"Artist, The" (Khudozhnik) I.A.1 1965; II.A 1966, 1967, 1968; B 1967.
"At evening he watches, immobile in the doorway" (Pod vecher on vidit, zastyvshi v dveriakh) I.A.1 1965, 1970; II.A. 1966.
"Ballad, A" (Romans) I.A. 1 1965.
"Ballad for Rat-Catcher and Chorus" (Romans dlia krysolova i khor.—Sec. 39 of *Shestvie*), I.A.1 1965; II.A 1968; B 1970.
"Before Taking a Walk in One's Cell" (Pered progulkoi po kamere) I.A.2 1967.
Bol'shaia elegiia Dzhonu Donnu (Elegy for John Donne) I.A.1 1965, 1970; II.A 1966, 1967, 1968, 1969, 1971; B 1965, 1969.
"Book, The" (Kniga) I.A.1 1965; II.A 1966, 1968, 1969; B 1966, 1967.
"Byl chernyi nebosvod svetli tekh nog"; *see* "V tot vecher vozle nashego ognia."
"Candlestick, The" (Podsvechnik) I.A.1 1970; II.A 1971; B 1970.
"Christmas Ballad, A" (Rozhdestvenskii romans) I.A.1 1965, 1970; II.A 1966, 1967; B 1965.
"Clouds are Sailing, The" (Proplyvaiut oblaka) I.A.1 1965, 1970; II.A 1966, 1969, 1971; B 1970.
"Columbine's Ballad" (Romans Kolumbiny—Sec. 5 of *Shestvie*) I.A.1 1965; II.A 1971; B 1970.
"Da, my ne stali glushe ili starshe" (We have not grown older or more deaf) I.A.1 1965; II.A 1966, 1968, 1969.
"Definition of Poetry" (Opredelenie poezii) I.A.1 1965; II.A 1966, 1968, 1969; B 1967.
"Derev'ia v moem okne, v dereviannom okne" (The trees in my window, in my wooden-framed window) I.A.1 1970; II.B 1971.
"Dialog" (Dialogue) I.A.1 1965; II.A 1967, 1969, 1971.
"Dlia shkol'nogo vozrasta" (For the School Age) I.A.1 1970.
"Dni begut nado mnoi" (The days glide over me) I.A.1 1970.
"Doiti ne tomom, ne domom" (To get there not by book or by building) I.A.2 1965; II.A 1966, 1967, 1969.
"Dorogomu D. B." (To Dear D. B.) I.A.1 1965; II.A 1966.
Dva chasa v rezervuare (Two Hours by the Reservoir) I.A.1 1970; II.A 1970, 1971.
"Dva vsadnika skachut v prostranstve nochnom" (Two riders gallop in the vastness of the night) I.A.1 1965, 1970.
"Earth, The" (Zemlia) I.A.2 1965; II.A 1966, 1967.
Einem alten Architekten in Rom I.A.1 1970; II.A 1971.
"Elegiia" (Elegy) I.A.1 1970.

Elegy for John Donne (Bol'shaia elegiia Dzhonu Donnu) I.A.1 1965, 1970; II.A 1966, 1967, 1968, 1969, 1971; B 1965, 1969.
"Enei i Dodona" (Aeneas and Dido) I.A.1 1970; II.B 1971.
"Enigma for an Angel" (Zagadka angelu) I.A.1 1965, 1970; II.A 1967, 1971; B 1965, 1970.
"Evening" (Vecherom) I.A.1 1970; II.A 1967.
"Evreiskoe kladbishche okolo Leningrada" (The Jewish Cemetery near Leningrad) I.A.1 1965; II.A 1966, 1967, 1968, 1969, 1971; B 1967.
"Exhaustion now is a more frequent guest" (Teper' vse chashche chuvstvuiu ustalost') I.A.1 1965, 1970; II.A 1971.
"Fame" (Slava) I.A.1 1965.
"Farewell" (Proshchai) I.A.1 1965; II.A 1966, 1967, 1968, 1971.
"Fish in Winter" (Ryby zimoi) I.A.1 1965; II.A 1966, 1967, 1968, 1969, 1971; B 1967.
"Fontan" (The Fountain) I.A.1 1970; II.B 1968.
"For the School Age" (Dlia shkol'nogo vozrasta) I.A.1 1970.
"Fountain, The" (Fontan) I.A.1 1970; II.B 1968.
From the Outskirts to the Center (Ot okrainy k tsentru) I.A.1 1965, 1970; II.A 1967, 1969.
"From 'Old English Songs': Winter Wedding" (Iz 'Starykh angliiskikh pesen': Zimniaia svad'ba) I.A.1 1970.
From "The School Anthology" (Iz "Shkol'noi antologii") I.A.1 1970.
"Gladiatory" (Gladiators) I.A.1 1965; II.A 1966, 1967, 1968, 1969; B 1967.
"Glagoly" (Verbs) I.A.1 1965, 1970; II.A 1966, 1968, 1971; B 1967, 1968.
Gorbunov i Gorchakov (Gorbunov and Gorchakov) I.A.1 1970; II.B 1971.
Gost' (The Guest) I.A.1 1965.
Halt in the Wilderness (Ostanovka v pustyne) I.A.1 1970; II.A 1969, 1971; B 1968, 1969, 1971.
"He did not want to be too early" (Ne zhazhdal iavliat'sia do sroka) I.A.1 1965; II.A 1967.
Hills, The (Kholmy) I.A.1 1965, 1970; II.A 1966, 1967, 1968, 1969, 1971; B 1967.
"I bent to kiss your shoulders, and I saw" (Ia obnial eti plechi i vzglianul) I.A.1 1965, 1970; I.A.2 1966; II.A 1966, 1967, 1968, 1969; B 1965.
"I, like Ulysses" (Ia kak Uliss) I.A.1 1965; II.A 1966; B 1964.
"I now am leaving Moscow" (Teper' ia uezzhaiu iz Moskvy) I.A.1 1965.
"I vechnyi boi" (And endless battle) I.A.1 1965; II.A 1966, 1967, 1968, 1969.
"Ia kak Uliss" (I, like Ulysses) I.A.1 1965; II.A 1966; B 1964.
"Ia obnial eti plechi i vzglianul" (I bent to kiss your shoulders, and I saw) I.A.1 1965, 1970; I.A.2 1966; II.A 1966, 1967, 1968, 1969; B 1965.
"Iiul'skoe intermetstso" (Intermezzo in July) I.A.2 1968; II.A 1969.
"Iiul'skoiu noch'iu v poselke temno" (On a July night it is dark in the village) I.A.1 1965, 1970; II.A 1966, 1968; B 1967.
"In an empty park, closed for drying" (V pustom, zakrytom na prosushku parke) II.A 1971; B 1971.
"In February it's a long way to Spring" (V fevrale daleko do vesny) I.A.2 1967; II.A 1969.
"In Memory of Fedya Dobrovolsky" (Pamiati Fedi Dobrovol'skogo) I.A.1 1965; II.A 1966, 1968, 1969; B 1967.
"In order that an empty talker" (Zatem, chtob pustym razgovortsem) I.A.1 1965.
"In solitary one wants to sleep" (V odinochke zhelanie spat') I.A.2 1967; II.A 1969, 1971.
"In villages God lives not just in ikon corners" (V derevne Bog zhivet ne po uglam), I.A.1 1970; I.A.2 1967; II.A 1969, 1971; B 1967, 1968.
"Instructions to the Prisoner" (Instruktsiia zakliuchennomu) I.A.2 1967.
"Instruktsiia zakliuchennomu" (Instructions to the Prisoner) I.A.2 1967.
"Intermezzo in July" (Iiul'skoe intermetstso) I.A.2 1968; II.A 1969.
Isaak i Avraam (Isaac and Abraham) I.A.1 1965, 1970; II.A 1969, 1971; B 1970.
Iz "Shkol'noi antologii" (From "The School Anthology") I.A.1 1970.
"Iz 'Starykh angliiskikh pesen': Zimniaia svad'ba" (From 'Old English Songs': Winter Wedding) I.A.1 1970.
"January 1, 1965" (Pervoe ianvaria 1965 goda) I.A.1 1970; II.B 1971.
"Jewish Cemetery near Leningrad, The" (Evreiskoe kladbishche okolo Leningrada) I.A.1 1965; II.A 1966, 1967, 1968, 1969, 1971; B 1967.
"K Likomedu, na Skiros" (To Lycomedes on Scyros) I.A.1 1970; II.B 1968.

"K sadovoi ograde" (Toward the Park Fence) I.A.1 1965; II.A 1967, 1971; B 1965.

"K severnomu kraiu" (To the Northland) I.A.1 1970; II.A 1971; B 1970.

"Kak tiuremnyi zasov" (Like a prison bolt) I.A.2 1967; II.A 1971.

Kholmy (The Hills) I.A.1 1965, 1970; II.A 1966, 1967, 1968, 1969, 1971; B 1967.

"Khudozhnik" (The Artist) I.A.1 1965; II.A 1966, 1967, 1968; B 1967.

"Kniga" (The Book) I.A.1 1965; II.A 1966, 1968, 1969; B 1966, 1967.

"Knocking" (Stuk) I.A.2 1968.

"Kogda podoidet k izgolov'iu" (When at the head of your bed) I.A.1 1965; II.A 1967, 1969.

"Kolesnik umer, bondar' " (The wheelwright's dead, the cooper) I.A.1 1965; II.A 1966, 1967; B 1965.

"Lamentation" (Plach—Sec. 28 of *Shestvie*) I.A.1 1965; II.A 1966, 1971; B 1970.

Letter in a Bottle, A (Pis'mo v butylke) I.A.1 1970; II.B 1971.

"Letter to A. D., A" (Pis'mo k A. D.) I.A.1 1965; II.A 1971.

"Like a prison bolt" (Kak tiuremnyi zasov) I.A.2 1967; II.A 1971.

"Lomtik medovogo mesiatsa" (A Slice of Honeymoon) I.A.1 1970.

"Lover's Ballad, The" (Romans liubovnika—Sec. 35 of *Shestvie*) I.A.1 1965; II.A 1971; B 1970.

"March is coming. Once again I serve" (Prikhodit mart. Ia syznova sluzhu) I.A.1 1965.

"Memories" (Vospominaniia) I.A.1 1965; II.A 1966, 1968; B 1967.

"Message to my Verses" (Poslanie k stikham) I.A.1 1970.

"Mne govoriat, chto nuzhno uezzhat' "(They say that I must leave) I.A.1 1965; II.A 1967, 1968.

"Monument, The" (Pamiatnik) I.A.1 1965; II.A 1966, 1967, 1968, 1969; B 1964, 1967, 1968.

"Na Prachechnom mostu, gde my s toboi" (On Washerwoman Bridge, where you and I) I.A.1 1970; II.B 1968.

"Nastupaet vesna" (Spring is Here) I.A.1 1965; II.A 1966, 1968.

"Ne zhazhdal iavliat'sia do sroka" (He did not want to be too early) I.A.1 1965; II.A 1967.

New Stanzas to Augusta (Novye stansy k Avguste) I.A.1 1970; II.A 1967; B 1970.

"New tenants find their houses wholly strange" (Vse chuzhdo v dome novomu zhil'tsu) I.A.1 1965, 1970; II.A 1966, 1967; B 1965.

Novye stansy k Avguste (New Stanzas to Augusta) I.A.1 1970; II.A 1967; B 1970.

"Now that I've walled myself off from the world" (Sumev otgorodit'sia ot liudei) I.A.1 1970; II.B 1970.

"Oboz" (Wagon Train) I.A.1 1965, 1970; II.A 1966; B 1965.

"Odinochestvo" (Solitude) I.A.2 1970; II.B 1965.

"Odna vorona (ikh byla gur'ba" (One crow—there was a swarm of them) I.A.1 1970; II.A 1971.

Odnoi poetesse (To a Certain Poetess) I.A.1 1970.

"Ogon', ty slyshish', nachal ugasat' " (The fire, as you can hear, is dying down) I.A.1 1970; II.B 1971.

"Okna" (Windows) I.A.1 1965; II.A 1967, 1971; B 1965.

"On a July night it is dark in the village" (Iiulskoiu noch'iu v poselke temno) I.A.1 1965, 1970; II.A 1966, 1968; B 1967.

"On Washerwoman Bridge, where you and I" (Na Prachechnom mostu, gde my s toboi) I.A.1 1970; II.B 1968.

Once more I have visited. See *From the Outskirts to the Center.*

"One crow (there was a swarm of them" (Odna vorona—ikh byla gur'ba) I.A.1 1970; II.A 1971.

"Opredelenie poezii" (Definition of Poetry) I.A.1 1965; II.A 1966, 1968, 1969; B 1967.

"Orfei i Artemida" (Orpheus and Artemis) I.A.1 1970.

Ostanovka v pustyne (Halt in the Wilderness) I.A.1 1970; II.A 1969, 1971; B 1968, 1969, 1971.

Ot okrainy k tsentru (From the Outskirts to the Center) I.A.1 1965, 1970; II.A 1967, 1969.

"Otkazom ot skorbnogo perechnia—zhest" (Refusing to catalogue all of men's woes) I.A.1 1970.

"Pamiati Fedi Dobrovol'skogo" (In Memory of Fedya Dobrovolsky) I.A.1 1965; II.A 1966, 1968, 1969; B 1967.

"Pamiatnik" (The Monument) I.A.1 1965; II.A 1966, 1967, 1968, 1969; B 1964, 1967, 1968.

"Pamiatnik Pushkinu" (The Pushkin Monument) I.A.1 1965; II.A 1966, 1967, 1968, 1969; B 1964, 1966, 1967.
"Park, The" (Sad) I.A.1 1965; II.A 1966, 1967, 1968, 1969.
Pen'e bez muzyki (Song without Music) I.A.2 1971; II.A 1971; B 1970.
"Pered progulkoi po kamere" (Before Taking a Walk in One's Cell) I.A.2 1967.
"Pervoe ianvaria 1965 goda" (January 1, 1965) I.A.1 1970; II.B 1971.
"Pervoe sentiabria" (September First) I.A.1 1970; II.B 1971.
"Pesenka" (Song) I.A.2 1967; II.B 1967.
"Pesenka o Fede Dobrovol'skom" (Song about Fedya Dobrovolsky) I.A.1 1965, 1970; II.A 1966, 1971.
"Pesni schastlivoi zimy" (Songs of a Happy Winter) I.A.1 1970.
"Petukhi" (Roosters) I.A.1 1965; II.A 1967.
"Piligrimy" (Pilgrims) I.A.1 1965; II.A 1966, 1967, 1968, 1969; B 1966, 1967.
"Pis'mo k A. D." (A Letter to A. D.) I.A.1 1965; II.A 1971.
Pis'mo v butylke (A Letter in a Bottle) I.A.1 1970; I.B 1971.
"Plach" (Lamentation—Sec. 28 of *Shestvie*) I.A.1 1965; II.A 1966, 1971; B 1970.
"Pochti elegiia" (Almost an Elegy) I.A.1 1970; II.A 1971; B 1970, 1971.
"Pod vecher on vidit, zastyvshi v dveriakh" (At evening he watches, immobile in the door-way) I.A.1 1965, 1970; II.A 1966.
"Podsvechnik" (The Candlestick) I.A.1 1970; II.A 1971; B 1970
"Poslanie k stikham" (Message to my Verses) I.A.1 1970.
"Posviashchenie Glebu Gorbovskomu" (To Gleb Gorbovsky) I.A.1 1965; II.A 1966; B 1966.
"Prikhodit mart. Ia syznova sluzhu" (March is coming. Once again I serve) I.A.1 1965.
"Prikhodit vremia sozhalenii" (The time for regret has come) I.A.1 1965; II.A 1966.
"Prince Hamlet's Ballad" (Romans Printsa Gamleta—Sec. 40 of *Shestvie)* I.A.1 1965; II.A 1969.
"Prishel son iz semi sel" (A dream has come from seven villages) II.A 1971; II.B 1971.
Procession, The (Shestvie) I.A.1 1965. [Translations of excerpts are listed separately under titles of sections.]
"Prophecy, A" (Prorochestvo) I.A.1 1970; II.A 1969, 1970; B 1967, 1969.
"Proplyvaiut oblaka" (The Clouds are Sailing) I.A.1 1965, 1970; II.A 1966, 1969, 1971; B 1970.
"Prorochestvo" (A Prophecy) I.A.1 1970; II.A 1969, 1970; B 1967, 1969.
"Proshchai" (Farewell) I.A.1 1965; II.A 1966, 1967, 1968, 1971.
Proshchaite, madmuazel' Veronika (Adieu, Mademoiselle Véronique) I.A.1 1970; II.B 1969, 1971.
"Pushkin Monument, The" (Pamiatnik Pushkinu) I.A.1 1965; II.A 1966, 1967, 1968, 1969; B 1964, 1966, 1967.
"Pustaia doroga pod sosnami spit" (The empty road slumbers beneath the pines) I.A.1 1965, 1970.
"Quilt-jacketed, a tree-surgeon" (Sadovnik v vatnike, kak drozd) I.A.1 1965, 1970; II.A 1966, 1967; B 1965.
"Refusing to catalogue all of men's woes (Otkazom ot skorbnogo perechnia—zhest) I.A.1 1970.
"Romans" (A Ballad) I.A.1 1965.
"Romans dlia krysolova i khor" (Ballad for Rat-Catcher and Chorus—Sec. 39 of *Shestvie)* I.A.1 1965; II.A 1968; B 1970.
"Romans Kolumbiny" (Columbine's Ballad—Sec 5 of *Shestvie)* I.A.1 1965; II.A 1971; B 1970.
"Romans liubovnika" (The Lover's Ballad—Sec. 35 of *Shestvie)* I.A.1 1965; II.A 1971; B 1970.
"Romans Printsa Gamleta" (Prince Hamlet's Ballad—Sec. 40 of *Shestvie)* I.A.1 1965; II.A 1969.
"Roosters" (Petukhi) I.A.1 1965; II.A 1967.
"Rozhdestvenskii romans" (A Christmas Ballad) I.A.1 1965, 1970; II.A 1966, 1967; B 1965.
"Ryby zimoi" (Fish in Winter) I.A.1 1965; II.A 1966, 1967, 1968, 1969, 1971; B 1967.
"S grust'iu i s nezhnost'iu" (Sadly and Tenderly) I.A.1 1965, 1970; II.A 1966; B 1965.
"Sad" (The Park) I.A.1 1965; II.A 1966, 1967, 1968, 1969.
"Sadly and Tenderly" (S grust'iu i s nezhnost'iu) I.A.1 1965, 1970; II.A 1966; B 1965.

"Sadovnik v vatnike, kak drozd" (Quilt-jacketed, a tree-surgeon) I.A.1 1965, 1970; II.A 1966, 1967; B 1965.

"Sem' let spustia" (Seven Years Later) I.A.1 1970.

"September First" (Pervoe sentiabria) I.A.1 1970; II.B 1971.

"Seven Years Later" (Sem' let spustia) I.A.1 1970.

Shestvie (The Procession) I.A.1 1965. [Translations of excerpts are listed separately under titles of sections.]

"Slava" (Fame) I.A.1 1965.

"Slice of Honeymoon, A" (Lomtik medovogo mesiatsa) I.A.1 1970.

"Solitude" (Odinochestvo) I.A.2 1970; II.B 1965.

"Sonet: Ia snova slyshu golos tvoi tosklivyi" (Sonnet: Once more I hear your melancholy voice) I.A.1 1965; II.A 1966, 1967, 1968; B 1967.

"Sonet k Glebu Gorbovskomu" (Sonnet for Gleb Gorbovsky) I.A.1 1965.

"Sonet: Kak zhal', chto tem, chem stalo dlia menia" (Sonnet: How sad that my life has not come to mean) I.A.1 1970; II.B 1968.

"Sonet: My snova prozhivaem u zaliva" (Sonnet: Once more we're living as by Naples Bay) I.A.1 1965, 1970; II.A 1966, 1969; B 1967, 1971.

"Sonet: Perezhivi vsekh" (Sonnet: Outlive them all) I.A.1 1965; II.A 1971.

"Sonet: Proshel ianvar' za oknami tiur'my" (Sonnet: The month of January has flown past the prison windows) I.A.1 1970.

"Sonet: Velikii Gektor strelami ubit" (Sonnet: Great-hearted Hector has been speared to death) I.A.1 1965, 1970; II.A 1966, 1968; B 1967.

"Song" (Pesenka) I.A.2 1967; II.B 1967.

"Song about Fedya Dobrovolsky" (Pesenka o Fede Dobrovol'skom) I.A.1 1965, 1970; II.A 1966, 1971.

Song without Music (Pen'e bez muzyki) I.A.2 1971; II.A 1971; B 1970.

"Songs of a Happy Winter" (Pesni schastlivoi zimy) I.A.1 1970.

"Sonnet for Gleb Gorbovsky" (Sonet k Glebu Gorbovskomu) I.A.1 1965.

"Sonnet: Great-hearted Hector has been speared to death" (Sonet: Velikii Gektor strelami ubit) I.A.1 1965, 1970; II.A 1966, 1968; B 1967.

"Sonnet: How sad that my life has not come to mean" (Sonet: Kak zhal', chto tem, chem stalo dlia menia) I.A.1 1970; II.B 1968.

"Sonnet: Once more I hear your melancholy voice" (Sonet: Ia snova slyshu golos tvoi tosklivyi) I.A.1 1965; II.A 1966, 1967, 1968; B 1967.

"Sonnet: Once more we're living as by Naples Bay" (Sonet: My snova prozhivaem u zaliva") I.A.1 1965, 1970; II.A 1966, 1969; B 1967, 1971.

"Sonnet: Outlive them all" (Sonet: Perezhivi vsekh) I.A.1 1965; II.A 1971.

"Sonnet: The month of January has flown past the prison windows" (Sonet: Proshel ianvar' za oknami tiur'my) I.A.1 1970.

"Spring is Here" (Nastupaet vesna) I.A. 1 1965; II.A 1966, 1968.

"Spring Season of Muddy Roads" (V rasputitsu) I.A.1 1970.

"Stansy" (Stanzas) I.A.1 1965.

"Stansy gorodu" (Stanzas to the City) I.A.1 1965.

"Stanzas" (Stansy) I.A.1 1965.

Stanzas (Strofy) I.A.1 1970; II.B 1970.

"Stanzas to the City" (Stansy gorodu) I.A.1 1965.

Stikhi na smert' T. S. Eliota (Verses on the Death of T. S. Eliot) I.A.1 1970; I.A.2 1967; II.A 1969, 1971; B 1968, 1969, 1970.

"Stikhi o priniatii mira" (Verses on Accepting the World) I.A.2 1965; II.A 1967, 1969; B 1964.

"Stikhi o slepykh muzykantakh" (Verses about Blind Musicians) I.A.1 1965; II.A 1966, 1967, 1968, 1969, 1971.

"Stikhi ob Ispantse—Miguele Servete, eretike sozhennom kal'vinistami" (Verses on the Spaniard Michael Servetus, a Heretic Burned by the Calvinists) I.A.2 1969.

"Stikhi pod epigrafom" (Verses beneath an Epigraph) I.A.1 1965, 1970; II.A 1966, 1967, 1969; B 1967.

"Stikhi v aprele" (Verses in April) I.A.1 1970; II.B 1971.

Stopping Place in the Desert, A. See Halt in the Wilderness

Strofy (Stanzas) I.A.1 1970; II.B 1970.

"Stuk" (Knocking) I.A.2 1968.

"Sumev otgorodit'sia ot liudei" (Now that I've walled myself off from the world) I.A.1 1970; II.B 1970.

"Teper' ia uezzhaiu iz Moskvy" (I now am leaving Moscow) I.A.1 1965.

"Teper' vse chashche chuvstvuiu ustalost' " (Exhaustion now is a more frequent guest) I.A.1 1965, 1970; II.A 1971.

"That evening, sprawling by an open fire" (V tot vecher vozle nashego ognia) I.A.1 1965, 1970; II.A 1966, 1967, 1968, 1969, 1971; B 1965, 1969, 1970.

"The days glide over me" (Dni begut nado mnoi) I.A.1 1970.

"The empty road slumbers beneath the pines" (Pustaia doroga pod sosnami spit) I.A.1 1965, 1970.

"The fire, as you can hear, is dying down" (Ogon', ty slyshish', nachal ugasat') I.A.1 1970; II.B 1971.

"The stove was lit. Flames trembled in the dark" (Topilas' pech'. Ogon' drozhal vo t'me) I.A.1 1965, 1970; II.A 1966; B 1965.

"The time for regret has come" (Prikhodit vremia sozhalenii) I.A.1 1965; II.A 1966.

"The trees in my window, in my wooden-framed window" (Derev'ia v moem okne, v dereviannom okne) I.A.1 1970; II.B 1971.

"The wheelwright's dead, the cooper" (Kolesnik umer, bondar') I.A.1 1965; II.A 1966, 1967; B. 1965.

"They say that I must leave" (Mne govoriat, chto nuzhno uezzhat') I.A.1 1965; II.A 1967, 1968.

Three Chapters (Tri glavy) I.A.1 1965; II.A 1971.

"To A. A. Akhmatova" (A. A. Akhmatovoi) I.A.1 1970; II.A 1966.

To a Certain Poetess (Odnoi poetesse) I.A.1 1970.

"To Dear D. B." (Dorogomu D. B.) I.A. 1 1965; II.A 1966.

"To get there not by book or by building" (Doiti ne tomom, ne domom) I.A.2 1965; II.A 1966, 1967, 1969.

"To Gleb Gorbovsky" (Posviashchenie Glebu Gorbovskomu) I.A.1 1965; II.A 1966; B 1966.

"To Lycomedes on Scyros" (K Likomedu, na Skiros) I.A.1 1970; II.B 1968.

"To the Northland" (K severnomu kraiu) I.A.1 1970; II.A 1971; B 1970.

"Topilas' pech'. Ogon' drozhal vo t'me" (The stove was lit. Flames trembled in the dark) I.A.1 1965, 1970; II.A 1966; B 1965.

"Toward the Park Fence" (K sadovoi ograde) I.A.1 1965; II.A 1967, 1971; B 1965.

Tri glavy (Three Chapters) I.A.1 1965; II.A 1971.

Two Hours by the Reservoir (Dva chasa v rezervuare) I.A.1 1970; II.A 1970, 1971.

"Two riders gallop in the vastness of the night" (Dva vsadnika skachut v prostranstve nochnom) I.A. 1 1965, 1970.

"Ty poskachesh' vo mrake po beskrainim kholodnym kholmam" (You gallop in the dark on the endless cold hills) I.A.1 1965, 1970; II.A 1966, 1969, 1971; II.B 1971.

"Ty vyporkhnesh', malinovka, iz trekh" (You'll flutter, robin redbreast, from those three) I.A.1 1970; II.B 1970.

"V derevne Bog zhivet ne po uglam" (In villages God lives not just in ikon corners) I.A.1 1970; I.A.2 1967; II.A 1969, 1971; B 1967, 1968.

"V fevrale daleko do vesny" (In February it's a long way to Spring) I.A.2 1967; II.A 1969.

"V odinochke zhelanie spat' " (In solitary one wants to sleep) I.A.2 1967; II.A 1969, 1971.

"V pustom, zakrytom na prosushku parke" (In an empty park, closed for drying) II.A 1971; II.B 1971.

"V rasputitsu" (Spring Season of Muddy Roads) I.A.1 1970.

"V tot vecher vozle nashego ognia" (That evening, sprawling by an open fire) I.A.1 1965, 1970; II.A 1966, 1967, 1968, 1969, 1971; B 1965, 1969, 1970.

"V tvoikh chasakh ne tol'ko khod, no tish' " (Your hours know calm as well as movement) I.A.2 1967.

"Vecherom" (Evening) I.A.1 1970; II.A 1967.

"Verbs" (Glagoly) I.A.1 1965, 1960; II.A 1966, 1968, 1971; B 1967, 1968.

"Verses about Blind Musicians" (Stikhi o slepykh muzykantakh) I.A.1 1965; II.A 1966, 1967, 1968, 1969, 1971.

"Verses beneath an Epigraph" (Stikhi pod epigrafom) I.A.1 1965, 1970; II.A 1966, 1967, 1969; B 1967.

"Verses in April" (Stikhi v aprele) I.A.1 1970; II.B 1971.

"Verses on Accepting the World" (Stikhi o priniatii mira) I.A.2 1965; II.A 1967, 1969; B 1964.

Verses on the Death of T. S. Eliot (Stikhi na smert' T. S. Eliota) I.A.1 1970; I.A.2 1967;
    II.A 1969, 1971; B 1968, 1969, 1970.
"Verses on the Spaniard Michael Servetus, a Heretic Burned by the Calvinists" (Stikhi ob
    Ispantse—Miguele Servete, eretike sozhennom kal'vinistami) I.A.2 1969.
"Vorotish'sia na rodinu. Nu chto zh" (You're coming home again. What does that mean?)
    I.A.1 1965, 1970; II.A 1967; B 1969.
"Vospominaniia" (Memories) I.A.1 1965; II.A 1966, 1968; B 1967.
Vot ia vnov' posetil. See *Ot okrainy k tsentru.*
"Vse chuzhdo v dome novomu zhil'tsu" (New tenants find their houses wholly strange) I.A.
    1 1965, 1970; II.A 1966, 1967; B 1965.
"Wagon Train" (Oboz) I.A.1 1965, 1970; II.A 1966; B 1965.
"We have not grown older or more deaf" (Da, my ne stali glushe ili starshe) I.A.1 1965;
    II.A 1966, 1968, 1969.
"When at the head of your bed" (Kogda podoidet k izgolov'iu) I.A.1 1965; II.A 1967,
    1969.
"Why are we changing places again" (Zachem opiat' meniaemsia mestami) I.A.1 1965;
    II.A 1966, 1967.
"Windows" (Okna) I.A.1 1965; II.A 1967, 1971; B 1965.
"Winter Evening in Yalta, A" (Zimnim vecherom v Ialte) I.A.1 1970; II.B 1970, 1971.
"You gallop in the dark on the endless cold hills" (Ty poskachesh' vo mrake po beskrainim
    kholodnym kholmam) I.A.1 1965, 1970; II.A 1966, 1969, 1971; B 1971.
"You'll flutter, robin redbreast, from those three" (Ty vyporkhnesh', malinovka, iz
    trekh) I.A.1 1970; II.B 1970.
"Your hours know calm as well as movement" (V tvoikh chasakh ne tol'ko khod, no
    tish') I.A.2 1967.
"You're coming home again. What does that mean?" (Vorotish'sia na rodinu. Nu chto zh)
    I.A.1 1965, 1970; II.A 1967; B 1969.
"Zachem opiat' meniaemsia mestami" (Why are we changing places again) I.A.1 1965;
    II.A 1966, 1967.
"Zagadka angelu" (Enigma for an Angel) I.A.1 1965, 1970; II.A 1967, 1971; B 1965,
    1970.
"Zatem, chtob pustym razgovortsem" (In order that an empty talker) I.A.1 1965.
"Zemlia" (The Earth) I.A.2 1965; II.A 1966, 1967.
"Zimnim vecherom v Ialte" (A Winter Evening in Yalta) I.A.1 1970; II.B 1970, 1971.

ADDENDA

PART I: TEXTS
    A. POETRY
        1. Books

1977

Iosif Brokskii, CHAST' RECHI. Ann Arbor: Ardis, 1977. 113 pp.
    Contents: "24 dekabria 1971 goda," "Odnomu tiranu," "Pokhorony Bobo,"
"Nabrosok," "Pis'ma rimskomu drugu," "Pesnia nevinnosti, ona zhe—opyta," "Sreten'e," "Odissei Telemaku," "1972 god," "V ozernom kraiu," "Osennii vecher v skrom-
nom gorodke...," "Ha smert' druga," "Babochka," "Tors," "Laguna," "Ha smert'
Zhukova," "Temza v Chelsi," "Dvadtsat' sonetov k Marii Stiuart," "Meksikanskii divertisment," "Klassicheskii balet est' zamok krasoty...," CHAST' RECHI: "Niotkuda s
liubov'iu, nadtsatogo martobria...," "Sever kroshit metall, no shchadit steklo...,"
"Uznaiu etot veter, naletaiushchii na travu...," "Eto—riad nabliudenii. B uglu—tep-
lo...," "Potomu chto kabluk ostavliaet sledy—zima...," "Dereviannyi laokoon,
sbrosiv na vremia goru s...," Ia rodilsia i vyros v baltiskikh bolotakh podle...," "Chto
kasaetsia zvezd, to oni vsegda...," "V gorodke, iz kotorogo smert' raspolzalas' po
shkol'noi karte...," "Okolo okeana, pri svete svechi; vokrug...," "Ty zabyla derev-
niu, zateriannuiu v bolotakh...," "Tikhotvorenie moe, moe nemoe...," "Temno-
sinee utro v zaindevevshei rame...,"
S tochki zreniia vozdukha, krai zemli...," "Zamorozki na pochve i oblysen'e lesa...,"
Vsegda ostaetsia vozmozhnost' vyiti iz domu na...," "Itak, prigrevaet. V pamiati, kak

na mezhe. . .," "Esli chto-nibud' pet', to peremenu vetra. . .," ". . . i pri slove 'griadu-shchee' iz russkogo iazyka. . .," "Ia ne to chto skhozhu s uma, no ustal za leto. . .," Kolybel'naia Treskovogo Mysa," "Dekabr' vo Florentsii."

Iosif Brodskii, KONETS PREKRASNOI EPOKHI. Ann Arbor: Ardis, 1977. 114 pp.
Contents:"Vtoroe Rozhdestvo na beregu. . .," "Rech' o prolitom moloke," "Ot-krytka iz goroda K.," "Pamiati T.B.," "Pesnia," "Pis'mo generalu Z.," "Posviashchaetsia Ialte," "S vidom na more," "Konets prekrasnoi epokhi," "Razgovor s nebozhitelem," "S fevralia po aprel'," "Pen'e bez muzyki," "Oktiabr'skaia pesnia," "Post aetatem nostram," "Chaepitie," "Debiut," "Vremia goda—zima. Na granitsakh spokoistvie. Sny. . .," "Litov-skii divertisment," "Ia vsegda tverdil, chto sud'ba—igra. . .," "Natiurmort," "Liubov'."

POETIC TRANSLATIONS BY BRODSKY:

Andrew Marvell's "Eyes and Tears" in RUSSIAN LITERATURE TRIQUAR-TERLY 6 (1973), pp. 639-40.

Translations from the Polish of poems by Alexander Wat, Zbigniew Herbert, and Czeslaw Milosz in TAM ZHE 8 (1976), pp. 7-11.

TRANSLATIONS OF BRODSKY'S POETRY:

1. In Books

Joseph Brodsky, DEBUT. Ann Arbor, Ardis, 1973. 14 pp. tr. Carl Proffer.
Contents: "Debut," "Sonnet: How sad it is that what my life and I. . .," "On Prachechny Bridge," "Sonnet: Possessor of luxurious, luscious form. . .," " Post Aeta-tem Nostram (excerpt)," "To a Certain Tyrant," "The Funeral of Bobo," "Odysseus to Telemachus."

EIGHTEEN CONTEMPORARY RUSSIAN POEMS. Youlgrave, England: Hub Publications, 1973. Contains Lydia Pasternak Slater's translation of "Podsvechnik."

THREE SLAVIC POETS. Chicago: Elpenor Books, 1975. Contains George Kline's translations of "Enei i Didona," and "Postscriptum."

B. PERIODICALS

1972

"Bol'shaia elegiia Dzhonu Donnu," LYRIKVANNEN (Sweden) 5 (1972), pp. 60-63.
"Razgovor s nebozhitelem," in NEW: AMERICAN AND CANADIAN POETRY 18
     (April 1972), pp. 22-28.
"Strakh," in DIE WELT (8 July 1972).
"Sonet: Proshel ianvar' za oknami tiur'my," Vorotish'sia na rodinu. Nu chto zh. . .,"
     "V rasputitsu," "Teper' vse chashche chuvstvuiu ustalost'," "Vecherom," "Ot-kazom ot skorbnogo prechniazhest," "Einem alten Architekten in Rom," in AN-TAEUS 6 (Summer 1972), pp. 100-13. Tr. George Kline.
"Nature Morte'," SATURDAY REVIEW: THE ARTS, Vol 55, No. 3 (August 12, 1972),
     p. 45.

"Pokhorony Bobo," MICHIGAN DAILY (Nov. 12, 1972), p. 15. Tr. Carl R. Proffer.

"Na Prachechnom mostu," MICHIGAN DAILY (June 14, 1972), p. 1. Tr. Carl R. Proffer.

"Odissei Telemaku," NEW YORK TIMES MAGAZINE (Oct. 1, 1972), p. 82. Tr. Carl R. Proffer.

"Two Hours in an Empty Tank," "A Tree-Surgeon," "September the First," NEW LEADER (Dec. 11, 1972), pp. 3-4.

1973

"Pokhorony Bobo," "Odnomu tiranu," "Odissei Telemaku," tr. Carl R. Proffer, "Liubov'," "Sreten'e," tr. John Updike, RUSSIAN LITERATURE TRIQUARTERLY 5 (Winter 1973), pp. 17-23.

"The days glide over me. . . ," "In villages God does not live only. . . ," "Gorbunov and Gorchakov (excerpt)," tr. George Kline, MADEMOISELLE (February 1973), p. 139.

"Liubov'," "Anno Domini," IOWA REVIEW 4:3 (Summer 1973), pp. 9-12. Tr. Daniel Weissbort.

"Enei i Didona," CHANGE (Summer 1973), p. 61. Tr. George Kline.

"Il viaggiatore solitario," NUOVI ARGAMENTI (Milano) 33-34 (May-August 1973), pp. 35-47. Tr. Pier Carlo Ponzini.

"Nunc Dimittis," VOGUE (Sept. 1973), p. 286.

"Elegies," ATLANTIS 6 (Winter 1973/4), pp. 43-46. Tr. Hugh Maxton.

1974

"Nature Morte," ENSEMBLE 5 (1974), pp. 113.

"S grust'iu i s nezhnost'iu," "Pochti elegia," "Stikhi v Aprele," "Sem' let spustiia," "Ostanovka v pustyne," "Einem Alten Architekten in Rom," ALMANACCO DELLA SPECCHIO 3 (1974), pp. 193-213. Tr. Giovanni Buttafava.

"A Christmas Ballad," COLORADO QUARTERLY XXI, 4 (Spring 1974), pp. 538-39. Tr. Eugene M. Kayden.

"An autumn evening in the modest square," CONFRONTATION (Spring 1974), pp. 20-21.

"North is south, and another couple. . . ," GHENT QUARTERLY 1 (Summer 1975), p. 65.

POEMS WRITTEN IN ENGLISH BY BRODSKY:

Stephen Spender, ed., W.H. AUDEN: A TRIBUTE. New York: MacMillan, 1975. "Elegy."